D1029196

CLAUDIAN POLICYMAKING
AND THE
EARLY IMPERIAL REPRESSION
OF JUDAISM AT ROME

SOUTH FLORIDA STUDIES IN THE HISTORY OF JUDAISM

Edited by
Jacob Neusner
Bruce D. Chilton, Darrell J. Fasching, William Scott Green,
Sara Mandell, James F. Strange

Number 160
Claudian Policymaking
and the
Early Imperial Repression
of Judaism at Rome

by
H. Dixon Slingerland

CLAUDIAN POLICYMAKING
AND THE
EARLY IMPERIAL REPRESSION
OF JUDAISM AT ROME

by

H. Dixon Slingerland

Scholars Press
Atlanta, Georgia

CLAUDIAN POLICYMAKING
AND THE
EARLY IMPERIAL REPRESSION
OF JUDAISM AT ROME

by
H. Dixon Slingerland

©1997
University of South Florida

Publication of this book was made possible by a grant from the Tisch Family Foundation, New York City. The University of South Florida acknowledges with thanks this important support for its scholarly projects.

Library of Congress Cataloging in Publication Data
Slingerland, H. Dixon.
    Claudian policymaking and the early Imperial repression of Judaism
at Rome / H. Dixon Slingerland.
        p.   cm. — (South Florida studies in the history of Judaism ;
no. 160)
    Includes bibliographical references and index.
    ISBN 0-7885-0425-8 (cloth : alk. paper)
    1. Jews—Italy—Rome—History. 2. Jews—Persecutions—Italy—
Rome. 3. Rome—History—Claudius, 41–54. 4. Rome—Ethnic
relations.   I. Title. II. Series.
DS135.I85R6629   1997
937'.004924—dc21   97-44291
                                          CIP

Printed in the United States of America
on acid-free paper

In memory of

Howard Dixon Slingerland
1908-1954

Maybelle Louise Carroll Slingerland
1904-1981

Bonnie Lee Farwell Slingerland
1944-1984

Table of Contents

Acknowledgments

This research could not have been contemplated or completed without assistance of many different kinds. Dr. Arthur Vööbus introduced me to the critical analysis of the Biblical texts. Professor J. Louis Martyn expanded this to include the larger world of the non-canonical Judeo-Christian writings, and Dr. Morton Smith encouraged me to situate these materials within the broader world of ancient Roman religiosity. Finally, a 1972-1973 year of research with Professor Martin Hengel at the Institutum Iudaicum of Tübingen University in Germany provided a beginning for the framework of the volume.

The immediate antecedent was a 1980 seminar of the National Endowment for the Humanities conducted by Dr. Smith. Likewise, its capstone became a 1995 program at the American Academy in Rome. Directed by Professors John Bodel of Rutgers University and Dean Richard Saller of the University of Chicago and supported by the outstanding resources of the Academy, it too was funded by means of the National Endowment for the Humanities. The program provided me with the opportunity to explore at first hand the resources of the great city which was the stage for the events discussed in this book. At the same time it permitted me to test out portions of the materials discussed here with my delightful colleagues at the Academy.

Hiram College, where I have instructed since 1979, also played a significant role in the project's completion. Besides the general encouragement of my co-workers and their patience in listening to reports of work-in-progress, the College provided me with summer research grants in 1987, 1989, 1994, and 1996, as well as a sabbatical for the 1992-1993 academic year. In other ways also the College has contributed directly to its progress. Robert Sawyer, our professor of classics, and Joyce Dyer, the writing director, have assisted me at several points, as have two former deans, Edward Smerek and Vivian Makosky, and our president, G. Benjamin Oliver. Furthermore, the college librarians and, in particular, Mary Lou Selander did an incredible job of making available through interlibrary loan the long list of books and articles without which such a study would certainly have been impossible. Finally, the staff of the Dray Computer Center aided me in a variety of ways.

I wish to thank also my colleagues in the Hellenistic Judaism Section of the Society of Biblical Literature, Alan Avery-Peck for the many ways in which he assisted me with this manuscript, John Bodel for his careful reading of chapter 9, Jacob Neusner for agreeing to publish the study as part of the South Florida Studies in the History of Judaism/Scholars Press series, the *Jewish Quarterly Review* for permission to print as chapters 4 and 5 modified versions respectively of "Suetonius *Claudius* 25.4 and the Account in Cassius Dio" and "Suetonius *Claudius* 25.4, Acts 18, and Paulus Orosius' *Historiarum adversum paganos libri VII*: Dating the Claudian Expulsion(s) of Roman Jews," both of which first appeared in that journal, and the University Press of America for permission to print as chapter 10 a much revised version of the article "Chrestus: Christus?"

Abbreviations

ANRW	*Aufstieg und Niedergang der römischen Welt*
CAH	*Cambridge Ancient History*
CII	*Corpus Inscriptionum Iudaicarum*
CIL	*Corpus Inscriptionum Latinarum*
CPJ	*Corpus Papyrorum Judaicarum*
CSEL	*Corpus Scriptorum Ecclesiasticorum Latinorum*
GCS	Griechischen christlichen Schriftsteller
IG	*Inscriptiones Graecae*
ILS	Dessau, *Inscriptiones Latinae Selectae*
LCL	Loeb Classical Library
LSJ	Liddell and Scott, *Greek-English Lexicon*, 9th ed.
OCD²	*Oxford Classical Dictionary*, 2d ed.
PIR	*Prosopographia Imperii Romani*
PIR²	*Prosopographia Imperii Romani*, 2d ed.
PW	Pauly, Wissowa, and Kroll, *Real-Encyclopädie der klassischen Altertumswissenschaft*

Introduction

In their book *Religion in the Ancient Greek City*, Louise Bruit Zaidman and Pauline Schmitt Pantel make mention of an interview with Jean-Pierre Vernant during which he said that he had turned to the study of Greek religion because "the complexity of ancient Greek culture seemed to me to be better expressed in that area than in any other."[1] From this perspective we are able to appreciate Arnaldo Momigliano's related assertion that analysis of the religious policy of the emperor Claudius best reveals the ideals governing his entire administration.[2] More directly related to the purposes of the present study, Momigliano also claims that, because of the nature of the sources, this religious policy is itself best appreciated through the clarification of Claudius' attitude towards Jews and Judaism.[3] In other words, examination of Claudius in terms of his relationship with Jews and their religion provides singular entree into the appreciation of his policymaking as a whole.

Concentrating on the circumstances of Roman Jews under the emperor Claudius (41-54 CE), the present volume does in fact reveal as much about him and his imperial predecessors as it does about these Jews themselves. Two lines of investigation converge here. The first focuses on the Acts of the Apostles, an important early Christian document relevant also to Greco-Roman and Jewish historiography. It has produced three articles, "'The Jews' in the Pauline Portion of

---

[1]Louise Bruit Zaidman and Pauline Schmitt Pantel, *Religion in the Ancient Greek City*, trans. Paul Cartledge (Cambridge: Cambridge University Press, 1992), p. 22.

[2]Arnaldo Momigliano, *Claudius: The Emperor and His Achievement* (1943; new preface, 1961; reprint ed., Westport, CT: Greenwood Press, 1981), pp. 26-27.

[3]Ibid., pp. 29-30.

Acts,"[4] a sequel, "The Composition of Acts: Some Redaction-critical Observations,"[5] as well as "Acts 18:1-18, the Gallio Inscription, and Absolute Pauline Chronology."[6] The former two of these highlight the tendency of Acts to rewrite history from an anti-Jewish perspective. For current purposes, however, it is the last which is most relevant. Parallel with *Claudius* 25.4, the Suetonian statement that "since the Jews constantly made disturbances at the instigation of Chrestus, he [Claudius] expelled them from Rome,"[7] Acts 18:1-18 reports likewise that "Claudius had ordered all Jews to leave Rome."[8] Because it also refers specifically to the Achaian proconsulship of Gallio, scholars have drawn significant chronological conclusions about the Claudian expulsion from Acts 18:1-18. Nevertheless, except insofar as its results are concerned, this first line of investigation remains in the background of our examination.

The second line is therefore central. Begun as a short inquiry into the scholarly consensus that the Chrestus of *Claudius* 25.4 was Jesus Christus, it has evolved into a comprehensive examination of Claudian policy vis-à-vis Jews and their religious practices at Rome. Demonstrating that Chrestus was neither Jesus nor any other such messianic figure and, consequently, that the practically universal *interpretatio christiana* has taken *Claudius* 25.4 out of context,[9] this

---

[4]Dixon Slingerland, "'The Jews' in the Pauline Portion of Acts," *Journal of the American Academy of Religion* 54 (1986):305-321.

[5]Dixon Slingerland, "The Composition of Acts: Some Redaction-critical Observations," *Journal of the American Academy of Religion* 56 (1988):99-113.

[6]Dixon Slingerland, "Acts 18:1-18, the Gallio Inscription, and Absolute Pauline Chronology," *Journal of Biblical Literature* 110 (1991):439-449. Cf. Slingerland, "Acts 18:1-17 and Luedemann's Pauline Chronology," *Journal of Biblical Literature* 109 (1990):686-690.

[7]"Iudaeos impulsore Chresto assidue tumultuantes Roma expulit." Except as otherwise noted, English translations of Suetonius' *De vita caesarum* are those of J[ohn] C. Rolfe in the LCL. We shall have reason to evaluate his translation of *Claudius* 25.4 later.

[8]"...διὰ τὸ διατεταχέναι Κλαύδιον χωρίζεσθαι πάντας τοὺς Ἰουδαίους ἀπὸ τῆς Ῥώμης." Unless otherwise indicated, Biblical quotations follow the translation of the New Revised Standard Version (NRSV).

[9]For preliminary results, see Dixon Slingerland, "Chrestus: Christus?" in *The Literature of Early Rabbinic Judaism: Issues in Talmudic Redaction and Interpretation*, ed. Alan J. Avery-Peck, Studies in Judaism: New Perspectives on Ancient Judaism, vol. 4 (Lanham, MD: University Press of America, 1989), pp. 133-144. Chapter 10 of this study provides the final results. Please note also that significant portions of chapter 4 appeared in Dixon Slingerland, "Suetonius *Clau-*

study restores the claim of Suetonius to various settings genuinely appropriate to it.

Some of the settings are relatively narrow. For example, though typically treated in abstraction, *Claudius* 25.4 makes good sense only within the literary context of *Claudius* 22-25, the immediate unit of which it is a part. Again, the proper interpretation of its vocabulary, grammar, and syntax depends upon an understanding of Suetonian usage in the *De vita caesarum* as a whole. Finally, one element of vocabulary in particular, the personal name *Chrestus*, introduces onomastics into the discussion.[10]

It is the exploration of the several broader contexts to which *Claudius* 25.4 belongs that makes this volume into a comprehensive examination of how the emperor Claudius fashioned his policies toward Roman Jews and their foreign cult. One of these contexts is historiographic. With its extensive bibliography spanning several disciplines, i.e., history of religions, Jewish studies, early church history, and Roman studies, the modern historiography on our subject has of course expanded several times upon the writers of antiquity. Distanced from the ancient Jewish and Gentile texts by very many centuries, we have to look closely in order to discern the quite fascinating tendencies which govern their different versions of Judeo-Roman history. Discovery of the tendencies which control the modern reconstructions of the same history is hardly less interesting or challenging. Nonetheless, once we realize how the tendentiousness of the ancients has fed directly into modernity, we are better able to comprehend in turn how the latter has distorted our image of Roman Jews, of their predicament under imperial rule, and, more broadly, of the nature of that rule itself.

Armed with these corrective tools, we are in a position to begin the detailed reconstruction of the religio-political realities under which Roman Jews functioned during the late Republican and early imperial period. Among the sources for the years prior to the time of Claudius we encounter the contemporary Valerius Maximus, Philo, and Seneca,

---

dius 25.4 and the Account in Cassius Dio," *Jewish Quarterly Review* 79 (1989): 305-322. Likewise, chapter 5 is a revision of Dixon Slingerland, "Suetonius *Claudius* 25.4, Acts 18, and Paulus Orosius' *Historiarum adversum paganos libri VII*: Dating the Claudian Expulsion(s) of Roman Jews," *Jewish Quarterly Review* 83 (1992):127-144.

[10]Because Suetonius nowhere identified Chrestus, interpretation of that name requires two different kinds of analysis. One, quite limited in scope, examines the general principles according to which Suetonius himself employed proper names in *De vita caesarum*. The other applies Greco-Roman onomastics as a whole to the question of the social and political parameters of this name at Rome.

also John Malalas, Eusebius in both his *Ecclesiastical History* and the *Chronicle*, as well as the ubiquitous Tacitus, Suetonius, Dio Cassius, and Josephus. Their conflicting tendencies exposed, these sources do reveal identifiable patterns of pre-Claudian policymaking with respect, in particular, to the Jewish cult at Rome. In so doing, they make clear the imperial precedents and so establish the appropriate background against which to interpret the subsequent policy of Claudius himself.

For purposes of that interpretation, we are fortunate to possess even more source materials than Momigliano and others have thought. Investigated within the context of Claudius' Republican and imperial predecessors, these then enable us to make sense of his own general tendencies vis-à-vis Roman Jewry. Philo, a contemporary of Claudius, plays a significant role here, as do Josephus, the Acts of the Apostles, Suetonius, Dio Cassius, Paulus Orosius, and Eusebius' *Chronicle*, less so Tacitus and Juvenal.

The sources become particularly rich in information about the behavior of Claudius at the crucial time of his rise to power in 41 CE. Here, Dio 60.6.6 and Philo's again contemporary *Legatio* 155-158 are central. So also is P. Lond. 1912, a near autograph of the remarkable Claudian letter to Alexandria, with its ominous allusion to Jews that he might "proceed against them in every way as fomenting a common plague for the whole world." Thus, just as we are able to place the general behavior of Claudius within the broader context of his predecessors, these materials constitute the wider Claudian context in which we may interpret the expulsion of Roman Jews documented by *Claudius* 25.4, the Acts of the Apostles, Paulus Orosius, probably Philo, and, perhaps, Juvenal.

The result: having provided ourselves with reliable controls for the interpretation of the Jewish policy behind that event, we permit Suetonius' claim to assume its rightful place in both the history of Rome and the history of the Jewish people. So situated among a long series of associated accounts, it plays an important part in clarifying how the emperor Claudius fashioned his policies toward Roman Jews and their cult.

As previously indicated, the bibliography associated with our subject is extensive. Particularly interesting is the fact that it arises out of several disciplines often isolated from one another. I refer here to historiography, the history of religions, Jewish studies, early church history, and Roman studies. The contextual approach described above requires the demolition of various walls among these fields, and the result demonstrates the advantage of that extra labor. In other words, to make sense of *Claudius* 25.4 requires the integration of several academic disciplines, and the sense so made adds in turn to our understanding within each of these disciplines.

In terms of historiography, we find that the proper interpretation of the relationships between Roman Jews and their imperial masters depends upon the recognition and evaluation of key presuppositions behind the claims of the writers both ancient and modern. It is, in particular, the discovery of the extent and ramifications of these presuppositions among nineteenth- and twentieth-century writers that adds an interesting chapter to the study of the study of history.

This whole work is, to some degree, an exercise in the history of religions. More particularly, we are unable to deal with the foreign *superstitio* of Judaism at Rome exclusive of similar phenomena, and especially the Egyptian cult of Isis. Hence, what we learn in detail about governmental policy vis-à-vis Roman Jews and their religion sheds light on the entire religious landscape of early imperial Rome.

Insofar as Jewish studies is concerned, we must keep in mind that Roman Jewry made up a significant portion not only of that city's population but also of the Diaspora as a whole. Hence, the religio-political background provided by the integration of disciplines carried out here establishes the fundamental context within which this very important Jewish community lived out the various aspects of its life under Claudius and his predecessors.

Early church history is equally well served by the establishment of this context. Precisely at the time of interest to us, Christianity began as a minor Jewish sect. Arriving in Rome roughly contemporary with the 41-54 CE rule of Claudius, its first preachers and adherents there were no doubt Jewish Christians subject to the imperial policies affecting the other Roman Jews. Thus, the clarification of these same policies becomes a prerequisite for understanding both the origins of Roman Christianity and Paul's epoch-making epistle to that city.

Finally, the case for the importance of the present research to Roman studies has been made in part already, for we began with the claim of Momigliano that the emperor Claudius is most transparent when viewed from the angle of his Jewish policy. In fact, how he dealt with Jews and their cult at Rome is well documented, and we learn much about Claudian absolutism from this documentation. Moreover, establishing the imperial context within which he functioned, we also learn much about his predecessors.

Chapter One

Historical Ramifications of the Tendentious Portrayal of Jews and Their Cult

"Events unfold in contexts."[1] Hence, if context is not everything, it is nearly everything, and anything examined out of context will certainly be distorted. As a result, to understand Claudian policymaking vis-à-vis Roman Jews in general and as illuminated through *Claudius* 25.4 in particular, we must proceed contextually. Since our ancient Jewish and Gentile as well as modern sources belong to this context, we begin with critical observations of a historiographic character.

By way of introduction to the Jewish materials, it is helpful to recall that, for the sake of Christianity's future within the Roman empire, the person who wrote both the Gospel according to Luke and the Acts of the Apostles was well advised to accentuate the positive and play down or eliminate the negative. That is precisely what this writer did. Specifically, Revelation, 1 Peter, Tacitus (*Annals* 15.44), Suetonius (*Nero* 16.2), Pliny (*Letters* 10.96-97) and the Hadrianic rescript preserved by Eusebius (*Ecclesiastical History* 4.9.1-3) make clear that the new Jewish sect received an unfriendly welcome from Rome's upper-class and imperial leadership. Nevertheless, the author of Luke-Acts left readers with the quite different image of a Christian religion that was neither harmful to, nor perceived as such by, its Roman masters.

A primary example is the treatment of Jesus' death. Not able to deny that he had been executed under imperial jurisdiction, Luke-Acts

---

[1] Jim Campbell, "America's Long History of Burning Black Churches," *The Plain Dealer* (Cleveland), 19 June 1996.

mitigates this major stumbling block to the credibility of Christianity by indicating that the representative of Roman authority, Pilate, had been forced much against the evidence to give in to Jewish demands (Luke 23:4-5, 13-16, 20-24).[2] As Tacitus (*Annals* 15.44) made clear, however, there were more matter-of-fact ways of describing the same event: "Christus, the founder of the name, had undergone the death penalty in the reign of Tiberius, by sentence of the procurator Pontius Pilatus, and the pernicious superstition [exitiabilis superstitio] was checked for a moment."[3]

The treatment of Paul in Luke-Acts is all the more conspicuous. Fundamental to it is the often repeated protestation that the apostle was a proud citizen of Rome who depended for his safety upon that citizenship (Acts 16:37, 16:38, 22:25, 22:26, 22:27, 22:28, 22:29, 23:27).[4] Not surprisingly, therefore, in Acts 18:14-15 the primary representative of Roman authority in Achaia, Gallio, is made to attest to the innocuousness of Paul and his new religion. Brought before the court by Corinthian Jews, Paul was summarily exonerated by Gallio in terms meant to express how the author of Acts wanted Rome to perceive Christianity: "If it were a matter of crime or serious villainy, I would be justified in accepting the complaint of you Jews; but since it is a matter of questions about words and names and your own law, see to it yourselves; I do not wish to be a judge of these matters."

Lest readers miss the point, Acts 23:26-30 then provides similar testimony from a Roman tribune:

> Claudius Lysias to his Excellency the governor Felix, greetings. This man [Paul] was seized by the Jews and was about to be killed by them, but when I had learned that he was a Roman citizen, I came with the guard and rescued him.... I found that he was accused concerning questions of their law, but was charged with nothing deserving death or imprisonment.

This is a nice response; necessitated however by the life-and-death needs of early Christian apologetic, it is also incredible. We know, that is, how persons such as Tacitus really felt and governors like Pliny

---

[2]Though related motifs appear in Matthew and Q (the common source behind the gospels of Matthew and Luke), most of this material is unique to the account within Luke.

[3]Unless otherwise noted, English translations of the *Annals* are those of John Jackson in the LCL.

[4]Since Paul's own letters do not indicate that he was a Roman, we cannot be sure if Acts was simply stressing a detail useful to its own apologetic or if it was inventing one.

really behaved towards what from the Roman perspective amounted to an "exitiabilis superstitio."[5]

If we consider Acts 9:23-25, it is all the more incredible. As an account of Paul's flight from Damascus, this passage claims the escape became necessary only because "the Jews plotted to kill him."[6] In 2 Corinthians 11:32-33, however, we possess Paul's own version of the same occurrence. According to him, and he was there, "In Damascus, the governor under King Aretas guarded the city of Damascus in order to seize me, but I was let down in a basket...and escaped from his hands." Why did Acts substitute the Damascene Jewish population as culprit and so omit reference to the proxy for Roman rule? Because the author of Acts knew that a picture of the Christian hero fleeing imperially established governmental authority raised serious questions about the innocuousness of Christianity.

Acts does finally admit that Roman officials caught up with and took Paul to Italy for trial. Even so, the end of the story in Acts 28 is curiously truncated, for it leaves readers in the dark as to the outcome of events at Rome. Nonetheless, since Paul was almost certainly executed by imperial decision, we can understand why Acts omits the end of his life from its otherwise fairly detailed biography.[7] After all, a cult whose founder, Jesus, and chief propagandist, Paul, were both executed under imperial authority was in a very precarious position.

Hence, insofar as possible, Luke-Acts attempts to reshape how Roman authority perceived and managed the Christian *superstitio*. Furthermore, E. Mary Smallwood inadvertently witnesses to Luke-Acts' success in this regard when, on the basis of it, she affirms that "the way in which both Felix and Festus treated St. Paul when he was under arrest shows the Roman government in a good light. They were firm and impartial, and they were anxious to save their prisoner from merciless treatment at the Jews' hands...."[8] From Gentile authors like Tacitus and from Christian texts like Revelation, we know things were not as Luke-Acts claims. Still, with the major exception of the blame

---

[5]*Annals* 15.44 above.

[6]In the second half of Acts it seems that Jews had little more to do than spend their lives plotting Paul's destruction. See Slingerland, "'The Jews' in the Pauline Portion of Acts," passim.

[7]The same may well be true of Peter. He strangely disappears following the apostolic council in Acts 15.

[8]E. Mary Smallwood, "Jews and Romans in the Early Empire," *History Today* 15 (1965):315. W. H. C. Frend (*Martyrdom and Persecution in the Early Church: A Study of a Conflict from the Maccabees to Donatus* [Garden City: Anchor Books, 1967], pp. 120-121) is similar.

transposed to Jews, we must sympathize with a text which seeks to put the best face possible on what was in reality a dangerous situation for the new sect and its adherents.

The purpose of this introductory discussion of the Christian Luke-Acts is to clarify an analogous problem which the Jewish sources faced in their confrontation with imperial authorities little more sympathetic to the Jewish than to the Christian *superstitio*.[9] Simply put, Roman authors of history like Tacitus and Suetonius did not report early imperial attitudes towards Jews and their cult in the positive light of Philo and Josephus, the Jewish authors upon whom we are required to depend for most of our information in this matter. Smallwood writes,

> It is a striking and important fact that most of our information about Rome's dealing with the Jews and Judaism comes from Jewish sources. The Jews are almost unique among Rome's subjects in having left a fairly extensive native literature. It is particularly rich in the first century A.D., with Philo the Alexandrian Jew, Josephus the Palestinian Jew, and the New Testament. Without that literature, practically nothing would be known about the Jews in the early Empire, in Palestine or elsewhere. For Roman literature has very little to say about the unimportant province of Judaea, or about the scattered Jewish minorities–just an odd reference here and there, and the first few pages of Tacitus' account of the siege of Jerusalem in A.D. 70. To Roman writers the Jews mattered, and therefore were mentioned, only when they gave serious trouble.[10]

If we set aside the attribution of guilt implied by her claim that Jews "gave serious trouble," Smallwood is quite right that Roman sources filed Jewish life under the word "trouble." Hence, interpreted more accurately to mean that these sources had little good to say about Jews, especially as practitioners of a particular foreign *superstitio*, this word is, as we shall soon see, accurate.

However, Smallwood then completely misses the mark with her additional statement that "our Jewish sources are, understandably,

---

[9]This is not to imply that Jews and Christians faced the same legal situation. On the one hand, our sources indicate that Judaism had a legal existence within the empire (cf. Theodosian Code 16.8.9: "Iudaeorum sectam nulla lege prohibitam satis constat."). On the other, Pliny had to ask the emperor Trajan about the status of Christianity, and their correspondence was hardly promising in this regard (cf. Simeon L. Guterman, *Religious Toleration and Persecution in Ancient Rome* [London: Aiglon Press Ltd., 1951], p. 121, n. 72). Instead, the Jews and Christians appear to have faced the same attitudinal situation, and it was no doubt these imperial attitudes which determined imperial actions.

[10]Smallwood, "Jews and Romans," pp. 233-234.

biased in favor of the Jews, and it is an impressive testimony to
Rome's kindly attitude to Judaism that they nevertheless give no
evidence of religious persecution, but tell of efforts on the part of
Rome to protect Jewish religious liberty."[11] That is, having already
indicated that the Roman sources consistently said otherwise and now
admitting the tendentiousness of Philo and Josephus, she fails to
realize how this bias manifests itself precisely in the fact that the
Jewish writers did "give no evidence of religious persecution." Of
course they did not comment on this mistreatment to the same degree
as their Roman counterparts,[12] nor should we expect them to have
done so. This is because, just as with the Christian Luke-Acts,[13] it

---

[11]Smallwood, "Jews and Romans," p. 234 (cf. her "Some Notes on the Jews under Tiberius," *Latomus* 15 [1956]:320-321). She then blames Jewish difficulties on
Roman hostility to proselytizing. Guterman (*Religious Toleration*, p. 157) claims
"Rome tolerated and even encouraged Judaism," A. N. Sherwin-White (*Racial Prejudice in Imperial Rome* [Cambridge: Cambridge University Press, 1967], p. 96)
mentions "the general philo-Judaic attitude of the government," S. Davis (*Race-
Relations in Ancient Egypt: Greek, Egyptian, Hebrew, Roman* [New York: Philosophical Library, 1952], pp. 152-153) assumes "Roman relations with the Jews till
the tragedy of A.D. 70 were, on the whole, conciliatory, if not friendly," and
Vincent M. Scramuzza ("The Policy of the Early Roman Emperors towards Judaism" in *The Beginnings of Christianity*, ed. F. J. Foakes Jackson and Kirsopp
Lake, 5 vols. [London: Macmillan, 1920-1933], 5:278, 284-285) agrees: Tiberius and
Claudius followed the tolerant attitude of Augustus. Hence, Gaius was an exception, but, considering how he treated Roman Jews, so was Tiberius (p. 289).

[12]Though the Jewish sources had good reason for their harmonious recasting
of past history, we shall see in subsequent chapters that, just as Luke-Acts could
not deny Roman participation in the execution of Jesus, so Philo and Josephus
were unable to ignore Jewish persecution.

[13]An informative parallel exists between Josephus' apologetic portrayal of
Petronius, the governor of Syria, and Acts' treatment of his Achaian counterpart,
Gallio. Tricked by the needs of Josephus, Emil Schürer (*The History of the Jewish
People in the Age of Jesus Christ*, ed. Geza Vermes, Fergus Millar, Matthew Black,
and Martin Goodman, 3 vols. [Edinburgh: T. and T. Clark, 1973-1987], 1:394)
writes, "it was with a heavy heart that Petronius, who was a reasonable man,
obeyed this childish demand" of Gaius to set up the emperor's image in Jerusalem,
for that is exactly the picture of this governor which Josephus wanted his readers
to glean from *Antiquities* 18.276-283. Key elements of this image are incredible.
For example, though effective apologetically, it is impossible that Petronius
addressed himself to Jews as "serving the sovereign of all, almighty God, whose
temple I should not have had the heart to see fall a prey to the insolence of
imperial authority" (18.280) or that he made a public remark about the "capricious
human plots" of his emperor (18.281). That Gaius' representative in Syria may not
have thought it sound to provoke war in the East is possible; that he spoke as a
devotee of the God of Israel and openly ridiculed the man who had given him such
an important position is preposterous. Though J. P. V. D. Balsdon (*The Emperor*

would have been entirely unproductive in terms of the basic apologetic purposes of either one of these writers.

Thus, in the process of commenting on how Josephus dealt with the Roman Jewish difficulties which arose during the years when Tiberius was emperor, Horst Moehring makes the highly important observation that the historian "was hardly able to deny that the Jews had been involved in some kind of religious persecution under Tiberius. He could not dare to claim that this persecution had been entirely unfounded, but neither could he allow to keep up the generally held opinion that the Jews in Rome had been involved in a moral scandal."[14] Philo chose to deal with the matter not much differently from Josephus. Specifically, Elmer Truesdell Merrill is quite correct when he writes of him that Philo "had a diplomatic reason for not recording any severe action against the Jews for which Tiberius must be held personally responsible. It would interrupt the array of uniformly favorable precedents of imperial procedure that he was concerned as an advocate to present."[15]

Similarly, but thinking in particular of the Roman edicts which Josephus claimed to preserve for readers (*Antiquities* 12-20), Alfredo Rabello reminds us that the Josephan task fell into the category "of apologetics; the documents help him to defend the Jews, and thus he cites only documents in their favour, omitting all documents directed against them."[16] Guterman too recognizes that these materials "are cited from motives frankly apologetic and are designed to present the Jew in as enviable a light as possible." Nevertheless, on the basis of his statement that "these *Acta* represent the whole extent of our knowledge of the laws governing the Jews in the Empire," he refuses to permit what he considers to be minor corruptions in the texts of these decrees to invalidate their utilization for purposes of historical reconstruction. As a result, he expresses no reservations about their

---

Gaius (Caligula) [Oxford: Clarendon Press, 1934], p. 138) also appears to recognize a problem with the reporting of Josephus, Hugo Willrich's historicizing approach ("Caligula," *Klio* 3 [1903]:417) implies Petronius did indeed take the Jewish side. Why? Because Jews bribed him.

[14]Horst R. Moehring, "The Persecution of the Jews and the Adherents of the Isis Cult at Rome A.D. 19," *Novum Testamentum* 3 (1959):303.

[15]Elmer Truesdell Merrill, "The Expulsion of Jews from Rome under Tiberius," *Classical Philology* 14 (1919):372. See also the similar view of W. Seston, "L'Empereur Claude et les Chrétiens," *Revue d'histoire et de philosophie religieuses* 11 (1931):291.

[16]Alfredo Mordechai Rabello, "The Legal Condition of the Jews in the Roman Empire" in *ANRW*, 2.30:682.

"essential authenticity."[17] Still, his approach is flawed. First, even if these decrees were unique, that would be irrelevant to the question of their authenticity. Second, they are not, for "laws governing the Jews" play a significant part in P. Lond. 1912, the certainly authentic copy of a letter sent by Claudius to Alexandria in 41 CE.[18] Again, familiar with the "design" of these decrees, Guterman should also have realized the doubtful value of any information drawn from them. This is above all true since such information, completely false or merely adjusted, becomes misinformation or disinformation, in other words, apologetic or propaganda, the very thing even Guterman recognizes it to be.

Moehring, therefore, is on the right track when he insists that

> it is wrong to read Josephus without always keeping his apologetic purpose in mind. That means, however, that the documents in Josephus must first and foremost be read as part of his apologetic scheme. Their direct use as historical evidence is impossible. They can be used for that purpose only after full allowances have been made for their apologetic character....[19]

---

[17]Guterman, *Religious Toleration*, p. 109. See, similarly, the generalizations of Élie Bikerman [Bickerman], "Une question d'authenticité: Les privilèges juifs," *Annuaire de l'Institut de philologie et d'histoire orientales et slaves* 13 = *Mélanges Isidore Lévy* (1953):11-34.

[18]The editio princeps is H. Idris Bell, *Jews and Christians in Egypt: The Jewish Troubles in Alexandria and the Athanasian Controversy Illustrated by Texts from Greek Papyri in the British Museum* (1924; reprint ed., Westport, CT: Greenwood Press, 1976), pp. 1-37. Both it and *CPJ*, 2:36-55 (#153) provide English translations and commentary. The latter has an extensive bibliography. Text and translation alone appear in *Select Papyri*, trans. A. S. Hunt and C. C. Edgar, LCL, 5 vols. (Cambridge: Harvard University Press, 1963), 2:79-89 (#212).

[19]Horst R. Moehring, "The *Acta pro Judaeis* in the *Antiquities* of Flavius Josephus: A Study in Hellenistic and Modern Apologetic Historiography" in *Christianity, Judaism and Other Greco-Roman Cults: Studies for Morton Smith at Sixty: Judaism before 70*, ed. Jacob Neusner, Studies in Judaism in Late Antiquity, vol. 12.3 (Leiden: E. J. Brill, 1975), pp. 156-157 and passim. Louis H. Feldman ("Flavius Josephus Revisited: The Man, His Writings, and His Significance" in *ANRW*, 2.21^2:816-817) also appreciates the apologetic needs which governed important elements of Josephus' work, and so does Seston ("L'Empereur Claude," p. 291). Scramuzza expresses the same thought (*The Emperor Claudius* [Cambridge: Harvard University Press, 1940], p. 12): "More than a historian he [Josephus] was a propagandist." Shaye J. D. Cohen (*Josephus in Galilee and Rome: His Vita and Development as a Historian*, Columbia Studies in the Classical Tradition, vol. 8 [Leiden: E. J. Brill, 1979], passim) is particularly interesting in this regard. For general comments upon the tendencies of Philo and Josephus, see J. N. Sevenster, *The Roots of Pagan Anti-Semitism in the Ancient World*, Supplements to Novum Testamentum, vol. 41 (Leiden: E. J. Brill, 1975), pp. 19-30.

Antiquities 14.186-267 is a good example of these things. This unit consists of a long catena of largely Asia-related official documents, all of which claim Roman authorities supported Jews particularly in the practice of their religious customs. So formulated, the text leaves a distinct impression that Josephus was forced to compose it in order to defend against the claims to the contrary. Furthermore, there is no particular reason that we should have to speculate concerning this because his conclusion to the unit (14.267) is explicit: "I cannot suppose that anyone is so stupid that he will actually refuse to believe the statements about the friendliness of the Romans towards us, when they have demonstrated this in a good many decrees relating to us."[20] In other words, these "stupid" people really did exist in his own time, and they obviously had good reason to interpret the Roman treatment of Jewish *sacra* in a quite different light. Otherwise, Josephus would hardly have found it necessary to compose a lengthy apologetic against their position.

Obvious in this regard, and particularly relevant in terms of the present volume, is the situation of historical reporting concerning Claudius. If we had at our disposal only the Jewish sources, we would find it practically impossible to discern the serious difficulties facing the Jewish population of Rome and elsewhere during the years 41-54 CE. Specifically, assuming that when he wrote both the *Flaccus* and *Legatio* some of these problems had already arisen, we may conclude that Philo made reference to them only in the oblique fashion to be discussed shortly. Josephus, however, who certainly wrote after these hardships, simply omitted them.[21]

In their place, he substituted at *Antiquities* 19.279-291 what purport to be two early Claudian edicts of a definitely philo-Judaic nature. The first affirms previously established Jewish rights in Alexandria and Syria (19.279-285), and the second does the same for the remainder of the Roman world (19.286-291). These are, therefore, at least as problematic as the other Josephan *Acta*. F. F. Bruce does take the first to be "substantially accurate,"[22] and Théodore Reinach agrees. At the same time, however, the latter also mentions "graves

---

[20]LCL translation by Ralph Marcus. This friendship of the Romans towards the Jewish people of which Josephus here speaks has a suspiciously neat counterpart in Claudius' first edict, where comment is made about Jewish friendship towards Rome (*Antiquities* 19.289).

[21]We shall deal with the supposed Josephan quotation of Paulus Orosius in chapter 5.

[22]F. F. Bruce, "Christianity under Claudius," *Bulletin of the John Rylands Library* 44 (1962):311.

doutes" and implies that the way Josephus introduced both edicts was governed by "l'absurdité" of diaspora Jews portrayed as citizens of all the cities in which they lived.[23] Not surprisingly, therefore, Victor Tcherikover concludes that the first but not the second document was entirely forged or "worked over by forgers."[24] Dieter Hennig alludes similarly to "massive Fälschungen" in the first text,[25] provides excellent examples of these, points out parallels with P. Lond. 1912, and finally suggests Josephus invented it on the basis of that certainly genuine Claudian letter.[26] Insofar as the second edict is concerned, Hennig offers excellent evidence that it too is fictional.[27] Overall, then, the ambiguity even among scholars who support the authenticity of one or both edicts provides some of the best evidence for Moehring's thesis. At the same time, it forbids reliance upon this material in particular when contradicted by other evidence which is of an entirely unambiguous kind.

Ultimately, that is, the positive impression left in particular by the Josephan omissions and additions does not make sense in terms of what we know from other sources. Specifically, Dio informed his readers that, within months of his becoming emperor, Claudius had initiated measures against the practice of Judaism in Rome; Philo referred in oblique fashion to a religion-motivated, almost certainly Claudian expulsion of the Jewish population of the city; Suetonius

---

[23]Théodore Reinach, "L'empereur Claude et les Juifs d'après un nouveau document," *Revue des études juives* 79 (1924):125-126.

[24]Victor Tcherikover, *Hellenistic Civilization and the Jews*, trans. S. Applebaum (New York: Atheneum, 1959), pp. 409-415. Scramuzza ("Policy" in *Beginnings of Christianity*, 5:291-292) makes a similar point. Jean Juster (*Les Juifs dans l'Empire romain: leur condition juridique, économique et sociale*, 2 vols. [Paris: Librairie Paul Geuthner, 1914], 1:233-234) likewise draws attention in particular to the second edict as authentic evidence of the privileged status of Jews ever since the time of Julius Caesar.

[25]Dieter Hennig, "Zu neuveröffentlichten Bruchstücken der <Acta Alexandrinorum>," *Chiron* 5 (1975):328. See S. Applebaum ("The Legal Status of the Jewish Communities in the Diaspora" in *The Jewish People in the First Century: Historical Geography, Political History, Social, Cultural and Religious Life and Institutions*, ed. S. Safrai and M. Stern, Compendia Rerum Iudaicarum ad Novum Testamentum: Section One, 2 vols. [Philadelphia: Fortress Press, 1974-1987], 1:458) on the use to which Josephus put this edict in *Antiquities* 19.310.

[26]Hennig, "Bruchstücken," p. 326, n. 20; p. 328; pp. 329-330.

[27]Ibid., pp. 332-335. Gaston May ("La politique religieuse de l'Empereur Claude," *Revue historique de droit français et étranger* 17 [1938]:35-36) also expresses no confidence in either document.

reported a Claudian expulsion of the same people, as did the author of the Acts of the Apostles, and Paulus Orosius too. Furthermore, in his certainly authentic Alexandrian letter, Claudius expressed himself most negatively when he declared concerning Jews that he was willing to "proceed against them in every way as fomenting a common plague for the whole world."[28] Josephus let slip not a single word about any such things.

Having recognized the tendentiousness of the Jewish materials, we might be inclined to rely all the more heavily on the Gentile sources for the reconstruction of Jewish life under the early empire. Yet, before deciding to do this, we need to return to Smallwood's claim, for her clear sense that Roman writers mentioned Jews "only when they gave serious trouble" implies a significant element of tendentiousness on the part of these authors as well.

Since it has been done often and recently, this is not the place to summarize the various opinions of Greco-Roman writers on Jews[29] and on what Cicero in his *Pro Flacco* 28.67 had called their "barbaric superstition,"[30] or, to employ the language of Tacitus (*Histories* 5.5) almost two centuries later, their "absurd and filthy" religious custom: "Iudaeorum mos absurdus sordidusque." When we draw out salient

---

[28]P. Lond. 1912, lines 98-100. Throughout this study, unless otherwise indicated, English translations follow *CPJ*, 2:42-43.

[29]The interpretation of these writers in A. Bludau ("Die Juden Roms im ersten christlichen Jahrhundert," *Katholik* 1 [1903]:202-221) is particularly critical of them. Recent summaries include Jerry L. Daniel, "Anti-Semitism in the Hellenistic-Roman Period," *Journal of Biblical Literature* 98 (1979):45-65; F. F. Bruce, "Tacitus on Jewish History," *Journal of Semitic Studies* 29 (1984):33-44; John G. Gager, *The Origins of Anti-Semitism: Attitudes toward Judaism in Pagan and Christian Antiquity* (New York: Oxford University Press, 1985), pp. 39-88; Menahem Stern, "The Jews in Greek and Latin Literature" in *The Jewish People in the First Century: Historical Geography, Political History, Social, Cultural and Religious Life and Institutions*, ed. S. Safrai and M. Stern, Compendia Rerum Iudaicarum ad Novum Testamentum: Section One, 2 vols. (Philadelphia: Fortress Press, 1974-1987), 2:1101-1159, as well as his "Antisemitism in Rome" in *Antisemitism through the Ages*, ed. Shmuel Almog (Oxford: Pergamon Press, 1988), pp. 13-25. Romano Penna ("Les Juifs a Rome au temps de l'Apotre Paul," *New Testament Studies* 28 [1982]:323-326) summarizes Jewish and Gentile sources on Roman Jewry, and Sherwin-White (*Racial Prejudice*, pp. 86-101) traces the supposed differences between the Greek and Roman attitudes towards Jews.

[30]We may not negate the reality of the attitude behind this expression by arguing it was a rhetorical tool for gaining acquittal of Cicero's client. Whether or not Cicero personally maintained such an antagonistic view towards Judaism, he certainly assumed that his jurors did. See Anthony J. Marshall, "Flaccus and the Jews of Asia (Cicero *Pro Flacco* 28.67-69)," *Phoenix* 29 (1975):141-142.

points of these largely upper-class[31] ideas, it is easy to demonstrate that the immediate background of both Gentile writing and imperial decision-making vis-à-vis Roman and other Jews was clouded by outrageous claims against these people and, in particular, against their religious practices.[32]

In the air precisely at the time of interest to us was, among other things, the opinion that Jews, as part of their cult in Jerusalem, practiced not only human sacrifice but also cannibalism.[33] Although this appears ridiculous to us, to the Romans it was not. In other words, among the Scythians, Carthaginians, and Gauls, Plutarch (*De superstitione* 13) took such practices quite seriously. Concerning the last of these peoples, and within the very context of Claudius' actions against Roman Jews, Suetonius also made known that this emperor "utterly abolished the cruel and inhuman religion of the Druids among the Gauls,"[34] a campaign of which Pliny the Elder (*Natural History* 30.13) was equally proud. Thus, the highly inflammatory rumor of Damocritus according to which "every seventh year they [Jews] caught a foreigner and sacrificed him"[35] could hardly have been a matter of indifference, especially when the Alexandrian anti-Jewish scholar Apion spread the damning information among the educated, including

---

[31]Cf. Peter Garnsey and Richard Saller, *The Roman Empire: Economy, Society and Culture* (Berkeley and Los Angeles: University of California Press, 1987), p. 108: "The literature was written by a tiny fraction of the population; the authors were uniformly men of the leisured elite, and their works convey the perceptions of the upper strata of society."

[32]Concerning Tacitus, Ronald Mellor (*Tacitus* [New York: Routledge, 1993], p. 380) writes, "His negative view of the Jews indiscriminately blurs together a few facts (Moses and Egypt; dietary laws; monotheism), biblical myths (Sodom and Gomorrah), preposterous nonsense (Jews originated in Crete), and anti-Semitic clichés (their lasciviousness)."

[33]For discussion, see Sevenster, *Roots of Pagan Anti-Semitism*, pp. 140-142.

[34]Suetonius *Claudius* 25.5. See the helpful remarks in Momigliano (*Claudius*, p. 28, n. 18); also, cf. Stern (*Greek and Latin Authors on Jews and Judaism*, 3 vols. [Jerusalem: Israel Academy of Sciences and Humanities, 1976-1984], 1:530, n. 1). May ("Politique religieuse," pp. 11-12) indicates that Claudius' abolition of Druidism was not a religious persecution but amounted instead to a humanitarian measure against human sacrifice. This means, of course, that the suppression of the supposedly cannibalistic rites of Judaism would have been easily justified on the same grounds.

[35]*Suidae Lexicon*, ed. Ada Adler, 5 parts (Leipzig: B. G. Teubner, 1928-1938) Δαμόκριτος (ad loc.). The present translation is that which appears in Stern, *Authors*, #247 (1:531).

those who lived in Rome,[36] that no less of a person than Antiochus Epiphanes entered the temple in Jerusalem only to discover a Greek captive being fattened for slaughter.[37] Asked for details, the unhappy man told about

> the unutterable law of the Jews, for the sake of which he was being fed. The practice was repeated annually at a fixed season. They would kidnap a Greek foreigner, fatten him up for a year, and then convey him to a wood, where they slew him, sacrificed his body with their customary ritual, partook of his flesh, and, while immolating the Greek, swore an oath of hostility to the Greeks. The remains of their victim were then thrown into a pit.[38]

It requires no analysis on our part in order to reject the idea that the practice of human sacrifice and cannibalism belonged to the rites of the Jewish cult. Moreover, it would be a very poor use of time to seek to discover some flaw within the Judaism of the Greco-Roman world that might account for this claim. It can only have arisen out of the meanest kind of prejudice, cf. the related statement of Géza Alföldy, "particularly marked were prejudices against the Jews,"[39] and it

---

[36]*Antiquities* 18.257-260 is explicit that Apion brought his famous anti-Judaism (cf. *Apion* 2.1-144) to Rome in the time of Gaius, and Schürer (*History*, 3¹:605), Stern (*Authors*, 1:389), as well as *OCD²* (s.v. "Apion") take for granted the *Suda*'s claim (*Suidae Lexicon* 'Απίων [ad loc.]) that he was to be found there also under Tiberius and Claudius. Concerning Tiberius, in any case, Pliny (*Natural History*, preface 25) claimed that this emperor knew Apion well enough to refer to him as "cymbalum mundi."

[37]Modern conceptions of the wicked Antiochus arise largely from the rightly hostile accounts of him in the Jewish sources (*OCD²*, s.v. "Antiochus IV"). That some influential Romans did not feel this way is clear from the comments of Tacitus: "King Antiochus endeavored to abolish Jewish superstition and to introduce Greek civilization; the war with the Parthians, however, prevented his improving this basest of peoples" (*Histories* 5.8; English translations of the *Histories* by Clifford H. Moore in the LCL). Within the same context Diodorus Siculus had written previously of Antiochus as "a magnanimous and mild-mannered person" (34/35.1.5; English translations by Francis R. Walton in the LCL). I am reminded also of a highly respectful, early imperial, Greco-Roman miniature bronze of Antiochus which recently toured as part of a collection of these objects (*The Gods Delight: The Human Figure in Classical Bronze*, organized by Arielle P. Kozloff and David Gordon Mitten [Cleveland: The Cleveland Museum of Art, 1988], pp. 172-175).

[38]Josephus *Apion* 2.94-95; LCL translation by H. St. J. Thackeray.

[39]Géza Alföldy, *The Social History of Rome*, trans. David Braund and Frank Pollock (Baltimore: Johns Hopkins University Press, 1991), p. 113.

certainly represented nothing less than the most outrageous slander against the religion of the Jewish people. Still, considering that the analogous Christian blood libels have had an extended and successful history, there is no reason to think Apion's ancient contemporaries were any less fooled.[40]

Another religious slander claimed that the Jewish god was an ass.[41] Damocritus said Jews worshipped a gilded image of the head of this animal.[42] Again, Diodorus Siculus wrote how Antiochus had found in the holy of holies "a marble statue of a heavily bearded man seated on an ass."[43] Likewise, Apion insisted, and once again on the authority of Antiochus Epiphanes, that within the temple "the Jews kept an ass's head, worshipping that animal and deeming it worthy of the deepest reverence."[44]

Near the beginning of the second century Plutarch was still assuming the truth of such views,[45] and about the same time Tacitus provided readers with the founding story behind this "absurd and filthy" cult. As the Jewish people were leaving Egypt after abandoning the traditional gods,

> nothing caused them so much distress as scarcity of water, and in fact they had already fallen exhausted over the plain nigh unto death, when a herd of wild asses moved from their pasturage to a rock that was shaded by a grove of trees. Moses followed them, and, conjecturing the truth from the grassy ground, discovered abundant streams of water. This relieved them, and they then marched six days continuously, and on the seventh seized a country, expelling the former inhabitants; there they founded a city and dedicated a temple.

---

[40]For further discussion of similar charges, see Tcherikover, *Hellenistic Civilization*, pp. 366-367. Juster (*Les Juifs*, 2:204-205) refers briefly to the relationship between the pagan and later Christian accusations against Jews, and Guterman (*Religious Toleration*, p. 46, n. 139) likewise makes clear the serious part which the related and just as equally outrageous claim of infanticide played in hostilities directed against Christianity. Still, calling this type of charge the "fortuitous factor," he fails to do justice to the fact that these accusations were at least as likely to produce hatred and violence as were any more subtle charges associated with monotheism.

[41]For more discussion and bibliography see Sevenster (*Roots of Pagan Anti-Semitism*, pp. 8-10) and Tcherikover (*Hellenistic Civilization*, pp. 365-366).

[42]See p. 17, n. 35.

[43]Diodorus Siculus 34/35.1.3.

[44]Josephus *Apion* 2.80.

[45]*Quaestiones conviviales* 4.5.2.

Within it they consecrated "a statue of that creature whose guidance enabled them to put an end to their wanderings and thirst."[46] What sense should we make of the widespread claim that at the center of the Jewish cult lay the golden image of an ass? Just as much as we can of the equally preposterous insistence that human sacrifice and cannibalism were vital to the same *superstitio*. Elsewhere, after all, Tacitus noted that when Pompey entered the temple in Jerusalem he discovered "the place was empty and the secret shrine contained nothing."[47] This means that several of the most influential writers of the early empire passed on false rumors about the Jewish religion even, as in the case of Tacitus, where they knew better. With good reason, therefore, is Bludau astonished by such a phenomenon: "Gar wunderlich sind die Ansichten, die Tacitus über den Ursprung der Juden...anführt."[48]

Insofar as the Sabbath is concerned, imperial attitudes of an equally slanderous nature have survived and, along with them, hints of the dangers these posed for Jews and others. By way of background we need to keep in mind the remarks of various influential Romans. Seneca wrote, "Let us forbid lamps to be lighted on the Sabbath, since the gods do not need light, neither do men take pleasure in soot."[49] Objectively, we might well ask why a bit of light should not have been preferred to darkness. Indeed, though he intended otherwise, Seneca's contemporary, Persius, described a warm scene among the otherwise drab *insulae* of Rome: it was the Sabbath when "the lamps wreathed with violets and ranged round the greasy window-sills have spat forth their thick clouds of smoke, when the floppy tunnies' tails are curled round the dishes of red ware, and the white jars are swollen out with wine."[50] Try as he did to conjure up an ugly image, it consisted in fact of lights, flowers, decorated plates of fish, and the fruit of the vine all nicely set out. What is it that justifies the attitude of Persius? Or, as Tcherikover properly phrases the question, "Why should the custom

---

[46]*Histories* 5.3-4.

[47]Ibid., 5.9; cf. *Histories* 5.5 on imageless worship. So too Bludau, "Die Juden Roms," p. 207.

[48]Bludau, "Die Juden Roms," pp. 202-203. He continues (pp. 204-205), "Eines Gefühles des Unmutes können wir uns nicht erwehren, dass der geistreiche und gelehrte Historiker so alberne und lächerliche Märchen über der Juden Ursprung und Eigentümlichkeiten...gläubig weitererzählt."

[49]*Epistulae morales* 95.47; except where otherwise noted, English translations of the *Epistulae* are those of Richard M. Gummere in the LCL.

[50]*Satires* 5.180-184; LCL translation by G. G. Ramsey.

of observing the Sabbath, so full of dignity and calm, have aroused contempt and mockery?"[51]

Particularly interesting, therefore, is the fact that Rome's first emperor had demonstrated a similar contempt for this fundamental religious observance. According to Suetonius, that is, Augustus made the jaundiced comment, "Not even a Jew, my dear Tiberius, fasts so scrupulously on his sabbaths as I have today."[52] The Sabbath was not a day of fasting, but neither Augustus nor the other Gentiles who assumed it was had taken the time to learn about what they were criticizing.[53] In the case of the Sabbath, therefore, the later Seneca and Persius were simply passing on old misunderstandings and prejudices that had made their way very early into imperial circles.

Clearer are imperial attitudes towards another basic religious observance, the dietary laws. We have evidence of disapproval in this regard associated not only with Augustus but also with his successors Tiberius and Gaius. Macrobius knew the jibe of Augustus, based on Herod the Great's penchant for killing his own children, that it were better to be Herod's pig than his son.[54] Though this comment may not have been as hostile as Daniel indicates,[55] the fact that Rome's first emperor made either it or the one about the Sabbath does have significance. This is the case because they both reveal the disparaging attitude of the earliest of Rome's new rulers towards what from his perspective really ought to have been inconsequential Jewish religious practices. Within the realm of reason, after all, neither the family dinner on the Sabbath nor Jewish aversion to pork constituted a threat to emperor or empire.

This was not the end of the matter. Tiberius almost surely and Gaius without doubt picked up on and attached threats to those who practiced the very same eating habits. Thus, in his *Epistulae morales*

---

[51]Tcherikover, *Hellenistic Civilization*, p. 370.

[52]*Augustus* 76.2.

[53]For the sources which express this view, see Sevenster, *Roots of Pagan Anti-Semitism*, pp. 130-132. Though he, like Harry J[oshua] Leon (*The Jews of Ancient Rome* [1960; reprint ed. with new introduction by Carolyn A. Osiek, Peabody, MA: Hendrickson Publishers, Inc., 1995], pp. 13-14), is surprised at the misunderstanding, it does not appear to dawn on him that this aspect of the Gentile attack upon the Sabbath was unwarranted. Contrary to his view, therefore, it is not in the present case the Jewish "strangeness" (p. 144) but instead the Jewish straw man which was at fault.

[54]*Saturnalia* 2.4.11.

[55]Daniel, "Anti-Semitism," p. 56.

108.22 Seneca related that he had once become a vegetarian only to be forced by the threat of false prosecution to give up his new diet:

> Do you ask how I came to abandon the practice? It was this way: The days of my youth coincided with the early part of the reign of Tiberius Caesar. Some foreign rites [alienigena sacra] were at that time being expelled [movebantur],[56] and abstinence from certain kinds of animal food was set down among evidence of the superstition [inter argumenta superstitionis].[57] So at the request of my father, who did not fear prosecution [calumniam], but who detested philosophy, I returned to my previous habits.

As an eyewitness account of datable occurrences within the religious history of imperial Rome, this text informs us that the early years of Tiberius witnessed an attack against the practices of foreign religion within the city. Moreover, it was sufficiently severe that the city's leading families took cognizance of their diet rather than submit themselves to the dangers of false prosecution[58] on the grounds of adherence to such practices.

Especially interesting is the chronological allusion because it makes this attack contemporary with the 19 CE Tiberian measures against the Jewish, Egyptian, and perhaps other foreign rites to be discussed in the next two chapters. As a result, we may suppose an imperial endeavor to rid Rome of certain foreign *superstitiones*. In this light Seneca's statement that "abstinence from certain kinds of animal food was set down among evidence of the superstition" becomes quite significant. Although he did not mention by name the prosecuted foreign *superstitio* concerning which he wrote, he did specify that one

---

[56]Stern (*Authors*, 1:434) follows the LCL in translating *movebantur* by "inaugurated," but, as Max Radin (*The Jews among the Greeks and Romans* [Philadelphia: Jewish Publication Society, 1915], p. 310) indicates, the contextually more likely sense is "expelled."

[57]We must be careful to draw no false conclusions from the "inter argumenta superstitionis" which means no more than "among evidence of the superstition." Specifically, the LCL translation ("as a proof of interest in the strange cult"), followed also by Stern, is eisegetic; its unsupported word *interest* implies that Seneca had in mind religious novices or proselytes exploring the possibilities of the superstition. All he really claimed was that the Roman authorities could use dietary customs to spot practitioners of the cult and that even members of the most highly placed families were not above suspicion. Hence, as to whether these were old or new adherents of the *superstitio* Seneca had nothing to say, for this matter is entirely separate from and may not be confused with what Seneca wrote about himself here, i.e., that he had recently become a Pythagorean.

[58]*Calumnia* refers to false charges.

religious custom in particular, i.e., abstention from certain meats, easily identified it for powerful Roman enemies. At the very least, therefore, Seneca constitutes unequivocal testimony to the reality of hostile Roman attitudes towards religiously based foreign dietary customs as well as to the hostile actions which arose in association with these attitudes during the early years of Tiberius' rule. Even more relevant, given in dietary matters Judaism's high profile among Gentile observers, it is entirely reasonable that scholarship has placed Seneca's account within the context of the 19 CE expulsion of Jewish rites from Rome.[59]

Circumstantial evidence in favor of this interpretation of Seneca arises out of an eyewitness account in Philo. It describes a Roman hearing held by the next emperor, Gaius, in order to deal, ostensibly, with the issue of Jewish rights at Alexandria.[60] Present were, besides

---

[59]So, for example, Frederic Huidekoper (*Judaism at Rome B.C. 76 to A.D. 140*, 3d ed. [New York: James Miller, 1880], p. 188), Gustav Volkmar ("Die Religions-verfolgung unter Kaiser Tiberius und die Chronologie des Fl. Josephus in der Pilatus-Periode," *Jahrbücher für protestantische Theologie* 11 [1885]:137), Merrill ("Expulsion," p. 369, n. 1), Smallwood ("Some Notes on the Jews under Tiberius," p. 320; so also her *The Jews under Roman Rule from Pompey to Diocletian: A Study in Political Relations*, Studies in Judaism in Late Antiquity, vol. 20 [Leiden: E. J. Brill, 1981], p. 205), Leon (*Jews of Ancient Rome*, p. 19, n. 4), Stern (*Authors*, 1:434), Schürer (*History*, 3¹:76, n. 86), and Margaret H. Williams ("The Expulsion of the Jews from Rome in A.D. 19," *Latomus* 48 [1989]: 765). The modification of Radin (*Jews among Greeks and Romans*, p. 310), based upon Seneca's plural "alienigena sacra movebantur," that the action was directed against more than one foreign religion, finds support in the Suetonian statement (*Tiberius* 36) that Tiberius "Externas caerimonias ...compescuit" ("He abolished foreign cults."). To the extent they include both Jewish and Isiac rites, the accounts of Tacitus and Josephus agree. Hence, since the cult of Isis had its own food laws, we may not be so sure as Smallwood ("Some Notes on the Jews under Tiberius," p. 320, n. 2; *Jews under Roman Rule*, p. 205, n. 12) that Seneca had in mind only Judaism. Of course his singular *superstitio* might indicate "alienigena sacra" refers to the foreign practices of a single cult rather than to various foreign *superstitiones*. More likely, however, Seneca had little interest in the niceties of foreign religiosity except as these had played a central part in the governmental measures affecting him. Thus, given the early actions against practices of the Egyptian and Jewish cults as well as the probability Seneca was recounting events mentioned in Tacitus, Suetonius, Dio, and Josephus, it is perhaps likely, so also Michel Malaise (*Les conditions de pénétration et de diffusion des cultes égyptiens en Italie*, Études préliminaires aux religions orientales dans l'empire Romain, vol. 22 [Leiden: E. J. Brill, 1972], p. 391), that Seneca's reference includes the dietary customs of at least these two foreign cults.

[60]Philo provides us with this unique, eyewitness account of a direct Jewish-imperial encounter in his *Legatio* 349-367. P. Lond. 1912 alone is comparable in primary source value.

the emperor and his own friends, the members of both the Greek and Jewish delegations from that city. For the latter group this was a frightening time: "the moment we entered we knew from his [Gaius'] look and movements that we had come into the presence not of a judge but of an accuser more hostile than those arrayed against us" and that "the actual proceedings showed a ruthless tyrant with a menacing frown on his despotic brow."[61] Again, arguments completed, "we gave up, for there was no strength left in us and...we all the time expected nothing else but death."[62]

In terms of the genuine issues, Gaius first attacked the Jewish delegation on the grounds it had failed to sacrifice to him as a god.[63] His next concern was the one of interest in the present context, for the emperor now inquired, "Why do you refuse to eat pork?"[64] Regardless of how inconsequential such an inquiry might appear, and in spite of the laughter it immediately provoked among those who were present with the emperor, this was from Philo's uncomfortable perspective a "grave and momentous question."[65] We need only to recall that other autocrat of two hundred years earlier, the Greek ruler Antiochus Epiphanes, who likewise had had an aversion to the religiously based Jewish diet. The result at that time, terrible trials for pious Jews caught between the opposing requirements of their god and of their earthly master, remains infamous. In any case, it was only after he had introduced these two matters that Gaius finally came to the supposedly central issue of Jewish rights in the city of Alexandria.

---

[61]Philo *Legatio* 349-350. Unless otherwise noted, English translations of Philo's *Legatio* and *Flaccus* are those of F. H. Colson in the LCL.

[62]*Legatio* 366. This is not a complete exaggeration. The *Acta Isidori* (cf. *The Acts of the Pagan Martyrs: Acta Alexandrinorum*, ed. Herbert A. Musurillo [1954; reprint ed., New York: Arno Press, 1979], pp. 18-26, 117-140, and *CPJ*, 2:66-81, for Greek texts, English translations, and introductions) report how a similar meeting conducted later by Claudius resulted in the immediate death of the losers in the debate, the Alexandrians Isidoros and Lampon. The former, incidently, was part of the opposing delegation at the present hearing (*Legatio* 355).

[63]*Legatio* 353-357.

[64]Ibid., 361.

[65]In terms of the emperors prior to Caligula, Anthony A. Barrett (*Caligula: The Corruption of Power* [1989; reprint ed., New York: Simon & Schuster, 1991], p. 184) treats inquiries about the practices of Jews as "fairly good-natured mockery of what were considered their outlandish religious views." Whether this is true or not, we must take seriously the word of one who had personally experienced the mockery that its results could be devastating, for so Philo wrote in *Legatio* 176-177 and 349-367.

Philo then concluded his narrative with the assertion that he had now "told in a summary way the cause of the enmity which Gaius had for the whole nation of the Jews."[66] Therefore, central to that cause were fundamental matters of religious practice, in particular, for present purposes, the prejudice of Gaius in a dietary matter of no consequence to the welfare of his empire.[67]

It is appropriate that we end this examination of upper-class and imperial attitudes towards the Jewish people and their cult with a fictional antecedent of both in Egyptian history. Traceable back to the third century BCE priest Manetho is the hostile account according to which the Pharaohs had found it necessary to expel Moses and his band of lepers from that country.[68] Specifically, Diodorus Siculus passed on to his readers how "the ancestors of the Jews had been driven out of all Egypt as men who were impious and detested by the gods. For by way of purging the country all persons who had white or leprous marks on their bodies had been assembled and driven across the border, as being under a curse."[69]

Another Augustan historian, Pompeius Trogus, also passed on information of a similar kind.[70] Likewise, Chaeremon, the mid-first-century CE Alexandrian who was perhaps a member of that city's delegation to Claudius and without doubt a tutor to Nero in later times, wrote in his history of Egypt how it had become necessary to expel the diseased Jews from that country.[71] Again, Apion, his older Alexandrian contemporary who, as noted already, was also active in Rome, reaffirmed in his own history both the disease-caused expulsion of Jews[72] and the equally unpleasant origins of the Sabbath:"'After a six days' march,' he [Apion] says, 'they developed tumours in the groin, and that was why, after safely reaching the country now called Judaea, they rested on the seventh day, and called that day *sabbaton*,

---

[66]*Legatio* 373.

[67]Discussing the Jewish aversion to pork, Sevenster (*Roots of Pagan Anti-Semitism*, pp. 136-139) notes the oddity that, among groups with dietary restrictions, the Romans centered their criticism on Jews.

[68]Josephus *Apion* 1.227-250; cf. the Egyptian Lysimachus (*Apion* 1.304-311).

[69]Diodorus Siculus 34/35.1.1.

[70]*M. Iuniani Iustini epitoma historiarum Philippicarum Pompei Trogi*, ed. Otto Seel (Leipzig: B. G. Teubner, 1935) 36.2.12.

[71]Josephus *Apion* 1.289-290.

[72]Ibid., 2.15.

preserving the Egyptian terminology; for disease of the groin in Egypt is called *sabbo*."[73]

That this material continued to play a part within the Roman mainstream is clearly demonstrated by the evaluation of one of its principal historians. After listing the theories about Jewish origins, Tacitus concluded approvingly, "Most authors agree that once during a *plague* [tabes] in Egypt which caused bodily disfigurement, King Bocchoris approached the oracle of Ammon and asked for a remedy, whereupon he was told to purge his kingdom and to transport this [Jewish] race into other lands, since it was hateful to the gods."[74] Hateful to the gods. History tells us of many instances where one group made the unequivocal religious claim against another that the gods hated it. Normally we recognize here that deity has received a bum rap, and we file the claims under such labels as "prejudice" and "intolerance." This, in reality, is where all of these claims concerning disease-laden Jews belong, even when supported by the intellectual authority of Tacitus or the political authority of the emperor Claudius who, as mentioned already, conceived of Jews as "fomenting a common *plague* for the whole world."[75]

Thus, whatever other reasons might be suggested for the anti-Jewish attitudes of Rome's writers and rulers, the most fundamental accusations spelled out here, i.e., rites of human sacrifice combined with cannibalism, the worship of a donkey, "tumors of the groin" as the etymology of the word *Sabbath*, the dingy Sabbath dinner, the distaste of pork, Jewish origins traced back to the spreading of leprosy, and Jewish expulsion based on the same argument, are so ludicrous as to tell us absolutely nothing credible or threatening about Jews and Judaism. Wolfgang Wiefel recognizes the same essential reality: "Vielmehr erscheint die Judenschaft in Rom schon am Anfang ihrer Geschichte von Missverständnissen umgeben."[76] Surrounded by

---

[73]Josephus *Apion* 2.21.

[74]*Histories* 5.3. As to Tacitus' approval, see Isidore Lévy, "Tacite et l'origine du peuple juif," *Latomus* 5 (1946):339-340. He reminds us that Tacitus chose the Alexandrian and most hostile source for his explanation of Jewish origins.

[75]P. 16.

[76]Wolfgang Wiefel, "Die jüdische Gemeinschaft im antiken Rom und die Anfänge des römischen Christentums: Bemerkungen zu Anlass und Zweck des Römerbriefs," *Judaica* 26 (1970):67. Hence, the general assessment of the situation by Daniel ("Anti-Semitism," p. 46; cf. to the contrary, Patricia A. Johnston, "The Concept of Empire in Vergil's *Eclogues*: Immigrants, Emigrants, and a Child to Guide Them," *Humanitas: Newsletter of the Ohio Classical Conference* 15 [1990-1991]:26-41) is accurate: "A survey of the comments about Jews in the Hellenistic-

misunderstandings, to say the very least. These many accusations do, however, raise serious questions concerning the credibility of those who disseminated them, and, as Claudius' reference to the Jewish plague indicates, they certainly proved threatening to Jews and the practice of their religion.

From the perspective of historical methodology these are vital observations. They mean that our analysis of the Roman sources must always make allowance for both anti-Jewish reporting of and anti-Judaism behind imperial measures. In other words, we face a two-headed tendentiousness that played its part not only in imperial actions against Jews and their religious practices but also in the Gentile reporting of those actions.

This tendentiousness of the ancient Jewish and Gentile sources contributes much to the difficulty of reconstructing any aspect of Jewish life under the early Roman empire. The task is made all the more difficult by a similar problem which runs through the modern reconstructions. Manifested in the common assumption that Jews were responsible for the hostile attitudes and actions which they faced, tendentiousness takes the general form of a statement like that of Barrett, who comments on "the problems presented by the Jewish people" and "the rigidity of the Jewish faith."[77] Again, George La Piana refers to "the inflexible temper of Judaism,"[78] Heikki Solin takes for granted "die Exklusivität der Juden, ihr Festhalten an der grundsätzlichen Besonderheit allen anderen gegenüber,"[79] and Daniel blames the problems on five areas of Jewish life: origins, strangeness, religion and ritual, exclusiveness, and proselytizing: "Jews remained

---

Roman literature shows that they were almost universally disliked, or at least viewed with an amused contempt. Some modern scholars have attempted to minimize the dislike, and relatively few have recognized just how deep and widespread the anti-Semitic feelings were." Nevertheless, his apparent assumption (pp. 48, 49, 57, 58, 59, 62) that Jews caused the situation is clearly invalid, for it does not take with sufficient seriousness the preposterous nature of the basic charges made against them.

[77]Barrett, *Caligula*, pp. 183-184. We shall refer to the problematic nature of his judgments about Jews in chapter 3; cf. p. 84, n. 54.

[78]George La Piana, "Foreign Groups in Rome during the First Centuries of the Empire," *Harvard Theological Review* 20 (1927):393. This inflexible Judaism he compares tendentiously with "so great an institution as the Christian church" (p. 399), i.e., with that "new instrument of world domination fit to supersede" the glories of Rome (p. 395).

[79]Heikki Solin, "Juden und Syrer im westlichen Teil der römischen Welt. Eine ethnisch-demographische Studie mit besonderer Berücksichtigung der sprachlichen Zustände" in *ANRW*, 2.29²:617.

Jews," he claims, "sufficiently different to attract attention, most of which was unpleasant."[80]

For a similar view we may return to the statement of Smallwood that the Roman writers mentioned Jews "only when they gave serious trouble." The matter-of-fact way in which she herself makes reference here to Jews as troublemakers represents the very same variety of tendentiousness. Specifically, though this blame-the-Jew motif is only one interpretation of the reality that these people were greatly discomforted under the early Roman empire, scholarship has granted it nearly canonical status.[81] For example, Smallwood uses the same motif a second time in order to justify the Claudian anti-Jewish measures referred to in Dio 60.6.6-7. She writes that "Dio, by giving no indication of the Jews' offence, creates the impression that Claudius attacked them gratuitously. But such an action would be uncharacteristic of Claudius with his sense of justice and his concern for the underdogs of society.... Some unrecorded provocation must have occurred."[82] This is certainly a remarkable statement, for, as we shall observe subsequently, Dio's reference is to imperial measures intended to curtail Jewish religious practices at Rome. That aside, Smallwood goes so far as to place blame on Jews even where she recognizes that the Gentile source did not indicate such responsibility. Moreover, she does this on the doubtful, as we shall later discover, presupposition of Claudius' justice and mercy.

Similar is Williams' repristination of the contention that hostility towards them was the reasonable Gentile response to the "turbulence-prone Jews" and their resultant penchant for riotousness; Jews, she assumes, were one among a variety of "troublesome groups."[83] Or, to cite Solin once again, "Die Juden [Roms] waren immer ein Ferment der Unruhe, und so entstanden des öfteren Situationen, in denen die römischen Beamten sich gezwungen sahen, zu Strafmaßnahmen zu greifen."[84] Likewise, May, who in 1936 made quite clear that he did not consider himself hostile either to ancient or modern absolute

---

[80]Daniel, "Anti-Semitism," pp. 49-64, p. 49. Cf. Sevenster, *Roots of Pagan Anti-Semitism*, passim; cf. Tcherikover, *Hellenistic Civilization*, pp. 357-377.

[81]For the view that this image of Jews as troublemakers achieved literal canonical status within the Acts of the Apostles see Slingerland, "'The Jews' in the Pauline Portion of Acts," pp. 314-318.

[82]Smallwood, *Jews under Roman Rule*, p. 215.

[83]Williams, "Expulsion," pp. 782-784.

[84]Solin, "Juden und Syrer" in *ANRW*, 2.29²:686; cf. his p. 690 for the same "Ferment der Unruhe."

power,[85] can account for Claudius' anti-Jewish activities only on the basis of the Jewish tendency to disturb the public order.[86]

Momigliano also makes an odd appeal to "the nature of Jewish activities,"[87] and the same ideas manifest themselves in Willrich's treatment of both the 38 CE pogrom against the Alexandrian Jews and the demand of Gaius that his statue be placed in the Jerusalem temple.[88] In a similar context Balsdon accuses the eastern Jews of a general inability to compromise,[89] and Carl Kraeling implies that the suffering of Jews in Antioch was the result of "a sense of their own self-importance."[90] Similar thoughts are found in Th. Reinach's interpretation of Claudius' letter to Alexandria, Dio 60.6.6-7, and *Claudius* 25.4.[91] They then appear one further time in the generalization of Scramuzza that "for one reason or another, the Jewish population scattered throughout the empire gave much concern to every emperor in the first century of the Christian era."[92]

As the discussion of Sevenster makes manifest, these modern generalizations correspond poorly to the realities of antiquity. That is, in spite of the sundry malicious things which certain circles enjoyed repeating, many Roman and other Gentiles were to be found whose experiences with Jews and Judaism were of a quite different kind.[93]

---

[85]Gaston May, "L'activité juridique de l'Empereur Claude," *Revue historique de droit français et étranger* 15 [1936]:66. Here we encounter a curious correlation between the rise of modern fascism and the improved image of Rome's emperors.

[86]May, "Politique religieuse," passim.

[87]Momigliano, *Claudius*, p. 32.

[88]Willrich, "Caligula," pp. 401, 412. Odd in regard to 38 CE Alexandria are the comments of Jean Juster (*Les Juifs*, 2:182-183) concerning the rebelliousness of Alexandrian Jews as exemplified by their massacre. Solin ("Juden und Syrer" in *ANRW*, 2.29²:715, n. 286a), referring to oppressed Jews as "fanatischen Rebellen," cites Juster approvingly. For a recent summary of and commentary on Juster's entire work see Rabello, "Legal Condition" in *ANRW*, 2.30:662-762.

[89]Balsdon, *Gaius*, p. 139. The fallaciousness of the ideas behind this claim will be demonstrated in chapter 3; cf. p. 86, n. 56.

[90]Carl H. Kraeling, "The Jewish Community at Antioch," *Journal of Biblical Literature* 51 (1932):148.

[91]Th. Reinach, "L'empereur Claude," p. 131.

[92]Scramuzza, "Policy" in *Beginnings of Christianity*, 5:287.

[93]Sevenster, *Roots of Pagan Anti-Semitism*, pp. 191-218; cf. Gager, *Origins of Anti-Semitism*, pp. 36, 58-66.

Seneca himself was certainly aware of the fact: "The customs of this accursed race have gained such influence that they are now received throughout all the world. The vanquished have given laws to their victors."[94] To this extent of course Bruce errs when he summarizes that "Jews were unpopular in Rome: they had been so ever since Pompey's incorporation of Judaea within the Roman Empire brought increasing numbers of them to Rome."[95]

Thus, it is perhaps better than anyone else that Bludau captures a basic sense of the way in which many ancients perceived the Jewish people and their religion:

> If the firm faith in an invisible, eternal, and all encompassing god, creator of heaven and earth and his holy moral code, as well as the theological simplicity of this faith must have drawn people to Judaism, there existed even a better sermon for converts than the written or verbal instruction, and this was the life where Judaism was practiced with sincerity. Its seriousness, its unchanging piety, its good morality, it firm obedience to the law, its modesty, beneficence, and harmony found approval in wide circles.[96]

Furthermore, and regardless of the claim of Smallwood regarding the Claudian "sense of justice and his concern for the underdogs of society," analogies which might be drawn from the nature of modern absolutism require us to take seriously the much more reasonable possibility that the repeatedly maligned Jews were simply victims of imperial mistreatment. Bell is specific about this in regard to Flaccus' actions in Alexandria,[97] and so too, of all people, was Tacitus: he accused bad procuratorial administration of causing the outbreak of the Jewish war.[98]

In this regard Goodenough reminds us that

> the spirit of Roman rule corresponds most closely in modern times to fascism, for Augustus and his successors were fascist rulers in the sense that they had no constitutional warrant for their totalitarian authority.... This fascist power, which began with proscriptions, exiles, and civil murders on a great scale, operated effectively, and, once settled, quite liberally on any point except its own despotic

---

[94]So Augustine *City of God* 6.11; LCL translation by William M. Green.

[95]Bruce, "Tacitus," p. 39.

[96]Bludau, "Die Juden Roms," p. 222 (my translation).

[97]H. Idris Bell, "Egypt under the Early Principate" in *CAH*, 10:310.

[98]*Histories* 5.9-10.

power. From subject peoples little was asked except complete sub-
mission and the prompt payment of very high taxes.[99]

In fact, the well disposed Ankaran title to the *Res gestae* of Augustus
expresses precisely this view: "Concerning the Accomplishments of the
Divine Augustus by which He *subjected* the World to the Mastery of
the Roman people."[100]

As a result, we are compelled to take seriously the implications
of Momigliano's statement that Claudius "felt the need to concentrate
the real government of the State in the Emperor's hands, and to base
that government upon the army...transformed into a means of maintaining the equilibrium of the whole Empire."[101] While it is true that
absolute rulers are able to accomplish their goals, it is equally true
that those subjected to this absolutism often fare poorly. Philo, dealing
with the emperor Gaius, knew this first hand: "What greater curse can
a slave have than a hostile master? Subjects are slaves of the absolute
emperor...."[102] Thus, Momigliano's already mentioned appeal to "the
nature of Jewish activities," Williams' explanation that the plight of
Jews resulted from the simple fact that they were one among various
"troublesome groups," and Smallwood's need to read into Dio 60.6.6-7
a Jewish "offence" provoking the benign Claudius do not take seriously
enough the actual relationships between absolute power and those
subjected to it.

Though he typically identifies Jews with political agitation, May
makes the interesting observation that the discrete nature of Jewish

---

[99]Erwin R. Goodenough, *An Introduction to Philo Judaeus*, 2d ed. (Oxford:
Basil Blackwell, 1962), p. 53. Cf. Alföldy (*Social History*, pp. 99-100): "The
princeps enjoyed power which was, in practice, unlimited: there was no power in
the Roman state which could be employed as an alternative to that of the emper-
or. The contemporary view is revealed by Tacitus' account of the behaviour of the
'weak' Claudius when conservative senators took a stand against his policy which
admitted the Gallic aristocracy to senatorial offices. He duly heard the contrary
arguments but did not allow himself to be swayed by them and immediately contradicted them. Thereupon, the Senate passed a decree in accordance with his pro-
posal (Tac., *Ann.*, 11.23ff.)." Tacitus was aware of this absolutism (Mellor, *Tacitus*,
p. 60; Ronald Martin, *Tacitus* [Berkeley and Los Angeles: University of California
Press, 1981], p. 143). For Gaius' "total absolutism," cf. Albino Garzetti, *From
Tiberius to the Antonines*, trans. J. R. Foster (London: Methuen, 1974), p. 86.

[100]My translation of the Latin text in *Velleius Paterculus, Compendium of
Roman History; Res gestae Divi Augusti*, trans. Frederick W. Shipley, LCL (London: William Heinemann, 1924).

[101]Momigliano, *Claudius*, p. 24.

[102]*Legatio* 119.

religious rites would have resulted in a lack of attention as compared to the public ceremonies of other eastern cults.[103] Penna underlines this: "selon la documentation, dont nous disposons, le judaïsme romain du Ier siècle nous révèle un panorama plutôt pâle et plat. Rien n'émerge en dehors de l'attachement quotidien et ordinaire aux composantes les plus élémentaires de l'identité propre."[104] In any case, the clear examples of slander already referred to, i.e., what Sevenster also recognizes as cases of "foolish and libellous contentions,"[105] require that we be suspicious of all charges of Jewish responsibility. In other words, such contentions reveal that prejudice rather than anything which Jews actually did played a central part in upper-class Roman hostility towards them.

Even in less obvious cases the situation may not have been what is generally supposed. Specifically, it is often assumed that one source of Gentile hostility was an absolute monotheism which caused Jews to despise the various traditional Gods.[106] Nevertheless, Josephus interpreted Moses to have declared, "Let none blaspheme the gods which other cities revere, nor rob foreign temples, nor take treasure that has been dedicated in the name of any god."[107] This was not a Josephan peculiarity. Philo could also write respectfully of Dionysus, Heracles, and the Dioscuri (*Legatio* 78-92), of Hermes, Apollo, and Ares (*Legatio* 93-113), as well as of attendant powers (*Legatio* 6).[108] In particular, he could refer to the deified Augustus as surpassing human nature (*Legatio* 143)[109] and as the "savior and benefactor" (*Flaccus* 74), he could heap honor on the imperial cult center in Alexandria (*Legatio* 151) and write approvingly of Jewish religious piety towards the revered imperial house ("τῆς εἰς τὸν Σεβαστὸν οἶκον ὁσιότητός," *Flaccus* 49). Hence, these two most important witnesses to the first-century Jewish encounter with the Gentile world manifest no little respect for its religiosity.

---

[103]May, "Politique religieuse," pp. 14-15, 20, 36.

[104]Penna, "Les Juifs a Rome," p. 336.

[105]Sevenster, *Roots of Pagan Anti-Semitism*, p. 140.

[106]Cf. Smallwood, "Jews and Romans," p. 233.

[107]*Antiquities* 2.207. LCL translation by H. St. J. Thackeray.

[108]Cf 1 Corinthians 15:24 and the associated views of Paul. He was another diaspora Jew.

[109]Cf. Frend (*Martyrdom*, p. 90) for helpful references to the similar religious implications among Gentiles of the title *augustus*.

Were Josephus and Philo disingenuous? Though it really makes no difference, I think not. Were they unique in their tolerance? No, for there survives the most remarkable statement of the *Letter of Aristeas* 15 quoted approvingly by Josephus that the god of the Jewish people is identical with Zeus.[110] We may also recall the Gentile theophoric names like Aphrodisia, Dionysias, and Isidora witnessed by the Jewish catacombs of Rome.[111] Relatedly, sacrifice associated with the Roman *augusti* belonged to each day's cult in Jerusalem.[112]

In fact, it is the catacombs of Roman Jews which give us some of our best primary source evidence against charges associated with Jewish particularism. In general, Roman Jewish devotion to a single god is entirely unremarkable in a city where the physical remains of antiquity attest the worship of large numbers of individual foreign and domestic deities.[113] Again, concerning the architecture of the Roman catacombs, Paul Styger is unwilling to concede the possibility that the Christian catacombs of the city were patterned after the Jewish ones. He argues, therefore, that both the Jewish and Christian structures must have been borrowed from the pagan models.[114] However, since obvious examples of pagan catacombs do not exist, his evidence is insufficient to make the case. Still, implicitly following Styger, Margaret H. Williams does make the certainly relevant observation that, "as for the forms of these [Jewish] family tombs, throughout the cities of the Diaspora they tended to be the same as those most favoured by the gentile population."[115]

---

[110]*Antiquities* 12.22. Cf. Marcel Simon, "Jupiter-Yahvé: Sur un essai de théologie pagano-juive," *Numen* 23 (1976):43 and 50; likewise, Martin Hengel, *Judaism and Hellenism: Studies in Their Encounter in Palestine during the Early Hellenistic Period*, trans. John Bowden, 2 vols. (Philadelphia: Fortress Press, 1981), 1:264-265.

[111]Leon, *Jews of Ancient Rome*, p. 121; Penna, "Les Juifs a Rome," p. 335.

[112]Chapter 2 provides further discussion; cf. p. 48.

[113]Cf. the topographies of ancient Rome for the ubiquity of individual deities and their cult centers.

[114]Paul Styger, "Heidnische und christliche Katakomben," *Pisciculi: Studien zur Religion und Kultur des Altertums, Franz Joseph Dölger zum sechzigsten Geburtstage dargeboten von Freunden, Verehrern und Schülern*, Ergänzungsband 1, ed. Theodor Klausner and Adolf Rücker (Münster: Verlag Aschendorf, 1939), pp. 266-275.

[115]Margaret H. Williams, "The Organization of Jewish Burials in Ancient Rome in the Light of Evidence from Palestine and the Diaspora," *Zeitschrift für Papyrologie und Epigraphik* 101 (1994):173, 177.

Furthermore, mentioning Roman synagogues of the Augustesians and Agrippesians,[116] the inscriptions of the catacombs have nothing of a foreign or subversive sound to them. Likewise, the synagogues of the Campesians and Siburesians drew their members from the regions of the Campus Martius and the Subura. These were thriving areas of the city in which Jews could hardly have hoped to isolate themselves from Gentile neighbors and religions.[117] Concerning another region, the modern Trastevere, Leonard Rutgers states the matter clearly:

> Even for those Jews who had freely come to Rome, pagans were never far off, for just as the tombs of deceased Jews and non-Jews were situated close to one another, so were the houses of the living. In Rome, one of the centers of Jewish settlement was in *Transtiberim*, present-day Trastevere, Augustus's *regio* XIV. This piece of land, located on the left side of the Tiber and outside the *pomerium*, attracted foreigners from all over the world, making it Rome's most cosmopolitan district.... The living conditions in Trastevere being what they were, Jewish families could hardly avoid communicating with neighbors having radically different religious preferences.[118]

Again, the cognomina of the epitaphs are almost entirely Latin or Greek,[119] which informs us that the various Jews called Maximus, Victor, or Iulia[120] were not intent upon distinguishing themselves from other Romans of the same name. Of course the epitaphic formula

---

[116]Leon, *Jews of Ancient Rome*, pp. 140-142. Cf. Williams, "Organization of Jewish Burials," pp. 166-167.

[117]Leon, *Jews of Ancient Rome*, pp. 144-145, 151-153; Suzanne Collon, "Remarques sur les quartiers juifs de la Rome antique," *Mélanges d'archéologie et d'histoire de l'École française de Rome* 57 (1940):86-89; Leonard Victor Rutgers, "Archaeological Evidence for the Interaction of Jews and Non-Jews in Late Antiquity," *American Journal of Archeology* 96 (1992):177, n. 128.

[118]Rutgers, "Archaeological Evidence," pp. 116-117. From this perspective it is very difficult to make sense of the unsupported and practically self-contradictory charge of Jewish isolation in the statement of Solin ("Juden und Syrer" in *ANRW*, 2.29²:602; likewise pp. 684-685, 695, 720, 780) that "die meisten Juden wohnten nicht in Palästina, sondern in der Diaspora, die eine einzigartige Erscheinung ist. Da die Juden sich in der Diaspora vielfach isolierten, vermischten sie sich nur wenig." Somewhat better, perhaps, is his view of the contrary tendencies within the Judaism of the Diaspora (p. 713; cf. p. 706): "Treue gegenüber nationalen Traditionen auf der einen und der Wunsch, sich der Umgebung anzupassen, auf der anderen Seite."

[119]Leon, *Jews of Ancient Rome*, p. 107.

[120]Ibid., pp. 98-99.

shalom / eirene / pax is distinctive,[121] but the formulas "Θάρσει οὐδεὶς ἀθάνατος" and "benemerens" are no more Jewish than is the standard "fecit" or other grammatical constructions of these inscriptions.[122] As to particular epithets, many of them made perfectly good sense in a Gentile environment.[123]

Perhaps most interesting in this regard are aspects of the art belonging to Jewish burial places. Granted, Judaism did bring with it a series of singular signs and symbols, i.e., the menorah, lulav, shofar, and Torah shrine of the catacombs.[124] Far more worthy of remark, however, is the fact that many key elements of this art cannot be distinguished from their Gentile counterparts. In general, Leon's comment is apropos: "When the painted rooms of the Appia catacomb were discovered, the first reaction was to regard them as of pagan origin, since it was felt that obviously such figures of animals and human beings...would hardly have been the work of Jewish artists or used by Jews to adorn a tomb chamber."[125] In particular, we might think of the beautiful figure evidently of the goddess Fortuna painted on a ceiling in the catacomb of the Via Appia.[126] There exists also

---

[121]Erich Dinkler, "Schalom–Eirene–Pax: Jüdische Sepulkralinschriften und ihr Verhältnis zum frühen Christentum," *Rivista di archeologia cristiana* 50 (1974): 121-144.

[122]For references, see Leon, *Jews of Ancient Rome*, pp. 126 and 130.

[123]Cf. Leonard Victor Rutgers, *The Jews in Late Ancient Rome: Evidence of Cultural Interaction in the Roman Diaspora*, Religions in the Graeco-Roman World, vol. 126 (Leiden: E. J. Brill, 1995), pp. 192-193 and 196-197.

[124]Cf. Leon, *Jews of Ancient Rome*, pp. 195-203.

[125]Leon, *Jews of Ancient Rome*, pp. 203-204; cf. Penna ("Les Juifs a Rome," p. 334), Hugo Gressmann ("Jewish Life in Ancient Rome" in *Jewish Studies in Memory of Israel Abrahams*, ed. George Alexander Kohut [New York: Press of the Jewish Institute of Religion, 1927], p. 190), Juster (*Les Juifs*, 1:338-354), La Piana ("Foreign Groups," pp. 376-377), Scramuzza ("Policy" in *Beginnings of Christianity*, 5:284), Joseph Gutmann ("Early Synagogue and Jewish Catacomb Art and its Relation to Christian Art" in *ANRW*, 2.21²:1313-1342), Rutgers ("Archaeological Evidence," passim), and of course Goodenough (*Jewish Symbols in the Greco-Roman Period*, Bollingen Series, vol. 37, 13 vols. [New York: Pantheon Books, 1965], 12:passim) along with the review of Morton Smith ("Goodenough's *Jewish Symbols* in Retrospect," *Journal of Biblical Literature* 86 [1967]:53-68). As a result, the assertion of Solin ("Juden und Syrer" in *ANRW*, 2.29²:623) that "die Trennung von allem Nichtjüdischen der Sinn der jüdischen Katakomben war" has little meaning.

[126]Leon, *Jews of Ancient Rome*, p. 205 and Figure 16. It was still well preserved when I saw it during the summer of 1995.

the Jewish sarcophagus resting in the courtyard of the Palazzo Spada. Its catacomb of origin uncertain, only the inscription distinguishes it from the countless other sarcophagi of the same strigilation design used in antiquity by Gentile Romans.[127] Very important also is the surviving front of the famous Season Sarcophagus, which is readily identified as Jewish by its central menorah-filled medallion. Otherwise, however, displaying a large variety of mythological figures celebrating the seasons of the year, it looks typically Gentile in appearance. Hence, Leon is obviously correct that "such pagan figures were not repugnant to the Jewish user."[128] Cumont is of equal interest in this regard because, after calling attention to the Dionysiac motif of wine pressing below the medallion, he draws the conclusion that the Jew who purchased this sarcophagus from some Gentile shop could not have been "d'une orthodoxie très rigoureuse."[129] The question is, orthodox by whose standards? The fact is, this rare piece of original testimony simply does not correspond to particularistic expectations.

Although a bit further afield, if it is true, as for example Th. Reinach asserts, that Alexandrian Jews wished to become citizens of that city for the sake of then becoming Roman citizens, another image of Jewish particularity disappears.[130] Relatedly, there exists a most interesting inscription of the Jewish woman Rufina. She was ruler of

---

[127]Leon, *Jews of Ancient Rome*, p. 218 and Figure 31. I photographed it there in the summer of 1995. On these sarcophagi in general, note the observation of Rutgers ("Archaeological Evidence," p. 104) that "the most striking feature of the approximately 40 Jewish sarcophagi from Rome is the dominance of pagan or at least religiously neutral imagery, in some cases to such an extent that it is impossible today to determine if these sarcophagi were used for Jewish or for non-Jewish burials."

[128]Leon, *Jews of Ancient Rome*, pp. 211-212 and Figure 44.

[129]Franz Cumont, *Recherches sur le symbolisme funéraire des romains* (Paris: Librairie orientaliste Paul Geuthner, 1942), pp. 485-486. For examples of other Jewish sarcophagi exhibiting Gentile workmanship and motifs see Hermann W. Beyer and Hans Lietzmann *(Jüdische Denkmäler I: Die jüdische Katakombe der Villa Torlonia in Rom* [Berlin: Walter de Gruyter & Co., 1930], pp. 42-45) as weil as Adia Konikoff *(Sarcophagi from the Jewish Catacombs of Ancient Rome: A Catalogue Raisonne*, 2d ed. [Stuttgart: Franz Steiner, 1990], pp. 27-29. Cf. Rutgers ("Archaeological Evidence," p. 108): "It must have been perfectly normal for a Jew to walk into a non-Jewish workshop to order a sarcophagus, just as there was nothing abnormal in the attempt of a non-Jewish salesman to fill such an order as satisfactorily as possible."

[130]Th. Reinach, "L'empereur Claude," p. 129. Sherwin-White *(Racial Prejudice*, p. 93) recognizes that this contradicts his own thesis of Jewish exclusiveness.

a synagogue in Asian Smyrna and had a clearly amicable relationship with the pagan authorities.[131] Again, we may recall the magnificent house of prayer in Asian Sardis built in the very center of the Gentile city.[132] Likewise, Apamea in Asian Phrygia drew upon the motif of Noah's Ark for an entire series of early third-century coinage.[133] This was a result of the Jewish presence in that place already prior to Cicero (*Pro Flacco* 28.68),[134] in whose time Asian Jews and Gentiles worked together to oppose Roman corruption. In sum, none of these rare, contemporary, and authentic glimpses corresponds very well to the picture of ancient Jews and Judaism painted typically by the modern reconstructions.

The historiographic considerations of this chapter provide the fundamental context within which to interpret Republican and early imperial policy vis-à-vis Roman Jews and their cult. Unfortunately, in other words, between us and the first century there is no direct line of sight. Instead, we look back through filters consisting of the ancient Jewish, ancient Gentile, and modern reconstructions of that policy. Each of these, as it turns out, distorts our vision of the relationship between Jews and their Roman masters. Aware of this historiography at all three levels, however, we are now in a position to adjust for its astigmatism and so put in proper perspective the central elements of that relationship.

---

[131]*CII*, 741. Concerning Rufina, see in particular Ross S. Kraemer, "Jewish Women in the Diaspora World of Late Antiquity" in *Jewish Women in Historical Perspective*, ed. Judith R. Baskin (Detroit: Wayne State University Press, 1991), pp. 43-67.

[132]See appendix 1.

[133]Schürer, *History*, 3¹:28-30.

[134]Marshall, "Flaccus," passim.

Chapter Two

Gentile Witnesses to Pre-Claudian Repression
of the
Jewish Cult at Rome

In order to appreciate the situation of Roman Jews under the emperor Claudius, we need to clarify their position prior to him. Initially, therefore, we shall examine what the ancient Gentile sources have to say about this matter. Based on various observations in the previous chapter, it should not be surprising that the primary reference is to governmental policies directed against these Jews as practitioners of a particular foreign *superstitio*.

We begin with Valerius Maximus, the earliest of such sources. He composed the *Factorum et dictorum memorabilium libri novem* as a protégé of Tiberius (14-37 CE).[1] Unlike Tacitus, Suetonius, and Dio Cassius, he was both an eyewitness to early imperial history and a Tiberian sympathizer.[2] His *Factorum* 1.3 is significant in terms of

---

[1]As to the dating of *Factorum*, Constant in *Valère Maxime: actions et paroles mémorables*, ed. Pierre Constant, 2 vols. (Paris: Librairie Garnier Frères, 1935), 2:346, n. 542, argues *Factorum* 9.11.4 refers to the 31 CE death of Tiberius' praetorian prefect Sejanus (for the life of L. Aelius Sejanus, cf. *PIR²* A 255; *PW* 1 [1894] 529-531) and so gives a *terminus post quem* for that portion of the text. He assigns 27-37 CE to the composition of the entire work but associates *Factorum* 2 with the time of Claudius (*Valère Maxime* 1.ii; cf. *OCD²*, s.v. "Valerius Maximus" and its placement of the entire composition shortly after Sejanus' death).

[2]For Valerius Maximus' highly eulogistic attitude toward Tiberius see his preface as well as *Factorum* 4.3.3, 5.5.3, and 9.11.4; cf. *Valère Maxime*, 1:ii; *OCD²*, s.v. "Valerius Maximus."

what it reports about the various foreign religious cults and practices banned at one time or another from the city of Rome. These consist of the Bacchanalia (1.3.1), divination by Fortuna Praenestina (1.3.2), astrology (1.3.3), the Jewish *sacra* and, perhaps, the cult of Jupiter Sabazius (1.3.3), the use of private altars in public places (1.3.3), and the cult of Isis and Serapis (1.3.4).

Like the rest of this unit, the portion associated with Judaism at Rome survives in the largely parallel epitomes of Julius Paris and Januarius Nepotianus.[3] According to the latter,

> [1] The same [Cornelius] Hispalus also
> [2] drove away from the city [urbe exterminavit]
> [3] The Jews [Iudaeos]
> [4] who had tried to transmit their sacred rites [sacra sua] to the Romans.

Paris preserved the passage similarly:

> [1] The same man [Cn. Cornelius Hispalus praetor peregrinus]
> [2] compelled [coegit] to return to their homes
> [3] the Jews [Iudaeos]
> [4] who had tried to infect Roman customs [mores] with the cult [cultu] of Jupiter Sabazius.[4]

There exists also, however, an alternative but very largely ignored manuscript of Paris in Codex Bernensis 366 which substitutes the devotees of Jupiter Sabazius for Jews.[5]

Dated to 139 BCE by Paris, in the two epitomes this event is associated chronologically with the expulsion of astrologers and in

---

[3]Significant differences between the epitomes are as follows: the reference to private altars does not appear in the epitome of Paris; that to Isis and Serapis is absent from Nepotianus; and, while the epitome of Nepotianus leaves open the origins of the Jews of whom it treats, Paris indicates that they were foreigners. Unclear in both is if Valerius Maximus imagined that all Jews were expelled or only those who had attempted ("qui...conati erant" in both epitomes) to propagate their religion.

[4]My translations, based largely on Stern, *Authors*, 1:358, but intended to make clear the parallels. The standard text is *Valerii Maximi: Factorvm et dictorvm memorabilivm libri novem cvm Ivlii Paridis et Ianvarii Nepotiani epitomis*, ed. Carolus Kempf, 2d ed., 2 vols. (1888; reprint ed., Stuttgart: B. G. Teubner, 1982). Kempf moved the relevant passages from their place within the epitomes (pp. 477, 597) back to the main text on pp. 16-17.

[5]Eugene N. Lane, "Sabazius and the Jews in Valerius Maximus: A Re-examination," *Journal of Roman Studies* 69 (1979):35-38.

Nepotianus with the removal of private altars from public places,[6] actions taken by the same *praetor peregrinus*. Furthermore, the standard manuscript of Paris (Vat. Lat. 4929)[7] would indicate that Valerius Maximus somehow identified the Jewish god with the Asian Zeus Sabazius prominent in late second century BCE Pergamum.[8] In fact, as Lane makes clear, even the alternate reading of Paris implies that Valerius Maximus associated the cults of the two gods.[9]

---

[6]The "their" which Stern (*Authors*, 1:358)–similarly, Théodore Reinach (*Textes d'auteurs grecs et romains relatifs au Judaïsme réunis, traduits et annotés* [1895; reprint ed., Hildesheim: Georg Olms Verlagsbuchhandlung, 1963], p. 259, n. 3), Leon (*Jews of Ancient Rome*, p. 3), and Smallwood (*Jews under Roman Rule*, pp. 129-130)–adds to his translation of Nepotianus links these altars to the worship of the Jewish god; however, the connection is not called for. This obviates what is in any case the *non sequitur* of Salvatore Alessandrí ("La presunta cacciata dei Giudei da Roma nel 139 a. Cr," *Studi classici e orientali* 17 [1968]:194-195) that, because Nepotianus' reference to Jewish altars makes no sense, the altar reference as a whole is an interpolation in the original text of Valerius Maximus.

[7]Lane, "Sabazius," p. 36.

[8]On the basis of the standard manuscript of Paris, scholarship has provided various explanations for Valerius Maximus' reference to Jupiter Sabazius. Franz Cumont (*The Oriental Religions in Roman Paganism* [1911; reprint ed., New York: Dover Publications, 1956], pp. 63-65, and also his *Recherches sur le symbolisme funéraire*, pp. 484-498), Gressmann ("Jewish Life," pp. 170-175), and, in part, Hengel (*Judaism and Hellenism*, 1:263-264) find evidence of Jewish syncretism. Simon ("Jupiter-Yahvé," pp. 52-56) sees it as the name by which orthodox Jewish preachers proclaimed the *Kurios Sabaoth* to Gentile hearers. Kurt Latte (*Römische Religionsgeschichte*, Handbuch der Altertumswissenschaft, vol. 5.4 [Munich: C. H. Beck'sche Verlagsbuchhandlung, 1960], p. 275) claims that *Sabazius* either represents Jewish syncretism or erroneously replaces the Hebrew *Sabaoth*. Both Schürer (*History*, 3¹:74) and Th. Reinach (*Textes*, p. 259, n. 3) see *Jupiter Sabazius=Kurios Sabazius* erroneously replacing the Septuagintal *Kurios Sabaoth*. Bludau ("Die Juden Roms," p. 115), Hermann Vogelstein and Paul Rieger (*Geschichte der Juden in Rom*, 2 vols. [Berlin: Mayer und Müller, 1896], 1:3, n. 1), Leon (*Jews of Ancient Rome*, p. 3), Smallwood (*Jews under Roman Rule*, p. 129), and also Wiefel ("Die jüdische Gemeinschaft," p. 67) are similar: *Sabazius* erroneously replaces *Shabbat* or *Sabaoth*. Wiefel then suggests Valerius Maximus' identification of the Jewish god with Jupiter Sabazius is an another example of the misunderstandings surrounding Roman Judaism since its arrival in the city.

[9]Assuming three recensions of *Factorum* 1.3.3 exist (Nepotianus, referring only to the expulsion of Jews; Paris in Codex Bernensis 366, referring to the expulsion of the cult of Jupiter Sabazius; Paris in Vat. Lat. 4929, combining the two cults), Lane ("Sabazius," pp. 35-38) uses the second to propose that Valerius Maximus mentioned separate expulsions of Jews and Sabazius worshipers and that the third recension is but a conflation of the first two. This is possible; however, Codex Bernensis 366 may also be read as a scribal correction of Vat. Lat. 4929 intended

In the context of what immediately precedes it, *Factorum* 1.3.3 sheds considerable light upon Valerius Maximus himself. That is, by means of *Factorum* 1.1.1-15 he made quite clear his devotion to the prosperity-bringing practices of traditional Roman religion.[10] He then turned to instances of charlatanism (*Factorum* 1.2.1-4) and, equally unsympathetically, justified various past suppressions of foreign *sacra* at Rome (*Factorum* 1.3).[11] Thus, in narrating past events Valerius Maximus at the same time revealed his own contemporary hostility towards those rites.[12]

---

to eliminate the problematic identification of the Jewish and Sabazian cults. Alessandrí ("La presunta cacciata," pp. 193-194) is open to similar criticism. Depending upon the epitome of Nepotianus and ignoring Codex Bernensis 366, he argues that Nepotianus best preserved the language of Valerius Maximus. His evidence: had it been authentic, Nepotianus could not have failed to preserve this unusual identification; the cult of Jupiter Sabazius reached Rome after 139 BCE; Valerius Maximus knew the difference between it and Judaism. These arguments are not convincing. The third is contradicted by the text, and the second overlooks the fact that Valerius Maximus described past history from a much later date. Still, Alessandrí's first argument best reveals the weakness of his thesis, for we might suppose the more difficult reading of Paris' epitome would better reflect what Valerius Maximus wrote than does the easier text of Nepotianus. In other words, Paris had little reason for introducing *Jupiter Sabazius* into a comprehensible text of Valerius Maximus like the one reproduced by Nepotianus. As Simon ("Jupiter-Yahvé," p. 54) indicates, however, Nepotianus did have cause to omit the difficult expression "cult of Jupiter Sabazius" from the text of Valerius Maximus before him and to replace it with the easier "sacred rites."

[10]Constant (*Valère Maxime*, 1:v) also recognizes this devotion "à la religion de la cité" and "à la politique religieuse inaugurée par Auguste." Nevertheless, he accuses Valerius Maximus of "faux zèle" and adds that he "appartient en effet à cette réaction religieuse du Ire siècle dont Renan a pu dire qu'elle tenta...de réhabiliter par raison d'État toutes les superstitions."

[11]In the surviving epitomes, the exclusion of the Bacchanalia, divination by Fortuna Praenestina, astrology, the Jewish *sacra*, and, perhaps, the cult of Jupiter Sabazius are justified. Preserved alone in Nepotianus, the prohibition against using private altars is unexplained. The measures against the Roman cult of Isis and Serapis surviving in Paris are also unexplained.

[12]Recalling relationships among Sabazius, Dionysus, and Bacchus (cf. Cumont, *Oriental Religions*, pp. 64-65; Erwin Ohlemutz, *Die Kulte und Heiligtümer der Götter in Pergamon* [1940; reprint ed., Darmstadt: Wissenschaftliche Buchgesellschaft, 1968], pp. 269-272; OCD^2, s.v. "Sabazius") and the association in *Factorum* 1.3 between Jews and the cult of Sabazius as well as between Jews and the Bacchanalia scandal of 186 BCE (*Factorum* 1.3.1; cf. 6.3.7), Valerius Maximus may have expressed this hostility less overtly as well. It was Livy, the source of much in Valerius Maximus (Stern, *Authors*, 1:359; Th. Reinach, *Textes*, p. 259, n. 3; Constant in *Valère Maxime*, 1:iii; OCD^2, s.v. "Valerius Maximus"), who (Book

Such an antagonism manifests itself in a more particular way as well. To appreciate this, we must first observe how Valerius Maximus artificially juxtaposed the earlier Roman repression of the Jewish (*Factorum* 1.3.3) and Isiac (*Factorum* 1.3.4) rites, for though together in Valerius Maximus, they were separated in time by the one hundred years between 139 BCE (the Jewish rites) and 50 BCE (Isiac rites).[13] Carried out by means, respectively, of expulsion and demolition, these measures therefore correspond closely to the way in which Tiberius, his imperial patron, acted against the same two cults in 19 CE.[14] As a result, Alessandrí maintains that Valerius Maximus invented his materials in order to establish a precedent for the contemporary measures of Tiberius.[15]

Concerning the charge of fabrication, however, his arguments are unconvincing.[16] Specifically, the fact that the Jewish expulsion may be found clearly in no other author[17] means very little within a field of scholarship where the few chance remains of antiquity play such a central part. That it does not correspond to the amicable relations

---

39.8-19) told readers of the drastic measures taken against the perverse and subversive Roman devotees of Bacchus in 186 BCE–attested also in *CIL*, I², 581 (I, 196) and *ILS*, 18 (cf. Arthur E. Gordon, *Illustrated Introduction to Latin Epigraphy* [Berkeley and Los Angeles: University of California Press, 1983], pp. 83-85 and Plate 6). So, aware of the association Sabazius-Dionysus-Bacchus and the ease of identifying *Sabazius* with the Hebrew *Sabaoth*, we may wonder if Valerius Maximus intended to slander Roman Jewry by associating it with this other foreign cult, the punishment of which he had already reported approvingly. Granted the strange Gentile references to donkey worship, human sacrifice, and cannibalism, and in light of the fact that Greco-Roman tradition also associated Judaism with the worship of Dionysus (Tacitus *Histories* 5.5; cf. David Flusser, "Paganism in Palestine" in *The Jewish People in the First Century: Historical Geography, Political History, Social, Cultural and Religious Life and Institutions*, ed. S. Safrai and M. Stern, Compendia Rerum Iudaicarum ad Novum Testamentum: Section One, 2 vols. [Philadelphia: Fortress Press, 1974-1987], 2:1068-1069), the correlation of Roman Judaism with the similarly damnable rites of Dionysus-Bacchus-Sabazius would have been credible.

[13]Cf. Latte, *Religionsgeschichte*, p. 282, n. 4.

[14]So, similarly, Radin, *Jews among Greeks and Romans*, p. 255; Smallwood, "Some Notes on the Jews under Tiberius," p. 321, and her *Jews under Roman Rule*, p. 130, n. 34.

[15]Alessandrí, "La presunta cacciata," p. 198. He is followed by Marshall, "Flaccus," pp. 140-141.

[16]So already Lane, "Sabazius," p. 35, n. 8.

[17]Alessandrí, "La presunta cacciata," pp. 188-190.

between Rome and Judea during this time period[18] begs the question of those relations. That the report is brief[19] has no real bearing on its veracity, and that its picture of Jews as proselytizers is spurious[20] requires demonstration. So, it is not a fabrication.[21]

Alessandrí stands on much firmer ground with his suggestion that Valerius Maximus intended these materials to establish a precedent for the contemporary measures of Tiberius. Such a close correspondence between *Factorum* 1.3.3-4 and the events of 19 CE is best interpreted to mean that he fashioned his account of ancient anti-Jewish/anti-Isiac measures on the basis of the contemporary Tiberian actions. Hence, explicitly affirming the former, he implicitly affirmed the latter as well.

Of course we might be tempted to attribute his approval of these actions to discretion; as the protégé of Tiberius, after all, Valerius Maximus had little choice except to affirm imperial policies against the practice of Jewish and other foreign rites. Nevertheless, within the context of his expressed devotion to the traditional rites of Roman religion, his aversion to those of foreign origin is entirely credible. Moreover, we have seen already that such upper-class Roman hostility towards Jewish *sacra* was hardly unique to this particular writer. In sum, *Factorum* 1.3.3 is very useful in terms of what it reveals about the outlook of an upper-class contemporary of the emperor Tiberius:

---

[18]Alessandrí, "La presunta cacciata," pp. 190-192, 197.

[19]Ibid., p. 195.

[20]Ibid., p. 196.

[21]Insofar as the reference to the expulsion of Roman Jews is concerned, Gaston May also claims it did not occur. He denies ("Politique religieuse," pp. 16-17; cf. Leon, *Jews of Ancient Rome*, p. 4) the account had anything to do with Jews because, first, *Sabazius* in the standard manuscript of Paris points rather to the cult of the Asian deity and, second, because Jews were not in Rome at this early date. Concerning his first claim, it does have the additional support of Codex Bernensis 366 but does not account for the Jewish reference in Vat. Lat. 4929 (Paris) or Nepotianus (cf. Lane, "Sabazius," p. 36; Juster, *Les Juifs*, 2:169, n. 2; Schürer, *History*, 3¹:74; Simon, "Jupiter-Yahvé," p. 54; Hengel, *Judaism and Hellenism*, 1:263, n. 42). The second argument, since we possess no information against which to check it, is purely conjectural. Hence, Juster (*Les Juifs*, 2:169) and Smallwood (*Jews under Roman Rule*, p. 129) are able to assume the basic accuracy of the account, Scramuzza ("Policy" in *Beginnings of Christianity*, 5:292, n. 5; cf. Radin, *Jews among Greeks and Romans*, p. 228; Schürer, *History*, 3¹:75; Marshall, "Flaccus," p. 140) assumes that the Jewish community visible to Cicero ca. 60 BCE could not have developed overnight, and Vogelstein and Rieger (*Geschichte*, 1:2-3) suggest several explanations for the early presence of a significant number of Jews within Rome.

it obviously made good sense to him that the introduction of foreign religious rites should have led Rome's ancient authorities to expel Jews and others from the city.

As to the occurrence which it narrates, *Factorum* 1.3.3 is equally significant. That is to say, this text provides us with our earliest information concerning the presence of Jews in the city:[22] by the second half of the second century BCE they constituted an identifiable entity there. In addition, and more important for our purposes, it makes a clear statement about the motivation behind the Republican banishment of Roman Jews.

Michel Malaise, typical of the modern consensus that authorities were generally troubled by Jews more from the political than from the religious angle,[23] suggests that the actual reason for the Republican expulsion of Jews and others might have been the secret political aspirations of the persons banished.[24] At least insofar as Jews are concerned, however, Valerius Maximus is explicit that the measure was a response to the introduction of Jewish religious practices. Deeming these offensive, the authorities proceeded against them in the most direct of ways by expelling from the city those who brought and practiced them there. In other words, Valerius Maximus informed readers that when earlier Roman authorities decided to take measures against the dissemination of Jewish rites in Rome, they resorted to the expulsion of those who practiced them. This would not be the last time that expulsion served a similar purpose.

In sum, *Factorum* 1.3.3 invites close consideration from several perspectives, i.e., from that of the 139 BCE Republican action which it records, from that of the 19 CE Tiberian measures to which it also alludes, as well as from that of a Tiberian protégé, Valerius Maximus himself. As such, this account provides a most revealing glimpse of

---

[22]This is with the exception of the tidbits preserved by 1 Maccabees 8 (cf. *Antiquities* 12.414-419), 12.1-18 (cf. *Antiquities* 13.163-170), 14.24, and 15.15-24 (cf. *Antiquities* 13.227) vis-à-vis Judean delegations sent to Rome (cf. Schürer, *History*, 3¹:73-74). As to the lack of association between the Jewish delegations to Rome reported by 1 Maccabees and those Jews expelled in 139 BCE, see Stern (*Authors*, 1:359-360) and Simon ("Jupiter-Yahvé," pp. 52-53; cf. Bludau, "Die Juden Roms," pp. 115-116 for the contrary view). Besides the fact that these embassies included nothing like the number of persons implied by the account of Valerius Maximus, Smallwood (*Jews under Roman Rule*, p. 129; cf. Vogelstein and Rieger, *Geschichte*, 1:3, n. 4) is correct that 1 Maccabees presupposes a thoroughly positive outcome to these visits.

[23]Cf. pp. 27-29.

[24]Malaise, *Les conditions*, p. 361. He implicitly assigns like reasons (p. 388) to the hostility of Augustus in the soon to be discussed *Augustus* 93 of Suetonius.

how both those in power and their upper-class associates reacted to the presence of Jewish *sacra* in Rome.

The next time Gentile writers mention Roman Jews is different. In *Julius* 84.5 Suetonius reported that at the death of Caesar many of them had played a conspicuous part among his mourners. It is certainly reasonable to assume, therefore, that Jews perceived Caesar as sympathetic or at least as more sympathetic to them than was the party responsible for his murder. An entirely different question is how Caesar had demonstrated this sympathy. Scramuzza[25] utilizes the rather confused official document quoted in *Antiquities* 14.213-216 to argue that this sympathy was associated with the time when Caesar, having prohibited the assembly of all other religious associations in Rome, exempted Jews and so allowed them alone to assemble: "Gaius Caesar, our consular praetor, by edict forbade religious societies to assemble [κωλύων θιάσους συνάγεσθαι] in the city, but these people alone he did not forbid to do so."[26]

The other source which Scramuzza cites in this regard raises serious doubts about the trustworthiness of Josephus' edict. That is, according to *Julius* 42.3, Caesar disbanded all except the most ancient *collegia*.[27] Thus, provided they do refer to the same ban, these texts agree that Julius Caesar prohibited certain Roman associations, but they contradict one another on two major points. First, Josephus asserted that Caesar exempted only a single entity from the ban, but Suetonius claimed that various *collegia* were permitted to remain in existence. Second, while Josephus indicated that the exemption was for Jews alone, Suetonius mentioned that it was for Rome's ancient associations. This of course would exclude those meetings devoted to the practice of Judaism.

Whom are we to believe? Aware of Josephus' tendency to portray Jews in the best possible light vis-à-vis Roman authorities, it would be difficult to think Caesar closed down all of the ancient Roman

---

[25]Scramuzza, "Policy" in *Beginnings of Christianity*, 5:293; similarly, Malaise, *Les conditions*, p. 377.

[26]LCL translation by Ralph Marcus. Philo (*Legatio* 311-313) paraphrased what he claimed to be a letter of Augustus to Rome's Asian governors also according to which, because of the proper religiosity practiced there, only the gatherings of Jews were to be permitted.

[27]*Augustus* 32.1 indicates that Augustus also disbanded all *collegia* except those which were ancient and legitimate. This was, in Suetonius' view, because the recently established *collegia* were no more than *factiones* created for the purpose of criminal activity. Still, according to Philo (*Legatio* 157), Augustus did not prohibit Roman Jews from gathering for the practice of their religious rites. Cf. *Legatio* 311-313 on the supposedly similar Augustan situation is Asia.

societies but permitted Jews to continue to meet. Thus, even if the scenario of Judaism's elevation above all other Roman societies were not in itself unbelievable,[28] it would be so dubious as to make practically useless any conjectures based upon it. The result: while *Julius* 84.5 may be correct that Roman Jews were noticeable among Caesar's mourners, the reason for their grief divined by Scramuzza from the very tendentious *Antiquities* 14.213-216 is without merit.

Equally without merit is Juster's generalization that the same *Julius* 84.5 shows Jews to have been "amis des Empereurs."[29] First, the text does not make the assertion that Julius Caesar considered Jews to be his own friends. Second, if it did, this would indicate nothing about the attitude of Rome's subsequent emperors. Third, much evidence does in fact exist to demonstrate that, particularly in matters of religion, these rulers had anything but a friendly attitude towards Jews.

Therefore, when we now turn to Caesar's adopted son Augustus who, as we saw already, deprecated the Sabbath and food laws, we possess the very revealing statement of Suetonius in *Augustus* 93 that this emperor

> treated with great respect such foreign rites [peregrinarum caeri-moniarum] as were ancient and well established, but held the rest in contempt [contemptui habuit]. For example, having been initiated at Athens.... But on the other hand he not only omitted to make a slight detour to visit Apis, when he was travelling through Egypt, but highly commended [conlaudavit] his grandson Gaius for not offering prayers at Jerusalem as he passed by Judaea.

To us Gaius is little more than a footnote to history. Still, had he not died prematurely, he instead of Tiberius might well have been the next Roman emperor.[30] For this reason, the information of Suetonius is revealing in several ways: it makes clear Augustus' own prejudiced attitude towards even the Jewish cult center in Jerusalem; it shows that the imperial heir-apparent had been trained in the same ideas; and it demonstrates how, when the right occasion arose, such negative views resulted in comparable actions of an intolerant and demeaning

---

[28]This claim is somewhat analogous to the one in *Antiquities* 18.280-281, which makes Petronius, the Roman legate of Syria, sound like a devout Jew.

[29]Juster, *Les Juifs*, 1:220; cf. 1:224.

[30]*Res gestae* 2.14; Edward T. Salmon, *A History of the Roman World from 30 B.C. to A.D. 138*, 6th ed. (1968; reprint ed., London: Routledge, 1989), pp. 35-37; Robin Seager, *Tiberius* (Berkeley and Los Angeles: University of California Press, 1972), p. 31.

kind.[31] Because there was no reason for the insult, this is all the more true. Evidently from Augustan times, sacrifice on behalf of Rome and its emperor was a daily part of the temple cult,[32] and special offerings were made there as well when the welfare of the empire appeared to be in question.[33] Thus, it is entirely understandable that, though they proudly described both Marcus Agrippa's earlier visit to Jerusalem and the magnificent sacrifice which he had made at the cult center there,[34] both Philo and Josephus passed over in complete silence what must surely have been the very humiliating scene which transpired upon Gaius' arrival in the neighborhood of the city.

---

[31]In order to maintain his theory that Augustus was sympathetic to Jews, Scramuzza ("Policy" in *Beginnings of Christianity*, 5:293) introduces the non sequitur that the present incident showed the emperor's aversion only to "their proselytizing activities." For the same purpose, but even more oddly, Williams ("Expulsion," p. 773, n. 44) seems to use this text as evidence that it was "Augustus' policy to favour the Jews." Indeed, they were "happy" under him (p. 774; cf. Smallwood [*Jews under Roman Rule*, p. 202] about the "happy relations" between Roman Jews and the government preceding the time of Tiberius).

[32]Specific reference to the daily sacrifice for Rome and the emperor appears in Josephus (*War* 2.197, 409-417 and *Apion* 2.77). Though without indicating that they were performed for Rome and its emperor, Philo (*Legatio* 157, 317-318) was evidently drawing attention to the same offerings as evidence of Augustus' respect for the god of Israel. In his view, that emperor had begun the practice of sponsoring these rites himself, but Josephus (*Apion* 2.77) claimed that the Jewish people absorbed the cost. It is possible that there were two different sacrifices associated with the emperor, the one in Philo which Augustus first dedicated and the other which Jews offered on behalf of the emperor and Rome. Alternatively, although Schürer (*History*, 1:380, 2:311-312) and Juster (*Les Juifs*, 1:347, n. 5) see no difficulty in the conflation of the reports in Philo and Josephus, we might suspect that Philo's interpretation had the apologetic purpose of demonstrating Augustus' approval of Judaism, a motif vital to him within the context of *Legatio* 155-158. In any case, as to the importance of these sacrifices for Rome and the emperor, Josephus is clear, for he relates that Eleazar's decision to terminate them not only constituted impiety (*War* 2.413, 414) but also (2.409) "laid the foundation of the war with the Romans" (LCL translation by H. St. J. Thackeray).

[33]During his interview with Gaius, Philo insisted that massive sacrifices had occurred on behalf of this one emperor three different times, i.e., when he began to govern, when he recovered from grave illness, and when he set out against the Germans (*Legatio* 356). Gaius' complaint that sacrifice was *to* the god of Israel *for* (ὑπὲρ) himself aside, these rites make clear the public goodwill of the Jewish people towards both the emperor and Rome. Incidently, Josephus also used the preposition ὑπὲρ in referring to the sacrifices for Rome and the emperor (*War* 2.409, 416) but also its synonym, περί (*War* 2.197). At *Apion* 2.77 the Latin translator's *pro* could stand for either.

[34]Philo *Legatio* 294-297; Josephus *Antiquities* 16.12-15.

Something of a mystery attaches itself to the scholarly interpretation of *Augustus* 93. Though it is a clear statement of Augustus'
contempt for Judaism not only at Rome but also within its own cult
center, Leon writes for example that on this occasion Augustus merely
"refrained from showing himself too friendly to the Jews." Similarly,
Stern insists that Suetonius' words are "not to be interpreted as the
expression of a specific anti-Jewish attitude on the part of Augustus."
Stranger still is Williams' deduction from this text: "there is no doubt
that it had been Augustus' policy to favour the Jews."[35] Frend makes
a similar assertion: "In this case, the foreign rites included Judaism
which he treated with marked favour both in Rome and the East."[36]
Of course *Augustus* 93 does not permit these conclusions. Instead,
Schürer's general reference to Augustus' "instinctive antipathy to
Judaism" and Stern's statement elsewhere that the ruler "had little
sympathy for the Jewish religion" provide the only legitimate interpretation of the passage.[37]

These implications of *Augustus* 93 are important. Keeping in
mind that Gaius was following the lead of his grandfather when he
shunned the god of Israel and gravely insulted the god's devotees, we
might expect the subsequent emperors and their families equally
concerned about the emulation of Augustus to have pursued a similar
course.[38] In fact, they did. Thus, our Gentile sources make clear that
under the emperor Tiberius, the actual successor of Augustus, the
practice of Judaism in Rome encountered grave resistance.[39]

----

[35]Leon, *Jews of Ancient Rome*, p. 11, n. 1; Stern, *Authors*, 2:111; Williams,
"Expulsion," p. 773. Williams also states (p. 774) that "Augustus' surviving words
reveal a man who regarded Jewish ways as odd rather than obnoxious–suitable
material for pleasantries and puns. So why the change in A.D. 19?" In fact, of
course, there was no change. Tiberius' actions at that time were consistent with
the attitude of his predecessor.

[36]Frend, *Martyrdom*, p. 89.

[37]Schürer, *History*, 2:312; Stern, "The Jewish Diaspora" in *The Jewish People
in the First Century: Historical Geography, Political History, Social, Cultural and
Religious Life and Institutions*, ed. S. Safrai and M. Stern, Compendia Rerum
Iudaicarum ad Novum Testamentum: Section One, 2 vols. [Philadelphia: Fortress
Press, 1974-1987], 1:163.

[38]About this emulation in religious matters see Garzetti, *Tiberius to the
Antonines*, p. 31 (Tiberius) and pp. 139-140 (Claudius). Insofar as the latter is
concerned, his Alexandrian letter (P. Lond. 1912, line 87) is explicit.

[39]This is the general view of Bludau ("Die Juden Roms," p. 122), Momigliano
(*Claudius*, p. 30), Leon (*Jews of Ancient Rome*, p. 16), and also Stern ("Jewish
Diaspora" in *Jewish People*, 1:163). Only by failing to appreciate the apologetic

As indicated already, Seneca was an eyewitness to early actions of Tiberius against the practice of foreign religiosity including, in all likelihood, Judaism. Moreover, Tacitus, Suetonius, Dio, and Josephus made specific assertions about the same things. Though this is not the occasion for deciphering all of our information on such matters,[40] it is important that we scrutinize at this time the assorted Greco-Roman sources[41] as a witness to the treatment which Tiberius and those in authority beneath him afforded the Roman practitioners of Judaism and other foreign cults.

Hence, describing a happening which he appears to have dated correctly to 19 CE,[42] Tacitus wrote,

---

requirements of Philo is Radin (*Jews among Greeks and Romans*, pp. 309-310) able to minimize the resistance.

[40]Williams ("Expulsion," passim) does an excellent job of categorizing the various issues raised by the accounts.

[41]The details of Josephus are reserved for the next chapter.

[42]A later date has Josephus' support (*Antiquities* 18.65 and 81-84). Versus Malaise (*Les conditions*, pp. 391-392; but cf. Stern, *Authors*, 2:71), their common reference to measures against Isiac and Jewish religion as well as the identical details about the four thousand men sent to Sardinia prohibit us from separating the accounts in Tacitus and Josephus. But, unless Volkmar ("Religionsverfolgung," pp. 138-143) is correct that he was reporting topically rather than chronologically, Josephus (*Antiquities* 18.65) placed this event during the 26-36 CE period when Pilate was procurator and, thus, within the same time frame as the anti-Jewish measures Philo (*Legatio* 159-161) reported in conjunction with the 31 CE death of the praetorian prefect Sejanus. Therefore, were it possible to identify the events described by Tacitus and Josephus with those in Philo, the precise context of whose *Legatio* 159-161 does not permit the alternative possibility of placing in 19 CE the events which it describes, the additional support thus given to the Josephan chronology would make it difficult to decide between the 19 CE and ca. 31 CE dates of Tacitus and Josephus respectively. In fact, Smallwood ("Some Notes on the Jews under Tiberius," pp. 322-329) argues convincingly that this identification is not possible. In agreement are Merrill ("Expulsion," p. 372), Sevenster (*Roots of Pagan Anti-Semitism*, p. 25), Ernst Bammel ("Judenverfolgung und Naherwartung: Zur Eschatologie des Ersten Thessalonicherbriefs," *Zeitschrift für Theologie und Kirche* 56 [1959]:297), Box (*Philonis Alexandrini: IN FLAC-CUM*, ed. Herbert Box [London: Oxford University Press, 1939], p. 68), Williams ("Expulsion," p. 774), Solin ("Juden und Syrer" in *ANRW*, 2.29²:686-688), and Stern (*Authors*, 2:71); to the contrary but without supporting evidence, Volkmar ("Religionsverfolgung," p. 137), W. A. Heidel ("Why Were the Jews Banished from Italy in 19 A.D.?" *American Journal of Philology* 41 [1920]:40), Scramuzza ("Policy" in *Beginnings of Christianity*, 5:294), Leon (*Jews of Ancient Rome*, pp. 19-20), Moehring ("Persecution," p. 302, n. 1), as well as Stern ("Jewish Diaspora" in *Jewish People*, 1:164). In addition, Smallwood is correct that Seneca's reference to the early period of Tiberius corroborates the date in Tacitus ("Notes," p. 315,

Another debate dealt with the proscription of the Egyptian and Jewish rites [sacris], and a senatorial edict directed that four thousand
descendants of enfranchised slaves, tainted with that superstition [ea
superstitione infecta] and suitable in point of age, were to be shipped
to Sardinia and there employed in suppressing brigandage: "if they
succumbed to the pestilential climate, it was a cheap loss." The rest
had orders to leave Italy, unless they had renounced their impious
ceremonial [profanos ritus] by a given date.[43]

As becomes explicit already in Tacitus' introduction, the intention of
this senatorial legislation was to put an end to Jewish and Egyptian
religious practices within Rome. In Tacitus' description, therefore, the
primary issue is the question of what was expelled, and his answer is
"profanos ritus," i.e., the rites which constituted the practice of Jewish
and Egyptian religion.[44]

---

n. 1), and she also appears to have the support of the chronological framework in
which John of Antioch situated his excerpt of Dio (p. 314; cf. *Cassii Dionis
Cocceiani: Historiarum romanarum quae supersunt*, ed. Ursulus Philippus Boissevain, 5 vols. [Berlin: Weidmannsche Buchhandlung, 1895-1931], 2:577; Stern,
Authors, 2:70; Williams, "Expulsion," p. 767). For these reasons, the present study
follows the consensus of scholarship (cf. Smallwood, "Some Notes on the Jews
under Tiberius," p. 315; Stern, *Authors*, 2:70; Louis H. Feldman, trans., in
Josephus, *The Life, Against Apion, The Jewish War, Jewish Antiquities*, trans. H.
St. J. Thackeray et al., LCL, 10 vols. [Cambridge: Harvard University Press, 1926-
1965], 9:50-51, n. d) in its preference for the dating proposed by Tacitus.

[43]*Annals* 2.85, LCL translation by John Jackson.

[44]Although "ea superstitione" is singular, Radin (*Jews among Greeks and
Romans*, p. 310) is correct that the texts of Tacitus and Suetonius do not allow us
to limit the measures to Jewish practices. Indeed, within his history of the ups
and downs of Isiac religion in Rome, Malaise (*Les conditions*, pp. 390-393) makes
perfectly good sense of these measures from the perspective of that cult. In any
case, as noted already (p. 23, n. 59), the same problem of singulars and plurals
appears in the related text of Seneca and is perhaps to be accounted for by the
unitary way in which these Romans perceived all foreign *superstitio*. It is true
that John of Antioch's soon to be discussed citation of Dio preserves information
only about the fate of Roman Jews. Nevertheless, whether Dio had referred also
to the measures against the cult of Isis and perhaps other foreign rites, we have
no way of knowing. In any case, and especially because we know that various cults
did face difficulty under Tiberius (Vogelstein and Rieger, *Geschichte*, 1:14; Seager,
Tiberius, p. 150), under no circumstances would it be legitimate to use the silence
of the excerpt of Dio to escape the sense of Tacitus, Suetonius, Josephus, and
Valerius Maximus that Judaism was not the only Roman religion targeted for
curtailment in 19 CE. This, it may be said ahead of time, does not require us to
imagine that the affected superstitions were all treated in just the same way.
Specifically, beginning with the statement of Suetonius, we may suppose that the
government took measures against several of these, but that the Isiac and Jewish

This then provides us with an *a priori* answer to the secondary question of who was expelled, for we must suppose that it would have been limited to those persons practicing the prohibited rites. That we are dealing with more than a supposition Tacitus made plain through his further statements about the two groups into which he divided those affected by the legislation. The first consisted of male citizens of military age characterized specifically as practitioners of superstition ("ea superstitione infecta"): conscription removed both them and their practice of profane rites from Rome.[45] The second, i.e., the "ceteri,"

---

religions received the particular attention maintained by Suetonius, Tacitus, and Josephus. Between these two, then, all of our sources are clear that expulsion was utilized against the practitioners of Judaism but less clear in this regard about worshipers of Isis. Perhaps, therefore, and contrary to Malaise (*Les conditions*, p. 390), expulsion was considered to be less effective or even unnecessary in the curtailment of the Egyptian cult which according to Josephus was crippled instead by the crucifixion of its priests and the burning of its central sanctuary. In sum, although our texts leave much room for conjecture concerning the nature of the measures used to curtail Jewish and Isiac religion in Rome, they permit no doubt that both foreign cults were central objects of imperial concern in 19 CE.

[45]That Tacitus understood them to be Roman citizens is clear from their status as members of the "libertini generis," i.e., "of the class of freedman," for whether this means literally that they themselves were freedman citizens or that they belonged to families of this class, the citizenship is not in question. Entirely unclear is their ultimate provenance. Having their origins among the class of Roman slaves, they or their families came perhaps from Judea, Egypt, Syria, Asia, or Greece. We simply cannot know. More important, these slave origins make it impossible for us to know either how or when they came by their Jewish or Isiac rites. To clarify the point we may take as our example one of the Roman citizen practitioners of Judaism. He had achieved the citizenship either at birth as the child of manumitted parents or at the time of his own manumission. Thus, if he or his parents were taken into slavery from Judea, we might suppose that he was born into the practice of Judaism. From anywhere else we have no means of knowing. Specifically, supposing that his origins were ultimately from Asia, it might be that his parents belonged to one of the old diaspora Jewish communities there or that they were Asian converts to Judaism. In both cases, it would be legitimate to suppose again that his practice of Judaism began early and that he came to Rome as a slave practitioner of Jewish rites. Of Asian Gentile origin, however, he himself had converted to Judaism prior to being enslaved and brought to Rome, or he had come as a Gentile slave and converted sometime thereafter. The point is that the slave origins of these Roman practitioners of Isiac and Jewish rites make it impossible for us to reach any conclusions about the circumstances of their involvement in these customs, for all the text tells us is that they were in fact so involved. In light of these considerations we may not place very much stock in Williams' claim ("Expulsion," p. 770-772; cf. Radin, *Jews among Greeks and Romans*, p. 308) that by his use of the verb *inficere* ("infecta") Tacitus intended to imply, albeit wrongly in her opinion, that these Roman citizen practitioners of foreign rites were proselytes. It is worthwhile to note that within

constituted the rest of these Roman *superstitiosi*. To them two escape clauses were available. On the one hand, if they were willing to leave Italy, they could continue to practice their rites; on the other, if they were willing to abandon their customs, they could continue to live in Rome.[46] Both of these underline the vital point that the legislation was directed not primarily against persons, i.e., against the Jews or Egyptians, but against the practice within Rome of rites associated with foreign *superstitio*.[47]

---

the context of the previously discussed account of Valerius Maximus *inficere* does have just that implication. Here, however, it does not, for from the perspective of a *senatus consultum* created with the purpose of driving foreign religious rites out of the city, any person practicing Jewish customs was certainly no less "tainted" with Judaism than was a proselyte. Rightly, therefore, do Smallwood (*Jews under Roman Rule*, p. 205; less clearly her "Some Notes on the Jews under Tiberius," p. 319) and Merrill ("Expulsion," p. 366) refer the term in broad fashion to the practitioners of Judaism.

[46]Smallwood (*Jews under Roman Rule*, p. 204) claims on the basis of Josephus that the expulsion was only from Rome.

[47]Here too Williams insists ("Expulsion," p. 770) that, because the Romans "at no time" prohibited Jews by birth from practicing their religion, "the offer of exemption from expulsion to 'the rest' if they gave up their *profanos ritus* makes little sense unless Tacitus has proselytes in mind." There is no basis for this line of thinking which limits to proselytes those whom Tacitus thought to have been affected by the *senatus consultum*. In the first place, besides claiming more than it can possibly know, her unqualified "at no time" begs the question about the present instance. Second, her argument depends upon the likewise unsupported thesis that Tacitus shared her unqualified conviction and depended for his own interpretation upon it. Most important, she fails to observe that the intention of the *senatus consultum* was not to prohibit the practice of foreign rites but to prohibit their practice in Rome. Ultimately, in any case, Williams argues that Tacitus wrongly limited those affected to proselytes and turns instead to Josephus for her conclusion that all Jews were in fact expelled (pp. 770-772). Nevertheless, this is as problematic as is her interpretation of Tacitus, for besides ignoring his insistence that it was primarily religious rites rather than persons, i.e., Jews (or Egyptians), who were banished, it also ignores not only what Williams herself recognizes elsewhere to be the highly problematic nature of the account in Josephus (pp. 775-778) but also its clearly religious dimension to be discussed shortly. Equally without merit does Leon (*Jews of Ancient Rome*, pp. 18 and 19) use the slightly different presupposition that "the practice of Judaism was no crime in Rome at that time [19 CE]" in order to limit the expulsion not to proselytes but, and just as arbitrarily, to "foreign Jews and freedmen, who did not enjoy the full rights of citizenship." Since this presupposition also begs the question of the present instance, there is no basis for the conclusion upon which he bases it. With the exception of his unfounded (cf. p. 23, n. 59) limitation of the senate's measures to Judaism, therefore, Merrill's reading ("Expulsion," p. 366) of the text is both simpler and more accurate: "When Tacitus speaks of the 4,000 as

Whether he was dependent upon the same source of information or not,[48] Suetonius also provided his readers with certain details about this event:

> He [Tiberius] abolished foreign cults [externas caerimonias], especially the Egyptian and the Jewish rites [ritus], compelling all who were addicted to such superstitions [superstitione ea] to burn their religious vestments and all their paraphernalia. Those of the Jews who were of military age [Iudaeorum iuventutem] he assigned to provinces of unhealthy climate, ostensibly to serve in the army; the others of that same race [reliquos gentis eiusdem] or of similar beliefs [similia sectantes] he banished from the city, on pain of slavery for life if they did not obey.[49]

Suetonius appears at first to have been slightly less clear concerning the focus of Tiberius' attack, but that is because of his tendency not to make a distinction between the ethnic and religious sense of the word *Iudaeus*.[50] Hence, his reference to the "Iudaeorum iuventutem" certainly implies the religious element. Again, his "reliquos gentis eiusdem" is explicitly ethnic, but the associated "similia sectantes" underlines the religious aspects of this Jewish *Gens*. Not surprisingly, therefore, Suetonius too maintained explicitly in his own introductory statement that the intention of Tiberius was to curb (*compesco*) the practices (*caerimonias/ritus*) of foreign cults at Rome. Within this context he then made clear that it was the Isiac and Jewish religious rites which were the particular butt of Tiberius' actions.

Moreover, these measures themselves indicate the same thing. Only to this end, after all, does it make sense that Tiberius demanded the destruction of the religious clothing ("religiosas vestes") and of all instruments ("instrumento omni") associated with these rites[51] and

---

'tainted with this superstition' (*ea superstitione infecta*), and says the rest (*ceteri*) were to be expelled, he certainly means only that these persons were all of the Jewish religion, not necessarily that they were all of Jewish blood, still less that they were all proselytes."

[48]Stern (*Authors*, 2:113; cf. Leon, *Jews of Ancient Rome*, p. 18 and Williams, "Expulsion," p. 766) argues this source, and Merrill ("Expulsion," p. 365) assumes that Josephus used it also.

[49]*Tiberius* 36.

[50]For discussion at length, see pp. 154-155.

[51]It is unclear on what basis Leon (*Jews of Ancient Rome*, p. 18), Smallwood (*Jews under Roman Rule*, p. 204, n. 10) and Stern (*Authors*, 2:113) think that Suetonius' expression "religiosas vestes cum instrumento omni" should not have applied to Jewish just as much as to other foreign religious accoutrement. We

likewise expelled the "similia sectantes," i.e., the Jewish proselytes[52] and the worshipers of the Egyptian deities.[53] In sum, Suetonius too contributed direct evidence that Tiberius "abolished foreign cults [caerimonias], especially the Egyptian and the Jewish rites [ritus]." The result: precisely as Smallwood suggests, "the Roman objection to Judaism at this time, therefore, was religious rather than racial."[54]

In addition, a fragment of Dio preserved by John of Antioch requires consideration within the present context: "As the Jews had flocked to Rome in great numbers and were converting many of the natives to their ways [ἔθη], he [Tiberius] banished most of them."[55] Because of the various claims which Smallwood and Williams make in relationship to this text, we can best deal with it by examining those claims.

On the basis of the standard assumption that Dio was referring to the same events as Tacitus and Suetonius, Smallwood turns to him instead of them for her interpretation of events in 19 CE. As she understands Dio, the anti-Jewish measures of the period happened because of the imperial hostility towards proselytizing,[56] but such an approach suffers from several significant flaws. In the first place, Smallwood associates this manner of reasoning with her more general

---

must be careful to avoid anachronism here, but in agreement with Bludau ("Die Juden Roms," pp. 123-124) we may not suppose that the houses of prayer were devoid of furnishings associated with Jewish religious practices.

[52]So Smallwood, "Some Notes on the Jews under Tiberius," p. 319. Similarly, Williams ("Expulsion," p. 773) identifies the three groups as Jews of military age, all other Jews, and converts. Bludau ("Die Juden Roms," p. 124, n. 3) also takes these *similia sectantes* to be proselytes.

[53]Malaise, *Les conditions*, p. 390.

[54]Smallwood, *Jews under Roman Rule*, p. 205.

[55]Dio 57.18.5a. Unless otherwise noted, English translations of Dio are those of Earnest Cary in the LCL.

[56]Smallwood, "Some Notes on the Jews under Tiberius," pp. 319-322, and *Jews under Roman Rule*, p. 203-207. In this she largely follows Vogelstein and Rieger (*Geschichte*, 1:14-16). Still following them but on the basis of the account in Josephus which she already discredited as a "*suppressio veri*" (*Jews under Roman Rule*, pp. 203-204), Smallwood (*Jews under Roman Rule*, p. 206) postulates that it was the dishonest proselytizer referred to there who first called Tiberius' attention to the fact that persons of high rank were turning to Judaism. Reacting to the conjecture of Ernest L. Abel ("Were the Jews Banished from Rome in 19 A.D.?" *Revue des études juives* 127 [1968]:383-384) that converts alone were expelled, Smallwood (*Jews under Roman Rule*, pp. 206-210) in any case believes that both Jews of long standing as well as steadfast proselytes were so treated.

position that "it was the regular policy of Rome...to protect the Jews in the practice of their religion."[57] By so doing, she presumes to distinguish between Tiberius' aversion to the spread of Jewish rites and his aversion to the rites themselves. Nonetheless, besides the fact that this is an overly fine distinction, we must keep in mind that the thesis itself has no independent merit. Instead, it requires case by case demonstration.

Second, she finds herself in the position to apply Dio as her interpretive key only on the basis of the prior claim that "neither Tacitus nor Suetonius gives any reason for Tiberius' measures against the Isis-cult or for those against the Jews."[58] Unsubstantiated and otherwise in evident contradiction to the clear sense of what both Tacitus and Suetonius expressed in their accounts, this position has very little to commend it. As a matter of fact, Smallwood herself turns to the narrative of Tacitus in order to express the awareness that it "was primarily the Jewish religion which was held to be offensive."[59] Such a comment corresponds to her previously cited statement that "the Roman objection to Judaism at this time, therefore, was religious rather than racial."

Of course she is not without company in her recognition of the religious element, for, in spite of the fact that scholarship has tended to ignore its full ramifications, there is no lack of awareness of imperial hostility towards Judaism and other foreign cults in the city of Rome. By way of example, although Theodor Mommsen makes the insupportable[60] statement that the Roman practice of Jewish *sacra* by non-citizens consistently remained legal,[61] he nevertheless refers in general, and correctly, to governmental interventions directed against the worship of foreign gods.[62] Just as aware of this is Williams. She writes entirely without nuisance that "the Romans...did not like *externae religiones* very much," and Garnsey and Saller like-

---

[57]Smallwood, "Some Notes on the Jews under Tiberius," p. 321.

[58]Ibid., p. 315; Smallwood, *Jews under Roman Rule*, p. 203.

[59]Smallwood, "Some Notes on the Jews under Tiberius," p. 317; cf. her *Jews under Roman Rule*, p. 204, according to which "the offence must have lain in the religion itself."

[60]Guterman, *Religious Toleration*, p. 148; cf. pp. 139-141 of this study.

[61]Theodor Mommsen, "Der Religionsfrevel nach römischen Recht" in *Gesammelte Schriften*, 8 vols. (1905-1913; reprint ed., Berlin: Weidmannsche Verlagsbuchhandlung, 1965), 3:401-405.

[62]Mommsen, "Religionsfrevel" in *Gesammelte Schriften*, 3:401, n. 2.

wise challenge the common view that the imperial authorities were tolerant of foreign cults.[63] Similarly, but referring to the events presently under discussion, Stern explains that "Tiberius' action against foreign cults was in line with the general religious policy of the Roman government after Actium" and that "the senate consistently tried to check the diffusion of oriental cults."[64] Again, La Piana refers to "the general policy of Tiberius, so hostile to all foreign cults" and makes the interesting observation in the same place that particular provocations to imperial hostility were secondary to this general policy.[65]

Third, and as Williams points out,[66] the approach of Smallwood depends upon the questionable methodology of interpreting the more complete accounts of Tacitus and Suetonius by the much less detailed fragment of Dio.[67] Finally, she establishes a false dichotomy by unnecessarily calling for a choice between the claims of Tacitus and Suetonius on the one hand and of Dio on the other. That is, the brief excerpt of Dio makes perfectly good sense when interpreted within the context not only of Tacitus and Suetonius but of Seneca as well, for it too is explicit that the measures of Tiberius had their origin in his opposition to the practice of foreign religious rites within the city of Rome.[68] Specifically, Dio wrote that the practitioners of Jewish customs at Rome were spreading their ways [ἔθη], i.e., in Seneca's terms their *sacra* or *consuetudines*, in Tacitus' words their *sacra* or *ritus*, and in the language of Suetonius, their *caerimonias* and *ritus*, among natives of the city.[69] Therefore, just as Tacitus and Suetonius

---

[63]Williams, "Expulsion," p. 775, and Garnsey and Saller, *Roman Empire*, pp. 170-174.

[64]Stern, *Authors*, 2:72.

[65]La Piana, "Foreign Groups," p. 375, n. 6.

[66]Williams, "Expulsion," p. 767.

[67]See p. 51, n. 44.

[68]Between her previously quoted statement that it "was primarily the Jewish religion which was held to be offensive" and her recognition of the reference to proselytes within the narratives of Suetonius, Tacitus, and Seneca, Smallwood ("Some Notes on the Jews under Tiberius," pp. 319-320) almost acknowledges the same thing.

[69]We ought to keep in mind that Valerius Maximus, contemporary with the events here described, had associated the original expulsion of Roman Jews with the same introduction of Jewish *sacra* (epitome of Nepotianus) or *mores* (Paris) into the life of the city and that he had done so within the context of reference to

indicated, it was part of his aversion to these rites that Tiberius was expressing when he expelled a majority of Jews from Rome.[70]

For some of the same reasons, the usage to which Williams puts the account from Dio is little more successful. She begins with the introduction of the interesting thesis that this text had in mind an event different from and of much smaller magnitude than the one in Tacitus and Suetonius. That is, as the result of "the immigration of a group of Jews who were causing a public nuisance by their aggressive proselytizing activities," Tiberius in a "relatively small operation" expelled the members of that group.[71]

Though a thesis which would underline Tiberius' commitment to the abolition of offensive foreign religious practices within Rome, it is probably not correct. First, by insisting upon the limited nature of the proselytizing activity and hence of the measures against it, Williams directly contradicts her source. Second, after she has made a case that the "scrap" in Dio is very fragmentary as compared with the materials in Tacitus and Suetonius, it is hardly legitimate, as she in fact admits,[72] to use what Dio did not write in order to distinguish the event which he recorded from the one in Tacitus and Suetonius. Third, and most important, we have observed already that, while the excerpt of Dio lacks the precision of both Tacitus and Suetonius, it does correspond to them in terms of the fundamental question of what motivated the actions of the government at this time,[73] for here too the intention was clearly to rid from Rome the rites of offensive foreign religiosity.

Thus, Williams is to be criticized above all in terms of her use of the expression "public nuisance," for even more problematic than its pejorative nature is the fact that it has no basis within the text of Dio. In other words, since to resist proselytizing was a single dimension of resisting the practice of various undesirable *sacra*, the imperial wrath

---

several foreign cults. Concerning the aversion of Dio himself to these cults see 52.36.1-2.

[70]Dio's statement that Tiberius "banished most of them" certainly applies to practitioners of Judaism but leaves open the unanswerable question of the identity of those spared expulsion. Thinking of Tacitus, we might conjecture that these were persons who chose to abandon Jewish customs. Equally likely, however, is the possibility that Dio's imprecision reflected his disinterest or ignorance.

[71]Williams, "Expulsion," p. 768.

[72]Ibid., p. 767.

[73]Williams ("Expulsion," p. 767) does recognize that the event described by Dio took place in the very same years as that in Tacitus and so forth.

was directed not at some stereotypical Jewish "nuisance" but, just as Tacitus, Suetonius, and Seneca indicated, at the practices of Jewish and other foreign rites in Rome.

Williams' way of treating the account in Dio has a direct bearing upon her interpretation of the 19 CE events in Tacitus and Suetonius. Disassociating Dio's material from those events, she also disassociates from them his clearly religious motivation for the actions of Tiberius. Similarly, by her position analogous to that of Smallwood that Tacitus and Suetonius failed to provide any immediate motivation for these measures,[74] she excludes from consideration those two texts as well. Again, construing Josephus as purely apologetic and at the same time ignoring Seneca on this point, she finds herself without any immediate explanation for the measures of Tiberius. As a result, for her own interpretation she turns to two sorts of general consideration, first, to the Ciceronian estimation of Jews as troublemakers, i.e., to "their well-attested propensity for unruly behaviour,"[75] and, second, to the contemporary social situation in Rome, that means, to Jewish poverty, the economic crisis of 19 CE,[76] the prediction of a revolt in that year, and Germanicus' popularity.[77]

This approach to the events of 19 CE leaves much to be desired. In the first place, it is based upon the doubtful thesis that Dio had in mind events different from those in Tacitus and Suetonius.[78] Second, and similar to the interpretation of Smallwood, it depends upon the

---

[74]Williams, "Expulsion," p. 774. What she means in particular is that the Roman hostility towards "*externae religiones*," i.e., "the Romans...did not like *externae religiones* very much" (p. 775), could not have produced concrete actions against them except under the stimulus of some more specific cause. Given both her failure to justify this important supposition and the clear sense to the contrary which we find in Seneca, Tacitus, and Suetonius, there is no basis for recourse to secondary causality.

[75]Williams, "Expulsion," p. 780.

[76]Ibid., pp. 781-782.

[77]Ibid., p. 783.

[78]It is certainly curious that, though Williams separates the event in Tacitus from the one described by Dio, she ultimately ascribes the grounds for both to the troublesome character of Jews. Hence, referring to the foreign Jewish proselytizers whom she envisions behind the occurrence in Dio, she takes advantage of the expression "obnoxious minority groups" and, similarly, "troublesome immigrant Jews" ("Expulsion," p. 768). Likewise, she characterizes the Roman Jews of the account of Tacitus et al. in terms of their "crowding and turbulence," "disorderly behaviour," "well-attested propensity for unruly behavior," "propensity for unruliness," and so forth (pp. 780-783).

unsupported and in fact insupportable proposition that Tacitus and Suetonius were silent about the intention of Tiberius' measures. Third, having placed the account of Seneca within the same context as that of Tacitus and Suetonius,[79] it then ignores the fact that this account is explicit about the religious intention of Tiberius' measures. Fourth, it ignores the clear sense of the latter two sources that Jews were but a single target of these actions. Fifth, disregarding the contextual explanation of the emperor's actions in Seneca, Tacitus, Suetonius, and Dio, it reaches back to the time of Cicero for its interpretive key. Finally, implicitly excluding all other members of the large Roman proletariat from circumstances similar to those in which Roman Jews at this time found themselves and also ignoring its own caveat that Jewish participation in these matters "cannot, of course, be proved," it then concludes that massive Jewish riots must have caused the expulsion of these people.[80]

Therefore, in spite of how Smallwood and Williams treat these matters, the eyewitness accounts of Seneca and Valerius Maximus as well as the later reports of Tacitus, Suetonius, and Dio agree that, not long after[81] he became emperor, Tiberius made clear his intention to exclude various foreign religious rites from Rome.[82] Moreover, among

---

[79]Williams, "Expulsion," p. 772.

[80]Ibid., p. 782.

[81]The early date is expressly stated by Seneca and Tacitus and apparently confirmed by John of Antioch; cf. p. 50, n. 42.

[82]Smallwood and Williams are hardly unique in disregarding the clear sense of Tacitus, Suetonius, Seneca, and Dio in this matter. Without providing any consideration of the texts themselves, for example, Guterman attributes the events of 19 CE to the fact that the synagogues had "probably become centres of unrest" (*Religious Toleration*, pp. 148-149). By way of contrast, using the account in Josephus as his interpretive key, Merrill ("Expulsion," p. 365; cf. Leon, *Jews of Ancient Rome*, p. 17) assumes that the action of Tiberius was no more than his response to the conversion of and embezzlement from a prominent Roman matron coupled perhaps with "other unrecorded scandals." Nevertheless, besides the fact that this Josephan idea hardly suffices to account for the expulsion of the entire Roman Jewish population (so already Heidel, "Why Were the Jews Banished?" p. 39, and Smallwood, *Jews under Roman Rule*, pp. 203-204), it also ignores the clear sense of the above sources and, as we shall soon see, disregards the highly apologetic nature of the account in Josephus. The same criticisms stand in the way of what really is the "fantastic suggestion" (Feldman, trans., in Josephus, *The Life, Against Apion, The Jewish War, Jewish Antiquities*, 9:58-59, n. b; also, Smallwood, *Jews under Roman Rule*, p. 203, n. 9, and Williams, "Expulsion," p. 775) of Heidel (pp. 42-47) that Tiberius expelled Roman Jews because one of them encouraged a Roman matron to become a temple prostitute in Jerusalem.

the various ways in which this might have been done, our sources indicate several actually employed by the new emperor. Perhaps less important or at least less remarkable were the several measures directed against the objects necessary to the performance of these foreign *sacra*. That is, Suetonius alone made readers aware of the fact that Tiberius had forced worshipers into burning their own religious vestments and other liturgical furnishings.[83] More important were the various measures which Tiberius took against both actual and would-be practitioners of these foreign rites. This is not surprising because the direct way of ridding the city of unwanted religious customs was to take remedial measures against those who already observed them and proleptic measures against the creation of new adherents to them.

Concerning prolepsis, Seneca informed his readers that members of the best Roman families felt they had to be on guard against even the appearance of practicing culinary customs associated with foreign superstition. Otherwise, they exposed themselves to false prosecution. Likewise, the "similia sectantes" of Suetonius were expelled from the city, and steps were naturally taken against anyone involved with leading them into the practice of foreign rites.[84] Concerning the other measures, our sources are equally clear: Tacitus preserved the quite valuable detail that the government employed the threat of general expulsion in order to convince *superstitiosi* to give up their practices, Seneca exemplified the reality of that threat, and both Tacitus and Suetonius wrote that the expulsion which took place subsequently was directed against persons practicing the despised foreign rites.[85] In sum, focusing all such observations upon the foreign cult of interest to the present study, we see from our Gentile sources in particular that the fundamental cause of Tiberius' 19 CE actions against Roman Jews was the fact that they were practicing the rites associated with

---

[83]Josephus (*Antiquities* 18.79) referred also to how Tiberius burned the temple of Isis and had the cult statue thrown into the Tiber. More ominously, he reported that the Isiac priests were crucified. This reality of physical danger finds further expression in Tacitus' well-known comment about the likely death of the draftees, Suetonius' reference to the threat of perpetual slavery, and Josephus' hint about the fate of young Jews unwilling to serve in the military.

[84]Dio was explicit about this, and Valerius Maximus most probably, albeit anachronistically, referred to the same thing. Moreover, and as already noted, there is nothing in the text of Tacitus or Suetonius which limits the punishments described in them to persons born into the practices of foreign *sacra*.

[85]Josephus (*Antiquities* 18.83) referred to the expulsion of the entire Jewish population, no doubt a bit of exaggeration suitable to his contrast with what little happened to the worshipers of Isis.

the Jewish religion, and it is equally clear that the intention of these actions was the eradication of those practices from the city.[86]

With the exception of what Tacitus narrated in his *Histories* 5.9, "When Caligula ordered the Jews to set up his statue in their temple, they chose rather to resort to arms, but the emperor's death put an end to their uprising," we are in possession of no information from Greco-Roman historical sources concerning the imperial treatment of Jews and their religious practices under Rome's next emperor, Gaius (Caligula, 37-41 CE). Still, even that small piece of information is important to us. It was sufficiently bad already that the other Gaius, Augustus' heir-apparent, should have offended the Jewish people by ignoring the cult of their deity as he journeyed through Judea. It was, however, a far worse situation when the later Gaius Caligula began to organize the erection of a statue or statues of himself within the temple precincts of Jerusalem. Here we are reminded for the second time of Antiochus Epiphanes and the innovations, as well as the devastation, which the latter actually and the former very nearly succeeded in bringing upon Judea.

Having begun the present chapter with Valerius Maximus, the earliest of our Gentile sources for the pre-Claudian period, we may conclude it with the latest. The way in which the third century Dio Cassius described the earlier history does in fact constitute a fitting summary of it:

> I do not know the origins of this name ['Ιουδαῖοι] for them, but it also refers to the other persons, even foreigners, who eagerly pursue their customs [νόμιμα]. And this people is even among the Romans.

---

[86]In the midst of the Gentile sources, we shall not at present introduce either Josephus' description of this event or the indications from Philo that Tiberius also took action against Jewish religiosity on a later occasion. Furthermore, because, as will be indicated shortly, imperial treatment of Jewish royalty had little relationship to how other Jews were handled, I omit here the tradition of Dio 59.8.2 that Tiberius had imprisoned in Rome the Jewish prince Agrippa I. It is interesting, nonetheless, that, though Dio simply stated this hostile action as a fact, Josephus attempted to explain it away. As he told the story in *War* 2.179-180, Agrippa's servant reported to Tiberius how his master had prayed for the death of the emperor. In this form of the account, readers were left to suspect that the slave had made up such an unlikely charge. In *Antiquities* 18.168-169/179-204 such suspicions are confirmed. There, it turns out, the servant was seeking imperial favor against Agrippa who had rightly accused him of theft (18.169). The result: though Dio is easily understood otherwise, Josephus insisted that Tiberius' imprisonment of Agrippa had nothing to do with the fact he was a Jew. Instead, it occurred because of a false accusation of treason. According to the clever Josephan apologetic, therefore, neither the emperor nor Agrippa had really done anything wrong.

Though often curtailed, it increased to the greatest extent so as to win by force the freedom of its religious belief [νομίσεως].[87]

In this passage Dio broadened the ethnic definition of the word *Jew* by giving it a separate religious meaning. That is, he used the term to designate persons ethnically conceived, but for him it meant also those others as well, i.e., Gentiles, who followed the religious way of life typically associated with the ethnic group.[88] Thus, looking back over the history of these practitioners of Judaism among the Romans, Dio wrote that an earlier period had been characterized by the repression of the various individuals who carried out Jewish rites.[89] Through imperial eyes, again, the problem was the *superstitio*.

As a basic step towards understanding imperial policy vis-à-vis Roman Jews under the emperor Claudius, we have investigated all the Gentile sources in terms of what they reveal about the relationship between these Jews and their pre-Claudian masters. In so doing, we have found that this relationship was governed by three grammatical elements: Republican or imperial authority is the subject, Jews as practitioners of a particular foreign *superstitio* are the object, and the predicate is one or another hostile act of the former against the latter. From observations in the last chapter we know that Jews were in a precarious position. This was not because of their supposed penchant for troublemaking but on account of the outrageous attitudes which the upper class and emperors of Rome maintained towards the Jewish cult. We were aware also that such hostile attitudes threatened to provoke measures of a like kind. Hence, the present chapter confirms these conclusions, for, according to the Gentile sources, hypothetical Jewish inclinations towards troublemaking constitute no background against which to view the subsequent policy of the emperor Claudius. This is furnished instead by the very real upper-class and imperial prejudices which were acted out in concrete measures intended to suppress the practice of Jewish and other foreign *sacra* at Rome.

---

[87]Dio 37.16.5-17.1, my translation. See LSJ, s.v. "νόμισις" on the interpretation of this word as "religious belief." "Curtailed" translates "κολουσθὲν."

[88]The definition of Suetonius included only the ethnic sense to which was attached a fixed religious connotation. Gentile adherents of the cult he designated obliquely as "similia sectantes" (cf. pp. 54-55). For further discussion, cf. chapter 7 (pp. 154-155).

[89]Dio composed long after Claudius, and, as we shall see, gave specific details about this emperor's measures against the practice of Judaism at Rome.

Chapter Three

Pre-Claudian Repression from between the Lines of the Jewish Sources

We saw earlier the truth of Smallwood's assertion that the ancient Gentile writers did not portray early imperial attitudes towards Jews and their cult in the positive light of the Jewish sources. Having recognized their apologetic purposes and reading between the lines, however, we find that the Jewish writers actually confirm the Gentile portrayal. In other words, these witnesses also make clear the difficult situation of Roman and other Jews prior to the time when Claudius became emperor. They too, furthermore, corroborate the primarily religion-based causes of these difficulties.

Granted, neither Philo nor Josephus referred to what from the Jewish perspective must have been the shocking and yet imperially approved behavior of Augustus' heir-apparent towards the Jewish cult center in Jerusalem. On the other hand, Victor Tcherikover is most likely correct that Augustus' abolition of the Jewish ethnarchy in Alexandria, which Philo did report (*Flaccus* 72), posed a threat to the previous status of the large Jewish population in that city.[1] More importantly, silent about that action of Augustus in Alexandria, the Gentile sources also provide no particulars concerning what under the

---

[1]Tcherikover, *Hellenistic Civilization*, pp. 412-413; cf. p. 302. The fact that Claudius' Alexandrian edict in *Antiquities* 19.279-285 denies any such action on Augustus' part (19.283) leads Tcherikover to recognize apologetic forgery. Seen from another angle, that Josephus thought the denial a necessity points to the negative implications of the change, ones which Josephus himself associated with the disturbance of the traditional Jewish way of life (19.283).

65

emperor Tiberius was an equally hostile act of his heir-apparent in the same city.

Specifically, according to *Tiberius* 52.2, Germanicus travelled to Alexandria in 19 CE because of an immense famine which had struck there. Tacitus (*Annals* 2.59) added that, in order to cope with it, he had opened the granaries. In this way Germanicus was able to bring down the price of food and so make it available to the common people (*vulgus*). Most fortunately, therefore, Josephus, in his attack upon the anti-Jewish accusations of the Alexandrian Apion, also wrote about the same event. Reading carefully, we observe that the sympathetic hunger fighter of Suetonius and Tacitus had done something odd in this matter: "If Germanicus was unable to distribute corn to all the inhabitants of Alexandria, that merely proves a barren year and a dearth of corn, and cannot be made *an accusation against the Jews.*"[2]

So expressing himself, Josephus let slip the awkward fact that the popular Germanicus, father of the emperor Gaius and brother to Claudius, had excluded Jews from a share in his deed of mercy.[3] Unwilling to reveal imperial hostility towards Jews, Josephus chose to excuse Germanicus on the grounds of scarcity.[4] Because there was insufficient corn to go around, he gave Jews none of it. As we read the account in Josephus, Apion must have used this event to demonstrate that Jews were not citizens of Alexandria.[5] Against him Josephus then responded as indicated. Back of this entire matter, however, stands an event on which both men agreed. In a time of great hunger, Germanicus denied food specifically to the Jewish population of the city. But, just as the letter of Claudius illustrates,[6] this was hardly

---

[2]*Apion* 2.63.

[3]Bell ("Egypt" in *CAH*, 10:309) also notes the exclusion. *Legatio* 155-158 implies a similar exclusion of Jews from the dole in Claudian Rome (cf. p. 95).

[4]Though Conrad Cichorius (*Römische Studien: Historisches, Epigraphisches, Literargeschichtliches aus vier Jahrhunderten Roms*, 2d ed. [Darmstadt: Wissenschaftliche Buchgesellschaft, 1961], pp. 378-379, 384-385) and Barrett (*Caligula*, p. 184) take Josephus uncritically at his word, Cichorius' overall description of Germanicus' humanitarian action (pp. 375-388) is well worth reading. The edicts themselves appear along with discussion in Ulrich von Wilamowitz-Moellendorff and F. Zucker, "Zwei Edikte des Germanicus auf einem Papyrus des Berliner Museums," *Sitzungsberichte der preussischen Akademie der Wissenschaften* 33 (1911): 794-821. The first of these orders testifies to Germanicus' kindness towards the people of Alexandria and Egypt and so contrasts sharply with his treatment of the Jewish population.

[5]He used an occurrence from the time of Cleopatra similarly (*Apion* 2.60).

[6]P. Lond. 1912, lines 82-88.

consistent with the legitimate place long held by Jews within the city of Alexandria. Moreover, neither Suetonius nor Tacitus implied that only citizens were included in the relief effort. Philo, by the way, who was probably there at the time, employed a different apologetic tool in order to handle this imperial injustice. He ignored it.

We have referred previously to the religion-based expulsion of Roman Jews which occurred according to Tacitus at almost exactly the same time. Josephus too was aware (*Antiquities* 18.65, 81-84) that, in conjunction with measures against practitioners of the cult of Isis, Tiberius had

> ordered the whole Jewish community [πᾶν τὸ ᾿Ιουδαϊκὸν τῆς ᾿Ρώμης] to leave Rome. The consuls drafted four thousand of these Jews for military service and sent them to the island of Sardinia; but they penalized a good many of them, who refused to serve for fear of breaking the Jewish law [τῶν πατρίων νόμων].

Not surprisingly, the story as Josephus told it looks quite different from the version presented by our various Gentile sources.[7]

In particular, whereas the latter accounts place the Tiberian measures against Jewish cult practices within the same context as those against the rites of Isis, Josephus made a very sharp distinction between the two. While *Antiquities* 18.65 introduces them together, *Antiquities* 18.66-80 and 18.81-84 each provide entirely self-contained narratives about the Roman cult of Isis and Judaism respectively. As a result, although our Gentile sources assume an undifferentiated attitude toward these foreign cults, Josephus did not. Instead, he disassociated the one from the other so as to affirm the legitimacy of imperial action against Egyptian religion but to explain away the measures taken against all things Jewish in Rome ("πᾶν τὸ ᾿Ιουδαϊκὸν τῆς ᾿Ρώμης").[8]

Briefly, as he told the story, it was the greedy priests of Rome's great temple of Isis who played a key part in the scandalous actions

---

[7]So already Radin (*Jews among Greeks and Romans*, p. 306), who makes an interesting comment that "Josephus is probably the nearest in time to the events he is describing, but also the most remote in comprehension." In reality, he was able to understand only too well. Concerning the fact that Tacitus and Josephus were describing the same 19 CE event, see p. 50, n. 42.

[8]Within its present context ᾿Ιουδαϊκός obviously includes persons, but contrary to the LCL translation the neuter "everything Jewish" need not be limited to them alone. That is, though *War* 2.105 is best understood that way, in *Antiquities* 12.34 the adjective is applied to the Jewish Scriptures and in 14.228 to Jewish religious rites. In our text, therefore, "everything Jewish" would appear to refer to persons, religious documents, other *instrumenta* (cf. p. 54, n. 51), and *sacra*.

which led to their own crucifixion, the burning of their temple, the dispatch of their cult statue, but the expulsion of only a single person.[9] What great evil, therefore, must the practitioners of Judaism have committed to cause the expulsion of "everything Jewish" from the city? Nothing, for in their case this widespread measure resulted from the actions not of the authentic religious leadership but of a greedy Jewish charlatan new to Rome and present there only because of prosecution in his homeland.[10] As Josephus told the story, therefore, corruption at the heart of Rome's Isiac cult had resulted in the expulsion of one truly guilty person. By way of contrast, the actions of a stranger to the city's Jewish community had caused the wrongful banishment of all things Jewish.

Thus, with the exceptions of the correlation between anti-Isiac and anti-Jewish measures, the common references to Sardinia and to the four thousand draftees, and the indications that it was matters associated with religion which resulted in actions against the two cults,[11] it is not easy to recognize that Josephus and Tacitus et al. were describing the same event. In terms of the apologetic needs of the Jewish historian, this is to be expected. After all, it was hardly a good idea to leave the impression that grounds of a substantive nature had provoked Tiberius' expulsion of τὸ Ἰουδαϊκόν, or that he had acted in an arbitrarily hostile manner against everything Jewish within Rome, or that he had perceived Judaism to be but one among various disreputable foreign cults. Hence, according to Josephus' well thought out apologetic, this expulsion had nothing to do with things authentically Jewish but was to be accounted for instead by the actions of a single renegade Jew and his accomplices: "So because of

---

[9]For the details concerning it, see Samuel Ball Platner (*A Topographical Dictionary of Ancient Rome*, completed and revised by Thomas Ashby [1929; reprint ed., Rome: "L'Erma" di Bretschneider, 1965], pp. 283-284), Ernest Nash (*Pictorial Dictionary of Ancient Rome*, 2d ed., 2 vols. [New York: Frederick A. Praeger, 1961-1962], 1:510), and Lawrence Richardson, Jr. (*A New Topographical Dictionary of Ancient Rome* [Baltimore and London: The Johns Hopkins University Press, 1992], pp. 211-212). The first of these reminds us that it was located outside of the religious boundaries, i.e., the pomerium, of the city (cf. p. 393) and had alleged associations with prostitution. This latter fact no doubt played some part in Josephus' use of the temple prostitution motif.

[10]Incidently, though it is easy to assume that he came from Judea and had broken religious law, Josephus identified neither his homeland nor the nature of his crimes.

[11]A deception arising out of the Isiac rite of cult prostitution was the basis of measures against that cult, and a deception based upon religious devotion to the temple in Jerusalem produced the others.

the wickedness of four men the Jews were banished from the city" (*Antiquities* 18.84). Having been trivialized in such a manner, this expulsion therefore revealed no inherent hostility on the part of the emperor Tiberius and provided no precedent for future actions of a similar nature.[12]

Whereas Josephus decided to deal with the 19 CE expulsion of the Roman Jews by explaining it away, Philo took a much more direct route: he ignored it completely. That is, having already extolled the situation under the emperor Augustus, in *Legatio* 159-161 Philo went on to write that

> everyone...was afraid to engage in destroying any of our institutions [τῶν ᾽Ιουδαϊκῶν νομίμων], and indeed [μέντοι] it was the same under Tiberius though [καίτοι] matters in Italy became troublesome when Sejanus was organizing his onslaughts. For Tiberius knew the truth, he knew at once after Sejanus's death that the accusations made against the Jewish inhabitants of Rome were false slanders, invented by him because he wished to make away with the nation, knowing that it would take the sole or the principal part in opposing his unholy plots and actions, and would defend the emperor when in danger of becoming the victim of treachery. And he [Tiberius] charged his procurators in every place to which they were appointed to speak comfortably to the members of our nation in the different cities, assuring them that the penal measures did not extend to all but only to the guilty, who were few, and to disturb none of the established customs [ἔθους] but even to regard them as a trust committed to their care, the people as naturally peaceable, and the institutions [νόμιμα] as an influence promoting orderly conduct.

Describing events which occurred ca. 31 CE,[13] Philo wrote here as if the earlier expulsion had never taken place.

This way of handling things, however, should not be much of a surprise to us, for we observed already the apologetic value of ignoring happenings that reflected imperial disapproval of the Jewish way of

---

[12]My interpretation of the apologetic of Josephus follows the line proposed by Smallwood (*Jews under Roman Rule*, pp. 203-204), Moehring ("Persecution," pp. 300-304; cf. his "Joseph ben Matthia and Flavius Josephus: The Jewish Prophet and the Roman Historian" in *ANRW*, 2.21²:905), Williams ("Expulsion," pp. 775-778), and also Feldman ("Flavius Josephus Revisited" in *ANRW*, 2.21²:817). Heidel ("Why Were the Jews Banished?" p. 39) claims conjecturally that cult prostitution hides itself behind the account of Josephus. Nonetheless, he also recognizes the problematic nature of that narrative. Assuming the correctness of the Jewish historian, Schürer (*History*, 3¹:75-76), Merrill ("Expulsion," p. 365), and Stern ("Jewish Diaspora" in *Jewish People*, 1:164) in particular build their interpretation of 19 CE around him.

[13]See p. 50, n. 42.

life.[14] Furthermore, the present passage belongs, like *Legatio* 33, 141-142, and 298-308, within the context of Philo's polemic against Gaius, a principal ingredient of which is the clear contrast between this emperor and his predecessors. Reference to the Tiberian action of 19 CE would hardly have supported such a distinction: "Philo must have kept silent about the measure taken by Tiberius against the Jews. There is a very plausible reason for this. Philo was particularly concerned to demonstrate that, with the exception of the villain Caligula, all Claudius' predecessors were favourably inclined towards the Jews."[15]

Nonetheless, having aptly avoided the mention of this measure, Philo succeeded only in opening a new can of worms. That is, by means of the μέντοι/καίτοι construction, he drew a contrast between two different ways, as he proposed, that Jews were treated under Tiberius. Specifically, according to the manner in which Liddell and Scott express it, καίτοι is used "to mark an objection introduced by the speaker himself."[16] Thus, as even Scramuzza recognizes with his comment about the potential for a "calculated euphemism" here,[17] it is a strange eulogy which begins by objecting to itself. In terms of the narrative as a whole, however, we see that Philo could hardly have expressed himself otherwise, for the picture which he alone painted of the later Tiberian threat to Italian Jewish customs (νόμιμα/ἔθη) and their practitioners is surely authentic.[18] Bammel is quite correct,

---

[14]Similarly on the present passage, Smallwood, "Some Notes on the Jews under Tiberius," pp. 328-329.

[15]Sevenster, *Roots of Pagan Anti-Semitism*, p. 25. Smallwood ("Some Notes on the Jews under Tiberius," p. 329) makes the same claim in terms of "Philo's thesis that the Emperors were by tradition the champions of the Jews." Only by means of disregarding these considerations can Radin (*Jews among Greeks and Romans*, pp. 309-310) write, "the alleged expulsion is not mentioned by Philo in the extant fragments. The allusion to some oppressive acts of Sejanus...is not clear. But it is difficult to understand the highly eulogistic [Philonic] references to Tiberius, then long dead, if a general Jewish expulsion had been ordered by that emperor." As is typical, Scramuzza ("Policy" in *Beginnings of Christianity*, 5:294) also uses Philo to argue against Tiberius' hostility.

[16]LSJ, s.v. "καίτοι."

[17]Scramuzza, "Policy" in *Beginnings of Christianity*, 5:294.

[18]Eusebius twice paraphrased Philo on Sejanus' anti-Jewish policy. First, in his *Ecclesiastical History* 2.5.6-7, referring specifically to information gleaned from the *Legatio*, Eusebius explained that "in the time of Tiberius, in the city of the Romans, Sejanus, the most influential of the Emperor's court at the time, took measures completely to destroy the whole [Jewish] race." So also, in Jerome's

after all, that Philo would not have invented materials so contrary to his own purposes.[19]

In order to neutralize these facts, Philo made two attempts at apologetic dissimulation, but neither succeeds. The first drew a sharp line between the good emperor and the bad prefect of the Praetorian Guard. Though a safe procedure because Sejanus had been discredited prior to the writing of the *Legatio*, it is not a convincing one,[20] and for various reasons. Most obviously, it fails to account for Tiberius' 19 CE expulsion of the practitioners of Judaism from Rome, an event our sources nowhere attribute to Sejanus.[21] Equally important, it was the emperor himself who had chosen and then elevated this prefect,[22] a decision which we could more easily attribute to ignorance had he not thereafter elected as his prefect of Egypt another friend of similar ilk, Flaccus. As Philo himself (*Flaccus* 1-2) indicated,

---

Latin translation and revision of Eusebius' *Chronicle* we find the following notation under the twenty-first year of Tiberius: "Sejanus, the prefect of Tiberius, who had very much influence with him, encouraged greatly that he destroy the Jewish people. Philo mentions this in the second book of the *Legatio*." (This is my translation of the Latin text in *Die Chronik des Hieronymus: Hieronymi Chronicon: Eusebius Werke* 7, ed. Rudolf Helm, GCS, vol. 47, 2d ed. [Berlin: Akademie-Verlag, 1956], p. 176. Although the passage is not found in the Armenian version, *Die Chronik aus dem armenischen übersetzt mit textkritischem Commentar: Eusebius Werke* 5, ed. Josef Karst, GCS, vol. 20 [Leipzig: J .C. Hinrichs'sche Buchhandlung, 1911], p. 213, the apparatus of Helm does attribute it to Eusebius rather than to the revisions of his work in Jerome's Latin text.) Because neither of these passages provides us with any information which Eusebius could not have absorbed from *Legatio* 159-161, it is safest for present purposes to treat them as extrapolations from that source (so too Smallwood, "Some Notes on the Jews under Tiberius," pp. 323-324), accounting for their perhaps heightened rhetoric by Eusebius' polemical view that the evil befell the Jewish people "in consequence of their crimes against Christ" (*Ecclesiastical History* 2.5.6). The only exception is that the *Chronicle* dates this material to Tiberius' twenty-first year, i.e., to perhaps 34-35 CE, and hence wrongly to the period after the 31 CE death of Sejanus. Apparently, then, Eusebius does not provide us with independent confirmation of the report in Philo.

[19]Bammel, "Judenverfolgung," p. 297, n. 2.

[20]For modern views which take Philo at his word, see Leon (*Jews of Ancient Rome*, pp. 16-17) and Gager (*Origins of Anti-Semitism*, p. 62).

[21]So already Williams, "Expulsion," p. 774. Because he had been praetorian prefect since 14 CE (*PIR*[2] A 255; *PW* 1 [1894] 529), we may not draw any absolute conclusion about this.

[22]Cf. Garnsey and Saller, *Roman Empire*, pp. 25-26.

the policy of attacking the Jews begun by Sejanus was taken over by Flaccus Avillius. He had not like his predecessor the power to ill-treat outright the whole nation, for he had less opportunities of doing so, but those whom he reached suffered the direct misery from the stabs which he dealt to them one and all.... This Flaccus, then, who had been given a place in the suite of Tiberius Caesar [literally, "chosen to be among the companions at the side of Tiberius Caesar"],[23] was...made prefect of Alexandria and the country round it.

Consequently, in light of the 19 CE events, there is every reason to think that Sejanus carried out his anti-Jewish actions at the behest of the emperor who discovered in him "ein willfähriges und tüchtiges Werkzeug."[24] In any case, *Legatio* 160 makes clear that Tiberius had concurred with the charges against Roman Jews,[25] and *Legatio* 161 leaves no doubt that Tiberius himself continued to pursue anti-Jewish measures in various cities after the death of Sejanus.[26] Therefore, in spite of his efforts to the contrary, Philo failed to make credible his dichotomy between the pro-Jewish Tiberius and the anti-Jewish prefect, Sejanus.

The second attempt at dissimulation was intended to minimize the extent of and to reveal as little as possible about the specific charges brought against Jewish populations at that time. In order to achieve these goals Philo introduced contradictory claims. On the one hand, he indicated that the anti-Jewish charges were simply false, i.e., that they were a mere subterfuge intended by Sejanus to rid himself of Roman Jews because they constituted the sole or at least principal defenders of Tiberius (*Legatio* 160). On the other, he did admit the legitimacy of the accusations as well as of the punishments incurred

---

[23]Cf. Box's edition of the text, *Philonis Alexandrini: IN FLACCUM*, p. 69.

[24]*PW* 1 (1894) 530. Cf. Martin (*Tacitus*, p. 132): "Sejanus was rather Tiberius' aider and abetter than the instigator in cruelty." This is not to exonerate him, for Sevenster (*Roots of Pagan Anti-Semitism*, pp. 11-14) rightly underlines Sejanus' own anti-Judaism as revealed uniquely by Philo in *Legatio* 159-161 and *Flaccus* 1. We are reminded in turn of the importance of Sevenster's claim (pp. 7-8, 14) that chance has preserved for us perhaps only the tip of the iceberg in these matters. Furthermore, the anti-Judaism of the extremely powerful Sejanus makes clear again where in Roman society this hostility had imbedded itself.

[25]Cf. Juster, *Les Juifs*, 1:224, n. 3.

[26]Precisely what happened and where it happened Philo leaves vague. In the view of Bammel ("Judenverfolgung," p. 297), *Legatio* 160 alludes to an action directed against Roman Jews, *Legatio* 159 reports an action apparently at a different time against other Jews of Italy, and *Flaccus* 1 deals with an event more universal in scope.

but minimized the numbers found guilty and left the nature of these charges relatively vague. *Legatio* 161 tells us, that is, how Tiberius ordered his procurators in the various affected cities to assure Jewish populations in them

> that the penal measures did not extend to all but only to the guilty, who were few, and to disturb none of the established customs [ἔθους] but even to regard them as a trust committed to their care, the people as naturally peaceable, and the institutions [νόμιμα] as an influence promoting orderly conduct.

The former of these claims does not work well. In the first place, its image of Roman Jews as the chief protectors of the emperor makes sense only as apologetic; in the second, while it does account for the anti-Jewish measures of Sejanus, it does not for those of Tiberius himself. Contradictions aside, however, the latter claim works nicely because, like Josephus' treatment of the 19 CE expulsion, it shifts the issue of accusations against entire Jewish communities to particular misdeeds of what Philo insisted were only the few genuinely guilty persons. In this way he could admit not only to the fact of Tiberius' actions but also to their legitimacy and at the same time leave the necessary impression that the emperor was otherwise well disposed to Jews and their traditional customs.[27]

Hence, though Philo found himself unable to escape the fact that accusations were made and punishments carried out against Jews not only in Rome but in other cities as well, he did succeed to some degree in distracting attention from the nature and severity of both. Still, Philo's intention to the contrary, we are not left completely in the dark concerning these matters. Concretely, we know in terms of the general background that Tiberius had already taken decisive action against the Roman practice of foreign religious rites, i.e., against the practice of what our various sources refer to by means of the words *ritus*, *sacra*, *consuetudines*, *caerimonias*, ἔθη, and πατρίους νόμους, some ten years earlier. Furthermore, though Philo wished his readers to think otherwise, we know also from his own report that any objections of Tiberius to the more widespread anti-Jewish measures of Sejanus arose at best after the death of the latter and even then only in part. In addition, the very fact that these measures were so widespread indicates that the unstated charges could be applied broadly against Jews. As a result, when we conjecture about the specific nature of the accusations which could have been raised simultaneously against Jewish populations in several cities, the absence of other reasonable

---

[27]We observed (p. 62, n. 86) how, in the somewhat analogous situation of Agrippa I, Josephus defended his cause without seeming to criticize Tiberius.

possibilities forces us to think once again of charges associated with religious practices.[28]

Moreover, the very context within which Philo referred to these matters points in the same direction, for it is governed by the theme of Gaius' hostility towards the Jewish people so identified primarily in the religious sense. Referring to Gaius' claim of divinity, *Legatio* 114-115 begins the section of interest to us. On the basis of this claim, Gaius had

> looked with disfavour on the Jews alone because they alone opposed him on principle, trained as they were we may say even from the cradle, by parents and tutors and instructors and by the far higher authority of the sacred laws [τῶν ἱερῶν νόμων] and also the unwritten customs [τῶν ἀγράφων ἐθῶν], to acknowledge one God who is the Father and Maker of the world.

Considered in isolation, the statement of Philo that Gaius "looked with disfavour on the Jews alone" might be interpreted as an allusion to that emperor's ethnically based dislike for Jews. Nevertheless, the context within which he wrote these words makes clear that Gaius' perspective was religious: what angered the emperor was the inability of practicing Jews, i.e., of Jews devoted to the written and unwritten laws of their religion, to affirm his divinity.

Similarly, *Legatio* 117 identifies the Jewish people with those who followed its ancient traditions ("τῶν πατρίων"), *Legatio* 118-119 identifies it with persons holding monotheistic views, and *Legatio* 132-134 associates attacks against the Jewish ἔθνος directly with attacks against Jewish religious institutions, i.e., against the houses of prayer, the laws ("τῶν νόμων"), and customs ("ἐθῶν"). Likewise, but by way of contrast, *Legatio* 153-154 alludes to Augustus' respect for foreign traditions ("τῶν πατρίων") and legal observances ("τῶν νομίμων") as a more general way of declaring that he respected Jewish religious beliefs associated with monotheism. *Legatio* 155-158 then follows this up with the several ways in which he showed his approval of "τῶν πατρίων" (*Legatio* 155) of the Jewish religion, i.e., the houses of prayer, Sabbath worship, and the offerings for Jerusalem.

---

[28]The only other common denominator among those accused might have been the fact that they were perceived as Jews in the ethnic rather than religious sense. Nonetheless, though a good example of ethnic disapproval appears in Cicero's *Pro Flacco*, where he constantly maligned the character of Asian Greeks, this would create a false dichotomy. In any case, that large numbers of Jews in many different cities were charged with "some definite crime" like fraud, as Radin (*Jews among Greeks and Romans*, pp. 310-311) contends, makes no sense. By the way, because it would not have suited Philo's purposes to say so, we have no means of knowing if other foreign cults were also involved at this time.

This context firmly established, *Legatio* 159-161 then introduces itself as follows:

> Therefore everyone everywhere, even if he was not naturally well disposed to the Jews, was afraid to engage in destroying any of our institutions [τῶν Ἰουδαϊκῶν νομίμων], and indeed it was the same under Tiberius though matters in Italy became troublesome when Sejanus was organizing his onslaughts.

The emphatic "therefore" which Philo employed to introduce *Legatio* 159-161 demonstrates that he placed this section within the same primarily religious context as everything else in *Legatio* 114-158.

Hence, his statement here about persons "not naturally well disposed to the Jews" parallels his previous comment in *Legatio* 115 that Gaius "looked with disfavour on the Jews" and, like it, may be supposed to have in mind Jews under the aspect of their practice of Judaism. The legitimacy of this interpretation is then confirmed by the statement immediately following that the subject under discussion is the attacks upon Jewish νόμιμα ("τῶν Ἰουδαϊκῶν νομίμων"), i.e., upon the broadly conceived *sacra*, ἔθη, and so forth, which constitute the religiously based Jewish way of life. As a result, unless we are willing to suppose an invisible shift in the subject matter not only between *Legatio* 114-158 and *Legatio* 159-161 but also, and all the more strangely, between the introductory first half of *Legatio* 159 and what follows in the remainder of *Legatio* 159-161, Philo perceived the ca. 31 CE charges against Jews as essentially religious in nature.

With this in mind, we may revisit two other key observations among the remarks of Philo about Tiberius. The first, *Legatio* 160, has to do with the fact that "Tiberius knew the truth, he knew at once after Sejanus's death that the accusations made against the Jewish [Ἰουδαίων] inhabitants of Rome were false slanders, invented by him because he wished to make away with the nation [ἔθνος]." Here Philo used the terms Ἰουδαῖος and ἔθνος in such a way that exclusive of the broader context there is no way to be sure whether he was referring to Sejanus' ethnic or religious disapproval of Jews. Within that larger context, however, we have seen already that Philo gave a religious connotation to both words. Moreover, his parallel statements about Gaius who "looked with disfavour on the Jews" (*Legatio* 115) and about persons "not naturally well disposed to the Jews" (*Legatio* 159) are closely related to his reference to Sejanus as someone else who "wished to make away with the nation." Thus, in light of the religious associations of *Legatio* 115 and 159, there is no reason to think that Philo had anything different in mind in *Legatio* 160.

Even clearer in this regard is the second statement of Philo in *Legatio* 161:

he [Tiberius] charged his procurators in every place to which they
were appointed to speak comfortably to the members of our nation
[τοῦ ἔθνους] in the different cities, assuring them that the penal
measures did not extend to all but only to the guilty, who were few,
and to disturb none of the established customs [ἔθους] but even to
regard them as a trust committed to their care, the people as naturally peaceable, and the institutions [νόμιμα] as an influence pro-
moting orderly conduct.

That is, although the religious connotation of ἔθνος makes itself felt
only on the basis of the broader context of *Legatio* 114-161, Philo's
references to Jewish customs and institutions cannot be separated
from the primarily religious context of which they are an integral part.
Furthermore, by means of his statement that Tiberius had given the
order to disturb neither the ἔθη nor the νόμιμα, Philo revealed that
they in particular had been the object, along with the persons who
participated in them, of the imperial accusations.

Why did Philo wish to play down the fact that the broad-based
accusations of this period largely concerned themselves with matters
of Jewish religiosity? In part for the reason that Josephus did the
same thing vis-à-vis events in 19 CE. That is, no precedent attached
itself to imperial reaction against a few Jewish lawbreakers, but if
this reaction was to something so intrinsic as the Jewish religious
practices, it created a most ominous precedent. More particularly,
Philo chose this path because the events of ca. 31 CE made a lie of his
claim that Tiberius was categorically different from Gaius in attitudes
towards and actions against Jews and their cult. In sum, though Philo
did not dwell on the charges brought against Jewish communities in
Rome and elsewhere in Italy, religion obviously played a central role
in them. As a result, Juster's statement that "Tibère voulut détruire
tous les Juifs"[29] requires the clarification of the more nuanced view
of La Piana concerning "the general policy of Tiberius, so hostile to all
foreign cults."[30] In other words, it was Jews as practitioners of a
particular foreign *superstitio* who became the object of Tiberian wrath.

Overall, though we can appreciate the apologetic needs of Philo,
it is not possible to accept his optimistic picture of the reign of
Tiberius except perhaps precisely in terms of the context within which
he placed it. That is, maybe in a relative sense Tiberius did show
greater respect for Jews and their religious observances than Gaius.
Even so, considering the affront of the imperial heir-apparent to the

---

[29]Juster, *Les Juifs*, 1:224, n. 3. The extremity of his view depends upon
Eusebius' interpretation which has its own tendency (cf. p. 70, n. 18).

[30]La Piana, "Foreign Groups," p. 375, n. 6. Though made within the context of
his discussion of the 19 CE events (cf. p. 57), the statement applies here too.

hungry Alexandrian Jews in 18-19 CE, the religiously based expulsion of Roman Jews in 19 CE, and the similarly grounded but apparently more widespread goings-on which clustered around the year 31 CE, not to mention Tiberius' somewhat later imprisonment of Agrippa,[31] it is clear that Philo could only have been expressing himself here in the most relative terms.[32]

Gaius, the subsequent emperor and son of the Germanicus who had permitted Alexandrian Jews to go hungry, we met previously as he terrified Philo with challenges about Jewish religious life.[33] He ruled at the time of the 38 CE pogrom against Alexandrian Jews and their religious institutions.[34] Moreover, and as noted already on the basis of the brief report in Tacitus,[35] he later ordered that his own statue be situated within the Jewish temple, another action which had inherently religious implications.

Concerning the pogrom of 38 CE, we find ourselves in something of a quandary because the way Philo narrated the story in the *Flaccus* implies that Gaius bore no responsibility for it.[36] As a matter of fact,

---

[31]Cf. p. 62, n. 86.

[32]Wrongly, therefore, *CPJ*, 1:65, n. 37. How Barrett (*Caligula*, p. 184) expresses himself appears equally incorrect: "To the extent that there was anti-semitism among the Romans before Caligula, it generally took the form of fairly good-natured mockery of what were considered their outlandish religious views." Moreover, Leon (*Jews of Ancient Rome*, p. 20) provides no justification for his optimistic statement that "by the beginning of the reign of Tiberius' successor, Gaius, the Jews formed a large element in the population of Rome and were again in full enjoyment of their well established rights." More realistic is the much less happy picture which Bammel ("Judenverfolgung," p. 297) paints of the Roman Jewish situation at the time of Tiberius' death.

[33]Pp. 23-25.

[34]References to the specifically religious aspects of the pogrom make themselves visible in *Flaccus* 41-53 (the desecration of the Alexandrian houses of prayer, including implications for other parts of the Roman empire), *Flaccus* 96 (forced consumption of pork), as well as in *Legatio* 132-137 (desecration of the houses of prayer).

[35]P. 62.

[36]Critical of Philo's truthfulness otherwise, Willrich ("Caligula," p. 402; likewise, Balsdon, *Gaius*, pp. 141-142) believes him here. Hence, claiming that the earlier imperial friendship towards Jews must also have determined the original attitude of Gaius, he blames the pogrom of 38 CE secondarily on the Alexandrian Gentiles but primarily upon Agrippa and Alexandrian Jews. We saw already, however, the impossibility of assuming early imperial friendship, and we shall now see from several different angles that the same is at least as true of Gaius.

since Gaius recalled, tried, sent into exile, and ultimately executed Flaccus, the prefect immediately involved with it, the *Flaccus* reads naturally as though the emperor had actually opposed the pogrom.[37] Nevertheless, this does not correspond very well to two details from Philo's account: first, it was on the occasion of a celebration honoring the birthday of the emperor when, in the most barbaric of manners, Flaccus caused the Alexandrian Jews great suffering (*Flaccus* 81-85); second, the well-connected prefect had reason to think this sport would make a quite acceptable present for Gaius (*Flaccus* 108). Even so, Philo wanted his readers to interpret the fall of the Roman official as the result of the mistreatment of these Jews (*Flaccus* 116), and he implied that it was directly to this mistreatment that Gaius had responded with the arrest of Flaccus (*Flaccus* 102-104). Furthermore, Philo left ambiguous the actual charge against Flaccus and let slip the problematic detail that his accusers before Gaius were not the persecuted Alexandrian Jews but their worst enemies (*Flaccus* 125, 135, 146).[38] Thus, although the *Flaccus* seeks to exonerate Gaius, the contorted manner in which it goes about doing so suggests imperial complicity in the pogrom.

Not surprisingly, then, the two glimpses of these matters in Josephus confirm our suspicions. First, *Antiquities* 19.276 reports that, when Claudius became emperor, he "liberated Alexander the alabarch, an old friend of his, who had acted as guardian for his mother Antonia and had been imprisoned by Gaius in a fit of anger." This passage reveals that Gaius intervened directly against at least one prominent Alexandrian Jew, Alexander, who was also the brother of Philo.[39] We

---

[37]So too Goodenough, *Introduction to Philo Judaeus*, p. 58. For discussions of events in Alexandria under Gaius see Willrich ("Caligula," pp. 400-414), Balsdon (*Gaius*, pp. 125-135, and "Notes concerning the Principate of Gaius," *Journal of Roman Studies* 24 [1934]:19-24), Bell ("Egypt" in *CAH*, 10:309-311), Box's edition of the *Flaccus*, *Philonis Alexandrini: IN FLACCUM*, pp. xxxviii-l, Garzetti (*Tiberius to the Antonines*, pp. 92-97), Smallwood (*Jews under Roman Rule*, pp. 235-245), Schürer (*History*, 1:389-394), Barrett (*Caligula*, pp. 184-188), Hennig ("Bruchstücken," pp. 320-322), and, more generally, *CPJ* (1:48-93).

[38]So in part already H. Stuart Jones, "Claudius and the Jewish Question at Alexandria," *Journal of Roman Studies* 16 (1926):23-24. Willrich's well considered doubt ("Caligula," pp. 400-401) about the manner in which Philo portrayed the camaraderie of Flaccus and the Alexandrian anti-Jews raises the same questions. Still, Bell ("Egypt" in *CAH*, 10:310), conjecturing Agrippa's intervention, appears to think that Flaccus' mistreatment of Jews did play a part in his demise.

[39]*Antiquities* 18.259. Josephus mentioned Alexander and his family several times (*Antiquities* 18.159-160, 19.276, 20.100, and *War* 5.205). Cf. J. Schwartz, "Note sur la famille de Philon d'Alexandrie," *Annuaire de l'Institut de philologie*

do not know why.[40] Even more significant is *Antiquities* 19.278, for when Claudius became emperor, "there arose a feud between Jews and Greeks in the city of Alexandria. For upon the death of Gaius, the Jews, who had been humiliated under his rule and grievously abused by the Alexandrians, took heart again and at once armed themselves." The *Flaccus* attests to the part of Josephus' statement concerning Alexandrian abuse of the Jewish population but fails to mention the emperor's own involvement in their severe trials.

Oddly enough, the best evidence for this latter fact is provided by Philo himself. Quite differently from the *Flaccus*, the *Legatio* makes clear that Gaius played an active part against Alexandrian Jews.[41] Gaius dead, his brother freed,[42] and gloves off, Philo could now express himself in an open fashion.[43] This emperor had "looked

---

et d'histoire orientales et slaves 13 = *Mélanges Isidore Lévy* (1953):591-602; E. G. Turner, "Tiberivs Ivlivs Alexander," *Journal of Roman Studies* 44 (1954):54-64.

[40]Concerning the cause, Josephus reported only that it was the result of wrath or anger (ὀργή). In Josephus' earlier description of Philo's embassy, the same motif also appears: "Gaius cut him [Philo] short, told him to get out of his way, and, being exceedingly angry, made it clear that he would visit some outrage upon them" (*Antiquities* 18.260). Since Philo's eyewitness narrative (*Legatio* 349-350, 366) also shows the members of the embassy in real danger, May ("Politique religieuse," p. 25), Turner ("Tiberivs Ivlivs Alexander," p. 58), and Smallwood (*Jews under Roman Rule*, p. 242, n. 87) are perhaps right that Alexander was imprisoned as a member of Philo's delegation.

[41]So too Seston, "L'Empereur Claude," pp. 294-295; Goodenough, *Introduction to Philo Judaeus*, p. 58.

[42]It is germane to the way in which Philo wrote the *Flaccus* that Alexander was his brother. So long as Gaius lived and held Alexander in custody, Philo was in no position to express himself overtly against the emperor.

[43]The clear *terminus post quem* of the *Legatio* is Claudius' assumption of power (*Legatio* 107, 206; cf. Box's edition of the *Flaccus*, *Philonis Alexandrini: IN FLACCUM*, p. xxxii). To extend it as Seston does ("L'Empereur Claude," pp. 294-299) until the end of 41 CE is clever but not convincing. In any case, by the time that Philo wrote the *Legatio* Jews were out of Gaius' reach. Contrary to Seston again (p. 294), the *Flaccus* may well have been written while Gaius ruled. *Flaccus* 8 tells us that Flaccus ceased to be prefect of Egypt sometime during Gaius' first year as emperor, i.e., sometime evidently during 38 CE. He was still governing in June of 38 (*Flaccus* 56) and at the end of August (*Flaccus* 81-83). His arrest then came in the fall when Jews were celebrating the Feast of Tabernacles (*Flaccus* 116) and his journey to Rome in early winter (*Flaccus* 125). After this Philo reported the trial, the exile, and the order of Gaius to execute Flaccus but without reference to absolute dates. As a result, the *terminus post quem* of the *Flaccus* is an unspecified amount of time that passed between early winter of 38 CE and the death of the prefect. Though Gaius' own death in January of 41 CE marks the last

with disfavour on the Jews alone" (*Legatio* 115, cf. 133), the nation which was his worst enemy (*Legatio* 256), with the result that "a vast and truceless war was prepared against the nation" (*Legatio* 119). *Legatio* 119-121 describes the outcome for Alexandrian Jews as follows:

> Considering that he himself [Gaius] was a law, he abrogated those laid down by the legislators in the several states, treating them as empty talk. And we were ranked not only as slaves but as the most degraded slaves when the ruler changed into a despotic master. The promiscuous and unstable rabble of the Alexandrians perceived this, and thinking that a very suitable opportunity had occurred, attacked us.... For treating us as persons given over by the emperor to suffer the extremity of calamity undisguised or as overpowered in war, they worked our ruin with insane and most brutal rage.

Besides the fact that this picture of the emperor Gaius' ultimate responsibility for the horrors in Alexandria makes good sense of the difficulties in the *Flaccus* as well as of the direct statements within Josephus, it also has the important support of Claudius' 41 CE letter to the inhabitants of the city. Specifically, in the just-quoted passage Philo claimed that Gaius had changed the arrangements under which Alexandrian (and other) Jews lived. Following Gaius' death, therefore, Claudius informed the Alexandrians that he intended to restore the old order:

---

time when this could have occurred, we may guess that the execution took place more probably during the several months following Flaccus' early winter 38 CE return to Rome, i.e., perhaps by the fall of 39 CE. If this last estimation is of value, Philo may have written the *Flaccus* as early as winter, 39-40 CE. Though in no way conclusive, support for an early date is provided by the fact that this writing seems to know nothing of Gaius' plan to set up his statue in Jerusalem. Still, having seen the good use to which Philo could put silence, we must be very cautious of this particular *terminus ante quem* for the composition of the *Flaccus*. On the other hand, *Flaccus* 94 inspires a bit more confidence in this regard, for it does seem to be ignorant of the Alexandrian Jewish uprising which, according to Josephus *Antiquities* 19.278, occurred at the time of Gaius' death in January, 41 CE. If true, the *Flaccus* was written at least prior to that date. *Flaccus* 103 may imply an even earlier time. Referring to Agrippa's summer of 38 CE visit at Alexandria, Philo claimed that it was then that the Jewish community gave to him its decree in honor of Gaius. He then wrote that Agrippa "promising to send the decree, did sent it, as we hear." The vividness of this sudden present tense as well as its lack of historical perspective or resolution, i.e., Philo had not yet ascertained what became of the decree, indicate that these matters did not belong to past history. Hence, evidence of all these kinds hints that the *Flaccus* was written at least by the time of Gaius' death. Combined with the fact that the tone of the *Flaccus* differs from that of the clearly posthumous and sharply critical treatment of Gaius in the *Legatio*, this conclusion becomes even more appealing.

I conjure the Alexandrians to behave gently and kindly towards the Jews who have inhabited the same city for many years, and not to dishonour any of their customs [τῶν νενομισμένων] in their worship of their god [Θρησκείαν τοῦ θεοῦ], but to allow them to keep their own ways [ἔθεσιν], as they did in the time of the god Augustus and as I too, having heard both sides, have confirmed.[44]

In other words, imperial chicanery in 38 CE had opened the door for the expression of the previously latent hostility of certain Alexandrian Gentiles against their Jewish neighbors. Or, perhaps more accurately, this chicanery was in its own way an imperial imperative directed at these Alexandrians.[45] Either way, the fact that Claudius issued his own order to them in 41 CE indicates that Jewish problems in that city had not come to an end with the removal of Flaccus, something that the imprisonment of the alabarch Alexander until the same year (*Antiquities* 19.276) also implies.[46]

---

[44]P. Lond. 1912, lines 82-88.

[45]Though not generally considered, the difference is an important one. What came first: Gentile hostility to which Gaius gave full reign or Gaius' hostility which became an imperative for the Alexandrians? The fact is, as Smallwood for example demonstrates (*Jews under Roman Rule*, pp. 230-237), that we recognize nothing of previous Jewish difficulties in that city. On the contrary, Jews flourished there. Granted that important anti-Jews were associated with the place, it was not until the time of Gaius that they were able to act. In one way or another, therefore, Schürer (*History*, 1:389) is almost surely correct when he writes that "a bloody pogrom broke out in Alexandria, apparently staged by the Alexandrian mob, but actually instigated by the emperor himself." Consequently, the common opinion found, for example, in Smallwood (*Jews under Roman Rule*, pp. 223-224) and Barrett (*Caligula*, pp. 184-185) that Alexandrian Jews joined themselves to their Roman conquerors against Alexandrian Gentiles probably deserves re-examination. Smallwood fails to notice that the Ptolemies with which Alexandrian Jews fared well (p. 223) were the Greeks with whom she says they did not (p. 224). It appears instead that there may have been divisions within the Greek community of which Romans wishing to do so could take advantage. In light of all of these considerations it is in any case very difficult to accept the suggestion of Willrich ("Caligula," p. 402) that Caligula had been a friend of Jews until Alexandrian Gentiles turned him against them.

[46]So too Willrich ("Caligula," p. 414). Thus, Jones ("Claudius," p. 24; cf. Hennig, "Bruchstücken," p. 322) points out that according to both Philo (*Legatio* 367) and Josephus (*Antiquities* 18.257-260) the Jewish delegation obtained no satisfaction from its meeting with Gaius. In addition, *Antiquities* 19.278 indicates the same thing, for it refers to Gaius' rule in general and tells us that Alexandrian Jews were in a position to counterattack only after his murder. Contrary to Balsdon (*Gaius*, p. 144), therefore, the Jewish violence in 41 CE was nothing more than the first possible response to the violence perpetrated against them until the end of his reign. This is a reasonable interpretation (so too Schürer, *History*, 1:393) of

Legatio 162-165 then makes good sense of the success of the anti-Jewish accusers of Flaccus, for it indicates that Gaius had accepted their adulation as expressed specifically by means of the placement of imperial statues within the Alexandrian Jewish houses of prayer. Remarkable in this regard is the later statement of Philo (*Legatio* 346) about the emperor that

> having conceived a violent enmity to them he took possession of the synagogues in the other cities after beginning with those of Alexandria, by filling them with images and statues of himself in bodily form. For by permitting others to install them he virtually did it himself.

This passage gives us some indication of how Gaius involved himself with anti-Jewish activities in the city of Alexandria, for it reveals what we would have to assume otherwise, that imperial assent was of itself sufficient.

More important is the fact that *Legatio* 346 also preserves the informative detail concerning similar attacks against synagogues in other cities under Roman rule. On the basis of this statement, what the sixth-century historian John Malalas of Syrian Antioch reported in his *Chronicle* 10.244.22-245.2 for the third year of Gaius becomes relevant: "And there took place a great public disturbance, and a disaster occurred within the city, for the Greeks of Antioch, having engaged in public battle with the Jews there, murdered many Jews and burned their synagogues."[47] Having been reported by a writer concerned with the past history of his own great city and sounding very much like the roughly contemporary events in Alexandria, this text provides an almost certain recollection of the kind of attack on

---

what the letter of Claudius (P. Lond. 1912) saw in the year 41 as the ongoing Alexandrian hostilities, for in it the new emperor ordered these to cease, and in *Antiquities* 19.279 he commanded his Egyptian prefect to assume responsibility. Analogously, we must keep in mind that, even after Gaius agreed not to place his statue within the temple precincts of Jerusalem, having warned the Jews not to interfere, he continued to encourage its placement in the neighborhood (*Legatio* 334). Not surprisingly, as Tacitus indicated (*Histories* 5.9), it was only the 41 CE demise of Gaius that brought peace: "When Caligula ordered the Jews to set up his statue in their temple, they chose rather to resort to arms, but the emperor's death put an end to their uprising."

[47]My translation of *Chronicle* 10.244.22-245.2 from *Die römische Kaisergeschichte bei Malalas: Griechischer Text der Bücher IX-XII und Untersuchungen*, ed. Alexander Schenk Graf von Stauffenberg (Stuttgart: W. Kohlhammer Verlag, 1931); cf. the Slavonic version in English in the *Chronicle of John Malalas: Books VIII-XVIII*, trans. Matthew Spinka and Glanville Downey (Chicago: University of Chicago Press, 1940).

synagogues which Philo referred to in *Legatio* 346.[48] Thus, the above evidence clarifies what Philo's *Flaccus* leaves ambiguous: that Gaius did play a part in the sufferings of Alexandrian and other Jews as well as in the desecration of their religious centers.[49]

Turning to the same emperor's attempted interference with the Jerusalem cult, we would have difficulty imagining that matters could have been much different.[50] Since the intention of the present section is to demonstrate from the Jewish sources the existence of imperial

---

[48]Von Stauffenberg, ed., *Kaisergeschichte*, pp. 188-190, apparently unaware of *Legatio* 346, provides good arguments for the authenticity of events in *Chronicle* 10.244.22-245.2 and observes that they have much in common with the things that happened in Alexandria. Equally unaware of *Legatio* 346, Kraeling ("Jewish Community at Antioch," pp. 148-149; cf. Barrett, *Caligula*, p. 189, and also Von Stauffenberg, ed., *Kaisergeschichte*, p. 190) associates the massacre with events in Jerusalem. He does observe (pp. 149-150), however, that according to Josephus (*Antiquities* 19.279) the Alexandrian edict of Claudius (*Antiquities* 19.280-285) was directed also to Syria, i.e., to Antioch, and that we may therefore suppose Jews in both places faced similar difficulties. The full text (*Chronicle* 10.244.15-245.21) connects the events with struggles between the factions of the Blues and of the Greens (cf. the fifth century parallel in *Chronicle* 15.389-390) and also includes the apparently confused account (so Von Stauffenberg, ed., *Kaisergeschichte*, pp. 190-192) of a Judean attack against Antioch in retaliation for the Jewish murders. Although Kraeling (p. 148) implies that "a sense of their own self-importance" played a part in their suffering, the text of Malalas provides no basis for placing such blame on the Jewish population of Antioch.

[49]So too Juster, *Les Juifs*, 1:351, n. 5 and 2.7. Schürer (*History*, 1:390) seems correct therefore that Flaccus took his cue from the emperor himself. This would account for the change Philo claimed took place in the prefect after Gaius assumed power, it would have its motive in the need to improve his precarious position with the new emperor, but it would mean also that his recall was not based upon his bad treatment of Alexandrian Jews, something we suspect in any case since the charges against Flaccus were brought not by Jews but by their enemies. The way Willrich ("Caligula," p. 403) describes Flaccus' position is doubtful. His sense is that the prefect felt compelled to permit Gentile abuse of Jewish houses of prayer lest he appear to oppose the spread of the imperial cult. In terms of the need to improve his relationship with the emperor, however, he probably encouraged the measures. Even so, this may not have matched the expectations of the Alexandrian anti-Jews who then became his successful accusers before Gaius.

[50]Beside its previously referred to mention in Tacitus (*Histories* 5.9), the episode appears at length in Josephus' *Antiquities* 18.261-309 and Philo's *Flaccus* 188-348 as well as summarily in the former's *War* 2.184-203. *Legatio* 346 shows that Philo apparently patterned his account after the scenario of Antiochus Epiphanes two centuries earlier, for here the emperor is billed as "Gaius, the new epiphany of God." A useful comparison of details among the reports is found in the commentary to *Antiquities* 18.261-309 of Feldman, trans., in Josephus, *The Life, Against Apion, The Jewish War, Jewish Antiquities*, 9:154-179.

attitudes and actions of an anti-Jewish nature, and because it speaks quite clearly for itself in this regard, we need not dwell on Gaius' decision to order the erection of his own image in the temple.[51] It might be observed, however, that in addition to an interpretation of this plan according to which Gaius intended to demand explicit Jewish worship of his own divinity, it is also possible on the basis of the account in Tacitus, as well as from between the lines in Philo and Josephus, to suggest that the emperor demanded no more than the placement his statue or statues (*War* 2.185, 194) within the precincts of the temple. This would have occurred on analogy with the common practice among Gentiles of dedicating statuary of notable persons in the sanctuaries of their gods. Ohlemutz provides a good example of this art, some nevertheless having its own religious denotation, at the cult center of Athene on the acropolis of Pergamum. Particularly relevant is the fact that Livilla, sister to Gaius, was enthroned beside Athene there.[52] In any case, and no matter how we might interpret it, meddling of this type was guaranteed–as Gaius himself must no doubt have known[53]–to provoke precisely the kind of Jewish reaction which, even according to Tacitus, it did.

What might we suppose was to be acheived by "this childish demand"[54] on the part of the emperor? Looked at from the military

---

[51]The discussion following does not depend upon the resolution of a variety of questions raised by this event. For summaries and further discussion see Willrich ("Caligula," pp. 414-419, 467-470), Balsdon ("Notes concerning the Principate of Gaius," pp. 19-24) as well as his *Gaius* (pp. 135-141), Smallwood ("The Chronology of Gaius' Attempt to Desecrate the Temple," *Latomus* 16 [1957]:3-17), Schürer (*History*, 1:394-396), and Barrett (*Caligula*, pp. 188-191).

[52]Ohlemutz, *Kulte und Heiligtümer*, pp. 54-55, 58-59. Josephus in *War* 2.412-413 referred to the dedicatory gifts of foreigners which likewise surrounded the temple in Jerusalem.

[53]See, for example, Willrich, "Caligula," p. 414.

[54]So, rightly, Schürer (*History*, 1:394). It is uncertain what Barrett has in mind when he summarily rejects Philo's view that Gaius hated the Jewish people and was prepared for a war with them. Concerning these things he writes (*Caligula*, p. 190), "this is clearly absurd. Roman policy was basically one of reciprocity, and Roman *protection* of the Jewish religion was conditional on their limiting their *zeal*." To what *protection* does he refer in the context of *Gaius' zeal* to have his statue(s) erected within the temple precincts of Jerusalem? Again, how does this implicit approval of Gaius' actions against Jews make any sense in terms of Barrett's own criticism of the emperor elsewhere? "Caligula was clearly capable of acting right to the end in a rational manner. Why then does he seem so often to have behaved otherwise? What emerges clearly from the sources is that while he was *not clinically mad* he was so obsessed with a sense of his own importance

perspective, it surely could not have been very advantageous to the interests of the empire to withdraw troops from the dangerous eastern border, and this is all the more true should they actually have been forced into combat in Judea. Again, from an economic perspective, such a war would not have been a particularly good means of imperial revenue enhancement. Interestingly, however, while Tacitus provided no explanation for Gaius' decision either to set up his own image in Jerusalem or to do so by force of arms if necessary, both Philo and Josephus did offer such a rationale. On the one hand, in *Legatio* 199-203, Philo indicated the emperor's plan arose in response to the fact that Jews had destroyed an imperial altar at Jamnia. On the other hand, in *Antiquities* 18.260-261, Josephus associated the scheme with contemporary events in the city of Alexandria, and especially with the devastating confrontation between Gaius and the Alexandrian Jewish delegation led by Philo.[55]

Whether it was the Jewish resistance to his statues within the Alexandrian houses of prayer, to an imperial altar set up among them in Jamnia, or to like activities in other cities (*Legatio* 346), it is impossible to imagine how any kind of reasonable analysis might have led Gaius to the further step of installing his image in the sacred precinct of Jerusalem. Among all the vagaries of the case, therefore, one thing is sure: only out of the most extreme antipathy towards the religious sensibilities of the Jewish people could Gaius have conceived

---

as to be practically devoid of any sense of moral responsibility" (*Caligula*, p. 240). In terms of such a deservedly severe judgment, it becomes all the more difficult to understand Barrett's defense of Gaius against the criticism of Philo, and this is particularly so because the latter had direct dealings with the emperor who "was not *clinically* mad." Perhaps Philo, ignorant of Freud, failed to recognize this neat distinction, but then again so did many Romans (Barrett, *Caligula*, p. 216). Overall, therefore, whatever we may think of the merit of Barrett's attempt (cf. pp. xv-xxvi and 213-241) along the lines of Willrich and Balsdon to restore the image of Gaius, his own observations really prohibit doing this at the expense of legitimate Jewish grievances.

[55]Could it be that Gaius' decision arose in part at least as a punitive measure out of his encounter with Philo's delegation and that Philo's reference to Jamnia might have served to minimize the part which the Alexandrian situation played in this potentially even greater disaster? Willrich ("Caligula," p. 412), Balsdon (*Gaius*, p. 136), Bell ("Egypt" in *CAH*, 10:662), Schürer (*History*, 1:394), and Barrett (*Caligula*, pp. 188-189) ignore the explanation in Josephus. Smallwood ("Chronology," pp. 4, 6, 8) refers to but then, explicitly following Balsdon, fails to consider it. Juster (*Les Juifs*, 1:351, n. 5) does allude indirectly to it. In his view, it was as a result of events in Alexandria and Jamnia that Caligula ordered the erection of statues both in the temple and the diaspora synagogues. Garzetti's view (*Tiberius to the Antonines*, p. 96) is similar.

the undertaking.[56] We must also keep in mind at the same time that, though this particular approach was new, the imperial antipathy behind it was not, for we have seen already the relativity of Philo's claim that Tiberius had treated Jews better than Gaius did. In sum, though the apologetic purposes of the Jewish sources were best served by playing down imperial hostility towards Jews and their religion, these sources in fact add much to our knowledge of the ways in which this hostility demonstrated itself during the years prior to when Claudius became emperor. Thus, Josephus not only revealed inadvertently that the heir-apparent, Germanicus, had let Alexandrian Jews go hungry during a great famine but also confirmed the witness

---

[56]Referring to Gaius' *ersatz* measure of encouraging other cities of Judea to construct altars in his honor (*Legatio* 334-337), Willrich ("Caligula," p. 418) makes the same point. Nevertheless, concerning the latter action Balsdon (*Gaius*, p. 139) writes, "This was eminently fair, and Philo's unreasonable criticism only indicates the impossibility of reconciling the eastern Jews to any sensible arrangement of give and take." For several reasons Balsdon's praise of Gaius and condemnation of eastern Jews make no sense. First, because under absolute rule things go only one way, the expression "give and take" has no meaning in the present context. Second, he disregards the patently unfair measures which Gaius had beforehand taken against Jews. Third, this particular measure could only have been expected to bring about the same results which had occurred previously because, fourth, it remained a direct affront to Jewish religious sensibilities. Fifth, how then Balsdon expects Philo to have classified the actions under the word *reconciliation* is unclear, for, sixth, as an almost sure way of bringing about chaos on the already dangerous eastern border of the empire, it was extremely unwise. Seventh, having accepted Philo's account of Gaius' "fairness," he immediately makes light of that portion of the same report which refers to the emperor's continued intention of installing his statue in Jerusalem. Finally, that Jews were unreasonable in the refusal to give up allegiance to the demands of their own god for the sake of rites associated with the New Zeus Epiphanes Gaius is a matter of opinion with which reasonable persons might well disagree. Overall, therefore, given the reality of a Roman empire populated by peoples with widely different ways of life, Gaius' unwillingness to leave the Jewish people alone–they were *not* cannibals, after all–hardly smacks of fairness as much as of foolishness, intolerance, and pro-vocation. In fact, insofar at least as Alexandria is concerned, by calling for a restoration of the situation as it had existed there prior to Gaius, even Claudius' letter to that city (P. Lond. 1912, line 87) admitted as much. Similarly, but referring now to Gaius' original order for the erection of his statue in Jerusalem, Balsdon himself admits (*Gaius*, p. 143) that this emperor had probably not "anticipated the stubbornness of the Jewish opposition." Contrary to Balsdon, however, the poor decision-making may not be justified by his pejorative and ill-chosen analogy from modern history according to which "Jewish psychology" was no more comprehensible to Romans than is "Indian psychology" to the English, for the real analogy is not the inferior psychology of imperial subjects but imperialism itself. Balsdon, writing in 1934, may have thought rather too well of the British empire in India and on that basis have formulated his analogy.

of the Gentile sources that Tiberius had simultaneously excluded all things Jewish from the city of Rome. Likewise, Philo let slip that some ten years later the very same emperor had subjected Roman and other Jews to a second series of undefined hardships inseparably associated with the practices of their religion. He also reported the attacks upon Jews and their synagogues in Alexandria and elsewhere, indicated Gaius' part in these, and provided details of the offense to Jewish religious sensibilities constituted by that emperor's demands on the cult center in Jerusalem.

In other words, and whether examined from the perspective of Gentile or Jewish sources, the life of the Roman and of other Jewish communities in the pre-Claudian period was repeatedly tried by the hostile attitudes and resultant actions which these engendered among the ruling class of the empire. Furthermore, the sources provide no evidence for the theory that this hostility had its origin in one or another hypothetical character flaw of Jews. Instead, it arose within the context of continuous imperial antipathy towards the foreign cult to which these Jews belonged.

Chapter Four

Fundamental Reflections of Claudian Policymaking vis-à-vis Roman Jews and Judaism

Turning now to Claudius, we have little reason to presume that this emperor's attitudes or actions would have been radically different from those of his predecessors. Already in a general way Tacitus informed his readers of the deleterious effects on traditional Roman religion which Claudius thought the growth of "externae superstitiones" helped to produce.[1] The apparent silence of our Jewish sources concerning Claudius' hostility towards Jews and their cult does, but only at first, leave the contrary impression. In any case, the Acts of the Apostles, Suetonius, Dio, Paulus Orosius, perhaps the scholium to Juvenal, and certainly the emperor's own Alexandrian letter make entirely clear the falsity of this impression.

Our most doubtful evidence for these matters is in the scholium to Juvenal's *Satire* 4.117. It preserves the tantalizing remnant of information that "Jews who, having been sent from the city, travelled to Aricia."[2] Excerpted from some source which is both unknown and undatable and then incorporated into the text of Juvenal by an early

---

[1]*Annals* 11.15. It is within the context of a *senatus consultum* stemming from the year 47 CE that Tacitus made mention of the emperor's attitude on this matter. The specific legislation concerned the measures intended to strengthen the *collegio haruspicum*.

[2]This is my literal translation from *Scholia in Iuvenalem vetustiora*, ed. Paul Wessner (1931; reprint ed., Stuttgart: B. G. Teubner, 1967), ad loc.; see also Stern, *Authors*, #538.

Roman scholiast evidently about 400 CE,[3] the passage implies that an expulsion of Roman Jews had led some of them to migrate to Aricia (modern Ariccia), just to the southeast of the city. Furthermore, it provides us with details about what actually happened to the castoffs, for we see them here having left the city but a short way behind and now forced to beg for a living in their new surroundings.[4] It is most unfortunate that we are not in a position to know whether this alludes to the Republican expulsion mentioned by Valerius Maximus, or to the similar occurrences which took place under Tiberius and Claudius, or to an otherwise unrecorded event.[5]

More interesting is Philo. His seeming silence about Claudian actions against Roman Jews and their cult might be accounted for by the fact that he composed both the *Flaccus* and *Legatio* prior to their occurrence. Nevertheless, because Philo did write the *Legatio* after Claudius had become emperor,[6] it is easy to construe one section in

---

[3]Mommsen, "Zeitalter des Scholiasten Juvenals" in his *Gesammelte Schriften*, 8 vols. (1905-1913; reprint ed., Berlin: Weidmannsche Verlagsbuchhandlung, 1965), 7:509-511; *Scholia in Iuvenalem*, pp. xxxvii, xl, xliii.

[4]Because the scholiast tended to refer to Jews within the context of begging (cf. the scholia to *Satire* 3.16, 3.296, and 6.542) this part of the account may be anachronistic. On the other hand, that individuals driven from their homes and employment would have been compelled to do something similar is entirely likely.

[5]Scholarship has ignored the first possibility. Momigliano (*Claudius*, p. 30) assumes the second, and Juster (*Les Juifs*, 1:180, n. 90) prefers the third while Smallwood (*Jews under Roman Rule*, p. 216, n. 46), Stern (*Authors*, 2:655), and Schürer (*History*, 3¹:78, n. 94) leave open the possibility of the fourth. Since the expulsion noted in the scholium was clearly *from Rome* but apparently not *from Italy*, it might correspond to the Republican one in either version of Valerius Maximus or to the 19 CE banishment under Tiberius as described by Josephus, Suetonius, and Dio. (Tacitus claimed that the latter was from Italy.) Again, reference to Claudian expulsion from Rome takes place explicitly in Acts and Suetonius. Nonetheless, we may not conclude overmuch on the basis of that detail because Acts also has Aquila and Priscilla leave Italy. Furthermore, Philo, though referring to an expulsion from Rome (*Legatio* 157), appears to have used Rome and Italy somewhat interchangeably (155).

[6]See p. 79, n. 43. As is indicated there, the *terminus post quem* of the *Legatio* is Claudius' assumption of power in early 41 CE. Within the *Legatio* are two possible hints that Philo may have composed it not too long after the ca. 40 CE events that it describes. First, he referred to himself as being in the same age bracket at the time of both the embassy to Gaius and the composition of the *Legatio* (1, 182). Second, *Legatio* 3 seems to imply that the events associated with this embassy were also relatively contemporary with the time of composition. On the other hand, *Legatio* 206 with its reference to the death of Helicon implies that some time had elapsed between the murder of Gaius and the composition of the

particular as a reflection of the latter's measures. Specifically, in the midst of discussing Alexandrian matters, Philo turned abruptly in *Legatio* 155-158 to the city of Rome for a reply to the question of how Augustus had shown his approval of Jews:

> He was aware that the great section of Rome on the other side of the Tiber is occupied and inhabited by Jews, most of whom were Roman citizens emancipated. For having been brought as captives to Italy they were liberated by their owners and were *not forced to violate any of their native institutions* [τῶν πατρίων]. He knew therefore that they have houses of prayer and meet together in them, particularly on the sacred sabbaths when they receive as a body a training in their ancestral philosophy. He knew too that they collect money for sacred purposes from their first-fruits and send them to Jerusalem by persons who would offer the sacrifices. Yet nevertheless he *neither ejected them from Rome* [ἐξῴκισε τῆς 'Ρώμης ἐκείνους] *nor deprived them of their Roman citizenship* because they were careful to pre-serve their Jewish citizenship also, *nor took any violent measures against the houses of prayer, nor prevented them from meeting to receive instructions in the laws, nor opposed their offerings of the first-fruits.* Indeed so religiously did he respect our interests that supported by wellnigh his whole household he adorned our temple through the costliness of his dedications.... Yet more, in the monthly doles in his own city when all the people each in turn receive money or corn, he *never put the Jews at a disadvantage in sharing the bounty,* but even if the distributions happened to come during the sabbath...he ordered the dispensers to reserve for the Jews till the morrow the charity which fell to all. (emphasis added)

In light of Philo's precise detail and phraseology here, it is easy to understand the reason Seston construes these measures *not* taken by Augustus as a contrast with the like steps actually carried out against Roman Jewry by some other emperor.[7]

So stated, however, this interpretation is not quite accurate. Specifically, *Legatio* 154 claims Augustus did not wish to be called a god, evidence of which was his approval of Jews who, he knew, could not do this. As such, *Legatio* 154 does provide an explicit contrast, but this is with *Legatio* 115 (cf. 162). In this passage Gaius insists upon

---

Legatio, and it is hard to imagine that Philo would have invented his alleged letter from Agrippa to Gaius (*Legatio* 276-329) prior to the death of the former in 44 CE. For whatever it is worth, Eusebius (*Ecclesiastical History* 2.17.1 and 2.18.8) thought that Philo lived at least well into the reign of Claudius and visited Rome during those years.

[7]Seston, "L'Empereur Claude," p. 300. A similar use of Augustus appears in *Legatio* 311-316. The main difference is that, on the basis of supposed evidence from Asia, it demonstrates his support of the cultic gathering of Jews.

divine recognition and, because their religiosity prohibits it, condemns Jews. Now Philo had to provide evidence of the Augustan approval. With this in mind, he composed *Legatio* 155-158, introducing it with the question, "How then did he show his approval?" Hence, Philo listed the salutary actions of Augustus in order to demonstrate the contrasting behaviors of Gaius and his supposed model (cf. *Legatio* 143 and 149).

Nevertheless, because of certain oddities associated with *Legatio* 155-158, we cannot ignore Seston's observation.[8] The first of these is its enumeration of negatives: this does not correspond well to the positive connotation normally associated with approval. The second is the choice and sharpness of its detail, for these are unnecessary to the comparison between the Gaius of *Legatio* 115 and the Augustus of *Legatio* 154. The last is the introduction of Rome: even supposing that Philo had in mind the additional contrast with the specific measures Gaius encouraged against the Alexandrian Jews and their houses of prayer,[9] it is strange he did not draw his negations from Augustan Alexandria. In *Legatio* 143-154, after all, he had already used the city in this way.

Thus, though it is clear how Philo employed *Legatio* 155-158 to support the contrast between Augustus in *Legatio* 154 and Gaius in *Legatio* 115, the turn to Rome and the detailed negations associated with it transcend that original contrast and so point to an additional one. Exactly in the sense meant by Seston, therefore, *Legatio* 155-158 "implique une comparaison" with anti-Jewish measures carried out in Rome by some other imperial personage.

As to the identity of this person, options are limited by the near certainty that Philo prepared the *Legatio* under Claudius.[10] Augustus

---

[8]His view in the same place that it was Augustus who placed Jews in a single ghetto for their own protection is a gross anachronism. In addition, it insinuates the existence of unspecified forces against whom Jews needed protection.

[9]As *Legatio* 132 (destruction of synagogues), 134-137 (erection of imperial cult statues), 138 (erection of cult statues), 141-142 (erection of imperial cult statues), 148-152 (erection of imperial cult statues), and 165 (general) indicate, the Gaian-supported Alexandrian measures against houses of prayer are important within the present context. Nonetheless, the measures enumerated in *Legatio* 155-158 make no reference to the cult statues.

[10]Since there is no way to be sure when Philo died (cf. Schwartz, "Note sur la famille de Philon," p. 598, n. 4, who makes clear the entirely relative nature of Philo's conception of old age in *Legatio* 1 and 182), it is possible that he wrote the *Legatio* under Nero (cf. Schwartz, p. 599, on the likelihood that his brother was alive as late as 63 CE). Were this the case, however, we might expect to discover *termini post quem* within the text giving some hint of this.

excluded, this leaves only Tiberius, Gaius, and Claudius himself. In Seston's own view it was the first of these, or at least his infamous praetorian prefect, Sejanus.[11] Nevertheless, this choice flies in the face of the positive use to which Philo put Tiberius in *Legatio* 141-142 and especially in 159b-161.[12] Hence, the periods of both Augustus and Tiberius excluded, we are left with those of Gaius and Claudius. Gaius is to be excluded immediately because in the *Legatio*'s harangue against him Philo had every reason as well as unlimited opportunity to refer explicitly to any Gaian measures against Roman Jews, their houses of prayer, and the activities associated with them. His failure to do so means that he, like us, was ignorant of and unable to refer to them in *Legatio* 155-158.[13]

As a result of this process of elimination, we are forced to take seriously the suggestion of Smallwood that the culprit was Claudius: "If the closure of the synagogues [Dio 60.6.6-7], or even an expulsion [*Claudius* 25.4], was in the air at the time of composition [of the *Legatio*], Philo had every reason for citing Claudius' model Augustus as a counter-precedent."[14] In fact, various additional considerations point in the same direction. First, and more generally, we are forced to wonder about the element of duality in Philo's reporting. To express this a bit differently, it is hard to imagine that a treatise much of which was dedicated to imperial abuse of Jews should have arisen in a political vacuum.

---

[11]Seston, "L'Empereur Claude," p. 300.

[12]It is also governed by what we shall see to be the faulty evaluation of Philo's ability to criticize a contemporary ruler (cf. pp. 104-105).

[13]Cecil Roth (*The History of the Jews of Italy* [Philadelphia: Jewish Publication Society of America, 1946], p. 10) and Marcus Borg ("A New Context for Romans XIII," *New Testament Studies* 19 [1972-1973]:210, n. 9) do suggest Gaian attacks on Roman synagogues. To the contrary, on the basis of the silence of the sources, and probably correctly, Scramuzza, "Policy" in *Beginnings of Christianity*, 5:294-295. And so too Bludau ("Die Juden Roms," p. 125) since Caligula had a positive relationship with Judean royalty in Rome, lifted the ban on collegia (Dio 59.6), and rejected the charges based upon claims of atheism (60.1). None of Bludau's arguments is convincing, the first because, as we shall soon see, imperial attitudes towards the Jewish royalty were not the same as those towards members of the Jewish proletariat, the second because the collegial status of Jewish community organizations is uncertain, the third because, as Bludau himself indicates (p. 205), Jews were not automatically perceived as atheists.

[14]Smallwood, *Jews under Roman Rule*, p. 214; cf. *Philonis Alexandrini: LEGATIO AD GAIUM*, ed. E. Mary Smallwood, 2d ed. (Leiden: Brill, 1970), p. 239. Her added comment here that this would be "making an implicit protest at which the new emperor could not possibly take offense" is irrelevant.

That such was not the case becomes apparent from two different types of text within the *Legatio*. On the one hand, several passages assert Jewish loyalty to good emperors. Philo affirmed, for example, the necessity of imperial rule (*Legatio* 6-7, 149), the favor with which all peoples including Jews originally greeted Gaius (8-13, 288-289), their sadness and prayers when he became ill (15-20), the practical divinity of Augustus (143, 318), Jewish respect and prayers for as well as piety towards the emperors (236, 279-280, 352), and even Gaius' own recognition of Jewish devotion to himself (356-357). On the other hand, *Legatio* 214-217, 225-226, and 281-284 (cf. 245) hint broadly concerning the threat to the stability of the Roman empire posed by myriads of ill-treated Jews.[15] Since both of these themes were quite meaningless insofar as the now deceased Gaius was concerned, it is reasonable to suppose Philo was composing with one eye on Claudius. In other words, and as Goodenough argues with respect to the second of them, "Philo wrote the treatise [the *Legatio*], I am sure, to be read by the emperor Claudius, or, less likely, Nero, to show to him what he showed to the prefect [in the *Flaccus*]; namely, that an emperor touched Jewish people and religious observances at his peril."[16]

Second, and more specifically, the *Legatio* has a most unpolitic way of dealing with Claudius. It mentions him by name but a single time and even then without any sign of the laudatory tones manifest in the references to Augustus.[17] Again, the purpose of *Legatio* 138-161 is to contrast the good rulers of Alexandria with the evil Gaius. In order to do this, it refers to the whole series of Ptolemaic kings

---

[15]Though *Legatio* 281-284 pretends to be part of Agrippa's letter to Gaius at the time of the latter's plan to place his statue in the temple, the other two passages make clear that this is a Philonic motif. Similar is Juster (*Les Juifs*, 1:352, n. 3; cf. Smallwood, *Jews under Roman Rule*, p. 214). He also adds that Josephus' account of the involvement of Agrippa in that situation (*Antiquities* 18.258-309) includes no such letter. As to the reality of the threat itself, see Alexander Fuks, "Aspects of the Jewish Revolt in A.D. 115-117," *Journal of Roman Studies* 51 (1961):98-104.

[16]Goodenough, *Introduction to Philo Judaeus*, p. 60.

[17]*Legatio* 206. Philo called him here "Claudius Germanicus Caesar." Moreover, though *Caesar* was by now a title of respect (Heinrich Chantraine, *Freigelassene und Sklaven im Dienst der römischen Kaiser*, Forschungen zur antiken Sklaverei, vol. 1 [Wiesbaden: Franz Steiner Verlag, 1967], p. 3), this usage is a diminution in terms of the formal way of referring to Claudius, i.e., to "Tiberius Claudius Caesar Augustus Germanicus" (P. Lond. 1912, lines 11-14; cf. Sir John Edwin Sandys, *Latin Epigraphy: An Introduction to the Study of Latin Inscriptions*, 2d ed. [1927; reprint ed., Chicago: Ares Publishers Inc., 1974], p. 236), and especially so since Philo also endowed the title *augustus* with much respect (*Legatio* 48, 143, 149, 309, 321-322).

(138-140), then to Tiberius (141-142, 159-161), and at great length to Augustus (143-158). Claudius is oddly absent. Finally, *Legatio* 119 (cf. 141) implicitly relegates him to the side of Gaius: "Subjects are slaves of the absolute emperor, and if this is not true of any of his [Gaius'] *predecessors* since they ruled with moderation and observance of the law, it was indeed true of Gaius." This certainly appears to strike a serious backhand blow against Claudius because, though he governed by this time, Philo ignored him and looked instead to the predecessors of Gaius for governance by "moderation and observance of the law."[18] The situation is odd because any good example drawn from Claudius would have improved by just that much more the contrast with Gaius so important to Philo at this point. In addition, it would have served his apologetic purposes, for anything positive asserted about Claudius' relationship with the Jewish community would have contributed to the image of contemporary philo-Judaic imperial authority.[19]

Third, among the measures which Philo insisted that Augustus had not utilized for the purpose of coercing the Roman Jews into the violation of their religious customs, i.e., of τῶν πατρίων (*Legatio* 155) or τῶν Ἰουδαϊκῶν νομίμων (*Legatio* 159), several are associated with actions which we know from other sources that Claudius did carry out. Specifically, *Legatio* 155-158 refers to ejection from Rome, depravation of citizenship, violence against the houses of prayer, prevention of meetings for religious instruction, opposition to the offering of first fruits, and exclusion from the corn dole. While we are in the dark about the depravation of citizenship and exclusion from the dole, we are aware of the Claudian expulsion of Roman Jews. As to the other three measures, they constitute the bulk of Philo's implied contrast and have as their common locus measures taken against the corporate religious life of the Roman Jewish community. Associated with them are Philo's additional references to houses of prayer,[20] gatherings in them (especially on the Sabbath for religious study), and the collection of the first fruits for Jerusalem.[21] These, as we shall discuss later,

----

[18]This would remain true even if the *Legatio* were written under Nero.

[19]By way of analogy, Josephus, whom it is impossible to excuse on the grounds of chronology, reported nothing untoward in Claudius' relationship with Roman Jews but did find the means (*Antiquities* 19.276, 279-292) to indicate that the new emperor immediately improved their lot within the empire.

[20]See appendix 1.

[21]*Legatio* 311-316 associates the Jerusalem offering very closely with the right of Asian Jews to gather in their houses of prayer. This implies that a principal purpose of the gatherings was the preparation of this offering. In *Antiquities* 16.160-173 Josephus also focused upon the permission which the emperor Augus-

have a very close parallel in Dio's description of the 41 CE measures which Claudius took against the practice of Judaism in the city. Why was Philo not more explicit in his reference to the Claudian measures against this practice? In the first place, it was perhaps a matter of wisdom and safety,[22] for we need to keep in mind that his *Flaccus*, written probably while Gaius ruled, pointed a finger at that emperor but only in an oblique manner. Nonetheless, once dead and to some degree discredited, Gaius was subject to open attack in the *Legatio*. It may well be, therefore, that the *Legatio* functioned in terms of Claudius as the *Flaccus* did with Gaius. More obviously, insofar as his contemporary readers were concerned, he was sufficiently explicit, for they were well aware of the historical context and immediately recognized the allusions to contemporary happenings. In sum, much evidence makes credible the view of Smallwood that *Legatio* 155-158 reflects directly the contemporary Claudian measures against Roman Jews, or, to be more precise, against Jews as practitioners of Judaism at Rome.

Even if *Legatio* 155-158 did not bear witness to any of them, the fact of these measures would remain beyond dispute. Thus, Acts 18:2 is explicit that when Paul reached Corinth "he found a Jew named Aquila, a native of Pontus, who had recently come from Italy with his wife Priscilla, because Claudius had ordered all Jews to leave Rome." Thereafter we have *Claudius* 25.4 and the assertion that "since the Jews constantly made disturbances at the instigation of Chrestus, he [Claudius] expelled them from Rome." Likewise, in Dio 60.6.6-7 it is reported that "as for the Jews, who had again increased so greatly that by reason of their multitude it would have been hard without raising a tumult to bar them from the city, he [Claudius] did not drive them out, but ordered them, while continuing their traditional mode of life, not to hold meetings." Last, and in part dependent upon Suetonius, is Paulus Orosius: "Josephus reports, 'In his ninth year the Jews were expelled by Claudius from the city.' But Suetonius, who speaks as follows, influences me more: 'Claudius expelled from Rome the Jews constantly rioting at the instigation of Christ [Christo].'"[23]

---

tus had given to the Jews of Asia and Cyrene for the collection and transport of these monies.

[22]Philo was not a coward; he was willing to face Gaius and later, defending Jewish rights, to openly criticize this former tyrant. That he did these things in a way that would not guarantee his execution is understandable. See Goodenough, *Introduction to Philo Judaeus*, pp. 54-57.

[23]My translation of *Historiarum adversum paganos libri VII* 7.6.15 from C. Zangemeister's critical edition of the text in *CSEL*, vol. 5.

Thus, in spite of the impression created particularly by Josephus and regardless of the relationships among and the details of the above accounts, it is impossible to avoid the conclusion that Roman Jewry and the *externa superstitio* to which it was devoted once again faced imperially orchestrated hardship after Claudius came to power. Our present concern is the relationship between the accounts in Suetonius and Dio Cassius. Because these two passages deal with an operation of the emperor Claudius against Roman Jews and likewise share vocabulary conveying Jewish tumultuousness associated with the language of expulsion, scholarship has tended to equate them.[24]

---

[24]Barry Baldwin, *Suetonius* (Amsterdam: Adolf M. Hakkert, 1983), p. 356; Stephen Benko, "The Edict of Claudius of A.D. 49 and the Instigator Chrestus," *Theologische Zeitschrift* 25 (1969):407; A. Berliner, *Geschichte der Juden in Rom von der ältesten Zeit bis zur Gegenwart*, 2 vols. (Frankfurt: J. Kaufmann, 1893), 1:25-26; Borg, "New Context for Romans XIII," p. 211 n. 2; F. F. Bruce, *Commentary on the Book of Acts* (1954; reprint ed., Grand Rapids: Wm. B. Eerdmans Publishing Co., 1966), p. 368, but otherwise in his "Christianity," p. 314; Guterman, *Religious Toleration*, p. 150; Ernst Haenchen, *Die Apostelgeschichte*, Kritisch-exegetischer Kommentar über das Neue Testament, 14th ed. (Göttingen: Vandenhoeck & Ruprecht, 1965), p. 58; Adolf Harnack, *The Mission and Expansion of Christianity in the First Three Centuries*, ed. and trans. James Moffatt, 2d ed., 2 vols. (New York: Putnam's Sons, 1908), 1:5; Robert O. Hoerber, "The Decree of Claudius in Acts 18:2," *Concordia Theological Monthly* 31 (1960):691-692; Henri Janne, "Impulsore Chresto," *Annuaire de l'Institut de philologie et d'histoire orientales* 2 (1933-1934):533; Juster, *Les Juifs*, 1:411; Lake, "The Chronology of Acts" in *The Beginnings of Christianity*, ed. F. J. Foakes Jackson and Kirsopp Lake, 5 vols. (London: Macmillan, 1920-1933), 5:459; Leon, *Jews of Ancient Rome*, p. 24; Gerd Luedemann, *Paul: Apostle to the Gentiles: Studies in Chronology*, trans. F. Stanley Jones (Philadelphia: Fortress Press, 1984), p. 165; May, "Politique religieuse," p. 43; Penna, "Les Juifs a Rome," p. 331; Schürer, *History*, 3¹:77; Scramuzza, *Claudius*, p. 151 and "Policy" in *Beginnings of Christianity*, 5:295-296; Seston, "L'Empereur Claude," p. 300; Smallwood, "Jews and Romans," p. 236; Stern, *Authors*, 2:116 and "Jewish Diaspora" in *Jewish People*, 1:182; Alfred Suhl, *Paulus und seine Briefe: Ein Beitrag zur paulinischen Chronologie*, Studien zum Neuen Testament, vol. 11 (Gütersloh: Gerd Mohn, 1975), p. 326; Vogelstein and Rieger, *Geschichte*, 1:20; Thaddée Zielinski, "L'empereur Claude et L'idée de la domination mondiale des Juifs," *Revue de l'Université de Bruxelles* 32 (1926-1927):143-144. Scholars who have assumed two separate events include J. P. V. D. Balsdon (*Romans and Aliens* [Chapel Hill: University of North Carolina Press, 1979], p. 106), Bammel ("Judenverfolgung," p. 296), Bruce ("Christianity," p. 314), Frend (*Martyrdom*, p. 122), Heinrich Graetz (*History of the Jews*, ed. and trans. Bella Lowy, 6 vols. [Philadelphia: The Jewish Publication Society of America, 1891-1898], 2:202), E. G. Hardy (*Studies in Roman History* [New York: Macmillan Company, 1906], p. 43), Huidekoper (*Judaism at Rome*, p. 222), Robert Jewett (*A Chronology of Paul's Life* [Philadelphia: Fortress Press, 1979], p. 37, n. 116), Jones ("Claudius," p. 31), Eduard Meyer (*Ursprung und Anfänge des Christentums*, 3 vols. [Stuttgart: J. G. Cotta'sche Buchhandlung Nachfolger, 1923],

The equation has highly significant ramifications. First, it would mean that we were dealing with a single imperial measure. As such, except for the fact that it reflected the behavior of Claudius' predecessors, there would be little of a real tendency apparent here. Found to be separate maneuvers, however, *Claudius* 25.4 and Dio 60.6.6-7 would reveal a clear propensity on the part of Claudius to follow, with a vengeance, the policies of his forerunners. The second ramification is chronological. An absolute date supplied by either account would of course establish that of the other as well.

We begin with chronological considerations the obvious limits of which are the reign of Claudius, 41-54 CE. As to *Claudius* 25.4 within the context of *Claudius* 25.3-5, it is most unfortunate that Suetonius narrated here in a topical rather than chronological fashion. As a result, at least on the basis of his own narration, there is no way to establish an absolute or even a relative date.[25] A variety of scholars which includes Janne, Meyer, Bruce, Momigliano, and Stern presume, however, that Dio provided exactly such information for the occurrence which he related.[26] It took place in 41 CE,[27] that is, directly after Claudius became Rome's emperor. Against this latter position range themselves only Suhl, Hoerber, and Schürer, the last of whom argues that the text in Dio belongs to an introductory topical section on the general character of Claudius rather than to the chronology of events for the year 41.[28] Hence, in his view Dio did not intend to imply any specific date for the emperor's action vis-à-vis Roman Jews.

Luedemann is nonetheless correct that from 60.3.2 forward Dio wrote in a chronological manner concerning events which took place

---

3:463, n. 2), Momigliano (*Claudius*, p. 31), Smallwood (*Jews under Roman Rule*, p. 215), and Wiefel ("Die jüdische Gemeinschaft," p. 78).

[25]See appendix 2.

[26]Janne, "Impulsore Chresto," p. 535; Meyer, *Ursprung*, 3:463; Bruce, *Commentary*, p. 368, and "Christianity," p. 314; Momigliano, *Claudius*, p. 31; Stern, *Authors*, 2:116.

[27]So also Bammel, "Judenverfolgung," p. 296; Benko, "Edict of Claudius," p. 407; Frend, *Martyrdom*, p. 122; Huidekoper, *Judaism at Rome*, p. 222; Jewett, *Chronology of Paul's Life*, p. 37; Jones, "Claudius," p. 31; Juster, *Les Juifs*, 1:411; Lake, "Chronology of Acts" in *Beginnings of Christianity*, 5:459; Leon, *Jews of Ancient Rome*, p. 24; Stern, "Jewish Diaspora" in *Jewish People*, 1:165; Smallwood, *Jews under Roman Rule*, p. 215.

[28]Suhl, *Paulus*, p. 326; Hoerber, "Decree of Claudius," p. 692; Schürer, *History*, 3^1:77, n. 91. Suhl and Hoerber imply without giving a reason that Dio's date may be inexact.

during the first year of Claudius.[29] Thus, following 60.3.1 and its introductory "I shall now take up his [Claudius'] actions in detail," Dio immediately narrated the death of those who had killed Gaius (60.3.4), the abolition of several of Gaius' decrees (60.4.1-2), and, "in the same year" (60.5.7), the betrothal of a daughter to Lucius Junius Silanus. Then occurred the decision of Claudius against Roman Jews (60.6.6), followed by the abolition of another one of Gaius' acts (60.6.8), and, "after this" (60.8.1), the restoration of Commagene to Antiochus as an additional step of restitution. Dio next narrated how Claudius gave land to Herod Agrippa I as well as to his brother Herod (60.8.2-3), both events dated independently by Josephus (*Antiquities* 19.274-277) to the year 41 CE. Two more chronological references follow, "then" (60.8.4) and "in this year" (60.8.7), with the entire section for 41 brought to a close by "in the next year" (60.9.1). Because the materials permit no other conclusion, it is understandable that so many scholars have assumed Dio dated the action of Claudius to the year 41.

Granted that Dio did in fact provide a definite date, the next question concerns his accuracy in this matter. Specifically, several lines of argumentation have been followed in order to demonstrate the improbability that Claudius committed an unfriendly act against Jews at such an early date. Principal among these is the view that the emperor was originally sympathetic to this segment of the Roman population and therefore would not have taken measures against it at that time. The source of this opinion is Josephus. In *Antiquities* 19.279-291 he provided the two previously discussed edicts purported to have been sent by the new emperor in 41 CE, one to Alexandria and Syria (19.279-285), and the other to the remainder of the Roman world (19.286-291).

On the basis of the view that these texts reveal the sympathy of Claudius for the Jewish people, several scholars have concluded that the friendly emperor who prepared them could not have acted during this same time in the hostile manner narrated by Dio. For example, Hoerber comments simply that "Claudius' pro-Jewish edict...seems inconsistent with the early date implied by Dio Cassius."[30] Similarly, Vogelstein makes mention of the emperor's *Wohlwollen*,[31] Wiefel of Claudius' "zunächst judenfreundlichen Haltung,"[32] Berliner of the

---

[29]Luedemann, *Paul*, p. 164, n. 67.

[30]Hoerber, "Decree of Claudius," p. 691. Benko ("Edict of Claudius," p. 407) makes the same point.

[31]Vogelstein and Rieger, *Geschichte*, 1:19.

[32]Wiefel, "Die jüdische Gemeinschaft," p. 78.

Toleranz-Edict and "freundliche Gesinnung" therein,[33] and Schürer writes that "an edict unfavorable to the Jews is not likely to belong to the earliest years of his reign, for it was just then that he published an edict of tolerance in their regard."[34]

As a matter of principle, however, it is illegitimate to use the Claudian edicts of Josephus as a corrective to Dio. We saw already that the ambiguity even among scholars who support the authenticity of one or both edicts forbids reliance upon them, especially when they contradict unambiguous evidence to the contrary.[35] In the case before us the procedure is particularly problematic. That is, dependent upon Josephus alone, we would know nothing of the hardships which faced Roman Jews under Claudius, for this writer provided no inkling of the measures which Dio described, and, unlike both Acts and Suetonius, Josephus was absolutely silent about any Claudian expulsion of the city's Jewish population.[36] Instead, he recorded his second Claudian edict (19.286-291) which contains directives of toleration for the cities, among others, of Italy and so left the entirely false impression of an imperially inspired, uniformly peaceful life for Roman Jews during the thirteen-year rule of Claudius.[37]

Furthermore, insofar as the Claudian edicts of toleration are concerned, chance has rescued us in a highly remarkable way from our dependency upon Josephus. We noted already how, in his clearly authentic 41 CE Alexandrian letter, Claudius did call upon citizens to "behave gently and kindly towards the Jews who have inhabited the same city for many years, and not to dishonour any of their customs in their worship of their god, but to allow them to keep their own ways, as they did in the time of the god Augustus and as I too...have confirmed."[38] Or, as Dio (60.5.1) put it, "Claudius, accordingly, undid the unjust acts performed by Gaius...." Thus, of the fact that Claudius during his first year restored Jewish religious and other rights in Alexandria there can be no doubt. He did so, however, not out of any particular friendship towards the Jews of Alexandria but because he

---

[33]Berliner, *Geschichte*, 1:25.

[34]Schürer, *History*, 3¹:77, n. 91.

[35]P. 15.

[36]Contrary to Orosius, as we shall see in the next chapter.

[37]The fact that the account in Dio demonstrates Claudius' own lack of tolerance in matters of Roman Jewish religious observance raises additional questions about the legitimacy of this second edict.

[38]P. Lond. 1912, lines 82-88; cf. pp. 80-81.

wished to reinstate the policy of Augustus, one which he no doubt felt to be in the best interests of the empire.[39] Even so, and as becomes obvious from what follows in the letter, toleration is at best a neutral term expressing neither friendliness nor sympathy.[40] That is, immediately after restoring the Jewish rights in Alexandria, he commanded the Jews of the city not to seek further privileges and, above all, not to enlarge the community by additions either from Egypt or Syria. Otherwise, he declared, he would develop "greater suspicions"[41] about the Jewish people presumably not only of Alexandria but also of Egypt and Syria, i.e., Judea, as well. This indicates clearly that, even while restoring Jewish rights, Claudius harbored grave misgivings about a significant portion of the empire's Jews.[42] In what follows, it becomes all the more obvious that this was so, for, if his addressees disobeyed him on this point, he would "proceed against them in every way as fomenting a common plague for the whole world."[43] Under these circumstances, expressions such as *Wohlwollen, judenfreundliche Haltung, freundliche Gesinnung* are not appropriate.[44] On the contrary, and as will be discussed further, the

---

[39]Civil order was no doubt a primary interest, above all in Alexandria, Rome's breadbasket. This is why the emperor insisted upon personal control of the city through his own prefect.

[40]Cf. Barry Schwartz, "Tolerance: Should We Approve of It, Put Up with It, or Tolerate It?" *Academe* 82 (1996):24-28.

[41]P. Lond. 1912, lines 88-98.

[42]This is also implied by Luedemann (*Paul*, p. 168).

[43]P. Lond. 1912, lines 98-100.

[44]So also Zielinski, "L'empereur Claude," pp. 132 and 143, n. 2. Insofar as the Josephan edicts are concerned, Berliner's expression *Toleranz-Edict* is largely accurate, for the essence of these two texts is their claim to restore rights granted Jewish populations prior to but then abrogated by Gaius. In fact, this goal finds clear expression in the first edict: "I desire that none of their rights should be lost to the Jews on account of the madness of Gaius, but that their former privileges also be preserved to them" (*Antiquities* 19.285; LCL translations here by Louis H. Feldman; Zielinski ["L'empereur Claude," p. 131] likely being correct on this text that Claudius would not have referred so negatively to a prior emperor). Nor is the second different (*Antiquities* 19.289). The extreme hostility of the clearly genuine letter manifests itself in neither of these, but the first edict does have Claudius warn Jews and Greeks in Alexandria to "take the greatest precaution to prevent any disturbance arising after the posting of my edict" (*Antiquities* 19.285), and the second has the emperor admonish Jews in particular "to avail themselves of this [imperial] kindness in a more reasonable spirit, and not to set at nought the beliefs about the gods held by other peoples but to keep their own laws" (*An-*

41 CE anti-Jewish measures described by Dio are not out of line with the menacing tone of Claudius' Alexandrian letter of the same year. Nonetheless, different lines of argumentation are also employed to discredit Dio's date. Benko provides two of these when he writes that in 41 CE

> the Jewish prince Agrippa was rewarded with a large kingdom. Alexander Lysimachus, alabarch of the Jews in Alexandria...was immediately released from prison where he had been sent by Gaius.... It is indeed unlikely that under these circumstances a restrictive ordinance would have been placed upon the Jews previously in Rome, which would have been most embarrassing to Agrippa and to the Jews elsewhere.[45]

Since Alexander is associated directly with the situation in Alexandria just now discussed, it is easiest to deal with him first. Specifically, Josephus, whom Benko cites for his source on this matter, explained in the same text (*Antiquities* 19.276) that Claudius freed the alabarch because he was his personal friend and also the guardian of Claudius' mother. Furthermore, Josephus indicated there that the imprisonment had occurred without justification.

Thus, Claudius' action reveals once again a desire to undo the harmful work of his predecessor, and it shows how he treated friends. It indicates nothing, however, about his sympathy towards Jews living in Rome or elsewhere. We need only recall that 41 CE witnessed the kindness of the emperor vis-à-vis an aristocratic, Alexandrian Jewish friend but also the hostility of the same man, expressed in his letter, towards the other Jews there. Since Claudius could draw such a sharp line between Alexander and the Alexandrian Jews in general, Benko has no cause to think that the emperor's attitude toward the alabarch would have made him any more sympathetic to the Jewish community of Rome or any less inclined to establish ordinances against it.

---

tiquities 19.290). In any case, even in Josephus there is little that might lead to the classification of the emperor as *judenfreundlich*. In the second edict Josephus does have Claudius express his pleasure at the loyalty and friendliness of the Jewish people toward Rome (*Antiquities* 19.289). Still, as is indicated on p. 14 (n. 20), this does look very much like the work of Josephus, especially because it corresponds in no way to the extreme suspicions manifested in the emperor's certainly authentic letter of the same period. To see a true expression of Claudius' friendliness, it is helpful to read that text in terms of its treatment of Tiberius Claudius Barbillus. Caring deeply for this man, Claudius was not able to grant him all that he wanted in terms of privileges for the Alexandrians. Fearing that the people of the city might think less of Barbillus, Claudius therefore underlined (P. Lond. 1912, lines 105-108) how hard he had worked on their behalf.

[45]Benko, "Edict of Claudius," p. 407-408.

Benko's other argument rests on the view that Herod Agrippa I was so close to Claudius that the emperor could never have taken action against Roman Jews while Agrippa lived. Having played some part in his rise to power, Agrippa was doubtless close to the new emperor.[46] Still, it is necessary to keep this relationship and its significance for the Jewish people in perspective. First, no matter how obliged Claudius may have felt himself to Agrippa, he was certainly unwilling to sacrifice the welfare of his empire for the sake of his friend's image and feelings. Specifically, Josephus told his readers (*Antiquities* 19.326-327) that, at the time when Agrippa fortified the walls of Jerusalem, "Claudius, suspecting that a revolution was on foot, earnestly charged Agrippa in a letter to desist from the building of the walls; and Agrippa thought it best not to disobey." Since it bore directly on matters in his own country, this rebuke with its command to stop construction was certainly embarrassing to the king. Claudius' action against Jews in Rome could not have been any more so.

Second, Benko does not deny that Claudius took action against Roman Jews. He claims only that, in light of the emperor's special attachment to Agrippa, the event could not have occurred prior to the Jewish king's death in 44 CE. Even Benko recognizes, however, that Agrippa was not Claudius' only Jewish friend. Besides the alabarch, these also included Herod of Chalcis, Agrippa II, as well as Tiberius Alexander. In other words, there was no one time in his reign when Claudius' action against Roman Jews could have avoided a conflict between personal friendship and public policy.

Third, Agrippa also became a close friend of Gaius (*Antiquities* 18.168, 289). Gaius appointed him governor over various tetrarchies (*Antiquities* 18.237, 252), and, in return, the Jewish king remained his loyal follower (*Antiquities* 19.237). The implication of Benko's view is, therefore, that the mutual attachment of the two should have provided protection for the Jewish populations of the empire. In fact, Gaius caused them the most extreme difficulties. Hence, Benko's arguments against a 41 CE date for the anti-Jewish measures of Dio 60.6.6-7 are groundless. Imperial friendship with individual members of the Jewish aristocracy was one thing, the handling of the masses something entirely different.

A final argument against the date of Dio comes from Seston's observations based on the previously cited *Legatio* 155-158. Since in this passage Philo provided readers with a list of the punishments that Augustus had not inflicted upon Roman Jews, Seston concludes,

---

[46]This information appears not only in Josephus (*Antiquities* 19.236-247, 274-275; *War* 2.206-217) but also in Dio (60.8.2-3).

on voit mal Philon écrivant cet éloge précis de la politique juive d'Auguste, si au même moment les Juifs de Rome–même certains d'entre eux–avaient été expulsés. C'eût été briser les liens d'amitié qui l'unissaient si fortement à Claude et blesser l'empereur dont nous savons, par ses biographes comme par sa lettre aux Alexandrins, l'attachement dévot à la mémoire d'Auguste. Philon était sûr au contraire de garder la faveur impériale....[47]

That is, Philo could not have written the *Legatio* at the same time ("au même moment") Claudius was taking action against the Jewry of Rome. Had he done so, his commendation of the Augustan treatment of these Jews would have constituted a criticism of Claudius. The possibility of that interpretation Seston rejects because, first, Philo's close bond of friendship with the emperor prohibited the expression of thoughts so likely to injure his feelings, and, second, Philo was unwilling to risk the loss of imperial favor generated by such criticism.

This line of argumentation is without merit. In the first place, Seston substantiates neither of his latter two assertions. Insofar as the former is concerned, he is accurate that Claudius was close to the brother of Philo, Alexander, the alabarch of Alexandria,[48] but he provides evidence of no particular bond with Philo himself. Moreover, the fact that Philo had led a delegation to Gaius on behalf of fellow Jews certainly indicates that he was willing to risk far more than imperial favor for the sake of his people and their religion.[49] In addition, Dio reported that, although Claudius rejoiced at the death of his predecessor, he killed those who had murdered Gaius because they had dared to lay hands on *an* emperor. It was as if, wrote Dio, "he had caught Chaerea plotting against himself."[50] As no more than a narration of imperial abuse under Gaius, therefore, the *Legatio* in its entirety was a dangerous project, for Claudius might easily have construed it as compromising his own position.[51]

In the second place, we already affirmed Smallwood's view that the implied comparison in Philo's praise of Augustus (*Legatio* 155-158) points to Claudius. Finally, as the "au même moment" indicates, the presupposition behind Seston's entire argument is that Philo composed

---

[47]Seston, "L'Empereur Claude," p. 300.

[48]Ibid., p. 293-294; cf. p. 78 of this study.

[49]See *Legatio* 44.351, 353; 45.366; 46.370-372. Apparently independent attestation appears also in *Antiquities* 18.258-260.

[50]Dio 60.3.4.

[51]See especially *Legatio* 119 and 183.

the *Legatio* in 41/42 CE. This approach suffers from a fundamental weakness of methodology because it seeks to correct the clear date in Dio by what we have seen already to be the uncertain date when Philo wrote the *Legatio*. This was after the death of Gaius (*Legatio* 107) and the assumption of power by Claudius (*Legatio* 206). Seston also insists that it was after the publication of Claudius' letter, i.e., P. Lond. 1912, to Alexandria.[52] Whether he is correct of not, the evidence provides only a *terminus post quem*, i.e., January of 41 or, if Seston be right, November of 41.

What his case requires, however, is a *terminus ante quem* locking the *Legatio* into late 41 or early 42 CE. Without this, the "au même moment" upon which he constructs his argument has no support, and he ultimately grants as much. That is, having written how the *Legatio* was composed "sans doute dans le courant de l'année 42," he finds himself forced to add "en toute cas avant 49."[53] With this admission Seston's position against the 41 CE date of Dio collapses. In sum, Dio 60.6.6-7 witnesses to the fact that, as soon as he became emperor, Claudius took action against Roman Jewry.

Provided with such worthwhile information, we are inclined to equate the view of *Claudius* 25.4, "Iudaeos impulsore Chresto assidue tumultuantes Roma expulit," with the one in of Dio 60.6.6-7, "Τούς τε Ἰουδαίους πλεονάσαντας αὖθις ὥστε Χαλεπῶς ἂν ἄνευ ταραχῆς ὑπὸ τοῦ ὄχλου σφῶν τῆς πόλεως εἰρχθῆναι οὐκ ἐξήλασε μέν τῷ δὲ δὴ πατρίῳ βίῳ χρωμένους ἐκέλευσε μὴ συναθροίζεσθαι," so as to establish a concrete date for the expulsion in Suetonius. In fact, the two texts do have a great deal in common. That is, the implied subject in both passages is Claudius, verbs ("expulit"/"ἐξήλασε" and "εἰρχθῆναι") are associated with the idea of expulsion, "Jews" ("Iudaeos"/"Ἰουδαίους") is the direct object, and the place is Rome ("Roma"/"τῆς πόλεως"). Additionally, the notion of tumultuousness ("tumultuantes"/"ταραχῆς") appears in each. It is no wonder, then, that most scholars simply assume Suetonius and Dio described the same event.[54]

---

[52]Seston, "L'Empereur Claude," pp. 296, 299.

[53]Ibid., p. 299.

[54]Benko, "Edict of Claudius," p. 407; Berliner, *Geschichte*, 1:25; Borg, "New Context for Romans XIII," p. 211, n. 2; Bruce, *Commentary*, p. 368; Guterman, *Religious Toleration*, p. 150; Haenchen, *Apostelgeschichte*, p. 58; Harnack, *Mission and Expansion of Christianity*, 1:5; Hoerber, "Decree of Claudius," p. 692; Juster, *Les Juifs*, 1:411; Lake, "Chronology of Acts" in *Beginnings of Christianity*, 5:459; May, "Politique religieuse," p. 43; Scramuzza, *Claudius*, p. 151, and "The Policy" in *Beginnings of Christianity*, 5:296; Smallwood, "Jews and Romans," p. 236; Suhl, *Paulus*, p. 326; Vogelstein and Rieger, *Geschichte*, 1:20.

Nevertheless, closer examination reveals that the details of the two accounts are contradictory. Specifically, Suetonius stated that there were Jewish tumults, Dio that there existed only the potential for them; Suetonius that Claudius expelled Jews, Dio that he did not. A small number of scholars, therefore, seek to justify the equation of the accounts, but all resort ultimately to harmonization. The best justification arises from the question of probabilities. Schürer writes that "it would certainly be strange for one of them [i.e., Suetonius] to mention only the latter edict and the other [i.e., Dio], only the former."[55] The fact is that neither in *Claudius* 25.4 nor anywhere else in his reporting on Claudius did Suetonius reflect knowledge of the ban described by Dio. Similarly, Dio revealed no knowledge of an expulsion. Thus, Schürer may legitimately point out the strangeness of the circumstance that, were they really different, Suetonius could have failed to note the event described by Dio and vice versa.

The preliminary problem with this view lies in the fact that from 47 to 54 CE Dio's history exists only in later excerpts. Hence, there is no way to be sure that Dio at least did not report a second action of the emperor against Roman Jews.[56] Still, Schürer's real difficulty is his argument from silence. He insists that, because Dio did not record as a separate event the action narrated by Suetonius, it could hardly have occurred independent of the one which Dio actually did record.[57] Yet, equally strange is the fact that two historians, Josephus and Tacitus, were completely silent about *any* action of Claudius against Roman Jews. In light of this, the logic of Schürer would compel us to conclude that, just as the event in Suetonius did not take place independently, i.e., because Dio failed to record it independently, so too neither the event in Dio nor the one in Suetonius occurred at all, i.e., because Josephus and Tacitus were silent about both.

The other defense of the identification is based upon the view that Dio provided an intentional correction of the tradition found in Suetonius. Zielinski, who originated this, paraphrases Dio as follows: "Ici je trouve dans mes sources que Claude a chassé de Rome les Juifs séditieux, ce qui me paraît peu probable vu leur grande multitude. Je croix donc plutôt qu'il ne leur a pris que le droit de se réunir."[58] In maintaining the correctness of the paraphrase, Janne considers the

---

[55]Schürer, *History*, 3^1:77, n. 91.

[56]In fact, 60.6.6-7 provides no hint of a later action and so implies that Dio was silent about it.

[57]And, of course, vice versa.

[58]Zielinski, "L'empereur Claude," p. 143, n. 2.

emendation of Dio to be but pure conjecture[59] and Leon a "deliberate contradiction."[60] Although none of these scholars states it explicitly, the point of contrast comes in Dio's words that Claudius did *not* drive out the Roman Jews, a negative clause which, like the one discussed above in the *Legatio*, seems to imply a comparison. Thus, in light of the Suetonian statement that Claudius did drive them out, we may reasonably wonder if the third-century Dio was simply contradicting the tradition found in his second-century predecessor.

Now, if the context of these two references required their identification,[61] we should perhaps be forced to conclude that the one was a correction of the other. Since this is not the case, Zielinski's procedure is to take two passages sharing significant elements in common, set them side by side in an abstract manner, and then point out the supposed contradiction using that contradiction to equate them. Nonetheless, until it has been demonstrated that they are in fact related, there exists no contradiction. In other words, Zielinski argues in a circle. To demonstrate this, a quite different scenario—and one which does not demand the equation—can be fashioned on the very same assumption that Dio provided a contrast with the tradition in Suetonius. First came the event described by the latter: because of tumultuousness Claudius expelled Roman Jews. Then, precisely as Dio asserted, they returned in so large a number that the emperor feared further disorders should he try to drive them out again. Instead, he prohibited their gatherings.[62] This interpretation is as arbitrary as Zielinski's, but, also like his, it accounts for the contrast in Dio and, additionally, eliminates the contradiction between the two accounts.

What remains, then, is the same as what was there in the first place: Dio's statement that Claudius did not drive out the Roman Jews implies a comparison. Sound methodology dictates, however, that a search for the other element in that comparison begin not with the arbitrary juxtaposition of Dio and Suetonius but with the examination of Dio himself. In the first place, there is no way of knowing if Dio was familiar with any of the traditions in Suetonius.[63] In the second, he

---

[59]Janne, "Impulsore Chresto," p. 535.

[60]Leon, *Jews of Ancient Rome*, p. 24. Also Penna, "Les Juifs a Rome," p. 325.

[61]If they shared the same date or if both, for example, referred to Chrestus.

[62]This is a modified version of the reconstruction in Wiefel ("Die jüdische Gemeinschaft," p. 78).

[63]Baldwin (*Suetonius*, pp. 281, 356) perhaps implies that Dio was not familiar with Suetonius' materials; Balsdon (*Gaius*, p. 227) insists that Dio did not use them; Alcide Macé (*Essai sur Suétone* [Paris: Ancienne librairie Thorin et fils,

certainly was familiar with his own materials. And third, his usage of the adverbial "again" ("As for the Jews who had again increased so greatly....") suggests the value of examining those materials in search of a contextually sensible, i.e., non-arbitrary, explanation for the implied comparison. When this is done, the difficulty of the second element resolves itself immediately, for we observed already how, under the reign of Tiberius, Dio 57.18.5a records that "as the Jews had flocked to Rome in great numbers and were converting many of the natives to their ways, he [Tiberius] banished most of them."[64]

Thus, both passages use the verb ἐξελαύνω, the first passage makes perfectly good sense of the contrast in the second, and together they make perfectly reasonable sense without any arbitrary contextual gymnastics. That is, "As the Jews flocked to Rome in great numbers and were converting many of the natives to their ways, he [Tiberius] drove out most of them, [but by the time of Claudius the Jews] had *again* increased so greatly that...he did not drive them out but ordered them...not to hold meetings." Hence, since the elements common to Suetonius and Dio exist already in the earlier passage of the latter, it is entirely unnecessary to explain the implied contrast within Dio by resorting to the tradition in Suetonius. Such a tortuous procedure is hardly necessary when far simpler and more natural is the sensible explanation that Dio intended to contrast an action of Claudius with one he himself had previously reported concerning Tiberius.[65] In light of this, Zielinski's basis for equating the accounts in Suetonius and Dio disappears.

As just noted, among the many scholars who equate events in *Claudius* 25.4 and Dio 60.6.6-7, very few attempt to provide evidence for their position. Instead, they move immediately to processes of harmonization intended either to remove or to minimize to reasonable proportions the differences between the accounts. This assumes that, of itself, a sufficiently smooth harmony would justify the desired equation, yet in terms of the previous discussion alone it should be clear that these processes are doomed by their false presupposition. That is, based on an arbitrary juxtaposition of the two texts, they can produce no more than arbitrary harmonizations of them, and this is exactly what does happen.

1900], pp. 411-417) and Fergus Millar (*A Study of Cassius Dio* [Oxford: Clarendon Press, 1964], p. 86) are unsure; and Scramuzza (*Claudius*, pp. 32-33) indicates that Dio did "sometimes" use Suetonius.

[64]Cf. p. 55.

[65]This also puts to rest the complicated source analysis of Luedemann (*Paul*, pp. 165-166) discussed further in chapter 10 (cf. pp. 216-217).

Resultantly, each of the following harmonizations has been proposed by one scholar or another: Claudius restricted Roman Jewish worship and expelled rioters;[66] he closed one synagogue and expelled some of its members;[67] he closed some synagogues and drove out the rioters;[68] he closed all synagogues but expelled no one;[69] he closed all synagogues and threatened expulsion;[70] he closed all synagogues, threatened expulsion, and some Jews did leave or were ejected;[71] he closed all synagogues, and religious Jews left the city;[72] he closed all synagogues and expelled rioters;[73] he closed synagogues and expelled all Jews;[74] all the Jews were simply expelled.[75] Thus, depending on whether the particular harmonization demonstrates greater confidence in Suetonius and the fact of expulsion or in Dio and the utilization of prohibitions, the final picture tends to resemble more the one than the other scenario. Nonetheless, the actual result demonstrates both the vagaries of this process, and, more importantly, the irreconcilability of the two accounts.

We began the present section by pointing out the fundamental ramifications of the scholarly consensus that *Claudius* 25.4 and Dio 60.6.6-7 refer to the same imperial measure against Roman Jews. The fallacies of the consensus exposed, therefore, it is the ramifications of the contrary conclusion which are the basis for our further discussion.

---

[66]Scramuzza, *Claudius*, p. 151, as well as his "Policy" in *Beginnings of Christianity*, 5:296.

[67]Penna, "Les Juifs a Rome," p. 331; Luedemann, *Paul*, p. 166.

[68]Haenchen, *Apostelgeschichte*, p. 58.

[69]Juster, *Les Juifs*, 1:411; Guterman, *Religious Toleration*, p. 150.

[70]Harnack, *Mission and Expansion of Christianity*, 1:5.

[71]Stern, *Authors*, 2:116, and "Jewish Diaspora" in *Jewish People*, 1:182.

[72]Bruce, *Commentary*, p. 368; Schürer, *History*, 3¹:77; Vogelstein and Rieger, *Geschichte*, 1:20. According to this last, it was the Jewish leadership which left. Suhl (*Paulus*, pp. 326-327) agrees.

[73]Leon, *Jews of Ancient Rome*, p. 26; Berliner, *Geschichte*, 1:25; Hoerber, "Decree of Claudius," p. 692; May, "Politique religieuse," p. 43.

[74]Benko ("Edict of Claudius," pp. 407, 413) and Smallwood ("Jews and Romans," p. 236) but against her *Jews under Roman Rule* (p. 215) where she sees two different events.

[75]Zielinski, "L'empereur Claude," p. 144; Janne, "Impulsore Chresto," pp. 533-535; Borg, "New Context for Romans XIII," p. 211, n. 2.

Within the realm of chronology, that is, we saw how Claudius took the actions indicated by Dio in 41 CE, as soon as he became emperor; however, the expulsion of which Suetonius wrote did not occur at the same time. Hence, in the domain of Claudian policymaking, we find ourselves dealing not with a single decision but, instead, with an imperial propensity or tendency, i.e., with a repetitiveness reminiscent of Tiberius.

As it turns out, then, there is no basis for imagining that the attitudes and actions of Claudius were radically different from those of his predecessors. We noted his opinion concerning the deleterious effects which the increase of "externae superstitiones" had had on traditional Roman religion. We saw also how Philo's *Legatio* 155-158 appears to reflect contemporary Claudian measures against Roman Jews as, in particular, practitioners of one such foreign *superstitio*. We referred briefly to the Claudian expulsion texts in the Acts of the Apostles, Suetonius, and Paulus Orosius. The scholium to Juvenal, directly relevant to Claudius or not, also provided us with some sense of the wretched fate of Jews driven from Rome. Nor could we ignore the unique primary-source reference in Claudius' Alexandrian letter where he threatened to take action against Jews "in every way as fomenting a common plague for the whole world." And, finally, we examined both *Claudius* 25.4 and Dio 60.6.6-7. In light of our other observations, it should not surprise us that these texts also bear witness to the hostile propensities of the emperor Claudius in his policymaking with regard to Roman Jews.

Chapter Five

Witnesses to the Claudian Expulsion of Roman Jewry

In the last chapter we discovered that Dio 60.6.6-7 and *Claudius* 25.4 deal with separate measures of Claudius against Roman Jews. The former attaches itself firmly to 41 CE, a year of particular significance because it was then that Claudius first found himself in a position to make imperial policy. The Jews of Rome were one immediate object of the new policies. A separate decision, the expulsion of these Jews in *Claudius* 25.4, was made at some other time.

At present, therefore, we need to investigate the relationship between this last text and several others associated with it by their explicit or perhaps implicit claim that Claudius expelled Roman Jews. They include the accounts in the Acts of the Apostles, Paulus Orosius, Philo, and the scholium to Juvenal. The issues, largely introductory in nature, are analogous to those raised in chapter 4. We need to know if all these sources deal with a single expulsion and, relatedly, what kind of significant chronological information may be gleaned from them.

To be noted immediately is the fact that a 41 CE expulsion may not be excluded simply because the equation of events in Dio and Suetonius is false. Other evidence remains which might be interpreted to indicate that 41 CE saw not only the prohibitions referred to by Dio but also, and separately, an expulsion. First, Janne argues that Tacitus must also have reported this expulsion because in *Annals* 2.85 he had already noted the similar occurrence under Tiberius in 19 CE. Thus, since the later Claudian years, 47-54 CE, preserved within the remains of the *Annals* are silent about this matter, Tacitus must have reported it under one of that emperor's now missing earlier years.[1] In fact, however, Janne's argument supports at best only a 41-47 CE date,[2] and even this lacks merit. That is, in their absence we have no idea what events Tacitus mentioned under these lost years. Moreover, and by way of analogy, Josephus (*Antiquities* 18.65, 81-84) likewise narrated the 19 CE expulsion under Tiberius and, according to the above logic, should have referred to the similar one under Claudius. As we shall soon see, he did not. Thus, Janne makes no case for the 41 or even 41-47 CE date of a Claudian expulsion of Roman Jews.

A better argument for 41 CE arises from the fact that the same year witnessed the two other clear demonstrations of Claudian anti-Judaism visible in the emperor's letter to Alexandria and Dio 60.6.6-7. By itself, however, this evidence does not establish a temporal limit for any Claudian expulsion. In other words, given what we have seen already to be the traditional imperial attitudes and actions in these matters, it is at least as likely that the two measures which Claudius took when he became emperor were but initial manifestations of his own imperial tendencies.

Required in addition, therefore, is other evidence associating an expulsion with 41 CE. Zielinski alone attempts to supply it. His source is the previously referred to *Acta Isidori*[3] with its account of charges brought to the emperor Claudius by the Alexandrian Isidoros against a certain king Agrippa. The outcome of these charges was that the emperor defended his Jewish friend, Agrippa, and executed Isidoros. Interpreting this as a Claudian action favorable to Jewry in contrast to the unfavorable sentiments of the 41 CE Alexandrian letter, Zielinski assumes that during his last years and under the influence of Agrippa II the emperor must have turned "favorable aux Juifs." As a result, he places the expulsion "aux premières années de Claude."[4]

Of course even on its own terms this argumentation would not achieve its goal. The fact that during his latter years Claudius was influenced in a manner favorable to Jewry could set only the vaguest possible *terminus ante quem* to the earlier years of negative attitudes in the course of which an expulsion might have occurred. Further-

---

[1]Janne, "Impulsore Chresto," pp. 552-553. In agreement are Zielinski ("L'empereur Claude," p. 143, n. 2) and Stern (*Authors*, 2:116). Concerning *Annals* 2.85 see p. 51 of the present study.

[2]So, basically, Smallwood, *Jews under Roman Rule*, pp. 212-213.

[3]P. 24, n. 62.

[4]Zielinski, "L'empereur Claude," p. 143, n. 2. Cf. Bell, *Jews and Christians in Egypt*, p. 19.

more, Zielinski's argumentation is flawed by its own presuppositions. The first of these is that the *Acta Isidori* provide both historically reliable as well as dateable information concerning the event which they describe, but this is entirely open to discussion.[5]

The second is that the influence of Agrippa II became effective around the time of its manifestation at the Isidoros hearing. In fact, because it reveals nothing concerning when that influence might have begun, this event can provide no *terminus post quem*. Specifically, assuming momentarily with Zielinski that the hearing took place in the year 53,[6] we must remember that already in 48/49 CE Claudius gave Agrippa II kingship over Chalcis (*Antiquities* 20.1-4). At the same time (*Antiquities* 20.134-136) Agrippa used his contact with Agrippina to gain Claudius' favor for Jews in Judea. Furthermore, for 44/45 CE *Antiquities* 20.6-16 cites a similar case of Agrippa's influence with his ruler on behalf of Jews there, and *Antiquities* 19.360-362 indicates for the same period that, had Claudius had his own way, the seventeen-year-old son (*Antiquities* 19.354) would have inherited his father's dominions immediately. Even in 41 CE, however, the emperor was already favorably disposed towards the elder Agrippa. As a result, there is no basis for Zielinski's view that the *Acta Isidori* mark the beginning of Agrippan influence over Claudius.

Zielinski's third presupposition is that this influence of Jewish royalty would have contributed to a beneficial imperial attitude towards Jewry in general and so have prohibited actions of a hostile nature. The obvious difficulty with this view is that in 41 CE, already favorably disposed towards Agrippa I, the new emperor had acted against Roman Jewry and also menaced that of Alexandria. In other words, and as discussed previously,[7] there was very little correlation between imperial feelings toward members of the Jewish nobility and the treatment of the Jewish masses. In sum, the *Acta Isidori* do not place an expulsion of Roman Jews in the first or any other early year of Claudius.

Lacking further data concerning 41 CE, we have no grounds for assigning a Claudian expulsion to it. In fact, one major piece of evidence does exist, and it militates strongly against the likelihood that that year witnessed any expulsion of Roman Jews. Specifically, Dio 60.6.6-7 is explicit that Claudius excluded this particular measure

---

[5]Cf. *Acts of the Pagan Martyrs*, pp. 118-124.

[6]This is implied by his reference ("L'empereur Claude," p. 143, n. 2) to the views of M. Wilcken. Hennig ("Bruchstücken," p. 331, n. 30) makes clear that a 41 CE date is just as likely. It would destroy Zielinski's case.

[7]Pp. 102-103.

from those taken at that time. Hence, since we are aware already of the inadequacies of claims made against both the date and reliability of the account in Dio, we have no grounds for denying the account's basic accuracy in this matter. As a result, though the new emperor immediately threatened the Alexandrian Jews and acted concretely against the same population at Rome, we may not assign an expulsion to the year 41; however, sometime later, between 42 and his death in 54 CE, Claudius struck at least one more time. At that point, he did banish Jews from the city.

It remains to be observed that during the last century Karl Wieseler in particular employed a variety of circumstantial evidence in order to make the case that an expulsion occurred in 52 CE.[8] In the first place, and for the sake of providing a general temporal framework, Wieseler argues that Claudius would only have taken this measure during the 50-53 CE absence of Agrippa II from the city of Rome. Moreover, he limits the period even further by excluding both 50 and 53 CE on the grounds that Agrippa had left Rome during the former and was already back there by the start of the latter year.[9] His framework does suffer however from two major weaknesses. First, it depends upon what we have observed already to be the fallacious assumption that the influence of the Jewish royalty guaranteed the welfare of the Jewish masses. Likewise, it takes for granted that Josephus provided a complete timetable of Agrippa's comings and goings. He did not. In general, that is, we have no idea on what other occasions Agrippa might have absented himself from the city. In particular, Wieseler's own ideas of Agrippan departures and returns as well as when they occurred are assumptions, for neither *War* 2.223-245 nor *Antiquities* 20.104-135 supplies them.

His second argument associating an expulsion of Roman Jewry with 52 CE depends upon *Annals* 12.52. There Tacitus claimed that this year witnessed the banishment of astrologers from Rome. Since, according to Suetonius (*Tiberius* 36), Jews and astrologers were connected with "sacra peregrina" punished together under Tiberius, Wieseler concludes that the exclusion of the astrologers implies that

---

[8]Karl Wieseler, *Chronologie des apostolischen Zeitalters bis zum Tode der A-postel Paulus und Petrus* (Göttingen: Vandenhoeck und Ruprecht, 1848), pp. 125-127. He was subsequently followed by Thomas Lewin (*Fasti Sacri or A Key to the Chronology of the New Testament* [London: Longmans, Green, and Co., 1865], pp. lxii-lxiv), Huidekoper (*Judaism at Rome*, pp. 228-229), and Bludau ("Die Juden Roms," p. 125).

[9]Wieseler, *Chronologie*, pp. 124-125. He dates Agrippa's departure to rule Chalcis in 50 (cf. *War* 2.223, *Antiquities* 20.104) and his return to the time of the Cumanus hearing in 52 (cf. *War* 2.245, *Antiquities* 20.135).

of Jews as well.[10] Nevertheless, *Annals* 12.52 is what we might call *sacrum* specific: it explains that astrologers were expelled in 52 CE as a result of the part they played in the affair of Furius Scribonianus. Again, *Tiberius* 36 is topical in nature and, as a result, leaves open whether the measures taken against Jewish (and Egyptian) rites were contemporary with those against astrologers. In any case, without the clear grounds for doing so, it is illegitimate to use Suetonius in order to interpret Tacitus, especially since the former did in fact distinguish between the two groups.

Wieseler's last argument depends upon the Suetonian statement about Roman Jews being "assidue tumultuantes."[11] He assumes that these disturbances were associated with those that occurred among Palestinian Jews while Cumanus was procurator between 50 and 52 CE[12] as well as among the general Roman masses during the famine of 51/52 CE.[13] Wieseler, however, provides no justification for his combination of the entirely different disturbances in Palestine and Rome. Furthermore, the commotion of the Roman proletariat leaves unexplained why an expulsion was directed at Jews alone. That the Palestinian Jewish difficulties under Cumanus produced some kind of reaction among certain Roman Jews is perhaps likely,[14] but that this

---

[10]Wieseler, *Chronologie*, pp. 124-125; Lewin, *Fasti Sacri*, p. lxiii.

[11]Wieseler, *Chronologie*, pp. 126-127.

[12]Cf. the above texts of Josephus (*War* 2.223-245 and *Antiquities* 20.104-135).

[13]*Annals* 12.43 and *Claudius* 18.2. As an aside, on the basis of *Augustus* 42.3 and *Annals* 2.85-87, Wieseler (*Chronologie*, p. 127, n. 2) appends here that it was imperial policy in times of famine to appease the traditional Roman deities by the expulsion of foreign cults. Still, *Augustus* 42.3 does not claim this, and Tacitus drew no connection between the expulsion and the problem of the corn supply. Huidekoper takes us even further afield. In his view, it was not only the famine but also the earthquakes of 51 CE (*Annals* 12.43) which then produced messianic agitation within the Jewish community. This agitation in turn caused the tumults resulting in expulsion.

[14]In Lewin's view (*Fasti Sacri*, pp. lxii-lxiii) there is no need to posit any Roman Jewish reaction to account for the expulsion. Instead, since Augustus had expelled Gauls and Germans from the city at the time of the Varus' military disaster in their homeland (Dio 56.23), he assumes that Claudius did the same to Roman Jews at the time of the disturbances under Cumanus in theirs. This is not convincing because Dio himself clarified the extreme circumstances under which the Augustan expulsion occurred. Furthermore, Augustus did not expel Roman Jews at the time of the Judean disturbances following the death of Herod the Great. Finally, and as will be referred to again very shortly, in the case of Cumanus the emperor Claudius took the side of the Judeans.

manifested itself in anti-governmental tumultuousness followed by an expulsion is entirely conjectural.[15] Still, even as a conjecture it is most unlikely because in this instance Claudius assumed the side of Palestinian Jewry against Cumanus.

Overall, therefore, Wieseler's evidence in favor of a 52 CE date for the expulsion of Roman Jewry reveals itself to be at best vaguely circumstantial and at worst entirely conjectural in nature. In fact, a similar kind of inventiveness would be able to create chronological associations for each of the fourteen years during which Claudius ruled the Roman empire; these associations too, however, would leave us at the mercy of conjecture.

This explains why the information of Paulus Orosius assumes a singular role in these matters. That fifth-century Christian writer dated the expulsion of *Claudius* 25.4 to one specific year, 49 CE.[16] Furthermore, Acts 18:1-18 has often been read as corroborative of this Orosian detail because it too mentions a Claudian expulsion of Jews from Rome (18:2) within the absolute chronological context of Gallio's proconsulship of Achaia (18:12-17).

Beginning with the account in Acts, we must observe that its corroborative function depends upon two presuppositions. First, that both *Claudius* 25.4 and Acts 18:2 ("᾿Ακύλαν προσφάτως ἐληλυθότα ἀπὸ τῆς ᾿Ιταλίας...διὰ τὸ διατετάχεναι[17] Κλαύδιον χωρίζεσθαι πάντας τοὺς

---

[15]In general, the author of the Acts of the Apostles refers to Roman Jewish visitors in Jerusalem (2:10). They would have taken back to the city a clear awareness of events in the region. More precise in this regard are two additional indications (cf. Leon, *Jews of Ancient Rome*, pp. 14-15) provided by Josephus in *War* 2.80-81/*Antiquities* 17.300-301 and *War* 2.105/*Antiquities* 17.330-331. In the former case, and following directly upon extremely serious disturbances in Judea, eight thousand Jews at Rome gathered in the temple of the Palatine Apollo to demonstrate before Augustus their opposition to Archelaus' rule of Judea. Insofar as we are aware, these Jews were not considered tumultuous, and Augustus did not expel them from Rome. In the latter, related case, a man identifying himself as the Hasmonean prince Alexander, i.e., as the legitimate king of Judea, had arrived at Rome with a large retinue. As a result, the entire Jewish population of the city crowded the streets in order to see him. Again, these presumably excited Jews appear neither to have been accused of tumultuousness nor to have been banished from the city.

[16]W. M. Ramsay (*Pauline and Other Studies in Early Christian History* [London: Hodder and Stoughton, 1906], p. 361) indicates that Orosius meant 50 CE. For reasons indicated shortly, it is unnecessary to consider that possibility.

[17]The variant reading is τεταχέναι. It probably arose because of a grammatical difficulty in Acts 18:2. Specifically, διάτασσω takes a dative object (cf. Matthew 11:1, 1 Corinthians 9:14, 16:1), but πάντας τοὺς ᾿Ιουδαίους is in the accusative. As a result, since τάσσω does take the accusative case, the scribes apparently

'Ιουδαίους άπὸ τῆς 'Ρώμης"/"Aquila having recently come from Italy because Claudius had ordered all Jews to leave Rome") refer to the same event; second, the chronological details associated with Gallio establish reliable chronology of an absolute kind. Insofar as the former is concerned, the two texts do have much in common: they agree on the four details that Claudius expelled Jews from Rome. Moreover, the additional matter in Suetonius concerning the *impulsor* Chrestus and the claim that these Jews were "assidue tumultuantes" in no way contradicts Acts 18:2.

At only one point, in fact, might it be possible to differentiate between the occurrences preserved in Suetonius and Acts. To be specific, the latter indicates that the expulsion affected the entire Jewish population, in other words, "all the Jews." Suetonius is not quite so clear because, by itself, the expression "Iudaeos...assidue tumultuantes" might be interpreted either restrictively, i.e., "the Jews who were constantly making disturbances," or nonrestrictively, i.e., "the Jews, who were constantly making disturbances." Restrictively the sense would be that Claudius directed the expulsion only against tumultuous Jews, and, as previously indicated, various scholars have understood Suetonius in just this way.[18] Thus, if Acts remembered the measures against the entire community while *Claudius* 25.4 recalled those against only a portion of it, we would possess concrete evidence differentiating the two expulsions.[19]

The problem with this interpretation is twofold. First, Suetonius tended to employ "Iudaeus" inclusively, for among the other five places where this noun appears in his *De vita caesarum*[20] three require the inclusive interpretation (*Tiberius* 36, *Vespasian* 4.5 and 8.1), one prefers it (*Julius* 84.5), and the last (*Augustus* 76.2), though singular, is best understood in the same way.[21] Second, within the immediate context of Lycians, Rhodians, Trojans, Germans, and Druids, each one treated inclusively, it is natural to think that Suetonius expected

---

wanted to make a correction in the grammar by substituting the variant τεταχέναι for the original διατεταχέναι.

[18]P. 109.

[19]This is analogous to an argument which M. H. Williams ("Expulsion," pp. 767-768) uses to show that the Tiberian expulsion of Roman Jews reported by Dio was different from the one referred to in the other sources. At least in that case, the argument appears unsuccessful (cf. p. 58 of this study).

[20]Cf. Albertus Andreas Howard and Carolus Newell Jackson, *Index verborum C. Suetoni Tranquilli* (Cambridge: Harvard University Press, 1922), p. 127.

[21]"Ne Iudaeus quidem," i.e., "Not even *the* Jew." He cited Augustus here.

readers to understand "Iudaeos" similarly. As a result, since on this basis no distinction can be made between them, nothing stands in the way of the possibility that Acts 18:2 and *Claudius* 25.4 refer to a single Claudian expulsion.

Still, the possibility does not establish the certainty of this equation.[22] Specifically, besides the four-part statement shared by Acts 18:2 and *Claudius* 25.4[23] and containing the elements *Claudius*, *expulsion*, *Jews*, and *Rome*, chance has preserved three-, three/four-, and five-part claims of a related nature. The first of these we have encountered already in the scholium to Juvenal's *Satire* 4.117,[24] which refers to "Jews who, having been sent from the city, travelled to Aricia," i.e., to *expulsion*, *Jews*, and *Rome*. The three/four-part claim is found in the previously discussed *Legatio* 157 where its denial that Augustus "ἐξῴκισε τῆς 'Ρώμης ἐκείνους," that is, "ejected them [the Jewish population] from Rome," apparently contrasts the first emperor of Rome to another in association with *expulsion*, *Jews*, and *Rome*.[25] Hence, it shares the same three explicit details with the scholium. As indicated already, however, a fourth, implicit detail seems to be present in this instance as well, for the unnamed emperor is probably Claudius. Finally, a five-part claim appears in *Claudius* 25.4 because, in addition to its four details above, i.e., *Claudius*, *expulsion*, *Jews*, and *Rome*, Suetonius likewise added the reference about the *impulsor* Chrestus. Resultantly, since the scholium and *Claudius* 25.4 make the same three-part claim about Jews expelled from Rome, it is entirely possible that these texts have in mind the same event. Nevertheless, because the scholium might just as easily relate to the Republican expulsion mentioned by Valerius Maximus, or to the Tiberian one, or to an otherwise unrecorded event,[26] it is also entirely possible that they do not.

Although in an explicit sense *Legatio* 157 makes the same three-part claim as the scholium, its identification with the Suetonian event becomes far more probable since its subject is apparently the emperor Claudius.[27] In any case, Acts 18:2 does refer explicitly to Claudius.

---

[22]Insofar as I am aware, no one has either disputed or attempted to justify the identity of events in Acts 18:2 and *Claudius* 25.4.

[23]So also Josephus, according to Orosius.

[24]Pp. 89-90.

[25]Pp. 91-92.

[26]Cf. p. 90.

[27]Cf. pp. 92-96.

This means then that the identity of the occurrence in Acts 18:2 and *Claudius* 25.4 is slightly more probable than the identity of that in *Legatio* 157 and *Claudius* 25.4 and much more probable than that of the scholium and *Claudius* 25.4.

Finally, insofar as the five-part claim of Suetonius is concerned, let us suppose that *Legatio* 157 and Acts 18:2 had also mentioned the *impulsor* Chrestus. Then it would be all the more probable, that is, practically certain, that these three accounts had in mind the same Claudian expulsion. The point is, we are not dealing with certainties about the identification Acts 18:2 and *Claudius* 25.4 but with lesser and greater degrees of probability. In other words, the probability of equating the expulsions recorded by the author of Acts and Suetonius, or, in fact, by the author of Acts, Suetonius, and Philo, is simply that, a probability.

Alternatively, instead of making reference to the same Claudian expulsion, these passages might recount similar Claudian expulsions, for the agreements between them may perhaps point to tendency and repetition rather than to identity. Perhaps, in other words, portions at least of the already expelled Jewish population returned to Rome only to be banished by Claudius again at some later time. In the reporting of these matters, after all, chance rules. On the one hand, it has preserved for us the information that on at least two separate occasions Tiberius took significant measures against Roman Jews in the practice of their cult, that Claudius also acted against them at least twice, and that both emperors found expulsion suitable to their purposes.[28] On the other, the remnants of Dio report no expulsion during the first half of Claudius' reign, and those of Tacitus' *Annals* none for the second half.[29] Again, though Tacitus could have made excellent use of such a detail in his anti-Jewish diatribe of *Histories* 5, he made no mention of it. Likewise, Josephus reported no expulsion in either the *War* or *Antiquities*.

Resultantly, if Suetonius, Acts, and Paulus Orosius had not happened to preserve a brief glimpse of these things, we should have finished our reading of Philo,[30] Josephus, Tacitus, and Dio oblivious to the fact that Claudius ever expelled Jews from Rome. Consequently, granted the obviously unsystematic gathering of information among

---

[28]Concerning the Tiberian measures of ca. 19 and 31 CE, refer to chapters 2 and 3 respectively.

[29]Dio 60 covers through 46 CE, and *Annals* 11 begins during 47 CE. There are also excerpts of Dio for the following years. They know nothing of an expulsion.

[30]Without the information in these texts, the reference in *Legatio* 157 would probably go unnoticed.

these writers as well as the fortuitous nature of what has survived from them, it is not impossible that, just as Josephus, Tacitus, and Dio mentioned nothing about any Claudian expulsion, Philo, Suetonius, and the author of Acts referred to more than one expulsion. In sum, chance has preserved either separate accounts of the same Claudian measure or separate Claudian measures of a similar kind.

As to the second of these alternatives, the apostle Paul's letter to Rome apparently and Dio 60.6.6-7 certainly make clear that the imperial expulsions of Roman Jewry did not preclude the possibility of a return to and subsequent expulsion from the city. Thus, if the letter was written under Nero,[31] i.e., after the Claudian expulsion, it perhaps bears witness to Jews who had later returned to Rome. First, at least some of the persons addressed within the letter could have been Jewish.[32] Second, Romans 16:2-3 perhaps bears witness that the Prisca and Aquila found among victims of the Claudian expulsion of Acts 18:2-3 were now back in Rome.[33] In any case, we do possess the explicit evidence of Dio 57.18.5a and 60.6.6-7 with their previously discussed reference to the return by the time of Claudius of those Jews who had been expelled under the emperor Tiberius: "As the Jews flocked to Rome in great numbers and were converting many of the natives to their ways, he [Tiberius] drove out most of them, [but by the time of Claudius the Jews] had again increased so greatly that...he did not drive them out but ordered them...not to hold meetings."[34] The difficulty with this analogy is, however, that the return either of Claudian-expelled Jews under Nero or of Tiberian exiles by the time of Claudius differs from a return and second banishment of Roman Jews under the emperor Claudius alone.[35]

---

[31]This represents the consensus of scholarship. The problems of early Christian chronology raised in Slingerland, "Acts 18:1-18, the Gallio Inscription, and Absolute Pauline Chronology" may yet challenge it.

[32]Cf. Romans 2:17 (though its manner of argumentation was perhaps of a rhetorical nature).

[33]Provided Romans 16 belongs to the original letter, but it appears to make more sense as a Pauline note to Ephesus (cf. Werner Georg Kümmel, *Introduction to the New Testament*, trans. Howard Clark Kee [Nashville: Abingdon Press,1975], pp. 314-320). Solin ("Juden und Syrer" in *ANRW*, 2.29²: 661-665) assumes it is an authentic part of Romans.

[34]Cf. pp. 107-108.

[35]My "Suetonius *Claudius* 25.4, Acts 18, and Paulus Orosius' *Historiarum*" (p. 134, n. 36) uses other analogies to illustrate the possibility of more than one Jewish expulsion under Claudius. I no longer find these to be credible. First, vis-à-vis *Annals* 12.52 and Dio 61.33.3b, the expulsion of whole populations is hardly

Therefore, in the absence of different, more legitimate analogies along this line,[36] we are probably better served by the opposite kind of analogy. I refer to the fact that Josephus, Tacitus, Suetonius, and Dio reported what was without doubt the same Tiberian expulsion of Roman Jews.[37] This would appear to suggest that in the Acts of the Apostles, Suetonius, and the *Legatio* chance has preserved echoes of a single, obviously well-known Claudian measure rather than separate actions of a similar kind.

On the basis of the likelihood *Claudius* 25.4 and Acts 18:2 refer to the same event, we may return to the beginning of the present discussion and the use to which the latter has been put in order to corroborate Paulus Orosius' claim that the Suetonian expulsion took place in 49 CE.[38] Simply put, the usage is illegitimate, for under scrutiny the details of Acts 18:1-18 reveal themselves as unsuitable to the task of establishing absolute chronology. Specifically, I have made apparent elsewhere not only the historical tendentiousness[39] and the relative chronological imprecision[40] of Acts 18 but also the absolute

---

analogous to that of individual astrologers. Also, both texts may well refer to one event. Second, Williams' statement about Tiberius cited there ("Expulsion," p. 768: "The objection could be advanced that Tiberius is unlikely to have taken steps against the Jews twice within a few years but it is not valid. The early years of his principate saw action [Dio 57.15.8] against the astrologers on at least two separate occasions.") is triply illegitimate as an analogy for events in the time of Claudius. That is, it too fails to distinguish between measures directed against influential individuals as opposed to masses of people. Again, Dio 57.15.8 does not refer to a double expulsion. Finally, the use to which Williams puts this analogy, i.e., to contend that the Tiberian expulsion of Roman Jews reported by Dio was different from the banishment mentioned in the other sources, is simply not convincing (cf. p. 58).

[36]Cf. the previous note.

[37]Cf. pp. 50-62, 67-69.

[38]*Legatio* 157 provides no precise chronological help.

[39]Slingerland, "'The Jews' in the Pauline Portion of Acts," pp. 305-321; "Composition of Acts," pp. 99-113; "Acts 18:1-17 and Luedemann's Pauline Chronology," pp. 687-691; "Acts 18:1-18, the Gallio Inscription, and Absolute Pauline Chronology," pp. 439-449.

[40]Slingerland, "Acts 18:1-18, the Gallio Inscription, and Absolute Pauline Chronology," pp. 442-443. The brief response of Jerome Murphy-O'Connor ("Paul and Gallio," *Journal of Biblical Literature* 112 [1993]:315-317), intent upon resisting what it wrongly sees to be the "intellectual paralysis" (p. 317) resulting from this study, largely ignores my textual analysis and returns instead to the old probabilities which, as the details of the analysis make clear, are no longer so.

chronological imprecision of the Gallio inscription.[41] This invalidates every absolute chronological claim associated with the account in the Acts of the Apostles.[42]

Furthermore, other evidence intended to corroborate the 49 CE date supplied by Orosius is equally unconvincing. Thus, Momigliano's usage of the Nazareth inscription (*SEG*, 8.13, an undated imperial decree forbidding the molestation of graves) to support this date,[43] Momigliano himself repudiates in his 1961 preface.[44] Likewise, Bruce Metzger elaborates sensibly on Momigliano's position that there is no way to date the inscription or associate it with any specific event.[45] In fact, Momigliano's original use of the inscription rather presupposes than proves the 49 CE expulsion date.

Again, were scholarship in a position to demonstrate, first, that Paul actually wrote 1 Thessalonians not long after 49 CE and, second, that the well-known 1 Thessalonians 2:16, "God's wrath has overtaken them [the Jewish people] at last," recollected some catastrophe which

---

[41]Slingerland, "Acts 18:1-18, the Gallio Inscription, and Absolute Pauline Chronology," pp. 444-446.

[42]Even were it possible to accept the historicity of the account in Acts, its chronological imprecision combined with that of the Gallio inscription places Paul's arrival in Corinth only broadly between sometime shortly before December of 47 and April of 54 CE (Slingerland, "Acts 18:1-18, the Gallio Inscription, and Absolute Pauline Chronology," p. 449). If Acts could be trusted within these limits and Acts 18:2 means Aquila and Priscilla came directly from Rome, as προσφάτως implies, and so arrived in Corinth when Paul did, it would be possible to affirm that this expulsion occurred between 47 and the death of Claudius in 54 CE. The difficulty with the second point is the view of Janne ("Impulsore Chresto," p. 552, n. 5), Leon (*Jews of Ancient Rome*, p. 24), Smallwood (*Jews under Roman Rule*, pp. 212-213), Stern (*Authors*, 2:116) and Zielinski ("L'empereur Claude," p. 144) that Acts differentiates between when Jews left Rome and finally departed Italy, i.e., arrived in Corinth. Still, the sense of the passage does not favor this interpretation which arose to make possible the identification of the 41 CE event in Dio with the supposedly 49 CE banishment in Acts. Thus, provided that Acts 18:2 and *Claudius* 25.4 do refer to the same happening, anyone convinced of the absolute chronological merit of Acts 18:1-18 might conclude the expulsion occurred between late 47 and 54 CE.

[43]Momigliano, *Claudius*, p. 36; followed closely by Smallwood, *Jews under Roman Rule*, p. 213.

[44]Momigliano, *Claudius*, p. ix.

[45]Bruce M. Metzger, "The Nazareth Inscription Once Again" in *Jesus und Paulus: Festschrift für Werner Georg Kümmel zum 70. Geburtstag*, ed. E. Earle Ellis and Erich Grässer, 2d ed. (Göttingen: Vandenhoeck & Ruprecht, 1978), pp. 221-238.

had devastated Roman Jewry in particular,[46] the epistle might serve
as evidence of an expulsion in that year. The latter, in any case,
cannot be done. This is so because 1 Thessalonians 2:16 is open to
several interpretations including interpolation. No more convincing is
the view of Scramuzza that "the date A.D. 49 bears all the marks of
circumstantial credibility, for it was just in the period A.D. 47-52 that
Claudius was engaged in a very earnest campaign for the suppression
of foreign cults and the restoration of the old Roman religion."[47] The
evidence to which he alludes in support of this view is irrelevant; it
shows only how Claudius restored some rites, attacked the astrologers,
and did perhaps favor one foreign cult.[48] In sum, the chronological
claim of Paulus Orosius stands or falls on its own merits.

Orosius wrote as follows:

> Josephus reports, "In his ninth year the Jews were expelled by Clau-
> dius from the city." But Suetonius, who speaks as follows, influences
> me more: "Claudius expelled from Rome the Jews constantly rioting
> at the instigation of Christ [Christo]." As far as whether he had
> commanded that the Jews rioting against Christ [Christum] be re-
> strained and checked or also had wanted the Christians as persons
> of a cognate religion to be expelled, it is not at all to be discerned.[49]

The core of the material is two quotations. The one supposedly comes
from Josephus, and the other is *Claudius* 25.4. The latter is generally
accurate, but Orosius did make a single, significant change: Suetonius
wrote "Chrestus," and Orosius edited with "Christus," so applying a
Christian twist by the change of an "e" to an "i."[50]

---

[46]Bammel, "Judenverfolgung," p. 295.

[47]Scramuzza, "Policy" in *Beginnings of Christianity*, 5:296.

[48]Ibid., 5:460.

[49]*Historiarum adversum paganos libri VII* 7.6.15-16: "Anno eiusdem nono
expulsos per Claudium Urbe Iudaeos Iosephus refert. sed me magis Suetonius
movet, qui ait hoc modo: Claudius Iudaeos inpulsore Christo adsidue tumultuantes Roma expulit; quod, utrum contra Christum tumultuantes Iudaeos coher-
ceri et conprimi iusserit, an etiam Christanos simul velut cognatae religionis
homines voluerit expelli, nequaquam discernitur" (*Historiarum adversum paganos
libri vii: accedit eiusdem liber apologeticus*, ed. Carolus Zangemeister, *CSEL*, vol.
5 [1882; reprint ed., Hildesheim: Georg Olms Verlagsbuchhandlung, 1967], ad
loc.). Cf. *Paulus Orosius: The Seven Books of History against the Pagans*, trans.
Roy J. Deferrari (Washington: Catholic University of America, 1964) and *Historia
contra los paganos*, ed. E. Gallego-Blanco (Barcelona: Puvill libros, n.d.).

[50]The same twist occurs in Orosius' account (*Historiarum* 7.6.12) of the conversion of Helena of Adiabene to Christianity rather than Judaism.

Concerning the former, the first difficulty is that the extant texts of Josephus do not contain what is attributed to him here. Because of this, some scholars reject the information entirely.[51] Others assume its worth,[52] and a few argue that case. Among these last is Eisler. He is of the opinion that the quotation appeared in *War* 2.245-249, i.e., in the Cumanus account, or in the corresponding part of *Antiquities* 20 but was expunged by Christian scribes as a reference offensive to their religion.[53] Eisler nevertheless fails to observe that within the words attributed to Josephus there is nothing hostile to Christianity. That sense arises only in conjunction with Orosius' citation of Suetonius. Again, since he does not demonstrate the existence of a lacuna in either text, the only foundation for his hypothesis is confidence in the testimony of Orosius, but that is the question at issue.

Reflecting a similar trust, Smallwood suggests without evidence that Orosius used a text of Josephus into which the citation had been interpolated.[54] In fact, however, Orosius appears elsewhere to have made no direct use of Josephus, for Zangemeister's "Index scriptorum quibus Orosius usus est" indicates only two other locations in the *Historiarum* that contain references to Josephus. At 7.9.3 there is information about him, but it is taken from Suetonius. Even more revealing is 7.9.7 with its excerpt of the Jewish historian drawn verbatim from Jerome's Latin translation of Eusebius' *Chronicle*.[55]

The alternatives are, then, that Orosius invented this reference or erred in attributing it to Josephus. Harnack believes he used a no-longer extant version of Jerome's translation of the *Chronicle* which had been enriched by materials, including the reference to the Jewish historian, from Julius Africanus. As a result, the real authority behind the name "Josephus" and the note concerning Claudius' ninth year is probably ("Wir dürfen daher mit Wahrscheinlichkeit annehmen....") Africanus. But, as Harnack continues, since Josephus made no such

---

[51]Janne, "Impulsore Chresto," pp. 550-551; Leon, *Jews of Ancient Rome*, p. 24; Luedemann, *Paul*, pp. 6, 164; Stern, "Jewish Diaspora" in *Jewish People*, 1:182.

[52]Garzetti (*Tiberius to the Antonines*, pp. 140, 603), May ("Politique religieuse," pp. 38, 41), and Wiefel ("Die jüdische Gemeinschaft," p. 76).

[53]Robert Eisler, ΙΗΣΟΥΣ ΒΑΣΙΛΕΥΣ ΟΥ ΒΑΣΙΛΕΥΣΑΣ, Religionswissenschaftliche Bibliothek, vol. 9, 2 vols. (Heidelberg: Carl Winters Universitätsbuchhandlung, 1929), 1:132.

[54]Smallwood, *Jews under Roman Rule*, p. 210.

[55]*Die Chronik des Hieronymus*, under Vespasian's second year. To obtain some sense of Orosius' dependence on the *Chronicle* see the notes of Zangemeister, ed. (*Historiarum*) under "auctores" as well as his "Index scriptorum" above.

reference, whoever created the version employed by Orosius must have misquoted Africanus with the insertion of the name of Josephus where Africanus had written some other, perhaps "Justus of Tiberias."[56] Harnack's "wie dem aber auch sein mag"[57] does understate the highly conjectural nature of this source analysis built supposition upon supposition, the presupposition and weakness of which is the same as in the case of Eisler and Smallwood. To be more specific, Harnack is overly trusting when he writes, "Mithin hat er [Orosius] nichts 'erlogen'–es fehlten ihm auch zum Schwindeln Kentnisse und Virtuosität–, sondern einfach seine Quelle wiedergeben."[58] Rather, even a superficial reading of its prologue in *Historiarum* 1 certifies E. Gallego-Blanco's observation that the document is not a history: "El presbítero hispano ni es historiador ni se propuso serlo.... La obra de Orosio es una apología."[59] Negatively, this awareness prohibits any simple faith in Orosius' desire for historical accuracy. Positively, it underlines the need to figure out if the information attributed to Josephus came from a source other than his own apologetic interests.

The fact is that Orosius composed this passage in a very clever manner, for, having cited "Josephus," he used "Suetonius influences me more" in order to focus on his Christianized ("Chrestus" altered to "Christus") Suetonian text. And he did this because he could interpret the latter in two ways corresponding to separate apologetic interests visible elsewhere.[60] The first interpretation, demonstrating that the eviction of the Roman Jews constituted a legitimate punishment for the mistreatment of Christ/Christians, was typical of Orosius.[61] The

---

[56]Adolf Harnack, "Chronologische Berechnung des 'Tags von Damaskus,'" *Sitzungsberichte der preussischen Akademie der Wissenschaften* 34 (1912):675-676. Similarly, following him, Meyer, *Ursprung*, 3:38, n. 1; Jewett, *Chronology of Paul's Life*, p. 38; in part, Smallwood, *Jews under Roman Rule*, p. 210.

[57]Harnack, "Chronologische Berechnung," p. 676.

[58]Ibid., p. 675.

[59]Gallego-Blanco, ed., *Historia*, p. 18. Hans-Werner Goetz (*Die Geschichtstheologie des Orosius* [Darmstadt: Wissenschaftliche Buchgesellschaft, 1980], pp. 17-18) implies Orosian truth was a "bessere Wahrheit" refuting charges that contemporary evils arose with the Christianization of the empire.

[60]Hence, his "it is not at all to be discerned" does not represent the anguish of a historian struggling with sources.

[61]*Historiarum* 7.3.8 (destruction of Jerusalem/extinction of Jews caused by Jewish responsibility for the death of Jesus), 7.4.16 (same), 7.4.17 (expulsion from Rome vis-à-vis death of Jesus), 7.5.6 (Alexandrian slaughter and expulsion of Jews vis-à-vis death of Jesus). On this basis and because of his great popularity in the

second plays an even more fundamental part in his narrative. That is, having suggested that Claudius intended to harm Christians, Orosius immediately reported the nemesis involved for emperor and Roman populace alike: within the very next year ("sequenti anno") a dreadful famine occurred in Rome; Claudius was humiliated by the starving crowds; shortly thereafter several prominent Romans were executed unjustly; and the emperor was then poisoned.[62] As an exact parallel Orosius later explained how the Roman mistreatment of Peter and Paul under Nero immediately ("subsequente autumno") resulted in a multitude of evils for Rome, including pestilence in the city, disaster in Britain, defeat against the Parthians, earthquakes in Asia, and the humiliation and death of the emperor himself.[63]

Both of these instances he intended his readers to contrast with the salutary happenings which occurred when, at the very beginning of Claudius' rule, no impediment was placed in the way of Peter as he introduced Christianity into Rome: prominent Romans experienced a time of clemency, Athens received a long overdo amnesty, Rome was miraculously spared the horrors of civil war, Britain was subdued, and the Orcades added to the empire. All these, wrote Orosius, resulted directly from the unhindered arrival of Christianity in Rome.[64]

Consequently, either one of his interpretations of *Claudius* 25.4 was successful. The only question is why he bothered to introduce the present section with the statement that "in his ninth year the Jews were expelled by Claudius from the city." As for the event itself and his two interpretations of it, there was no reason for including the introduction. It merely repeats in less detail the information supplied by the other text. The one new thing added is the date ("anno eiusdem nono," i.e., 49 CE) presently under discussion, the best claim for the authenticity of which lies in the question of Harnack, "Wer sollte auch ein Interesse gehabt haben, es ["anno eiusdem nono"] zu erfinden?"[65]

Middle Ages, Orosius' part in the development of Christian anti-Judaism deserves further consideration.

[62]*Historiarum* 7.6.17-18. That Orosius linked Jew and pagan Roman in this way is clear from 7.5.1 where he wrote concerning the deserved punishment of "blasphemous Romans" and "persecuting Jews." The actual warning occurs already in 7.3.1.

[63]*Historiarum* 7.7.10-13.

[64]Ibid., 7.6.8, 11. Orosius adapted his source, the *Chronicle*, by moving Peter's arrival in Rome from Claudius' second to his first year so as to imply that the positive events of that year could be attributed to Peter's appearance.

[65]Harnack, "Chronologische Berechnung," p. 676.

Indeed, whose purposes could have been well served by something so apparently minor as the invention of a date?

Quite clearly, and cleverly, those of Orosius himself. In the first place, he was familiar with the apologetic value of manipulating his dates.[66] Second, the way in which he chose to compose the chapter on Claudius made necessary the insertion of chronological detail just at this point. That is, the other undated materials appear in the first half of the chapter (*Historiarum* 7.6.1-8). But, as noted above, the mood pervading that section is positive; it focuses upon the blessings brought about by the unhindered arrival of Christianity at Rome. Resultantly, although *Claudius* 25.4 shares with these materials a lack of absolute date, Orosius could not make use of it there because this would have contradicted his purpose of showing how the Roman embrace of Christianity had produced salutary results for Rome. At *Historiarum* 7.6.9, however, he turned to an annalistic style and so assigned a particular year for the remaining incidents which he narrated.[67] In terms of composition, therefore, if he wished to use Suetonius, he had to find space for it in *Historiarum* 7.6.9-18, and, to do that, he had to give it a date.

Third, the basic requirement of the date was that it serve his own purposes, and this would occur if it were possible to show some Roman disaster as the result of imperial hostility to Christianity. In terms of his principal source both for events and chronology in the time of Claudius, Orosius had limited options. For the emperor's first eight years, the *Chronicle* indicates no disasters,[68] and for his ninth year there is nothing. Year ten is different. It reads, "Magna fames Romae" ("great famine at Rome") and so provides an event for several reasons suitable to Orosius' apologetic redaction. That is, the famine was an evil which struck Rome directly, it was grave, and it was a personal disaster for Claudius. This Orosius was able to make clear by supplementing the account in the *Chronicle* with material from *Claudius* 18.2 which relates how, as a result of famine, the emperor

---

[66]See p. 126, n. 64.

[67]The exception is *Historiarum* 7.6.18 which, with the omission of date, foreshortens and so serves Orosius' purpose by associating the murder of Claudius with his abuse of Christians.

[68]For these years the *Chronicle* refers to only three negative events, and none of them brought direct sufferings to the Romans themselves. The first, under year four, is the famine prophesied by Agabus. The second, under year eight, is the massacre of Jews in Jerusalem while Cumanus was procurator. The last, under the same year, is a Greek famine. Orosius made use of the first and second, the first to show God's care for Christians, the second to remind readers of Jewish suffering following the death of Jesus.

was insulted and humiliated when the hungry mob pelted him with bread and forced him to flee from the Forum.[69] Fourth, it was near enough to the end of his fourteen years in power to permit the foreshortening of events by the omission of the *Chronicle*'s references to Felix and Paul in year ten through thirteen and the substitution for them of the Suetonian tradition (*Claudius* 29.2) concerning the most unfortunate fate of several Roman senators and knights. In Orosius they met this just after the terrible events of year ten.[70] Then came the death of the emperor, but whereas the *Chronicle* reports it as such, Orosius followed *Claudius* 44.2 with the apologetically useful tidbit that he had been poisoned.

In other words, taking his cue from and then supplementing the *Chronicle*'s reference to the great famine during Claudius' tenth year, he placed the undated *Claudius* 25.4 directly in front of that year and so fulfilled in the clearest possible terms his apologetic task. With far more intelligence than Harnack is willing to credit him, he invented the materials attributed to Josephus in order to be able to assign year nine to his Suetonian tradition.[71] Then, since "following" implies both temporal and causal relationship, he underlined this cause-effect motif by changing the *Chronicle*'s year ten to "sequenti anno."[72] Thus, it is no wonder that scholarship has been unable to discover where Orosius found his Josephan tradition because, in fact, he made it up.[73] Hence,

---

[69]Because Suetonius provided no date for this event either, it was left to Orosius to make the connection between the *Chronicle*'s reference and what happened to Claudius.

[70]Since Suetonius did not date this material, Orosius was again free to place it where his own purposes were best served.

[71]He was not the first to use Josephus in this way, for Eusebius (*Ecclesiastical History* 2.23.20) quoted him as stating that the siege of Jerusalem resulted from the murder of Jesus' brother James. Intrinsically impossible on the lips of Josephus but corresponding exactly to the view of Eusebius, it appears nowhere among the writings of the former and merits no historical consideration. Feldman (trans., in Josephus, *The Life, Against Apion, The Jewish War, Jewish Antiquities*, 10:109, n. e) does suggest that this and the same claim in Origen (*Against Celsus* 1.47) may have arisen over confusion with the statement concerning John the Baptist in *Antiquities* 18.116, but the fact that Eusebius' citation of Josephus exactly fits his own views and not those of the historian himself leads to the suspicion that "Josephus" was really an alter ego among early Christian apologists.

[72]As noted already, Orosius later used this method ("subsequente autumno") to explain the disaster befalling Rome and Nero after the death of Peter and Paul.

[73]So much then for Goetz' view (*Geschichtstheologie*, p. 25) that "tatsächlich scheint Orosius sich im allgemeinen bemüht zu haben, möglichst objektiv vorzu-

though Acts 18:2 and *Claudius* 25.4 likely make reference to the same event, neither Acts nor the elaboration of Suetonius in Paulus Orosius provides us with convincing evidence of an expulsion of Roman Jewry in 49 CE. As a result, 41 CE excluded, the years 49 and 52 no more or less probably witnessed this Claudian measure than did any other during the 41-54 CE rule of that emperor.[74]

Reviewing the last two chapters, we may suppose that Claudius' predecessors would have been proud of him, for, as soon as he was in power, Roman Jews became the clear object of his policymaking. More generally, Tacitus wrote of the emperor's anxiety about the deleterious effects of *externae superstitiones* on traditional Roman religion. Also, in his Alexandrian letter of 41 CE, we hear Claudius' very own voice: Jews were, he suspected, a potential plague on the whole world. More particularly, at the same time he took the measures against Roman Judaism known to us from Dio and almost certainly elaborated upon in *Legatio* 155-158. Thereafter, between 42 and 54 CE, came a second major blow, the apparently single expulsion remembered in Suetonius, the author of Acts, Paulus Orosius and, again, Philo. Concerning its results we are at least minimally informed by the scholium to Juvenal which, whether related to the Claudian expulsion or not, certainly does underscore the miserable fate of those Jews whom Claudius, with his "concern for the underdogs of society,"[75] had driven from the city.

---

gehen und trotz seiner apologetischen Tendenz die Quellen recht sinngemäss wiederzugeben." Far better is Serafino Prete, "Un episodio del sacco gotico di Roma del 410: Hieron., *Ep.* 127,13–Oros., *Histor.*, VII 39," *Storiografia e storia: Studi in onore di Eugenio Duprè Theseider*, ed. Massimo Petrocchi, 2 vols. (Rome: Bulzoni editore, 1974), 2:540: "In conclusione il testo orosiano è un pomposo rivestimento d'un episodio semplice, condotto con apparato retorico e con intento apologetico, al fine di innalzarlo a fatto simbolo dell'azione divina nella storia e, in particolare, nella economia della salvezza, nella quale risplende sempre la Provvidenza divina. Tutta l'opera orosiana è pervasa da questa idea."

[74]For a slight caveat see p. 122, n. 42.

[75]Cf. p. 28.

Chapter Six

41 CE: Claudius Establishes His Own Precedents for the Handling of Roman Jews and Their Cult

Having discovered that Suetonius and Dio wrote of separate Claudian measures against Roman Jews, we were able in the last chapter to focus on introductory questions linked with texts relating to *Claudius* 25.4 and the expulsion recounted there. We turn now to a discussion of Dio 60.6.6-7 and the year 41 CE with which it, P. Lond. 1912, and significant portions of *Legatio* 155-158 are associated. As indicated already, 41 CE is for our purposes a significant time. Claudius was then first able to establish his own precedents in the creation of imperial policy, and the surviving documentation reveals clearly that Roman Jews were one immediate object of those new policies.

Keeping in mind Tacitus' statement that Claudius was anxious about the harmful effects of *externae superstitiones* upon traditional Roman religion, we begin with the detailed analysis of what Dio 60.6.6 tells us of this matter: "Τούς τε ᾿Ιουδαίους πλεονάσαντας αὖθις, ὥστε Χαλεπῶς ἂν ἄνευ ταραχῆς ὑπὸ τοῦ ὄχλου σφῶν τῆς πόλεως εἰρχθῆναι, [Κλαύδιος] οὐκ ἐξήλασε μέν, τῷ δὲ δὴ πατρίῳ βίῳ χρωμένους ἐκέλευσε μὴ συναθροίζεσθαι." For the sake of convenience it has been possible so far to cite this passage according to the LCL translation, but for present purposes a more exact rendering is necessary. Specifically, the core of the text is a classical μέν-δέ parallel construction consisting of the contrast between what Claudius did and did not do. The two main verbs (ἐξήλασε, ἐκέλευσε) are aorists governing the same direct object (τούς τε ᾿Ιουδαίους) differentiated by the modification of two separate participles (πλεονάσαντας, χρωμένους):

131

Τούς τε ᾿Ιουδαίους πλεονάσαντας [Κλαύδιος] οὐκ ἐξήλασε μέν. Τούς τε ᾿Ιουδαίους τῷ δὲ δὴ πατρίῳ βίῳ χρωμένους [Κλαύδιος] ἐκέλευσε μὴ συναθροίζεσθαι.

He [Claudius] did not expel the having-become-excessive Jews. He [Claudius] did order the practicing-the-traditional-life Jews not to gather.

Or, with adverbs and particles added,

While he [Claudius] did not expel the again having-become-excessive Jews, he did in fact order the practicing-the-traditional-life Jews not to gather.[1]

Then, to the first of these two clauses, and by way of an aside, Dio added the further thought that, having become excessive again, Jews could hardly have been shut out of the city "without a disturbance by their crowd" ("ὥστε Χαλεπῶς ἂν ἄνευ ταραχῆς ὑπὸ τοῦ ὄχλου σφῶν τῆς πόλεως εἰρχθῆναι").

Looked at in terms of Dio's own attitude towards this happening, it is obvious that he had no great sympathy for its Roman Jewish victims. First, as Dio 60.6.1 and 60.8.4 indicate, he recorded it within the context of the positive actions of Claudius. Second, he could only account for the fact that Jews were not expelled by the consideration that there were just too many of them. Third, the verb πλεονάζω has a hostile sense of increase to the point of excess, an idea echoed in the phrase "disturbance by their crowd" and elsewhere in the previously cited Dio 37.17.1 and 57.18.5.[2] It is clear, then, that coupled with

---

[1]This is also the way Th. Reinach's French translation (*Textes*, p. 188, #107) understands the passage: "[Claudius] défendit *à ceux qui vivaient* d'après leurs coutumes nationales de se réunir." By passing over the parallel nature of the participles and the resultant differentiation between the Roman Jews in general and those in particular who practiced the traditional life, the LCL translation ("[Claudius] ordered them, *while continuing their traditional mode of life*, not to hold meetings.") muddles Dio's meaning, for it contradicts itself by implying that Claudius affirmed these ways while at the same time crippling the communal vehicles intended to facilitate them.

[2]Pp. 62-63, 55. Dio 52.35-36, words placed in the mouth of Augustus' friend Maecenas, provides an overview of Dio's religious views. No friend of the imperial cult (52.35), he affirmed traditional Roman practices and the imperial obligation to maintain them against the growth of foreign rites: "Do you not only yourself worship the Divine Power everywhere and in every way in accordance with the traditions of our fathers [τὰ πάτρια], but compel all others to honour it. Those who attempt to distort our religion with strange rites you should abhor and punish, not merely for the sake of the gods...but because such men, by bringing in new divinities in place of the old, persuade many to adopt foreign practices" (52.36.1-2).

Dio's report of an occurrence which took place in 41 CE are elements drawn directly out of his own third-century attitudes.[3] This raises the question of which information within the narrative reflects sources and which his own analysis, i.e., in Bell's terms, the question of fact as opposed to interpretation.[4]

The information itself is as follows: first, the Roman Jewish population had reached excess once again by the time when Claudius became emperor; second, it would hardly have been possible for the emperor to expel these people without disturbances; third, Claudius did not expel them; fourth, he did command the Jews practicing their traditional way of life not to assemble. Among these details, however, only the affirmation concerning Claudius' prohibition of assemblies of the pious reflects the source behind Dio's reporting, for everything else within the text is based upon a negation, i.e., "he [Claudius] did not expel the...Jews," and belongs therefore to Dio's own cogitations on the situation. Specifically, as indicated already,[5] there exists a direct contrastive relationship between the present text and Dio 57.18.5 with this latter's statement that Tiberius did expel the great numbers of Roman Jews. Hence, given the quite similar situations but different imperial actions, Dio 60.6.6 asserts simply that, contrary to Tiberius, Claudius did not banish Roman Jews.[6] Concerning why this emperor might not have preferred such a procedure, Dio then surmised, as the conditional ἄv tells us, that it was because the many Jews might have caused a disturbance.[7]

---

[3]Suetonius and Tacitus were not great friends of the Jewish people either. Macé (*Essai sur Suétone*, pp. 59-63; similarly, Andrew Wallace-Hadrill, *Suetonius: The Scholar and His Caesars* [London: Duckworth, 1983], pp. 131 and 190) associates Suetonius' aversion to Judaism with his devotion to traditional Roman rites. Pointing out that Suetonius' report of the Claudian expulsion was included among Claudius' good actions, Baldwin (*Suetonius*, pp. 354-355) notes the same hostility. Tacitus' "personal antipathy to the Jews" (Bruce, "Tacitus," p. 34; cf. Lévy, "Tacite," pp. 339-340) is familiar to all readers of his *Histories* 5.

[4]Bell, "Egypt" in *CAH*, 10:873.

[5]P. 108.

[6]When Smallwood (*Jews under Roman Rule*, p. 215) claims "Dio's statement that in 41 Claudius suspended the Jews' right of assembly because they were too numerous to expel may mean that he first threatened an expulsion," her "may" hints at the recognition of this. She is preferable to Momigliano (*Claudius*, pp. 31-32) who supposes that Dio had access to the mind of Claudius.

[7]So already Luedemann, *Paul*, p. 166, n. 74. We need to keep in mind also that in contexts like the present one the idea of excess is subjective. That is, it reveals more about the person describing the situation than about the situation itself.

Caveats aside, that is, Dio reported how in 41 CE Claudius did in fact "order the practicing-the-traditional-life Jews not to gather." As a result, though regularly overshadowed by *Claudius* 25.4 or simply overlooked,[8] Dio 60.6.6 provides us with revealing glimpses in two directions. On the one hand, it permits us to catch sight of the new emperor as he immediately set out to curtail the Roman practice of this particular *externa superstitio*. On the other, it reveals Roman Jews trapped between devotion to their god and subjection to their absolute ruler. Claudius was obviously aware, in other words, that he could strike a significant blow against the Roman Jewish cult by prohibiting its adherents from coming together. Even minimizing this, therefore, Scramuzza still finds himself forced to admit that Jewish worship was "hedged with certain rigid regulations."[9] Mommsen is more accurate; though minimizing in his own way, he recognizes that according to Dio it was the real intention of Claudius "den Juden die Ausübung ihres Gottesdienstes zu untersagen,"[10] i.e., to stop them from worshipping their god. Thus, even if we knew nothing more than what Dio 60.6.6 tells us, it would be clear that the object of Claudian hostility was Roman Judaism rather than the Roman Jews per se and that a prominent weapon used against this cult was the prohibition of synagogue-associated[11] activity.

Containing both of these elements, Philo's previously introduced *Legatio* 155-158[12] provides us with what certainly appears to be the mirror-sharp reflection of the measures mentioned by Dio, and it is a reflection all the more valuable for its contemporaneity and resultant vividness of detail. As to the first element, *Legatio* 155-158 is entirely clear that the measures which it describes were aimed not at Roman Jewry but rather at the practice of Judaism within Rome. Specifically, *Legatio* 155 states quite clearly concerning Augustus that he

> was aware that the great section of Rome on the other side of the Tiber is occupied and inhabited by Jews, most of whom were Roman

---

[8]From a historiographic perspective it is revealing that so much has been written about *Claudius* 25.4 and so little about Dio 60.6.6-7. This is perhaps to be accounted for by the claim that the former concerns earliest Christianity at Rome. Thus, even among the few scholars who recognize its independence from *Claudius* 25.4 (cf. p. 97, n. 24), there has been little consideration of Dio 60.6.6-7.

[9]Scramuzza, "Policy" in *Beginnings of Christianity*, 5:296.

[10]Mommsen, "Religionsfrevel" in *Gesammelte Schriften*, 3:411, n. 3.

[11]*Synagogue* used here as both the gathering and the gathering place.

[12]Cf. p. 90.

citizens emancipated. For having been brought as captives to Italy they were liberated by their owners and were not forced to violate any of their native institutions [τῶν πατρίων].

This text is important for what it reveals to us about how Philo interpreted the difficulties that faced contemporary Roman Jews: the imperial threat did not arise as a reaction to the presence of a large Jewish population in the city. Instead, its cause was anxiety about the customary practices ["τῶν πατρίων"] of this population. In other words, the measures to which Philo referred were not directed against Roman Jews as Roman Jews but as practitioners of a certain set of traditional customs. This also is what Dio communicated. He too was specific that the emperor Claudius had *not* taken measures against the big Roman Jewish population, i.e., against what he called the "having-become-excessive Jews," but against Roman Jews insofar as they practiced Judaism, i.e., against the "practicing-the-traditional-life Jews."

Dio 60.6.6 and *Legatio* 155-158 have as their second element in common that the imperial measures against Roman Judaism took the form of prohibiting synagogue associated activity. The third-century Dio expressed this summarily when he wrote that Claudius ordered "the practicing-the-traditional-life Jews not to gather." A contemporary of that order, Philo was in a position to know more about what its execution entailed. As indicated already,[13] that is, among the six measures which *Legatio* 155-158 insists Augustus had not used for the purpose of coercing Roman Jews into the violation of their religious customs, three, i.e., violence against the houses of prayer, prevention of meetings for religious instruction, and opposition to the offering of first fruits, have as their common locus actions taken against the corporate religious life of the Roman Jewish community. It is this issue, then, which constitutes the bulk of Philo's implied contrast, especially since associated with it are his additional references to houses of prayer, gatherings in them especially on the Sabbath for religious study, and the collection of the first fruits for Jerusalem.

In sum, combining this close correspondence between Dio 60.6.6 and *Legatio* 155-158 with the likelihood that the latter had Claudius specifically in mind,[14] it is reasonable to think that both texts are remembering the same occurrence. Either way, in any case, Claudius almost immediately after assuming control of the imperial machinery began to take steps against those Roman Jews who were insistent on the practice of their traditional mode of life, and he did so by ordering them not to assemble.

---

[13]P. 95.

[14]Pp. 93-96.

Tendentiousness run wild appears to be the only explanation for a free emendation of this material by modern interpreters. Ignoring the explicit statement of Dio that the Claudian measures were aimed against the Roman practice of Judaism, various modern writers fall back upon the stereotypical image of Jews as troublemakers in order to account for this particular imperial action. Guterman suggests a "turbulence in meetings,"[15] and Jewett refers to "some public disorder or infraction of Roman regulations."[16] Though unable to identify it, Schürer is certain that Claudius had good reasons for taking these measures against Roman Jews;[17] Juster makes an appeal to what he calls "troubles;"[18] Luedemann supposes that Claudius was responding to some "concrete incident that endangered the political peace of Rome;"[19] Momigliano states that the cause was "the same nuisance of Jewish unrest" which engendered the emperor's hostile letter to Alexandria;[20] and Barbara Levick claims to discover some unspecified

---

[15]Guterman, *Religious Toleration*, p. 150. Like others, he arrives at this conclusion on the basis of the false harmonization of the accounts in Dio and Suetonius. How unnecessary to his theory even this reason is becomes clear from the fact that he provides no foundation whatsoever for his explanation on the very same grounds of the 19 CE expulsion under Tiberius (p. 149).

[16]Jewett, *Chronology of Paul's Life*, p. 37. He goes on to indicate that "the specific cause for the disturbance in A.D. 41 is unknown." This is an interesting comment because it searches for the unknown cause of an unknown disturbance.

[17]Schürer, *History*, 3^1:1.77 and 3^1:1.77, n. 91.

[18]Juster, *Les Juifs*, 1:411. These troubles he presumably conceives in terms of his stereotype of Jews as "peuple séditieux" (2:182), a claim which he bases in part on the Alexandrian anti-Jew Apion and the fathers of the church (2:182, n. 2; cf. 1:220, n. 8) as well as upon the testimony of Cicero (cf. May, "Politique religieuse," p. 18), of Augustine and John Chrysostom in particular, and of the Acts of the Apostles (2:198-199; so also, May, "Politique religieuse," p. 39, n. 2), all of whom were tendentious observers. Insofar as how Acts molded its material so as to take advantage of and further propagate this stereotype, see Slingerland, "'The Jews' in the Pauline Portion of Acts," passim.

[19]Luedemann, *Paul*, p. 165.

[20]Momigliano, *Claudius*, pp. 32, 34. As will be discussed shortly, Smallwood (*Jews under Roman Rule*, p. 214; cf. Bruce, "Christianity," p. 314) also suggests an association between the Alexandrian letter and the event described by Dio. Momigliano is able to read Dio more accurately, for in the same place he suggests alternatively that the cause might have been associated with religious issues, i.e., with proselytism (Cf. Meyer, *Ursprung*, 3:463, who also refers to Jewish propaganda among Roman citizens). Incomplete in itself, this at least recognizes something of the religious dynamic.

"violence at Rome."[21] To sum up such opinions, in other words, rabble-rousing Jews were to be blamed, and the emperor was merely doing his best to restore the peace.

Smallwood alone, however, provides evidence in support of this view. She writes,

> Dio, by giving no indication of the Jews' offence, creates the impression that Claudius attacked them gratuitously. But such an action would be uncharacteristic of Claudius with his sense of justice and his concern for the underdogs of society, and would follow strangely on his recent edicts reaffirming Jewish rights in Alexandria and throughout the empire. Some unrecorded provocation must have occurred. It is probably no accident that Dio groups Claudius' treatment of the Jews with his disbandment of the perennial trouble-makers, the *collegia*, which Gaius had reintroduced, and his imposition of restrictions on taverns. All three rulings can be seen as police measures issued in answer to recent disorders.[22]

Thus, explicitly contradicting the clear sense of Dio 60.6.6, Smallwood appeals to the justice and goodness of Claudius, the Josephan edicts, and the broader context of Dio 60.6.6-7 in support of the typical view that Roman Jews were to be blamed for the attack of the new emperor upon them.

Nonetheless, insofar as Claudius' sense of justice and goodness are concerned, the arguments for this must be made on a case-for-case basis, and in the present instance it becomes obligatory that we take seriously Smallwood's own statement that, according to Dio, Claudius attacked Roman Jews *gratuitously*. As to her utilization of the edicts in Josephus,[23] it is inappropriate. Having previously observed the difficulty of basing any conclusions upon them and being likewise familiar with the hostile remarks of Claudius in his unquestionably genuine Alexandrian letter, we shall more wisely reverse Smallwood's argument and so conclude that Dio has furnished us with one more piece of evidence against their trustworthiness. Otherwise, they would represent at best the general modus operandi in these matters but would not, as the text of Dio itself indicates, preclude imperial measures of an anti-Jewish nature. In other words, the edicts under no circumstances are able to change the sense of Dio himself that the intention of Claudius was to prohibit the practice of Jewish rites within the city of Rome.

---

[21]Barbara Levick, *Claudius* (New Haven: Yale University Press, 1990), p. 184.

[22]Smallwood, *Jews under Roman Rule*, p. 215.

[23]She follows Momigliano (*Claudius*, pp. 30-31) and Schürer (*History* 3¹:77).

Again, concerning the broader context within which Dio made his remarks about the prohibition of Jewish gatherings, Smallwood's language is necessarily vague because it has no foundation within its source. Specifically, since Dio indicated that they were only potential, she has no basis within the text for her reference to "recent disorders." Instead, the common denominator of this topically arranged unit is Claudius' interdiction of various types of gathering at the beginning of his reign.[24] Each of these he prohibited for a different reason: the club in order to restore the imperial status quo prior to Gaius; the food establishment for the purpose of the reformation of daily life; the synagogue as a measure against Jewish religion.

In addition, Smallwood also faces difficulties with her claim that the prohibition in Dio amounted only to the "milder punishment of the temporary closure of the synagogues."[25] First, the picture which her statement engenders of buildings being boarded up is not accurate, for the prohibition was against religious meetings ("μὴ συναθροίζεσθαι"), and these, as already indicated, without doubt took place in a variety of different settings.[26] Second, "milder" has very little meaning except from the perspective of the third-century speculations of Dio but is completely misleading insofar as what it, according to Philo, actually signified for Roman Jews prohibited from following their traditional mode of life.[27] Finally, Smallwood's usage of the word "temporary" is without foundation.[28] All Dio remarked was that, soon after becoming emperor, Claudius took the necessary measures to keep Roman Jews from gathering for the practice of their traditional way of life. He

---

[24]On account of this arrangement, Jones ("Claudius," p. 31) associates the prohibition of the Jewish gatherings with the enforcement of "strict regulations in accordance with the law concerning *collegia*." The same is true of Guterman (*Religious Toleration*, p. 150). Huidekoper (*Judaism at Rome*, p. 222, n. 116) goes so far as to associate Judaism also with the taverns of the passage in Dio. In doing so, they miss the topical arrangement of Dio 60.6.6-7.

[25]Smallwood, *Jews under Roman Rule*, p. 215.

[26]See appendix 1.

[27]Momigliano (*Claudius*, p. 32) assumes that the prohibition was the result of Agrippa's benevolent influence upon Claudius, but he has no evidence to support this view. Furthermore, it is hard to grasp the kind of benevolence which would have made practically impossible important aspects of Jewish life in Rome.

[28]Juster (*Les Juifs*, 1:411) supports the temporary nature of the prohibition with his observation that Claudius' edict in *Antiquities* 19.286-291 would shortly have canceled it (1:411, n. 4). Nevertheless, besides the fact that this argument depends for its validity upon the questionable worth of the edict, it also fails to recognize that such decrees were not intended to govern Claudius' own actions.

provided no basis for the conclusion that Claudius either intended to or ever did rescind this regulation. Instead, insofar as we know, his next action vis-à-vis Roman Jews was to expel them. Such a sequence reminds us of the earlier ultimatum of the emperor Tiberius giving Jews and Egyptians the choice between abandoning their religious practices and being expelled from Rome. In so doing, it suggests strongly that the ultimate cause of the subsequent Claudian expulsion was likewise religious.

Thus, since Dio expressed himself only in a potential way about "provocation," "turbulence," and "some public disorder or infraction of Roman regulations," Smallwood's notion of Claudius' "sense of justice and his concern for the underdogs of society" has little to do with the event of which we learn in Dio 60.6.6 and *Legatio* 157.[29] The result: reality is much better served by her other statement that in this case Claudius acted gratuitously against Roman Jews, for what lies before us is not some infraction of Roman law but the imperial establishment of a new regulation, the intention of which was to cause the demise of Roman Jewish religious life.

This, to a significant degree, Mommsen also recognized. In his opinion it was primarily the Roman-citizen Jews, i.e., former slaves Jewish by birth or citizen proselytes, who were the object of this as well as of the other imperial operations against Roman Jews.[30] Why? Because as citizens having obligations to the deities of Rome[31] they

---

[29]Similar is the previously discussed view typified by Leon's statement (*Jews of Ancient Rome*, p. 21) that "the reign of Claudius...began auspiciously for the Jews," as well as his comment (p. 26) about Claudius' "liberal attitude." For his opinion he relies upon the two edicts of Claudius cited by Josephus. Thus, in referring to the emperor's Alexandrian letter, he is surprised by its "unexpected severity" (p. 23). In fact, we should be surprised to have found anything else in that text. It is beyond the scope of the present study to examine Leon's similar statement about the tranquil situation of Roman Jews under Nero (pp. 27-28) except insofar as to indicate that this would have been a most callous form of tranquility as thousands of friends and family members were threatened with slaughter at the very same time that the unspeakable destruction of the cult center loomed. (Cf. the Gospel of Mark, perhaps written in Rome and apparently very much concerned with events in the East at this time.) Moreover, after the expulsion under Claudius we do not know how many Jews remained in the city to be tranquil. Smallwood (*Jews under Roman Rule*, p. 216, n. 46) uses Romans 16 to indicate that Jews soon returned to that city; however, it is not clear either when Romans was written or if Romans 16 belonged originally to it. I share the view of those (cf. p. 120, n. 33) who believe that Romans 16 reads more easily as a note to Ephesus.

[30]Mommsen, "Religionsfrevel" in *Gesammelte Schriften*, 3:404-405, 412-413.

[31]Ibid., 3:390, 399, 400, 401, 406, 412.

were kept from fulfilling these by the monotheistic demands of Roman Judaism.[32] Formulated thusly, however, Mommsen's position is not entirely accurate. In the first place, and as already indicated,[33] the monotheistic demands of Judaism may well have been less absolute and more tolerant than Mommsen postulates. More important, this interpretation draws an insupportable line between the imperially approved practice of Judaism among non-citizens and the prohibition of that practice among citizens even of Jewish origin. In other words, it is not possible to see so neat a distinction within the previously traced history of imperial attitudes towards and actions against Roman and other diaspora Jews.[34]

---

[32]Mommsen, "Religionsfrevel" in *Gesammelte Schriften*, 3:404; cf. Mommsen, *Römisches Strafrecht*, Systematisches Handbuch der Deutschen Rechtswissenschaft, vol. 1.4 (Leipzig: Duncker und Humblot, 1899), pp. 573-574; similarly, Meyer, *Ursprung*, 3:516-517.

[33]See pp. 32-33.

[34]Vis-à-vis the 19 CE actions of Tiberius, Juster (*Les Juifs*, 2:164, n. 5) makes clear the overly neat character of Mommsen's claim ("Religionsfrevel" in *Gesammelte Schriften*, 3:404) that these were directed only against Jewish citizens of Rome. In any case, he is of the opinion that Roman citizens Jewish by birth *were* privileged to practice their own religion (*Les Juifs*, 1:245, 255-259, 2:15; so, similarly, La Piana, "Foreign Groups," p. 375; Bruce, *Commentary*, p. 368; Sherwin-White, *Racial Prejudice*, p. 100; cf. Guterman, *Religious Toleration*, pp. 14 and 90-91, who, while rejecting Juster's idea of privilege [p. 53], insists upon Judaism's consistent status as a *religio licita* open perhaps [pp. 39 and 119-120, but to the contrary, p. 122] to all citizens). Therefore, he also rejects (*Les Juifs*, 1:411, n. 2) Mommsen's interpretation of the passage presently under discussion. It should be noted, nonetheless, that for the period of interest to us, i.e., prior to 70 CE, Mommsen and Juster agree that the practice of Judaism in Rome was legal for foreign Jews and illegal for Gentile Roman citizens, i.e., proselytes (so too La Piana, "Foreign Groups," p. 387). They do disagree about the situation of foreign Jews who became Roman citizens. Contrary to Juster, Mommsen claims that such Jews had to give up this practice. Nevertheless, Merrill both implies (*Essays in Early Christian History* [London: Macmillan and Co., 1924], p. 44) and perhaps unintentionally demonstrates vis-à-vis the 19 CE banishment of all Roman Jews ("Expulsion," pp. 368-370) that the surviving sources refer neither much nor consistently to any of these distinctions. In fact, contrary to his own systematization otherwise, Guterman (*Religious Toleration*, pp. 118-119) does recognize for Roman Judaism what applied otherwise there to the cult of Isis: "It is clear then that the governmental policy toward the foreign cults, which were often admitted by law, was essentially the policy of individual magistrates or emperors, and this differed." (Cf. Frend, *Martyrdom*, p. 84: "The cult of Isis was the subject of a bewildering series of conflicting decisions.") Also important in this regard are the observations of May. Though it is impossible to accept his blanket view that imperial actions of an anti-Jewish nature were not directed against the practice of the religion, he does insist that the imperial treatment of these matters

Furthermore, having pronounced that Roman citizens could not be expelled from the city,[35] Mommsen can explain the Tiberian and Claudian expulsion of persons who according to his schema must have been such citizens only by denying that they had really been banished: "Die römischen Bürger jüdischen Glaubens...wurden nicht geradezu ausgewiesen, sondern indirect gezwungen."[36] This is sophistry, for as Applebaum rightly concludes from the same series of events, "No one precise and comprehensive law governing Jewish rights existed.... When in the fifth century Theodosius examined the basis of Jewish privileges, he had to fall back on a negative formula: The sect of the Jews has been prohibited by no law."[37]

Relatedly, Mommsen needs to have taken more seriously the "administrative Willkür" of which he himself writes.[38] Four examples will clarify this. First, having included "Proselytenmacher" among those who would have been expelled, Mommsen grants implicitly that the measure was directed also against non-citizens in this ill-defined category which, depending upon the discretion of the magistrate, might have included every Jew in Rome.[39] Second, and similarly, he in fact states that non-citizens in general were liable to expulsion.[40] Third, while he professes correctly that according to *Claudius* 25.5 Augustus had prohibited only Roman citizens from Druidism,[41] he fails to note the statement in the same place that Claudius chose to handle the matter differently, i.e., he forbade all persons to practice

---

tended to be administrative rather than juridical ("Politique religieuse," p. 1; "Activité," p. 254, n. 1; cf. his "Notes complémentaires sur les actes de l'Empereur Claude," *Revue historique de droit français et étranger* 22 [1943]:101-114). About the different set of legal vagaries vis-à-vis Christians, Guterman (*Religious Toleration*, p. 121, n. 72) makes the same point. For a succinct and largely credible description of and rationale for Rome's treatment of foreign cults in general, see Frend, *Martyrdom*, pp. 77-93.

[35]Mommsen, "Religionsfrevel" in *Gesammelte Schriften*, 3:411; but otherwise in his *Strafrecht*, p. 48; cf. Juster, *Les Juifs*, 2:164, n. 5.

[36]Mommsen, "Religionsfrevel" in *Gesammelte Schriften*, 3:411, n. 3.

[37]Applebaum, "Legal Status" in *Jewish People*, 1:457. His reference is to the Theodosian Code 16.8.9: "Iudaeorum sectam nulla lege prohibitam satis constat."

[38]Mommsen, "Religionsfrevel" in *Gesammelte Schriften*, 3:397. On imperial whim in a different setting, see Garnsey and Saller, *Roman Empire*, p. 32.

[39]Mommsen, "Religionsfrevel" in *Gesammelte Schriften*, 3:403, 404.

[40]Ibid., 3:405, n. 7.

[41]Ibid., 3:403.

it. Fourth is Mommsen's claim that, because the word "Jew" meant a citizen of Judea and citizenship was exclusive, persons from there who had become Roman citizens were no longer Jews but Romans and so necessarily abandoned old religious ways for the new Roman ones.[42] Besides the fact that Mommsen provides no evidence for this position, Philo (*Legatio* 157) claims the opposite, i.e., that Augustus treated practicing Jews who were also Roman citizens with respect. Thus, since Philo's statement was made by way of contrast with a later emperor, imperial "Willkür" is visible here also.

Returning to the account in Dio, we have no reason to disagree with the interpretation of Mommsen that the Claudian measure made mention of in that source was directed against the practitioners of Judaism in the city of Rome. Still, there is no basis for his refinement of this thesis to refer only to Roman-citizen practitioners of the Jewish cult, for that view is supported neither by his general considerations nor in fact by anything within either Dio[43] or *Legatio* 157. At least insofar as the present instance is concerned, therefore, we have to take very seriously both the insistence of May that the anti-Jewish activities of Claudius were of a severity bordering upon persecution[44] and the similar observation of Momigliano that the same emperor was "inclined to put Judaism on a level with Druidism and to deal with it so far as possible by the same methods."[45] Although each of these two

---

[42]Mommsen, "Religionsfrevel" in *Gesammelte Schriften*, 3:416-418.

[43]So also Guterman, *Religious Toleration*, p. 148.

[44]May, "Politique religieuse," p. 13. For the sake of the thesis that Claudius not only encouraged but was actually attracted by foreign cults such as Judaism, May (pp. 1, 7, 10, 45-46) declares that the anti-Jewish measures of Claudius and his predecessors were political in character. They were, that is, directed at Jewish troublemaking rather than the religious practices. This position requires him to exclude the account in Valerius Maximus 1.3.3 from the history of Roman Judaism (pp. 15-17), to imply a confusion which the texts themselves deny to the account of Tiberius' measures against Jews and worshippers of Isis (pp. 20-21), to skim over the specifically religious charges which Gaius made against Jews (pp. 24-25), to assume that the expulsion in *Claudius* 25.4 was caused by violent disputes over the messiahship of Jesus (pp. 37-42), and to charge that Roman Jewish religious establishments were but a front for political disorder (p. 43). Interpreting the word *plague* of P. Lond. 1912 similarly (p. 34), he is, as we shall see, closer to the truth.

[45]Momigliano, *Claudius*, p. 34. As to the inclination to which Momigliano refers, he seems to exaggerate only a little, but in terms of method he appears to go too far. Even so, we have to keep in mind that upper-class Roman attitudes associated Judaism not only with the worship of the head of an ass but also with human sacrifice, a rite imputed to Druidism as well. May ("Politique religieuse," pp. 10-11) also points out the unique company which Judaism kept with Druidism

statements may perhaps suffer from some slight exaggeration, neither is very far removed from the Roman Jewish realities of the year when Claudius became emperor.

Moving on to the consideration of P. Lond. 1912, the letter which the new emperor addressed to citizens of Alexandria in 41 CE, we may not ignore the reality that differences did exist between the 41 CE situation of Roman and Egyptian Jews. In other words, although Dio indicated that Claudius had acted gratuitously against Roman Jewish religiosity, the emperor's letter signals a reaction to overtly political events in the city of Alexandria. For present purposes, nevertheless, it is important to appreciate how a single mentality was at work in both places.

First, we need to clarify the nature of these events. To do so, we must look initially at the third section of Claudius' letter where it becomes obvious that the specific matter of the "disturbances and rioting, or rather, to speak the truth, the war" relating to [πρός][46] the Alexandrian Jewish population had been brought to the attention of the emperor by the members of the Greek delegation.[47] This fighting produced much hostility upon the part of Claudius: "I harbour within me a store of immutable indignation against those who renewed [τῶν ἀρξαμένων] the conflict" (lines 77-78). Either of the two ways in which we may interpret the aorist participle,[48] Claudius' intention is clear:

---

under Claudius. Nevertheless, typical of his interest otherwise, he then interprets the emperor's hostility as directed not against Roman Jewish religion but against politically minded, excess Jewish populations and their meeting places (p. 43; cf. pp. 10, 17-18, 34, 36, 41-42, 45), a strange, anachronistic, and revealing example of which is modern (1938) Jewish migration to Palestine (p. 34, n. 4; cf. p. 23).

[46]As the text of Hunt and Edgar (trans., *Select Papyri*, 2:85) indicates, the preposition πρός can have only this sense in the present context, for Claudius' letter takes up issues raised by the Greek delegation, one of which would not have been a war *against* (cf. the *CPJ* translation) the Alexandrian Jews. Furthermore, translated as if the Greeks had attacked Jews, it would affirm what Claudius immediately denied, that he blamed either party directly. *CPJ*, 2:47 (at line 73) provides a different interpretation but similar conclusion. For the unfounded view most recently repeated by Luedemann (*Paul*, p. 168) that the letter was associated with the arrival of Christianity in Alexandria, see Salomon Reinach, "La première allusion au christianisme dans l'histoire: sur un passage énigmatique d'une lettre de Claude," *Revue de l'histoire des religions* 90 (1924):108-122. He associates Dio 60.6.6-7 and *Claudius* 25.4 with the arrival of the same cult in Rome. Seston's "L'Empereur Claude" is largely a response to Reinach.

[47]P. Lond. 1912, lines 73-104.

[48]"Renewed," as here in *CPJ*, 2:43 and Bell, *Jews and Christians in Egypt*, p. 28; "renews," as in Hunt and Edgar, trans., *Select Papyri*, 2:85.

he wanted the cessation of the hostilities that were the subject of this particular section.[49] That he was bringing up a most recent stage only and hence precisely what Josephus narrated in *Antiquities* 19.278-279 is not impossible:[50]

> About this time, there arose a feud between Jews and Greeks in the city of Alexandria. For upon the death of Gaius, the Jews, who had been humiliated under his rule and grievously abused by the Alexandrians, took heart again and at once armed themselves. Claudius commanded the prefect of Egypt to put down the factional war.

Nevertheless, this reference is unlikely. First, it assumes a restoration of the Alexandrian Jewish fortunes after the pogrom of 38 CE, but, as already considered, there is no reason to suppose that any significant amelioration occurred as long as Gaius governed. In fact, the above quotation declares as much. Second, Josephus was describing here the situation at the time when Claudius assumed power. Thus, because the letter came sometime later, its reference to renewed conflict may have in mind the disturbance of the settlement previously achieved by Claudius' prefect of Egypt.

Moreover, even if we could be sure that Claudius was referring to the event in Josephus, it would not follow that he recognized the Jewish responsibility for the renewal of conflict and was directing his "immutable indignation [ὀργή]" only against them.[51] This is because the language of Josephus does not fix the blame one-sidedly upon Alexandrian Jews. In the first place, just as Claudius had done by means of his subsequent admonitions to both sides, so Josephus also indicated here that present events were part of a continuum. Second, στάσις and στασιάζω, which form the leitmotiv of this brief section in Josephus, denote in their present context both division and, as the LCL translation rightly indicates, factionalism. That is, as the letter indicates, two parties were involved in Alexandria, and it is precisely

---

[49]*CPJ*, 2:47 (at line 75). Likewise, A. Kasher, "The Jewish Attitude to the Alexandrian Gymnasium in the First Century A.D.," *American Journal of Ancient History* 1 (1976):155. His thesis: Claudius' warning against infiltrating the gymnasium referred to Jewish attempts at disruption, not participation.

[50]So *CPJ*, 2:47-48 (at lines 75-78). Similarly, Hennig ("Bruchstücken," p. 321) sees three major clashes between Alexandrian Gentiles and Jews before the time of Trajan: the pogrom of 38 CE, the Jewish attack after Gaius' death, and the disturbances when Tiberius Julius Alexander was prefect. Drawing a sharp line between the first and second, he supposes the embassy to Claudius focused only upon the latter (p. 323).

[51]*CPJ*, 2:47-48 (at lines 75-78) indicates otherwise.

for such a reason that Claudius felt himself compelled to strike out against both: "I merely say that, unless you stop this destructive and obstinate mutual enmity, I shall be forced to show what a benevolent ruler can be when he is turned to righteous indignation [ὀργή]" (lines 79-82). This wrath, whether "immutable" or "righteous," amounted to nothing less than the extreme anger of Claudius caused by the recent hostilities between the Greeks and Jews in Alexandria. Consequently, since it was potentially directed against both sides in the latter case (lines 79-82), we have no basis for construing it differently in the former (lines 77-78).[52]

Thus, on the basis of the principles which had prevailed under Augustus (lines 86-88; cf. lines 57-59), Claudius ordered both groups to respond: "I conjure the Alexandrians to behave gently and kindly towards the Jews.... The Jews, on the other hand, I order not to aim at more than they have previously had..." (lines 82-98). Moreover, to this response he attached a promise: "if you *both* give up your present ways and are willing to live in gentleness and kindness with one another, I for my part will care for the city as much as I can" (lines 100-104). As a result, because of the apparently balanced judgment which Claudius brought to this situation and the good wishes which he expressed for the future of Alexandria, we have no difficulty in understanding how the discovery of the Claudian letter has played a principal part in helping to redeem the image of this emperor.[53]

More to the point for our purposes, the fairness and goodwill of the new emperor are not the only parts of his character visible here. That is, besides these we also witness at first hand a virulent anger buttressed by sharp invective and blatantly intimidatory language insistent upon terrifying its addressees into compliance with the demands of an absolute ruler.[54] In other words, it was on the basis

---

[52]Based on its correct view that the image of a philo-Jewish Claudius is obsolete, *CPJ*, 2:48 (at line 78) declares, "the whole Letter of Claudius is hostile to the Jews." Hence, the "immutable indignation" of Claudius must have been directed only at them (2:49 [at lines 79-83]); however, this last conclusion is too strong. First, we just saw that Claudius' hostility towards Alexandrian Jews did not preclude anger against Gentiles. In fact, *CPJ* in the same place admits as much: "The threat is directed to both sides." Second, the *Acta alexandrinorum* make clear Rome's difficulties with some segments of the Gentile population.

[53]Momigliano, *Claudius*, p. xiii. So too Bell, *Jews and Christians in Egypt*, p. 22; Scramuzza, *Claudius*, pp. 64-79; *CPJ*, 2:38.

[54]So already Th. Reinach, "L'empereur Claude," p. 114. Jews were not the only objects of Claudius' hostility. Identified as Seneca or not, the contemporary who described the intended apotheosis of Claudius in the *Apocolocyntosis* saw this same side of the emperor's character. Suetonius did also.

of his "immutable" and "righteous" wrath that Claudius ordered Jews and Greeks either to follow the separate courses which he had set out for each or to face the consequence of their disobedience.[55]

Furthermore, although these threats were directed in principle against Greeks and Jews, the letter was heavily stacked in favor of its Gentile recipients and so gave Jews much more to fear. For example, several members of the Greek delegation, Tiberius Claudius Barbillus and Tiberius Claudius Archibios above all, were friends of Claudius (lines 105-108), and he certainly seems to have been trying to protect the honor of the Alexandrian delegation as a whole as well as of one Dionysios, son of Theon, in particular.[56] In addition, the first third of the letter (lines 16-51) reveals a personal appreciation for the honors which the Alexandrian Greeks wanted to bestow upon the new emperor. However, several of these, e.g., the sacred groves, Jews could hardly have supported with great enthusiasm. Similarly, the second section (lines 52-72) either approves or leaves open the possible approval of the Greek requests, this time including ones associated with the cult of "the god Augustus" (lines 59, 60-61, 62), and again therefore at odds with what Jews could best offer.[57]

Most important in this regard is the fact that, after having given orders to Greeks and Jews alike, Claudius then directed one particular threat towards the latter community; that is, "If they disobey, I shall proceed against them in every way as fomenting a common plague for the whole world."[58] When we recall both the devastation experienced by Alexandrian Jewish populations in the summer of 38 CE as well as the subsequent two and a half years of hardship in that city, we might suppose that the Jews present for the reading of this pronouncement were less shocked by its "brutale Ton"[59] than is the modern reader.

Still, they certainly could not have taken it as an omen of good things to come or as a sign of imperial favor. This is true for several reasons. In the first place, an "immutable" and "righteous" indignation

---

[55]*CPJ*, 2:49 (at line 82) asserts that the language of Claudius' order to the Greek citizens was "far more polite" than that to Jews, but the distinction is not an obvious one.

[56]Lines 73-78; cf. *CPJ*, 2:47 (at line 73). Josephus (*Antiquities* 19.276) wrote that Alexander Lysimachus, the Jewish alabarch of Alexandria, was likewise the friend of Claudius.

[57]For both reasons, Scramuzza (*Claudius*, p. 67) is incorrect that Claudius was concerned not to offend the religious sensibilities of Alexandrian Jews.

[58]P. Lond. 1912, lines 98-100.

[59]Hennig, "Bruchstücken," p. 333.

characteristic of the third section of the letter now channels itself directly against Jews, i.e., against the very people "proceeded against" since 38 CE. Second, in the hearing of the Alexandrian Gentiles this hostile language furnished excellent foundations for the continued debasement of their Jewish neighbors, for any kind of response on the part of the latter might well have been interpreted as "disobedience." Furthermore, the Jews and Gentiles in their separate ways no doubt appreciated the pun of the new emperor here. Specifically, the phrase "common plague" ("κοινὴν νόσον") was pregnant with meaning when directed to that part of the world in which the story of disease-laden Jews and their expulsion had its origin.[60] In fact, one of the chief proponents of that story, Chaeremon, may well have been the person of the same name whom Claudius mentioned (line 17) as a member of the Alexandrian delegation.[61]

Because in 41 CE Claudius was occupying himself with the large diaspora communities of both Rome and Alexandria, it is reasonable to inquire about the relationship between Dio 60.6.6 and P. Lond. 1912. According to Momigliano, it was causal:

> If we assume that in the year 41 the Jews of Rome had given Claudius some reason to prohibit them from assembling, we shall have an explanation of the tone of his letter to the people of Alexandria,

---

[60]Seston ("L'Empereur Claude," pp. 284-286, 292-293) takes Claudius' use of *plague* as a synonym for *civil war*. Not appreciating its background in the present context, this interpretation limits the sense of the term unnecessarily.

[61]Bell (*Jews and Christians in Egypt*, p. 29) argues the identification, Jones ("Claudius," p. 18) and *CPJ* (2:44, at line 17) assume it, and Stern (*Authors*, 1:417) recognizes the possibility. That the deck was stacked in favor of the Alexandrian delegation is in any case clear from the names of several of its members, for while Gaius Julius Dionysios and Gaius Julius Apollonios appear to have had family ties back to the beginnings of the Julio-Claudian period, Tiberius Claudius Barbillus, Tiberius Claudius Phanias, Tiberius Claudius Archibios, and, if not identical with the former, Tiberius Claudius Apollonios derived their names, as Jones indicates ("Claudius," p. 18), directly from the favor of Claudius himself. This imbalance is all the more certain because, as noted previously, (p. 101, n. 44), the letter reveals the close relationship between Barbillus and the emperor. Overall, therefore, it appears that something of an analogy exists between this Alexandrian delegation and the one sent earlier to Gaius, for in that situation as well (*Legatio* 349-368) the emperor had been able to identify with the Alexandrians and their anti-Jewish gibes. All of this corresponds to the contention of *CPJ* that while Jewish life in Alexandria and Egypt was in steady decline under Roman rule (1:48, 52, 54, 55, 60-61, 64; cf. Box's edition of the *Flaccus, Philonis Alexandrini: IN FLACCUM*, pp. xix, xxix, liv), most Alexandrian Greeks were on positive terms with their Roman rulers (1:48, 64-65). Relatedly, Hennig ("Bruchstücken," pp. 318-319) finds in the earliest excerpts of the *Acta alexandrinorum* little anti-Roman tendency.

which is...probably subsequent to the events in Rome. In that letter he quite unexpectedly assumes a tone of the utmost violence towards the Jews, whom he accuses of 'fomenting an universal plague'. Historians have been bewildered.... Nothing with which the letter deals ...could justify Claudius in using such harsh language. The explanation may perhaps be that he was disgusted with the events in Rome which must recently have provoked or were about to provoke the measures recorded by Cassius Dio; or, perhaps better, that he resented being compelled to deal with the same nuisance of Jewish unrest in two different parts of the Empire.[62]

In other words, the extremely hostile tone of the Alexandrian letter arose wholly or in part as a result of the fact that Claudius already had been provoked at home by the "nuisance of Jewish unrest."

Several difficulties stand in the way of this interpretation. For one thing, it depends upon a very specific chronological relationship between the events in Rome and the sending of the letter: according to Momigliano, the former preceded and determined the hostile tone of the latter. Yet, as his own "probably" indicates, there is no evidence to support this view. All we know is that in both Rome and Alexandria the new emperor was soon expressing hostility towards Jews. Only the two dates are clear: Claudius took power at the end of January, 41 CE, and his Egyptian prefect had received and published the letter by early November of the same year. All else is conjecture.[63]

---

[62]Momigliano, *Claudius*, p. 34; cf. Bruce, "Christianity," p. 314. Smallwood (*Jews under Roman Rule*, p. 214), in following Momigliano, writes: "Claudius' irritated tone and his sudden irrelevant reference to trouble caused by Jews outside Alexandria may reflect his annoyance at having an outbreak of Jewish unrest on his hands in Rome before he had finished with that in Alexandria." Momigliano (*Claudius*, pp. 33-34) and Smallwood (*Jews under Roman Rule*, pp. 214, 215, 250) are surprised by the difference in tone between Josephus' Claudian edict to Alexandria and the letter Claudius certainly did send there. Their explanation: meanwhile, in an undocumented way, Roman Jews had misbehaved. May is similar but less consistent. Although aware of the letter's hostility ("Politique religieuse," pp. 31-35) and of Josephus' virtual invention of both edicts (pp. 35-36), he affirms Claudius' benevolent attitude towards Alexandrian Jews and contrasts it with the emperor's irritation at supposed Jewish troubles in Rome (pp. 25-26, 42 and 44). As indicated already, however, knowing Josephus' tendency to invent an impression of positive relations between Jews and Roman masters, we may follow the tack of *CPJ*, 1:70 and attribute the contrast between Josephus' edict and Claudius' own letter to the apologetic inventiveness of Josephus. For the same reason, there is no basis for the view of Maurits Engers ("Der Brief des Kaisers Claudius an die Alexandriner," *Klio* 20 [1926]:173-176) that this contrast derives from the fickleness of Claudius.

[63]*CPJ*, 2:44 (at line 13) makes clear the problem of when the letter was originally composed. That is, published in Alexandria during November, it was

The second difficulty is the quite obvious tendentiousness of its characterizations. Like Smallwood thereafter, it presumes to justify Claudius at the expense of Roman Jewry. On the one hand, that is, Momigliano stereotypically presumes "Jewish unrest." On the other, he takes for granted that the emperor was acting reasonably when "he quite unexpectedly assumes a tone of the utmost violence towards the Jews." Claudius had "some [good] reason" for the action reported by Dio, some good grounds which "could justify Claudius in using such harsh language." He was either "disgusted" by "provocative" events in Rome or he "resented" the same Jewish "nuisance" in both Rome and Alexandria. Nevertheless, beginning with the opposite thesis that reasonableness took a definite back seat in the matter of imperial policymaking vis-à-vis Jews, we have no need either to vilify Roman Jews for the sake of justifying Claudius or to resolve the inner inconsistency of the letter by introducing matters external to it. In other words, when it comes to the choice between contrasting theses, Momigliano's own observation is critical: "Nothing with which the letter deals...could justify Claudius in using such harsh language."

The third difficulty with this interpretation is that it allows presuppositions concerning "Jewish unrest" to override the obvious sense of Dio. He wrote explicitly that what the new emperor found objectionable about Roman Jews was not a hypothetical penchant for troublemaking but a concrete devotion to a particular way of life. Indeed, Momigliano almost admits as much by introducing this section with "If we assume...." Unsupported by Dio, however, the only basis for this assumption is the presupposition that Claudius functioned reasonably in the establishment of policies affecting Roman Jews. It is that presupposition, however, which Claudius' decisions in this case challenge. In reality, then, what Momigliano correctly describes as the unexpectedly harsh tone of Claudius' letter corresponds to the equally unanticipated or, to use Smallwood's term, gratuitous action of the same emperor against Roman Jews in the practice of their cult.

Overall, therefore, it is impossible to accept Momigliano's view concerning a cause-effect relationship between the event in Rome and the letter to Alexandria. Still, a relationship between them does exist, for both originated with Claudius as soon as he became emperor, and both were directed against large diaspora communities. On the basis of this nexus, a fundamental common denominator appears: it is the

---

written at Rome perhaps during early October. Nonetheless, as a response to the important Alexandrian delegation which must have travelled immediately to Rome upon the succession of Claudius, the letter appears, if composed so late, to be very tardy. Moreover, considering the matters of moment with which it deals, this lateness seems unlikely.

hostile mentality of Claudius early expressed both verbally by means of his letter and administratively by means of his order prohibiting the practice of Judaism at Rome. Furthermore, this prohibition is consistent with the free use of imperial power expressed in the letter, for no doubt in Rome too the emperor was sure of the righteousness of his actions. We need observe only that, in contrast to Dio 60.6.6, P. Lond. 1912 does assert the right of Alexandrian Jews to practice their cult. Hence, it was these rites specifically in Rome which Claudius sought to check. What happened next? As to the outcome of events in the city of Alexandria we have little information.[64] Insofar as Rome is concerned, the situation certainly deteriorated. That is, having immediately ordered the suppression of the Jewish *superstitio* there, Claudius sometime later expelled its practitioners from the city.

The predecessors of Claudius established hostile precedents for the handling of Roman Judaism, and, as demonstrated by Dio 60.6.6 and *Legatio* 155-158, he made these his own. We observed already the strange ideas about this cult current among members of the upper-class and imperial elite. Consequently, it becomes understandable that, in defense of the traditional Roman rites, the self-righteous absolutism of Claudius should have combined with such prejudicial ideas and so produced immediate policies curtailing the practice of the Jewish religion in Rome.

---

[64]Silence concerning further hostilities there during the following thirteen years of Claudius' rule may perhaps be taken to mean that the menacing tone of his letter acheived its purpose. Blatant attacks against Alexandrian Jews did not occur, the Jews themselves submitted to the political realities of a unfriendly environment overseen by an unsympathetic emperor, and some Jews no doubt prospered. We may suppose that this was the situation of the Alexandrian Jewish alabarch, Alexander Lysimachus. As noted already, he was a personal friend of Claudius (*Antiquities* 19.276). The same appears to have been true also in terms of Alexander's son Marcus Julius Alexander (*Antiquities* 19.277) and was certainly true of his more famous son, Tiberius Alexander. Moreover, *Antiquities* 20.147 refers to a Jew by the name of Demetrius who near the end of Claudius' rule was the prosperous alabarch of Alexandria. Still, silence is no more than that. We have seen already the complete silence of Josephus concerning Claudius' actions against the Roman Jews, and it may well be that the silence of the Alexandrian Philo concerning the settlement in that city was something less than a vote of approval for it. In any case, even if the threats and arrangements of Claudius did put a cap upon the situation in Alexandria, it lasted only as long as Roman domination was able to keep it so, for as soon as war broke out in Judea in 66 CE uprisings began in Alexandria (*War* 2.487-498).

Chapter Seven

Claudius 25.4 in Its Literary Context

At the time he became emperor in the year 41 CE, Claudius set about to prohibit the practice of the Jewish *superstitio* at Rome. Reflective of the long-standing, upper-class and imperial antipathy towards that eastern cult, this measure was entirely consistent with such antipathy and, together with it, furnishes the fundamental background against which to comprehend the next documented measure that the emperor employed in opposition to Roman Jews.

That action was to command the expulsion of the Roman Jewish community. With the allusion to "Jews who, having been sent from the city, travelled to Aricia," the scholium to Juvenal's *Satire* 4.117 perhaps refers to it. Philo's *Legatio* 157 almost surely implies that Claudius "ejected them [the large Jewish population of Trastevere] from Rome." Acts 18:2 is quite explicit: "Claudius had ordered all Jews to leave Rome." So too are both *Claudius* 25.4, "[Claudius] Iudaeos impulsore Chresto assidue tumultuantes Roma expulit," and its echo in Paulus Orosius.[1] Introducing these materials within chapter 5, we discovered that the reference, expressed in terms of the four common elements that Claudius expelled Jews from Rome, is likely to a single imperial expulsion.

Looking for evidence by which to establish the absolute date of this occurrence, we were able to learn only that it took place at some undeterminable time between 42 and 54 CE. Suetonius was of no help here, the same is true of *Legatio* 157, the Orosian dating has proven

---

[1]Because he repeats the Suetonian text and invents a Josephan one, we need no longer consider Orosius.

to be fallacious, and the evidence from Acts takes us nowhere. In fact, with the exception of Suetonius, the others tell us practically nothing more than that Claudius did in fact banish Jews from Rome. For this reason, the present chapter introduces a thorough literary analysis of *Claudius* 25.4 within the larger context of Suetonius' *De vita caesarum* as a whole.

We begin with the observation that *Claudius* 25.4 is part of the larger unit *Claudius* 22 to 25.5b.[2] Within it Suetonius combined three subunits (*Claudius* 22a), i.e., "religious ceremonies [caerimonias]" (*Claudius* 22), "civil and military customs" (*Claudius* 23-25.2), and "the condition of all classes at home and abroad" (*Claudius* 25.3-5b). Suetonius did not intend these subunits to be self-contained. First, his own introduction in *Claudius* 22 brings them together. Second, and of particular import for purposes of the present study, topics of religion open and close the unit as a whole. The initial concrete references (*Claudius* 22) are to the emperor's responsibilities in certain Roman cult practices, i.e., to his selection of priests, to his supervision of the praetor on the occasion of earthquakes, and to his own sacerdotal obligation in times of ill omen. Likewise, the final reference (*Claudius* 25.5b) belongs within the same category, for it describes how this emperor concluded his treaties in the Forum by means of a sacrificial pig and recitation of an old religious formula. Just prior to that, reference is made to the restoration of the temple of Venus Erycina in Sicily, before that to the desire of Claudius to bring the Eleusinian mysteries to Rome, and before that to his abolition of Druidism among the Gauls. Shortly before this last, the text mentions the expulsion of Jews from Rome. Furthermore, in the same way the Druidic religion was inseparably associated with the Gauls, the Venus of Eryx with the Sicilians, and the great mysteries of Eleusis with the Athenians, so from the perspective of Suetonius was Judaism with Jews.[3] In sum, though his references to Roman Jews and to the Gauls belongs to the subtopic "the condition of all classes at home and abroad,"[4] it is impossible to disassociate either from the religious subject matter integral to the larger unit.

Its immediate literary context established, we may now turn to a whole series of intertwining lexical, grammatical, and syntactical observations which are associated directly with the view of Suetonius that Claudius "Iudaeos impulsore Chresto assidue tumultuantes Roma

---

[2]*Claudius* 25.5c ("Sed et haec....") creates a significant transitional bridge between this and the next unit.

[3]Cf. Suetonius' understanding of the word *Iudaeus* in the discussion following.

[4]Cf. appendix 2.

expulit." The place to begin is with the predicate of *Claudius* 25.4, i.e., with "expulit," the third person singular, perfect indicative active of *expellere*. As the following examples clearly illustrate, in grammatical contexts similar to the present one Suetonius made use of this verb often:[5] (1) "[Iulius] collegam...Foro expulit" (*Julius* 20.1); (2) "Claudius Caudex...freto traiecto Poenos Sicilia expulit" (*Tiberius* 2.1); (3) "[Tiberius] expulit et mathematicos" (*Tiberius* 36); (4) "[Nero] matrem...Palatio expulit" (*Nero* 34.1); (5) "Alexandrini regem suum...expulerant" (*Julius* 11); (6) "cum venalicias...[Augustus] urbe expulisset..." (*Augustus* 42.3); (7) "praefecto regis provincia expulso" (*Julius* 4.2); (8) "qui ob expellendum urbe Ciceronem" (*Tiberius* 2.4).

All of these cases make clear that the basic sense of *expellere* is "to drive out" or, literally, "to expel." Moreover, in #1 ("Foro"), #2 ("Sicilia"), #4 ("Palatio"), #6 ("urbe"), #7 ("provincia"), and #8 ("urbe") Suetonius employed this verb with the ablative of place from which. "Roma" has the same function in *Claudius* 25.4. Similarly, as in #1 (Julius), #3 (Tiberius), #4 (Nero), and #6 (Augustus) the text does not state but certainly assumes that its subject is the emperor Claudius. Again, as that which is driven out appears in the accusative case ("collegam," #1; "poenos," #2; "mathematicos," #3; "matrem," #4; ("regem," #5; "venalicias," #6), so does "Iudaeos" in *Claudius* 25.4. As a result, there is no doubt concerning the basic sense of "[Claudius] Iudaeos Roma expulit." It states conclusively that this particular emperor expelled *Iudaeos* from Rome.

Iudaeus, however, requires consideration at greater length. In order to understand what Suetonius meant by this term, we are also compelled to scrutinize his utilization of the related words *Iudaea* and *Iudaicus*. The former of these is the designation of the geo-political entity to which Suetonius on several occasions made reference.[6] In *Vitellius* 15.1, *Vespasianus* 6.3, and *Domitianus* 2.1 he also applied the adjective *Iudaicus* in reference to this entity, and in *Vespasianus* 4.5 as well as in 8.1 *Iudaeus/Iudaei* pertains to the inhabitants of the same place, i.e., to the Judeans.

Inseparable from the geo-political sense of these terms is an ethnic dimension, for it is within the context of references to the *Jewish* war of 66-70 CE that they often make their appearance.[7] This is confirmed by the fact that Suetonius twice made the explicit ethnic

---

[5]For all instances see Howard and Jackson, *Index verborum*, p. 89.

[6]For all instances of *Iudaea*, *Iudaeus*, and *Iudaicus* see Howard and Jackson, *Index verborum*, p. 127.

[7]*Iudaeus* in *Vespasianus* 4.5 and 8.1; *Iudaicus* in *Domitianus* 2.1 and 12.2. We shall return to further ramifications of this context shortly.

association. In *Julius* 84.5 he identified "Iudaei" in Rome as good examples of the mass of "exterarum gentium" who lamented the death of Caesar, and in *Domitianus* 12.2 he likewise referred to the tribute imposed upon the Jewish people ("imposita genti tributa"). In other words, when Suetonius used *Iudaeus*, his primary point of reference was Judea and the *gens* indigenous to it, i.e., the Judeans, conceived as foreign (*exterus*) from the Roman perspective.

In addition to this unified geo-political and ethnic element which Suetonius associated with *Iudaeus*, he also added to it a fundamental religious connotation. This becomes manifest in both *Tiberius* 36 and *Domitianus* 12.2. According to the latter, under the emperor Domitian "the *Iudaicus fiscus* was carried out most harshly. In this regard, those were indicted who either lived a Jewish life [Iudaicam vitam] privately or who, having concealed their origin [dissimulata origine], did not pay the tax imposed upon the people [genti]."[8] Here Suetonius concerned himself with two categories of persons who sought to avoid payment of the "Iudaicus fiscus" imposed according to Josephus (*War* 7.218) upon "Ἰουδαῖοι" everywhere following the termination of the war against Rome.

As was indicated already, Suetonius' description of the second category makes clear that, in his understanding, the *Iudaicus fiscus* affected *Iudaei* conceived as belonging to a particular *gens* or ethnic entity, a point which he made afresh with the statement that this category consisted of the *Iudaei* who pretended not to have had their origins ("dissimulata origine") in that *gens*. For present purposes, what matters is that Suetonius associated the concealment of origins, i.e., the pretending not to be what one really was, with the characteristic by which he identified persons within the first category. That is, this first category did live the "Iudaicam vitam", i.e., it did practice the traditional life which Suetonius associated with *Iudaei*. As an example of the lengths to which Domitian was willing to go, Suetonius then narrated an incident he himself had witnessed as a child, presumably in Rome. Specifically, some old man endured great humiliation when examined publicly to determine if he had been circumcised. Thus, the fact that Suetonius utilized this example within the present context makes explicit what we would have otherwise assumed, that from his own perspective, religious rites, in this case circumcision, belonged to the essence of those traditional things which made up the *Iudaicam vitam* and so defined *Iudaei*.

Even clearer in this regard is the previously discussed *Tiberius* 36. In that account, which appears among positive imperial actions, Suetonius maintained that Tiberius had intended to curb "externas

---

[8]My translation.

caerimonias, Aegyptios Iudaicosque ritus," i.e., foreign *sacra* including Egyptian and Judean rites practiced in Rome. Hence, just as certain religious rites, regardless of where they appeared, belonged to Egypt and Egyptians, so did others to Judea and Judeans.[9] Both, anyway, were foreign (*externus*) to Rome. More meaningful at present is the further statement of Suetonius that Tiberius drove off "reliquos gentis eiusdem vel similia sectantes" ("the rest of the *same people* or those *practicing similar rites*"). This definitely defines the Jewish *gens* by means of its religious practices, i.e., by way of its foreign religious rites the expulsion of which Suetonius approved, and at the same time indicates Suetonius did not apply the title *Iudaeus* to those Gentile practitioners of the Jewish religion in Rome. For them he seems only to have had the oblique phrase "similia sectantes."[10]

So far it is certain that, when Suetonius used the word *Iudaeus*, what came to his mind was a Judean, i.e., a person essentially foreign (cf. *exterus* in *Julius* 84.5) to Rome, who belonged to the same *gens* as characteristically populated Judea, and who by definition practiced the foreign (cf. the *externus* of *Tiberius* 36) religious rites of that *gens*. Already, then, we have detected a pejorative connotation to the word, for at least insofar as the *Iudaei* in Rome were concerned, Suetonius did approve of their expulsion. This was because he understood they were the practitioners of a cult foreign to the city.

Furthermore, the most typical context within which Suetonius applied *Iudaea*, *Iudaeus*, and *Iudaicus* was that of the Jewish war of 66-70 CE.[11] Least obvious are the references to the Roman "exercitus Iudaicus" in *Vitellius* 15.1 and *Vespasianus* 6.3, but *Titus* 4.3 and 5.2 do contain explicit references to the war. The resultant triumph "de Iudaeis" or "Iudaicum" is found in *Vespasianus* 8.1 and *Domitianus* 2.1. The previously noted "Iudaicus fiscus" is in *Domitianus* 12.2, and the culmination of this tendency comes in *Vespasianus* 4.5:

> There had spread over all the Orient an old and established belief,
> that it was fated at that time for men coming from Judea to rule the
> world.[12] This prediction...the people of Judea took to themselves;

---

[9]In *Legatio* 277-279, Agrippa I makes the same point.

[10]Dio had a different usage. Under the term *Jew* he also included Gentiles who practiced Judaism (cf. p. 63, and Solin ["Juden und Syrer" in *ANRW*, 2.29²:613] who takes the religious rather than ethnic use to be typical of antiquity).

[11]Of sixteen usages recorded in Howard and Jackson, eight reflect that conflict.

[12]"To rule the world" is an interesting phrase. It raises the question of the extent to which this text has played a role in anti-Semitic theories of world Jewish domination. Zielinski ("L'empereur Claude," pp. 128-133) bases his discussion of

accordingly they revolted [Id...praedictum Iudaei ad se trahentes re-
bellarunt] and after killing their governor, they routed the consular
ruler of Syria as well, when he came to the rescue, and took one of
his eagles. Since to put down this rebellion....

The point is that when Suetonius used the word *Iudaeus* he had
even more in mind than the largely negative connotations formerly
discussed, for in terms of his own usage this and related terms had an
anachronistic association with the great Judean rebellion which had
occurred at the time of his birth.[13] Therefore, behind his apparently
neutral declaration that Claudius "Iudaeos Roma expulit" stands a
rather glorious event as Suetonius must have understood it. By means
thereof, after all, the emperor had rid Rome of Judeans, i.e., of *Iudaei*
who from Suetonius' perspective had remained essentially foreigners,
of *Iudaei* who had contaminated Rome with the foreign religious rites
typical of them, and of *Iudaei* hardly to be differentiated from their
kith and kin of the same name who had gravely threatened the order
of the state during his own infancy.

Within *Claudius* 25.4 *Iudaeos* belongs to the participial phrase
"Iudaeos assidue tumultuantes," that is, "*Iudaeos* impulsore Chresto
assidue tumultuantes Roma expulit." To be specific, in agreement with
and modifying *Iudaeos* is the present participle of *tumultuare*, itself
being modified by the adverb *assidue*. Because it has been discussed
already,[14] we need not repeat here why the phrase's non-restrictive
interpretation, inclusive of the entire Roman Jewish population, is
preferable. Nevertheless, for the sake of adding to our understanding
of how Suetonius perceived the Claudian expulsion, we do need to look
closely at the connotations of Suetonius in his use of both *tumultuare*
and *assiduus*.

We are fortunate that the verb *tumultuare* and different forms
from the same root appear often in Suetonius.[15] Common to all of
them is the idea of disturbance. Suetonius once (*Caligula* 55.1) used
this root to refer to a single Roman knight who apparently disturbed
some kind of musical performance. Likewise, *Claudius* 41.1 alludes
briefly to the disruption of an imperial reading brought about by the

---

Jewish attempts at world rule on P. Lond. 1912, but he appears at times to be as
interested in contemporary, i.e., 1926-1927, as in ancient political issues.

[13]Since his account concludes with the emperor Domitian, we have no idea of
the degree to which the horrors of the second Jewish war during Trajan's reign
influenced Suetonius' image. We may suppose they did.

[14]Pp. 117-118.

[15]For all instances see Howard and Jackson, *Index verborum*, p. 253.

collapse of benches in the auditorium, and *Caligula* 26.4 narrates a far less humorous but similar disorder in the circus. Suetonius also used the same root to refer to generally unspecified disturbances of a kind threatening the civil order within Rome. Specifically, *Augustus* 23.1 concerns the emperor's fear that the defeat of Varus would bring about disorder there; *Augustus* 25.2 expresses a similar fear associated with the results of famine in the city; and *Tiberius* 37.2 claims Tiberius was very concerned to suppress all manner of popular disorder.

When we examine the most common context in which Suetonius used words taken from the root of *tumultuare*, it becomes clear why he thought the emperors should have responded in this way. In all of those cases his connotation focused upon the theme of resistance to the established order. Thus, by the adjectival form *tumultuosus* (*Nero* 40.4) as well as the adverb *tumultuose* (*Julius* 16.2, *Caligula* 45.1, *Vespasianus* 8.2) he understood opposition to order embodied either in the Roman state or emperor. The noun *tumultus* is similar. It appears in the murder scene not only of Caligula (*Caligula* 58.3) but also of Galba (*Galba* 20.1). The latter case is interesting because just prior to it, in *Galba* 19.2, Suetonius had used *tumultuare* in reference to all those who had risen up against this emperor. Again, in *Julius* 38.1 and *Vespasianus* 10 we find *tumultus* refers to the Roman civil wars, in *Galba* 7.1 it denotes a provincial uprising and otherwise often describes hostility directed against the ruling emperor (*Augustus* 19.1, 34.1; *Tiberius* 65.2; *Nero* 43.1, 49.4). Moreover, when we turn to the verb *tumultuare* itself, the situation is much the same. *Julius* 39 refers to a military revolt against that leader; *Caligula* 9 and 51.3 describe the potential and actual revolts of the military at the time respectively of Augustus' and Caligula's death; finally, *Claudius* 17.1 and *Galba* 9.2 note respectively uprisings in Britain ("Britanniam... tumultuantem") and Gaul ("tumultuari Gallias").

Thus, within Suetonius' usage the fundamental connotation of the root of *tumultuare* was that of disturbance of a kind representing rebellion against the established order of Rome. This is significant in the present case because we have just seen that Suetonius attached a very similar connotation to the word *Iudaeus*. As he understood it, after all, this was hardly a neutral term: associated with it among other negative connotations was an anti-Roman rebelliousness derived explicitly and therefore at least in part anachronistically from the Jewish war of 66 to 70 CE.[16] As a result, "tumultuantes" looks less like the objective description of concrete activity than it does the tendentious objectification of the connotation of *Iudaeus* which came

---

[16]As just indicated (p. 156, n. 13), the massive uprising of 114-117 CE would almost surely have influenced him in the same way.

naturally to his mind when Suetonius was passing on the fact that Claudius "Iudaeos Roma expulit." In the reporting of Suetonius, to express it a bit differently, "Iudaeos tumultuantes" smacks of a slur or cliché.[17]

The same process was intensified when Suetonius stated that these "Iudaeos tumultuantes" were "Iudaeos *assidue* tumultuantes." As to the adverb *assidue* itself, Suetonius used both it and the adjective *assiduus* frequently.[18] Concerning the latter, he employed it in the three senses of regular/habitual/scheduled, repeated, and uninterrupted/ongoing. There is perhaps only a slight distinction to be made between the first two connotations. In *Caligula* 3.1 Suetonius meant that this emperor regularly rode his horse after dinner; in *Claudius* 32 his comment concerned a habitual round of banquets; and in *Vespasianus* 8.4 and 25 he referred to repeated but certainly not scheduled invasions and conspiracies. *Caligula* 23.3 and *Claudius* 18.2 are different: in the former Suetonius meant an uninterrupted cough and in the latter an ongoing famine.[19]

Suetonius understood the adverb *assidue* similarly. Most often he used it in reference to regular or habitual actions. As in the above case of *Claudius* 32, for example, Suetonius wrote of regularly given imperial banquets (*Julius* 48, *Augustus* 74, *Vespasianus* 19.1). Also, Claudius was repeatedly harassed (*Claudius* 9.1), and Tiberius was repeatedly attended by unwelcome visitors (*Tiberius* 12.2); however, Suetonius used *assidue* in the sense of *uninterruptedly* too. *Augustus* 72.1, for example, asserts that this emperor lived continuously in Rome, and *Vitellius* 2.5 mentions the fact that the emperor always carried the slipper of Messalina about with him.[20]

Applied to the "Iudaeos assidue tumultuantes" of *Claudius* 25.4, these considerations require us to ask whether Suetonius envisioned repeated acts of rebellion or continuous Jewish rebelliousness. Because

---

[17]Additional support for this view is provided by the fact that, as presently constituted, the very short *Claudius* 25.4 contains two causal factors, i.e., these "assidue tumultuantes" Jews and the *impulsor* Chrestus.

[18]For all instances see Howard and Jackson, *Index verborum*, p. 25.

[19]Other instances of *assiduus* in the sense of *regular/habitual* include *Augustus* 71.1, and *Tiberius* 11.3 and 50.2. *Assiduus* meaning *repeated* is found in *Augustus* 80 and *Galba* 18.1, and cases where it signifies *uninterrupted* are *Julius* 75.2, *Tiberius* 40, and *Galba* 6.3.

[20]Other instances of *assidue* in the sense of *regularly* are *Augustus* 84.2 and 91.2, *Caligula* 18.2, 52, and 55.2, *Claudius* 27.2 and 41.1, *Vespasianus* 2.1, as well as *Domitianus* 4.1. Best interpreted in the sense of *uninterruptedly* are *Augustus* 33.1 and 87.2, and *Nero* 53.

the contextual criteria by which this distinction may be made in other cases are absent here, no explicit answer is possible. Still, since as a modifier of "tumultuantes" the adverb "assidue" serves a fundamental purpose of contributing additional emphasis to the objectification of the rebelliousness already inherent in Suetonius' understanding of the word *Iudaeus*, the latter is perhaps more likely.

Overall, then, "[Claudius] Iudaeos assidue tumultuantes Roma expulit" contains both a statement of the fact that Claudius expelled Roman Jews and what appears to be a Suetonian commentary based upon his own anachronistic sense of the Judean character. Foreigners, practitioners of foreign rites, and rebels against the Roman order that they were, Claudius had rid the city of them.

To this report Suetonius then added an apparently mysterious bit of information: "Iudaeos *impulsore Chresto* assidue tumultuantes Roma expulit." Ablatives of *impulsor* and *Chrestus*, these two words are, unfortunately, Suetonian hapax legomena. They come together here in an ablative-absolute construction that is characterized by the juxtaposition of a proper and a common noun which have been linked predicatively by the verb *to be*, understood. Put more simply, we have an equation according to which *Chrestus* is identified as *impulsor*: "Chrestus being *impulsor*."

Appearing outside of *Claudius* 25.4 only twenty-five times,[21] ablative absolutes of the proper noun–common noun type are found relatively rarely in Suetonius' *De vita caesarum*. Most typical are thirteen practically identical occurrences sharing the common noun *consul*. As an example, *Augustus* 5: "Natus est Augustus *M. Tullio Cicerone C. Antonio conss. [consulibus]*," i.e., "Marcus Tullius Cicero [and] Gaius Antonius [being] the consuls, Augustus was born."[22] Depending on a consul-based Roman chronology, Suetonius used the ablative absolute to provide readers with the chronologically decisive circumstance that it was during the year when these two men were consuls, i.e., 63 BCE, that the birth of Augustus occurred. It is, in other words, a temporal adverb modifying "natus est," and so the LCL translates it: "Augustus was born...in the consulship of Marcus Tullius Cicero and Gaius Antonius," or, and just as accurately, "When Marcus Tullius Cicero and Gaius Antonius were consuls, Augustus was born."

---

[21] An examination guided by indications of the case of proper nouns within Howard and Jackson (*Index verborum*) yields the following instances: *Julius* 20.2 (twice), 80.4, *Augustus* 2.2, 5, 81.1, 94.12, 96.1, 100.1, 101.1, *Tiberius* 1.1 (twice), 5, 47, 73.1, *Gaius* 8.1, *Claudius* 2.1, 45, *Nero* 40.1, *Otho* 2.1, *Vitellius* 2.2, 3.2, *Vespasianus* 2.1, 4.1, *Domitianus* 15.2.

[22] The other twelve are *Julius* 20.2 (twice), *Augustus* 100.1, 101.1, *Tiberius* 5, 73.1, *Gaius* 8.1, *Claudius* 2.1, 45, *Otho* 2.1, *Vitellius* 3.2, and *Vespasianus* 2.1.

There is also a temporal element in *Augustus* 2.2, *Vespasianus* 4.1, and *Domitianus* 15.2. Suetonius may have intended that it be chronological in the first of these, for he stated there that the great grandfather of Augustus had served in the second Punic war "Aemilio Papo imperatore," i.e., under and therefore at the time Papus was the commander of the army.[23] The second seems more generally temporal, but the last is indirectly causal, for "Claudio principe" is shorthand intended to explain how a freedman, Narcissus, could have wangled an important military commission for Vespasian.[24] In other words, "because Claudius was at that time the *princeps*, his own favorite freedman Narcissus possessed otherwise unthinkable power."

Relatedly, Suetonius often used ablative absolutes of this type with the common noun *auctor*. The word itself can refer most literally either to an author or authority behind a story. More important is its extended use with the sense of authority behind an action, founder, source, or plotter of a death.[25] In these cases it is ideas associated primarily with causation which Suetonius had in mind when he used *auctor*. Since the ablative-absolute constructions regularly serve to introduce an adverbial element of causality, it is hardly surprising that Suetonius chose five times to use *auctor* in this way.

The first of these appears in *Augustus* 81.1: "auctore Antonio Musa" Augustus was compelled to submit to a particular course of medical treatment. In this instance, since Musa was the emperor's physician (*Augustus* 59; cf. Horace *Epistles* 1.15.1-4), *auctor* means the authority behind the action. It was, in other words, the physician who

---

[23]The other cases are *Julius* 80.4, *Augustus* 94.12, and *Nero* 40.1.

[24]If we did not know from elsewhere (cf. *Claudius* 25.5, 28) of Suetonius' insistence upon the power of the Claudian freedmen, the ablative absolute would appear only temporal.

[25]In order to reach this conclusion, I analyzed each occurrence of *auctor* in *De vita caesarum* (cf. Howard and Jackson, *Index verborum*, p. 27). The results, excluding its usage in the ablative-absolute construction of interest to us, are as follows: Suetonius used *auctor* as *author* in *Julius* 56.1, *Augustus* 31.1, 55, 70.1, 89.2, *Tiberius* 56, 61.3, 70.2, *Gaius* 8.5, *Nero* 39.2, and *Domitianus* 8.3; as the *authority behind a story* in *Julius* 9.3, 81.2, *Augustus* 94.3, *Gaius* 6.1, 12.3, *Claudius* 37.1, and *Nero* 34.4; as the *authority behind an action* in *Julius* 16.1, *Galba* 19.2; as *founder* in *Augustus* 28.2 (of government), *Claudius* 25.3 (of the Roman people), *Domitianus* 5 (of a temple), *Nero* 1.1 (of a family), *Vitellius* 2.1 (of a family); as the *source* in *Julius* 19.1 (of a promise), *Augustus* 36 (of new administrative measures), *Tiberius* 35.1 (of legal measures), *Gaius* 15.3 (of legal measures), *Claudius* 25.5 (of religious measures), *Galba* 10.3 (of rebellion), *Otho* 1.2 (of rebellion), 8.1 (of diplomatic measures), *Vespasianus* 11 (of legal measures), and *Domitianus* 8.2 (of legal measures); as *plotter of a death* in *Julius* 20.5, *Nero* 33.1, *Titus* 9.1, and *Domitianus* 23.1.

induced Augustus to take the step. In *Augustus* 96.1, "auctore Divo Caesare" Thessalus prophesied the same emperor's impending victory at Philippi: the ascended Julius caused Thessalus to make such an announcement. Again, Suetonius claimed in *Tiberius* 1.1 that "auctore Tito Tatio" the *gens Claudia* moved to Rome; Tatius caused it to do so. Likewise, *Tiberius* 47 states that "auctore Augusto" Hortalus bore four children. Specifically, as Tacitus (*Annals* 2.37) informs us, the emperor had given Hortalus sufficient money to raise a family. He was, then, the ultimate cause of the poor man's paternity. Finally, "auctore Tiberio" it seemed good to remove certain persons from the list of senators (*Vitellius* 2.2).[26]

Thus, in each of these cases the ablative absolute expresses the cause of or the agent behind the action of the clause or phrase in which it is found. Excluding the remaining three instances where the ablative absolute is more generally circumstantial,[27] we see then that of these twenty-five constructions the majority are chronological or at least generally temporal in nature and that otherwise they express causality typically by means of the common noun *auctor*.

Keeping the motif of causality in mind, we turn now to lexical considerations associated with the *impulsor* of "impulsore Chresto." Because it is a hapax legomenon within Suetonius, we are at a real disadvantage, but the study of his employment of the related verb *impellere* and noun *impulsus* largely makes up for this drawback.[28] The latter appears in two instances. In *Galba* 18.1 it was by means of the movement ("impulsu," ablative of means) of a crowd that a soldier nearly wounded the emperor with his lance. That is, the *impulsor* was the crowd which nearly caused the soldier to injure Galba. Similarly, in *Vitellius* 17.2 it was by means of the movement ("impulsu," ablative of means) of a chariot that this ruler came to have a crippled leg. The *impulsor*, in other words, was a rival chariot, the movement of which caused the injury.

Insofar as the verb is concerned, Suetonius used it with the ablative of means as well as the closely related ablative of personal

---

[26]The same form with the pronoun replacing the proper noun appears in *Tiberius* 27 ("Auctore eo [Tiberius]," someone went to the senate.) and *Gaius* 34.1 (Except "auctore se [Gaius]," no one could erect a statue.).

[27]*Julius* 80.4: "Gaius Cassius and Marcus and Decimus Brutus being the leaders of the conspiracy, more than sixty plotted against him [Caesar]"; *Augustus* 94.12: "Agrippa being his companion, Augustus ascended..."; *Nero* 40.1: "Julius Vindex being the leader, the Gauls made a beginning" (my translations).

[28]I examine here the five instances cited by Howard and Jackson, *Index verborum*, pp. 111-113.

agency.[29] The former appears in *Nero* 31.4 where we are instructed that this emperor was moved ("impulsus est") to a harmful spending spree by means of the hope ("spe," ablative of means) aroused through the information ("ex indicio") of a Roman knight. In other words, hope was the direct *impulsor* which caused Nero to be extravagant, and behind it was the information of a certain knight. He, therefore, was the ultimate *impulsor* behind the action of the emperor. *Nero* 35.4 uses the ablative of personal agency, for the emperor declares here that the unfortunate Aulus Plautius had been moved ("impulsum") to an expectation of imperial succession by Nero's mother, Agrippina ("ab ea," ablative of personal agency). Thus, the *impulsor* was Agrippina who caused Plautius to develop a deadly expectation. Finally, both ablatives appear in *Caligula* 57.3. In this case, Suetonius narrated Gaius' dream according to which he had been in heaven when moved ("impulsum") by Jupiter ("ab eo," ablative of personal agency) by means of the latter's foot ("dextri pedis pollice," ablative of means) and so booted down to the earth. Here the foot of Jupiter serves as the immediate *impulsor*, and the god himself becomes the ultimate one.

These consistent similarities in the manner in which Suetonius employed both *impellere* and *impulsus* do not obscure the fact that two significant differences also manifest themselves. The first concerns the nature of the relationship between the *impulsor* and its object. In two of the cases above Suetonius conceived of the relationship between the *impulsor* and the one so moved as a positive one. That is, the knight was a confidant of Nero, and Agrippina was thought to be the lover of Aulus Plautius. Nonetheless, in each of the other three instances the relationship was unfriendly. The crowd was only inadvertently so, but within the context of a chariot race Suetonius no doubt thought the hostility to be real, and the same is all the more true of Jupiter's expulsion of Gaius from heaven.

Associated with this is the fact that the nature of the causation differs. So far we have expressed this causation with undifferentiated paraphrases using the idea of movement. Now greater precision may be warranted. Specifically, in the two cases of a positive relationship, the movement took the primary form of verbal encouragement. Nero was moved by what the knight had told him about the hidden fortune, and, likewise, Aulus Plautius by the insistence of Agrippina. The situation is different in cases where the relationship was inadvertently or patently hostile. This is least clear in *Galba* 18.1, where we might envision the slow pressure of the crowd; however, the fact that this movement produced a spear thrust in the direction of the emperor implies that Suetonius envisioned a violent surge against the soldier

---

[29]The latter supplies the *ab*.

holding it. In any case, this is preciously the sense of *Vitellius* 17.2 and *Caligula* 57.3, for the former requires us to imagine a severe blow of the offending chariot and the latter another blow hard enough to send Gaius falling to the earth.

Applying these observations to the Suetonian *impulsor*, we see that its fundamental connotation is causal. In this most basic sense, therefore, the ablative absolute of which it is a part has much in common with those other ablative absolutes of the same type in which *auctor* is the common noun. Whether "impulsore Chresto" or "auctore Chresto," after all, the basic sense is that Chrestus somehow caused the action which this phrase modifies in the manner of an adverb.[30] Consequently, the general sense of "impulsore Chresto" is "Chrestus being the cause." Beyond this, however, the more precise connotation may be construed in opposite ways. On the one hand, Suetonius might have had in mind the idea of the encouragement of an ally, that is, "at the encouragement of Chrestus" or "Chrestus being the one doing the encouraging."[31] On the other, he may have been thinking of a blow against an opponent, i.e., "at the blow of Chrestus" or "Chrestus being the one striking the blow."

Setting aside for now this question of the *how* of causation, we turn to the *what*. "Chrestus being the cause" of what? What precisely then did Chrestus cause? From a strictly grammatical perspective, the answer is unclear. In the first place, and more generally, *Claudius* 25.4 consists of two units, the clause "Iudaeos assidue tumultuantes Roma expulit" and the absolute phrase "impulsore Chresto." Taking seriously the absolute nature of the phrase and following the model of the most common way in which Suetonius used the ablative absolute of this type, we are able to translate in a chronological sense, "When Chrestus was *impulsor*,"[32] and so add a temporal detail associated with the claim that "Claudius expelled from Rome the continuously rebelling Jews." Again, his choice of the word *impulsor* makes clear that Suetonius envisioned some kind of causal relationship between the phrase and the clause. In other words, "Chrestus being the cause," i.e., Chrestus playing some kind of causative role, "Claudius expelled

---

[30]It should perhaps be noted that the causation associated with *impulsor* consistently produces a negative result. The same is not true of *auctor*.

[31]As we shall see, scholarship has assumed this to be the only way of understanding the phrase.

[32]We observed already that Suetonius used ablative absolutes regularly with *consul* for chronological purposes: "Natus est Augustus *M. Tullio Cicerone C. Antonio conss. [consulibus]*," i.e., "When Marcus Tullius Cicero and Gaius Antonius were consuls, Augustus was born" (*Augustus* 5).

from Rome the continuously rebelling Jews." Because of the shorthand involved in the use of the absolute construction, however, the precise nature of that role is elusive.

In the second place, and more particularly, the ablative-absolute phrases are somewhat less absolute than their designation signifies. Functioning adverbially, they do modify a verbal element within the unit of which they are a part. Unfortunately, however, *Claudius* 25.4 contains two such elements, the primary, predicative one, "expulit," and also the secondary, participial "tumultuantes." Considerations of grammar alone cannot reveal to us which of these Suetonius intended "impulsore Chresto" to modify. In other words, he was claiming either that "Chrestus caused Claudius to expel from Rome the continuously rebelling Jews" or that "Claudius expelled from Rome the Jews whom Chrestus caused to rebel continuously."[33]

Did Suetonius know which of these it was that Chrestus caused? There is excellent reason to think that he did. Specifically, we have already come across two other instances where Suetonius was able to use ablative-absolute shorthand because a bond of common knowledge united him and his original readers. In the first case, Suetonius reported that it was on account of Antonius Musa ("auctore Antonio Musa") that Augustus submitted to a particular course of medical treatment (*Augustus* 81.1). Precisely what this meant depended upon the identity of Musa, but it was exactly this which Suetonius failed to supply. Why? Because he was aware his readers already knew it. That is, very attentive ones might perhaps have been relied upon to recall *Augustus* 59: there Suetonius indicated that Musa was the physician of this emperor. More generally, of course, he certainly thought the name of the renowned man would be sufficient to identify him and so to clarify the shorthand.

The second case is also interesting. With great brevity *Tiberius* 47 employs the ablative absolute "auctore Augusto" to state that this emperor was responsible for the fact that Hortalus bore four children. Because of the abbreviated "auctore Augusto" and the unidentified Hortalus, the account is incomprehensible to modern readers. In this case, even a most careful reading of *De vita caesarum* does not help, for *Hortalus* is a Suetonian hapax legomenon. Even so, we should not conclude that *Tiberius* 47 was equally incomprehensible to those for whom Suetonius wrote it. That is, invisible behind his shorthand we must assume a story familiar to both writer and readers, i.e., the story preserved by Tacitus (*Annals* 2.37), about how Augustus had provided Hortalus sufficient money to raise a family.

---

[33]Among the type of ablative absolutes of interest to us, I found no case where this construction modified more than a single verbal element.

Unfortunately, Tacitus is of no help when it comes to Chrestus. Were he, we would possess vital clues concerning the relationship of this man to Roman Jews and/or the emperor, and these would in turn help modern readers to comprehend what precisely Chrestus caused within the statement "Claudius expelled from Rome the continuously rebelling Jews." That is, we have seen concerning *Augustus* 81.1 that Suetonius was able to get away with the abbreviation afforded by his "auctore Antonio Musa" because he as well as his readers shared a common knowledge about the person's identity. Likewise, concerning *Tiberius* 47 we noted that similar common knowledge legitimated the extreme abbreviation produced by the appearance of the unidentified "Hortalum" and the equally unexplained "auctore Augusto." Therefore, combining these considerations with what we shall soon discover to have been Suetonius' consistent carefulness in the use of personal names, we may return to the "impulsore Chresto" with every reason to suspect that its grammatical ambiguity concerning precisely what Chrestus caused is merely the flip side of its clarity to the ancient writer and his readers.

Nevertheless, on this subject the universal presupposition of scholarship is entirely different. It simply takes for granted that Suetonius intended the ablative absolute to modify the participle of *tumultuare*, the quasi-verbal element of the sentence. Typically, the LCL translation of Rolfe supplies "Since the Jews constantly *made disturbances at the instigation of Chrestus,* he [Claudius] expelled them from Rome."[34] Or, to employ the translation already proposed, "Claudius expelled from Rome the Jews whom Chrestus caused to rebel continuously." What then did Chrestus cause? He caused Roman Jews to rebel continuously.

Now, it is not impossible to provide syntactical support for this interpretation. In *Augustus* 101.1, the other case where an absolute construction surfaces in a participial phrase, this construction is associated with the participle instead of the main verb of the sentence. Furthermore, some units containing both a main verb and participle or infinitive locate the ablative absolute in proximity to the specific verbal element which Suetonius intended it to modify.[35] Thus, since Suetonius situated *impulsore Chresto* inside the participial phrase "Iudaeos assidue tumultuantes" and thus in proximity to *tumultuare,*

---

[34]Similarly, Th. Reinach (*Textes,* #186 [p.329]) translates concerning "les Juifs, qui à *l'instigation de Chrestus excitaient des troubles* continuels." More particularly, and as we shall see subsequently, the *interpretatio christiana* and its offshoots simply presuppose but also depend absolutely upon it.

[35]*Julius* 20.2 (#2, "'Bibulo fieri consule'"), though a quotation; *Tiberius* 1.1; *Nero* 40.1.

i.e., "Iudaeos *impulsore Chresto* assidue tumultuantes," it is possible Suetonius intended it to modify "tumultuantes."

Even so, several factors speak against this understanding. In the first place, "Iudaeos impulsore Chresto assidue tumultuantes Roma expulit" contains three different actors, i.e., Jews, Chrestus, and Claudius, and we have no reason to suspect Suetonius invented any of these. Concerning the concrete actions which he assigned to each, however, the situation is not the same. Specifically, among his three assertions that the Jews *assidue tumultuarunt*, Claudius *expulit*, and Chrestus *impulit* (*impulsor* from *impello*) we have seen already that from the pen of Suetonius the ascription of "assidue tumultuantes" to "Iudaeos" appears to represent his own tendentiousness. If correct, this means that in Suetonius' source[36] the causal factor associated with Chrestus could not have been associated with the non-existent secondary verbal idea *tumultuare* but must have modified what was its main and originally only verb, *expellere*.

A second consideration valid independent of the correctness of the first is that Suetonius normally did use his ablative absolutes to modify the actual predicate of his sentences and clauses. This is most obvious in that majority of cases where there is only a single verbal form, but it is precisely in these that we witness Suetonius' tendency to formulate absolute constructions for the purpose of modifying his predicates.[37] Not surprisingly, therefore, in the majority of instances where a participle or infinitive appears alongside of the actual verb, the ablative absolute also modifies the latter.[38]

Another consideration arises out of the structural context within which Suetonius employed his information about Chrestus and Roman Jewry. Intending to develop a section of his narrative on the topic of the emperor's treatment of various foreign communities, Suetonius scanned his sources for the applicable materials, came up with the information now found in *Claudius* 25.3-5, and then presented it as a series of parallel statements:

Peregrinae condicionis homines vetuit...;
Civitatem R. usurpantes...percussit;
Provincias Achaiam et Macedoniam... senatui reddidit;

---

[36]I use *source* loosely. Perhaps he had written materials such as those referred to in *Claudius* 3.2, but he was familiar with oral tradition (*Claudius* 15.3).

[37]*Julius* 20.2 (#1, a formula), 80.4, *Augustus* 2.2, 94.12, 96.1, 100.1, *Tiberius* 5, 47, *Gaius* 8.1, *Claudius* 2.1, 45, *Otho* 2.1, *Vitellius* 3.2, *Vespasianus* 2.1, 4.1.

[38]Main verb: *Augustus* 5, *Tiberius* 1.1 (twice), 73.1, *Vitellius* 2.2; participle or infinitive: *Julius* 20.2 (#2), *Augustus* 101.1, *Nero* 40.1; ambiguous: *Augustus* 81.1 and *Domitianus* 15.2.

Lyciis...libertatem ademit;
Rhodiis... [libertatem] reddidit;
Iliensibus...tributa remisit;
Iudaeos...expulit;
Germanorum legatis...permisit;
Druidarum religionem...abolevit. ·

As a result, this information and Suetonius' reporting of it are not quite identical. To use the obvious example, he wrote "expulit," but the sense of his source was that "Claudius expulit." Otherwise, he would not have associated the expulsion with Claudius. Why the omission of the name? Because the parallel accounts did the same thing.

Somewhat less conspicuous is the fact that a similar parallelism determined the central portion of the syntax of our text. Specifically, Suetonius began his sentences here very abruptly, as if by means of a subheading, with the name of the foreign group concerned in the accusative or dative case. For this reason "Iudaeos" too became a first word. Expressed a bit differently, the positioning of "Iudaeos" was controlled primarily by considerations of structure rather than of meaning. As a result, structure-based conclusions about this meaning are necessarily ambiguous.

Finally, the most important consideration is a play on words. In a sentence of only seven words Suetonius twice elected the root *pello*, and he did so in a manifestly intentional way by attaching to it the antonymic prefixes *in-* (*im-pul*) and *ex-* (*ex-pul*) so as to establish an explicit contrast between the actions of the *impulsor* Chrestus and the *expulsor* Claudius, i.e., "Chrestus impulit, Claudius expulit." Hence, Suetonius himself saw an essential relationship between the ablative absolute and the predicate of his sentence.

In sum, it is nearly certain that Suetonius intended the ablative absolute to modify the central verbal element *expellere*: "Chrestus caused Claudius to expel from Rome the continuously rebelling Jews," or, somewhat more faithful to the ablative absolute, "Chrestus being the cause, Claudius expelled from Rome the continuously rebelling Jews." In other words, Suetonius informed his readers that Chrestus caused Claudius to expel the continuously rebelling Jews.

Thus far, we have been able to make basic sense of most of the literary elements associated with the claim that Claudius "Iudaeos impulsore Chresto assidue tumultuantes Roma expulit." We saw how Suetonius placed this statement within a larger literary unit central to which was subject matter of a religious nature. Significantly, the Suetonian definition of *Iudaeus* also includes a fundamental religious component and so binds *Claudius* 25.4 to the religious theme of the larger unit. *Iudaeus* in all of its Suetonian connotations defined, we found the core statement, "[Claudius] Iudaeos Roma expulit," explicit.

That is, this emperor, the above measures of whom Suetonius clearly approved, expelled Roman Jewry. Nevertheless, his additional claim that these Jews were "assidue tumultuantes" creates an impossible image of continuous Jewish civil war at Rome. Moreover, in conjunction with the Suetonian connotation of *Iudaeus*, it bears obvious marks of tautology. As a result, "assidue tumultuantes" looks much more like an anachronistic slur arising out of Suetonius' impressions from the Jewish war of 66-70 CE than it does a detail based upon his source for earlier events under Claudius. As such, though we shall not be able to ignore the possible worth of such a detail, it probably adds nothing of historical value to the core statement that Claudius "Iudaeos Roma expulit."

Finally, although difficult on account of its two hapax legomena and ablative-absolute shorthand, "impulsore Chresto" does attach an important causative element to *Claudius* 25.4. As it turns out, of course, *impulsor* may refer to causation of two different kinds, the encouragement of a friend, apparently verbal in nature ("Chrestus being the one doing the encouraging"), and the perhaps more physical blow of an opponent ("Chrestus being the one striking the blow"). Not entirely certain either is just what Chrestus caused. Grammatically available to the secondary verbal element *tumultuare* as well as to the predicate *expellere* itself, the ablative absolute very likely modifies the latter, but we must explore the other possibility as well. Before we pursue these matters further, however, one important subject remains from our literary analysis of *Claudius* 25.4. That is, naturally, the second element of the ablative-absolute phrase and its second hapax legomenon, *Chrestus*. Exploration of this word may be expected to provide additional help in the interpretation of both *Claudius* 25.4 and the imperial expulsion to which it provides the most detailed witness.

Chapter Eight

Making Sense of a Curious Suetonian Silence

When Suetonius wrote that the emperor Claudius "Iudaeos impulsore Chresto assidue tumultuantes Roma expulit," his intention was to convey to his early-second-century readers a small bit of topically relevant information which stemmed from the middle of the previous century. Because he did assume certain shared understandings with those readers,[1] he could be quite succinct here. Specifically, in terms of the four proper nouns within the text, Suetonius certainly had no need to explain the identity of the implied subject, *Claudius*, or the significance of the word *Roma*. Similarly, and in spite of the special connotations which he attached to *Iudaeus*, the same thing is true of this term, for contemporary readers had at least the same relative idea of who was meant by it.[2] A priori, therefore, we may reasonably suppose that when, without any further explanation, Suetonius wrote *Chrestus*, he had good reason to think his readers would be able to make sense of the name.[3]

---

[1] On the reasons for these assumptions in Suetonius, see Wallace-Hadrill, *Suetonius*, p. 13.

[2] Relative in the sense that, while Suetonius used the word ethnically, Dio also applied its Greek equivalent to Gentiles who practiced the religion associated with Jews (cf. p. 63).

[3] Gordon (*Latin Epigraphy*, p. 20) notes the care of both Cicero and Pliny the Younger in the use of names. Concerning the latter see also A. N. Sherwin-White, *The Letters of Pliny: A Historical and Social Commentary* (Oxford: Clarendon Press, 1966), p. 113.

169

As to the manner in which they might have been able to do this, there are only two possibilities. First, perhaps Suetonius had already identified Chrestus.[4] We observed such a procedure in the instance of Antonius Musa. Similarly, Iulius Marathus appears only as the *auctor* in *Augustus* 94.3, but the previous *Augustus* 79.2 does establish his believability in that capacity by identifying him as the emperor's freedman and secretary. Even more obviously, referring to a certain Ptolemy at *Caligula* 35.1, Suetonius wrote specifically that he had previously identified the man ("de quo rettuli"). So he had, at *Caligula* 26.1. In the present instance Suetonius did not do this: *Claudius* 25.4 is the only instance in which he referred to Chrestus.[5]

Thus, unless Suetonius was simply careless, we are required to adopt the second possibility, which is that Chrestus was in need of no introduction. In other words, this mid-first-century character appears to have been sufficiently prominent that his name alone was to be depended upon to elicit recognition among second-century readers.[6] Nevertheless, more than appearance is involved here because close examination of the ways in which Suetonius identified his other characters leads to the same conclusion.

First come those cases where he reported an incident involving unnamed persons. For example, *Tiberius* 61.3 belongs to a section on the cruelty of that emperor. Commenting upon how a few careless words could result in death, Suetonius referred to two persons whom

---

[4]Suetonius did sometimes identify famous persons after the fact. Thrasyllus (*Augustus* 98.4, *Tiberius* 14.4, 62.3, *Gaius* 19.3) is an interesting case because, in order to appreciate his first appearance, readers needed to know that he was an astrologer; however, Suetonius withheld this information until later references. Other cases are those of Cornelius Balbus (*Julius* 78.1, 81.2) and King Archelaus (*Tiberius* 8, 37.4).

[5]Referring not at all to Chrestus, Tacitus and Dio Cassius provide no help with his identification, but it is illegitimate to conclude anything about Chrestus from their omission. By way of analogy, we have seen already how Tacitus (*Annals* 2.37) did happen to fill in the necessary blanks about the Hortalus of Suetonius *Tiberius* 47. Likewise, Tacitus (*Annals* 4.31, 11.1-7, 13.42-43) made clear that the Publius Suillius Rufus to be discussed shortly played a significant part in Claudius' Rome. Nonetheless, insofar as the reporting of Suetonius and Dio Cassius is concerned, Suillius appears never to have existed. Arguments from silence are therefore very precarious when it comes to the ancient sources, for the vagaries of the materials available to them as well as their own editorial interests and purposes leave much to chance.

[6]To impute our modern ignorance to the original readers of Suetonius would be, of course, highly anachronistic; cf. Kurt Linck, "De antiquissimis veterum quae ad Iesum Nazarenum spectant testimoniis," *Religionsgeschichtliche Versuche und Vorarbeiten* 14 (1913-1914):106.

Tiberius had executed. Instead of identifying them by their names, he indicated that the one was a poet and the other a historian. In this case the vocational identification was more germane than the personal one. Similarly, he narrated at some length an anecdote intended to demonstrate Titus' aversion to the death penalty (*Titus* 9.1-2). Though the concluding "sicut evenit" makes clear that he was telling less than he knew about the two persons whom he identified as patricians, he did not provide their names. Again, the inclusion of this information would have contributed nothing to the point of the story.

Related cases are those in which Suetonius avoided the personal name by his use of the indefinite pronoun *quidam.*[7] *Julius* 79.1, for example, narrates an incident initiated by "quidam e turba" ("some man from the crowd") which revealed Caesar's pretensions to royalty. Who this person was Suetonius failed to indicate. Why? Because there was no reason for tradition to have preserved it. In any case, insofar as Suetonius' own telling was concerned, the name really contributed nothing to the sense of the account. *Augustus* 79.1 is similar. Here an unnamed leader of the Gauls ("quidam e primoribus Galliarum") is claimed to have spared Augustus' life on account of the latter's fine demeanor. As to whether Suetonius knew the name of this particular Gaul, there is no way to know. Suetonius in any case had no reason to provide it because what mattered was the Gaul's identity as an authoritative figure able to evaluate the character of Augustus.

In cases observed up to the present point, Suetonius conveyed the intended sense of his narrative through the identification of necessary characters by means other than the use of their personal names. *Quidam* is nevertheless transitional since Suetonius also used it adjectivally to modify both common and proper, personal nouns.[8] Hence, referring to the insignificant persons who had tried to kill the emperor, *Augustus* 19.2 supplies the interesting example of a "lixa quidam," i.e., "a certain servant," caught with a knife very close to the bedroom of Augustus. Necessary here was the identification of the individual not by name but by rank, and that Suetonius carefully supplied. Again, for the sake of demonstrating the extreme brutality of Nero, Suetonius told the horror story of that emperor's inclination to throw persons alive to "a certain glutton" ("polyphago cuidam") of Egyptian origin (*Nero* 37.2). Here too, even if he knew it, Suetonius had no reason to supply the monster's real name, for the identification *polyphagus* conveyed precisely the unpleasant scene which he wished to describe.

---

[7]For all usages consult Howard and Jackson, *Index verborum*, p. 206.

[8]Again, for the usages see ibid.

As indicated above, he also utilized *quidam* with personal names and in this manner too implied that the noun itself was not really necessary to the account. He told, for example, of "a certain Octavius" ("Octavius quidam," *Julius* 49.2) who had insinuated that Caesar was effeminate. The proper noun adds nothing to the sense of the story and appears perhaps only because Suetonius remembered it from his stated source, Marcus Brutus. Similarly, in his section on Tiberius-the-dirty-old-man, he recounted the history of "a certain Mallonia" ("Mallonia quaedam," *Tiberius* 45) who, although she belonged to an illustrious family, became the prey of that emperor's desire and so committed suicide. Here too the proper noun was unnecessary to the sense of the story, and the same is true of the "certain Xeno" ("quidam Xeno," *Tiberius* 56) whom Suetonius used as one example of Tiberius' cruelty even to close friends.

It may well be that in both of these last cases Suetonius knew more about his subjects than he narrated, but for his purposes all that really counted was their identity as persons respectively of illustrious birth and close connection with the emperor. Names were available, so he used them, but each remains merely "a certain so-and-so," the meaning of the account enhanced in no way by this particular detail. As our final example we may call upon the famous Lucusta. That Suetonius knew well who she was and what she did becomes clear from references to her in *Nero* 33.3 and 47.1. Even so, her initial introduction is as "a certain Lucusta, chief of poisoners" ("quaedam Lucusta, index venenariorum," *Nero* 33.2), and this is more than sufficient because accounts of Suetonius in which she plays a role require little about her identification except that her appearance signalled mischief of a deadly kind.

A similar method of expression appears in Suetonius' far less common use of *nomine* with a personal name.[9] Citing omens prior to the death of Caligula, he related what had happened to "a certain Cassius by name" ("quidam Cassius nomine," *Caligula* 57.1). In terms of the intention of this one-sentence account, there was no real need to identify the dreamer by name, and Suetonius made this only too clear by what in this case is the tautological usage of *quidam* and *nomine*.[10] Analogously, Suetonius recounted various dangers which faced the emperor Tiberius, including one caused by a slave of Agrippa the Younger, "Clement by name" ("Clemens nomine," *Tiberius* 25.1).

---

[9]Among the instances of Suetonius' usage of the ablative *nomine* from *nomen* (cf. Howard and Jackson, *Index verborum*, p. 157), only four belong to this construction: *Augustus* 98.4, *Tiberius* 25.1, 61.5, *Gaius* 57.1.

[10]He might just as well have supplied the substantive *quidam*, i.e., "someone," but, having the personal name available, he preserved it.

As in the previous case, identifying the slave by his name was quite unnecessary to the story, and Suetonius expressed this by the use of *nomine*, which here also, therefore, becomes interchangeable with the adjectival use of *quidam*, i.e., "Clemens quidam."

Nevertheless, in the two other cases where Suetonius employed *nomine* with this construction its introduction does not turn out to be quite so insignificant as the previous uses might cause us to think. *Augustus* 98.4 belongs to a section on the *hilaritas* or good sense of humor of Augustus and so refers in an apparently off-handed way to an associate of the emperor, "Masgaba by name" ("Masgaban nomine"), whom Augustus had dubbed *Ktistes* (founder) of the Island of Capreae. Identification of this figure by name and title becomes the key to the subsequent debate between the astrologer of Tiberius, i.e., Thrasyllus, and Augustus concerning the meaning of some extemporaneous Greek verse composed by the emperor. Specifically, Suetonius intended to demonstrate here that Augustus had played a fine joke on Thrasyllus by successfully portraying Masgaba as a poetic subject of grand proportions. More to the point, Suetonius did sufficiently identify Masgaba so that his readers both ancient and modern could appreciate this bit of imperial humor. Consequently, *Augustus* 98.4 demonstrates Suetonius' care in the usage of proper, personal nouns, for although he identified Masgaba as a nobody, i.e., "Masgaba nomine," he was conscious also that the sense of his narrative required the name. So, he supplied it.

The same thing is true also of *Tiberius* 61.5, the final instance where Suetonius used *nomine* in conjunction with a personal name. He wrote here that Tiberius "thought death so light a punishment that when he heard that one of the accused, Carnulus by name, had anticipated [by suicide] his execution, he cried: 'Carnulus has given me the slip.'" In this case, the historian was aware of an old tag associated with the emperor Tiberius according to which the latter had at one time remarked, "Carnulus me evasit." Suetonius provided the comment with a real or imaginary context by including it in his discussion of how lightly Tiberius considered the application of the death penalty. That is, he identified Carnulus as a man who, about to be condemned to death by the emperor, took his own life instead. Beyond this, Suetonius had no reason to identify the poor victim further, so his initial introduction required and therefore provided only the "Carnulus nomine" by which to attach the name in the tag to the person in the vignette.

In the instances examined so far Suetonius showed himself very much aware of the need to provide his readers with an identification of characters sufficient for conveying the sense of his narrative. These same cases also make clear that the identification did not require the

provision of a specific name (e.g., *Tiberius* 61.3) and that, even when
this was provided, it might still be unnecessary to the story (e.g.,
Julius 49.2). Hence, related to the latter, it happens repeatedly in
Suetonius that otherwise unknown and insignificant characters are
introduced by name but then more relevantly identified for readers in
terms necessary to the sense of the particular account. *Julius* 39.1
concerns Furius Leptinus and Quintus Calpenus: "In the gladiatorial
contest in the Forum Furius Leptinus, a man of praetorian stock, and
Quintus Calpenus, a former senator and pleader at the bar, fought to
a finish." Wanting to underline the spectacular nature of Caesar's
shows, Suetonius found it necessary to identify these "gladiators" not
so much by personal name as by high rank.

Again, in support of his view that Augustus had been born at a
particular site in Rome, Suetonius mentioned the records of the senate
and the testimony of Gaius Laetorius contained therein (*Augustus* 5).
In this case too the name itself has no real meaning: only the identity
of Laetorius as the owner/authenticator of the emperor's reputed
birthplace gives significance to his mention in the account. And what
could his readers possibly have made of the appellation Telephus
(*Augustus* 19.1, 2) had Suetonius not identified him as the otherwise
unimportant slave, typical of persons even of the lowest rank, bent
upon assassinating Augustus? Then there is the promise to Tiberius
made by one Scribonius, but it gains its meaning only from the fact
that Suetonius identified him as an astrologer (*Tiberius* 14.2). There
are also Terpnus, important only in his identified capacity as greatest
lyre-player of his time (*Nero* 20.1), Spiculus, significant because
Suetonius identified him as that unimportant gladiator upon whom
Nero squandered much property (*Nero* 30.2), and Argivus, whose care
for the body of the murdered Galba makes little sense until his
identification as that emperor's steward (*Galba* 20.2). Thus, in case
after case of otherwise meaningless names, Suetonius, through some
additional mark of identification appropriate to the sense of the
account in which they occur, made clear to his readers the significance
of these persons.

Not surprisingly, there are also large numbers of names which
appear without any further identification because Suetonius assumed
the immediate reader-recognition of them. Among these, several are
readily recognizable to modern students too, for example, Pompey the
Great (*Julius* 19.2), Asinius Pollio (*Julius* 30.4), Scipio (*Julius* 35.2),
Gaius Cassius (*Julius* 80.4), Marcus Cicero (*Augustus* 3.2), Maecenas
(*Augustus* 66.3), Sejanus (*Tiberius* 48.2), Plinius Secundus (*Caligula*
8.1), Cincinnatus (*Caligula* 35.1), as well as the foreign ruler Queen
Berenice (*Titus* 7.1,2). Others names are perhaps less well known to
modernity: Aemilius Lepidus (*Caligula* 24.3), Silius (*Claudius* 26.2)

and Paetus Thrasea (*Nero* 37.1), and the foreigners Cottius (*Tiberius* 37.3) and Viriatus (*Galba* 3.2).[11]

Finally, and only apparently more problematic, are the figures of Hortalus and Vibius Crispus. We have observed previously a very abbreviated statement in *Tiberius* 47 that by means of Augustus the first of these men had fathered four children. We know also, however, that this text provides no basis for any theory of nomenclatorial carelessness because Tacitus (*Annals* 2.37), Suetonius' contemporary, was entirely familiar with the details of the case. Insofar as Vibius Crispus is concerned, *Domitian* 3.1 reports that

> at the beginning of his [Domitian's] reign he used to spend hours in seclusion every day, doing nothing but catch flies and stab them with a keenly-sharpened stylus. Consequently when someone once asked whether anyone was in there with Caesar, Vibius Crispus made the witty reply: "Not even a fly."

Who was this Vibius Crispus? Suetonius never identified him. Still, the text reads as if he thought readers knew the man. Thus, it should come as no surprise that contemporaries of Suetonius had no problem recognizing the name.[12] As a result, both Hortalus and Crispus turn out to be other instances like those of Pompey and Maecenas, for the problem of who they are arises not out of Suetonius' carelessness but from our own ignorance.

Thus far, we may conclude that in the matter of concern to us Suetonius was a careful writer, for he identified his characters to the extent required by the intended sense of his narrative. Consequently, with the Chrestus of *Claudius* 25.4 he very likely used the same care. Nonetheless, before reaching this conclusion we must search for other instances where Suetonius' failure to provide sufficient identification might perhaps have left his readers in a quandary. Two clear cases of this type do appear in *Augustus* 70.1 and *Claudius* 40.3, but, for the reasons discussed below, are irrelevant.

Concerning the former, Suetonius himself indicated that he was citing here an anonymously written but well-known poem. Among its six lines, one reads, "Sexque deos vidit Mallia sexque deas" ("Mallia saw six gods and six goddesses"), and the question naturally arises as to the identity of the Mallia mentioned therein. In the first place, however, there is no way to know if even he understood the exact reference to the word *Mallia*; after all, before Suetonius quoted it, the poem had been passed on in Roman society for at least one hundred

---

[11]Here in an adjectival form, "Viriatini belli."

[12]Cf. *PIR* V 379.

years.[13] In the second, whether he did or did not, it was the poem as a whole which underlined the theme of Suetonius in this section on Augustus' notorious adulteries. Thus, because the word *Mallia* was an integral part of the poem's structure, and because the poem as a whole was integral to his argument at this point, Suetonius was not in a position to omit the perhaps unidentified term.

Claudius 40.3, part of a section beginning at 38.3 and focusing on aspects of Claudius' stupidity as demonstrated by various of his utterances, is similar. Chapter 39 deals with imperial comments which arose out of thoughtlessness. Famous here is the occasion when, after having had his wife Messalina executed, he then complained about her failure to present herself for dinner. Chapter 40 then uses six imperial quotations in order to demonstrate that Claudius

> often showed such heedlessness in word and act that one would suppose that he did not know or care to whom, with whom, when, or where he was speaking.... In fact every day, and almost every hour and minute, he would make such remarks as these; "What! do you take me for a Telegenius?" ["Ego tibi Telegenius videor?"] "Scold me, but hands off!" and many others of the same kind which would be unbecoming ["multaque talia deformia"] even in private citizens.

In this case the issue is the identity of Telegenius; to readers without such information the odd expression "Ego tibi Telegenius videor?" is meaningless. For that reason Smilda and Rolfe assert that Claudius, Suetonius, and his original readers did know who the individual was, and the latter adds the reasonable suggestion that he was "some man proverbial for his folly."[14] Nonetheless, since Suetonius intended within the present context to demonstrate Claudius' *deformitas*, we may suppose that, because it was incomprehensible, he chose to cite this imperial quotation.[15] After all, the following "Scold me, but hands off!" is, to say the least, obscure.[16] In fact, it was Claudius' "obscurity" which Suetonius intended to highlight in this section: attributing to the emperor certain babblings about some meaningless

---

[13] Supposing it was written at the latest just prior to Augustus' death (14 CE).

[14] Henricus Smilda, *C. Suetonii Tranquilli: Vita Divi Claudii* (Groningen: J. B. Wolters, 1896), p. 163; Suetonius, *Lives of the Caesars, Lives of Illustrious Men*, trans. John C. Rolfe, LCL, 2 vols. (Cambridge: Harvard University Press, 1913-1914), 2:75, n. a.

[15] Suetonius used precisely that method, and for the same purpose, in *Claudius* 15.3: "I decide in favour of those who have told the truth."

[16] So Smilda, *C. Suetonii Tranquilli*, p. 163: "quid Claudius intellegi voluit, obscurum."

Telegenius did accomplish that goal.[17] Thus, *Augustus* 70.1 reveals no carelessness and *Claudius* 40.3 only an apparent lack of care on Suetonius' part in their identification of named subjects.

In sum, Suetonius consistently identified the various characters within his narrative to the extent required by the sense of the text. Because this is so, we must suppose that he thought *Chrestus* equally as recognizable to his second-century readers as were *Claudius, Roma,* and *Iudaeus*. This means, negatively, that our ignorance of Chrestus permits us to enter only incompletely into the conversation between Suetonius and his original readers. The very way in which Suetonius carried on his part of this conversation is informative, however, for the fact that Chrestus was still identifiable in the second century tells us, not insignificantly, of his ancient prominence.

---

[17]Smilda, *C. Suetonii Tranquilli*, p. 163, cites several Telegenii in *CIL*.

Chapter Nine

"Here a Chrestus, There a Chrestus"

On the basis of the likelihood that Suetonius and his original readers knew the identity of Chrestus, we must survey the relevant remains of antiquity in order to discover who Chrestus was. Failing that, we are obliged to establish at least the social and political parameters of the name, i.e., who he might have been. Before proceeding to this task, however, we need to consider a variety of general matters associated with the word *Chrestus* and with the principles of nomenclature in the Greek and Roman world.

The Latin *Chrestus* originates in a Greek personal name taken, as the instance in Plutarch's *Phocion* 10.2 shows, from the adjective χρηστός and the very broad range of qualities including usefulness, goodness, auspiciousness, successfulness, honesty, and kindness which were associated with it.[1] We are able to find the adjective on several Greek epitaphs in Rome, one good example of which is the dedication of a mother to her deceased son whom she describes as "χρηστὸς καὶ ἄμεμπτος."[2] Concerning Greek names generally, Pape wrote as follows:

---

[1]LSJ, s.v. χρηστός; cf. Heikki Solin, *Die griechischen Personennamen in Rom: Ein Namenbuch*, 3 vols. (Berlin and New York: Walter de Gruyter & Co., 1982), 2:861, 909.

[2]*IG*, XIV, 1639, and, similarly, 1859. See also 1495, 1595, 1797, 1928. Besides its use as an adjective to describe the deceased as he or she was when alive, χρηστός appears on Attic inscriptions of foreigners and slaves as an attribute of the dead and, elsewhere, in the vocative with χαῖρε as a greeting. Concerning both of these see Max Lambertz (*Die griechischen Sklavennamen* [Vienna: n.p., 1907], p. 4). For the vocative usage see also Iiro Kajanto (*A Study of the Greek Epitaphs*

jeder einzelne Grieche wurde von seinen Eltern mit einem an be-
sondere Umstände der Geburt, Familienverhältnisse und andere
ihnen wichtige Begebenheiten erinnernden oder ihre Wünsche für
das Kind ausdrückenden Namen belegt, oder erhielt auch von seinen
Mitbürgern einen sein Aeusseres oder seine geistige Eigenthüm-
lichkeit bezeichnenden Beinamen, mit welchem er nachher vor-
zugsweise benannt wurde. Erst die Gewohnheit hielt dann in einzelnen Familien bestimmte Namen fest, ohne sich um ihre ursprüng-
liche Bedeutung zu kümmern.[3]

Thus, in the case of *Chrestus* we have before us either a parental
wish name or the name later bestowed upon its bearer because of one
or another personal characteristic. Additionally, however, with little
and perhaps no regard for its original meaning, *Chrestus* might be a
customary family appellation. In particular, Pape observes that the
personal name Χρῆστος, like the others formed from adjectives, could
be identified by the recession of the accent from the ultima to the
penultima.[4] Fick adds that the full name of most Greeks was a single
word composed of two elements. According to him, the vast majority
of these names contained four or five syllables but, because they were
so long, tended to be abbreviated and personalized.[5] In this view,
therefore, Χρῆστος is one such personalization stemming perhaps from
Χρήστιμος (Χρηστό-τιμος) or Εὔχρηστος (Εὔ-χρηστος),[6] and its accent
has receded within the process of abbreviation.[7]

Relatedly, there is good reason to think that within the Greek-
speaking world Χρῆστος was not a name commonly given to slaves.
Besides the fact that it does not appear among those collected in
Lambertz' *Sklavennamen*, its accent over the penultima rather than
the ultima is also untypical of adjectivally derived slave names, the
tendency of which was to preserve the position of the accent as found

---

of Rome, Acta Instituti Romani Finlandiae, vol. 2.3 [Helsinki: Tilgmann, 1963], p.
18). In Rome, *IG*, XIV, 1480 and perhaps 1714 conform to the former; *IG*, XIV,
1810, 1873, and 1953 conform to the latter.

[3]W. Pape and G. Benseler, *Wörterbuch der griechischen Eigennamen*, 3d ed.,
2 vols. (1911; reprint ed., Graz: Akademische Druck- u. Verlagsanstalt, 1959),
1:xv.

[4]Ibid., 1:xvi-xvii.

[5]August Fick, *Die griechischen Personennamen nach ihrer Bildung erklärt und
systematisch geordnet*, ed. Fritz Bechtel and August Fick, 2d ed. (Göttingen: Vandenhoeck & Ruprecht, 1894), pp. 2 and 5.

[6]Ibid., p. 292.

[7]Ibid., p. 22.

on the adjective.[8] Consequently, although we are unable to maintain
categorically that Χρῆστος could never have been used as a slave
name,[9] it was not at home within that context.
While Greeks for the most part bore a single personal name,[10]
this was the practice in Roman nomenclature specifically for persons
who were either foreigners or slaves. Otherwise, emancipated male
slaves previously belonging to Roman citizens acquired not only their
own Roman citizenship but also the traditional Roman *tria nomina*,
i.e., the three-part Roman name consisting of praenomen, nomen, and
cognomen. It was customary for the freedman to take the praenomen
and nomen of his former master and now patron but also to preserve
the old slave name as cognomen.[11] For example, on the inscription
which bears his name, Lucius Marcius Ianuarius appears as "L[ucius]
Marcius L[ucii] l[ibertus] Ianuarius,"[12] that is, as "Lucius Marcius,
freedman of Lucius, Ianuarius." He was, in other words, the freedman
of the Lucius Marcius whose first two names he had as a matter of
custom taken. *Ianuarius*, on the other hand, had been probably his
slave name, but it was now his own cognomen as a Roman citizen. He
had received it perhaps in infancy or from a previous owner, perhaps
when renamed by his new purchaser, Lucius Marcius: "Als ein Sklave
auf dem Markt verkauft wurde, hatte er entweder einen Namen oder
er hatte keinen. Da er als *res* Eigentum seines Herrn war...es stand
dem Patron frei, den jeweiligen alten Namen zu genehmigen oder zu

[8]Lambertz, *Sklavennamen*, pp. 49-53. The adjectivally established slave form
Χρηστός is likewise unattested here; however, since Χρηστή, the feminine slave
construction, does appear twice, it is hard to imagine that the masculine was not
used in the same way.

[9]By way of example, we might imagine the circumstance in which it had been
given to the servant of someone whose own appellation was Χρῆστος (Lambertz,
Sklavennamen, p. 6).

[10]The full designation in Greek consisted of the personal name which was then
followed by both the patronymic or name of the father and thereafter by the ethnic
or place of origin, but only the first of these appeared in normal usage (Kajanto,
Greek Epitaphs, pp. 2-4).

[11]See Sandys (*Latin Epigraphy*, pp. 207-221) and Gordon (*Latin Epigraphy*, pp.
17-30) for good summaries of these matters. In pointing to the same tendency of
the freedmen to keep their former slave names as cognomina, Solin (*Beiträge zur
Kenntnis der griechischen Personennamen in Rom*, Commentationes Humanarum
Litterarum, vol. 48 [Helsinki: Societas Scientiarum Fennica, 1971], p. 134) seems
to argue against his own thesis concerning the social stigma perpetuated by the
use of Greek names.

[12]*CIL*, VI, 7918.

ändern."[13] In such a sense, therefore, Julius Baumgart familiarizes us with the masters who chose only Latin or only Greek names for their slaves or who preferred appellations of a religious nature.[14] What this means is that from the fact of a Latin or Greek slave name in itself we may draw few conclusions about the origins of the person so designated. In other words, Ianuarius may well have been a Gaul or a Greek, a Jew or an Egyptian.

The situation of course changed with the birth of a son to this *libertinus*. Although some disabilities were attached to the freedman status of parents, as free-born Roman citizens their children did not share in the same difficulties. These young people regularly received the new praenomen and nomen of their father along with a cognomen which was parentally chosen from the very large number of Greek and Latin names available in the city of Rome.[15] Thus, Ianuarius might well have given his son a cognomen different from his own so that he should have been called, let us suppose, Lucius Marcius Priscus. Also, he might have given his own cognomen to him,[16] in which case this son too became Lucius Marcius Ianuarius.

As a result, in terms of the father it may be said that *Ianuarius* first represented the name of a slave. Thereafter, however, it became the cognomen of this person as a freedman/Roman citizen of unknown ethnic background. He may have been either born or purchased in the month of January or perhaps was given this particular designation as a sign of "good omen."[17] Nevertheless, insofar as the son is concerned,

---

[13]Solin, *Beiträge zur Kenntnis der griechischen Personennamen*, p. 41, n. 2. He makes a similar point with his "Juden und Syrer" in *ANRW*, 2.29²:635. In the same place he also indicates that this accounts for why Semitic names were not common in the West.

[14]Julius Baumgart, *Die römischen Sklavennamen* (Breslau: R. Nischkowsky, 1936), p. 12.

[15]Iiro Kajanto (*The Latin Cognomina*, Commentationes Humanarum Litterarum, vol. 36.2 [Helsinki: Societas Scientiarum Fennica, 1965], pp. 379-417) lists perhaps 6,500 Latin cognomina. In addition to this, the statistics of Solin (*Beiträge zur Kenntnis der griechischen Personennamen*, pp. 97, 112) demonstrate that more than sixty percent of the Roman cognomina were derived from the Greek instead of the Latin language.

[16]We possess a good example of this in *CIL*, VI, 18022. Another instance is Cicero, i.e., Marcus Tullius Cicero. He had a brother, Quintus Tullius Cicero, with the same cognomen as his own. Their sons were called, respectively, Marcus Tullius Cicero and Quintus Tullius Cicero (*OCD²*, s.v. "Marcus Tullius Cicero" and "Quintus Tullius Cicero").

[17]Kajanto, *Cognomina*, p. 61.

the highly popular *Ianuarius* has become the cognomen of a second generation Roman.[18] In sum, his cognomen tells us very little about Ianuarius himself, for it might represent the single designation of a slave of undetermined origin, the cognomen of the same person within his new status as a freedman/Roman citizen, or the cognomen of some other Roman whose family had held the citizenship for an unspecified number of generations and who was given this name by his parents for reasons of connotation or family tradition.

In light of these considerations we can better understand the name *Chrestus* within its Roman context. First, granting its origins as the transliteration of the Greek personal name Χρῆστος, we need to keep in mind that behind any unelucidated appearance of a Chrestus in Rome might stand a free Greek foreigner (*peregrinus*) present within the city whose name was so transliterated into Latin script. This would have been the situation, for example, if Latin writers had recounted a visit to Rome by the Χρῆστος of Byzantium who was an important Athenian rhetorician of the second century.[19]

As a result of Hellenization, Greek names had also spread over the entire eastern Mediterranean world. For example, in terms of its parts associated with Judaism, Tcherikover writes, "In the Diaspora, as in Palestine, Hellenization found its first external expression in the changing of personal names.... Although Hebrew and Semitic names as a whole did not disappear throughout the Hellenistic period, by their side appears a multitude of Greek names such as Alexander, Ptolemy, Antipater, Demetrius, Jason and the like."[20] We should perhaps think of Jason and Menelaus in 2 Maccabees 4:7, 23, of the sons of John Hyrcanus, i.e., Aristobolus, Antigonus, and Alexander, of Herod and his sons Archelaus, Philip, and Antipas, or of Philo and his brother Alexander Lysimachus.[21] In a related sense Baumgart states

---

[18]According to Kajanto (*Cognomina*, pp. 29, 30, 60, 218), the "calendaric" *Ianuarius* was one of the eighteen most popular Roman cognomina. Not generally used by the senatorial class (1%), it appealed primarily to other Roman citizens (87%) but was in use at the same time as a slave name (7%).

[19]Philostratus *Lives of the Sophists* 2.11; *PW* 6 (1899) 2450.

[20]Tcherikover, *Hellenistic Civilization*, p. 346. See also Hengel, *Judaism and Hellenism*, 1:58-65, and Saul Lieberman, *Greek in Jewish Palestine: Studies in the Life and Manners of Jewish Palestine in the II-IV Centuries C.E.*, 2d ed. (New York: Philipp Feldheim, Inc., 1965), pp. 1-67.

[21]Within the context of Philo and his brother, the Apion and Chaeremon known to Josephus come to mind, both of whom appear to have been Egyptians (Stern, *Authors*, 1:389 and 417; *OCD*², s.v. "Apion" and "Chaeremon"). According to Willrich ("Caligula," p. 413, n. 2) Apion was a Greek.

that imperial Rome experienced a continuous "Einwanderung Freier, besonders aus dem Osten, in die Hauptstadt, die meist griech. Namen führten und griech. sprachen, obwohl der kleinste Teil von ihnen aus Griech. selbst stammte."[22] In other words, a free foreigner resident in Rome and bearing the Greek name Χρῆστος might or might not have been Greek in origin.

Additionally, in any case, Baumgart is certainly correct that he would not have wanted for company among other persons like himself: the Latin-Greek bilingualism of the city[23] no doubt caused Rome to be an attractive place for Greek speakers wishing to improve their lot. Hence, Seneca's description of the Roman populace at the time when the Chrestus of interest to us was there:

> Behold this concourse of men, for whom the houses of huge Rome scarcely suffice; most of this throng are now deprived of their country. From their towns and colonies, from the whole world, in fact, hither have they flocked. Some have been brought by ambition, some by the obligation of a public trust, some by an envoy's duty having been laid upon them, some, seeking a convenient and rich field for vice, by luxury, some by a desire for the higher studies, some by the public spectacles; some have been drawn by friendship, some, seeing the ample opportunity for displaying energy, by the chance to work; some have presented their beauty for sale, some their eloquence for sale—every class of person has swarmed into the city that offers high prizes for both virtues and vices.[24]

About the same things Tacitus later complained in referring to "the capital itself, where all things horrible or shameful in the world collect and find a vogue,"[25] an opinion likewise expressed in the famous words of Tacitus' contemporary, Juvenal: "I cannot abide, Quirites, a

---

[22]Baumgart, *Sklavennamen*, p. 83. In at least partial support of Baumgart may be cited also the statistics of Kajanto (*Greek Epitaphs*, pp. 2 and 5) who, from the few inscriptions which provide this type of information, reports that individuals bearing Greek names on the Greek epitaphs of Rome came not only from Greece (10) but also from Asia Minor (43), Syria (12), and Egypt (7) as well. It is unlikely, however, that all of these were free foreigners resident in Rome when they died. In any case, the facts alone that more than sixty percent of all Roman cognomina were Greek (cf. p. 182, n. 15) and that thirty-eight percent of Roman Jews had Greek names (Leon, *Jews of Ancient Rome*, p. 107) is revealing in a general way about the ubiquity of Greek names in Rome.

[23]Kajanto, *Greek Epitaphs*, pp. 6 and 44; Solin, *Beiträge zur Kenntnis der griechischen Personennamen*, pp. 49 and 68.

[24]Seneca *Ad Helviam* 6.2-3, LCL translation by John W. Basore.

[25]*Annals* 15.44.

Rome of Greeks; and yet what fraction of our dregs comes from
Greece? The Syrian Orontes has long since poured into the Tiber,
bringing with it its lingo and its manners, its flutes and its slanting
harp-strings; bringing too the timbrels of the breed, and the trulls who
are bidden ply their trade at the Circus."[26]
    Besides the free eastern foreigners who bore Greek names in
Rome, slaves as well were commonly given these names there. The
presupposition for understanding this matter is the fact already
alluded to that the slave owner was entirely free to determine the
name of his or her slave property. For a variety of different reasons[27]
Greek names became popular in this regard.[28] The result was that,
though Roman slave owners preferred the old Greek slave names and
also invented for their slaves new Greek ones based on Latin patterns,
they were quite willing to apply Greek personal names to their new
property.[29] *Chrestus*, therefore, might be the name not only of a free

---

[26]Juvenal *Satire* 3.60-65, LCL translation by G. G. Ramsay. In support of the
thesis of the universally servile sense of Greek names in Rome, Solin (*Beiträge zur
Kenntnis der griechischen Personennamen*, p. 41; cf. pp. 100, 108) plays down the
role of free foreigners with the statement, "Peregrinen gab es nicht viele in Rom,"
a position which he bases on the neither entirely relevant nor convincing (cf. his
own "Juden und Syrer" in *ANRW*, 2.29[2]:784) premise that Rome provided but few
possibilities for free foreign workers. In this particular as well as in his general
thesis he follows the classical position of Tenney Frank ("Race Mixture in the
Roman Empire," *American Historical Review* 21 (1915-1916):693-695). In light of
Tacitus, Juvenal and especially Seneca, however, there is no surprise in Kajanto's
conclusion (*Greek Epitaphs*, pp. 4-5) that Greek-speaking eastern immigrants
made up a significant proportion of the Roman population.

[27]Lambertz (*Sklavennamen*, p. 6, n. 7) and Solin (*Beiträge zur Kenntnis der
griechischen Personennamen*, pp. 86-99) trace these out.

[28]Solin, *Beiträge zur Kenntnis der griechischen Personennamen*, pp. 146-159;
Lambertz, *Sklavennamen*, p. 6.

[29]Lambertz, *Sklavennamen*, p. 6, n. 8; Solin, *Beiträge zur Kenntnis der
griechischen Personennamen*, pp. 105-106, although Solin is much more reticent
about the use of the personal names including the type to which Chrestus belongs.
Baumgart (*Sklavennamen*, pp. 16 and 21) does explain why masters might have
preferred a positive name like *Chrestus* for their slaves, though in so doing he
implicitly abolishes the difference in Greek between the personal name Χρῆστος
and the slave name Χρηστός, a distinction not expressible in the written form of
the Latin Chrestus although quite possibly so orally. That is, the given Roman
bilingualism, slave owners there may well have differentiated between the names
Chréstus/Χρῆστος and (*Chrestús*)/Χρηστός in speaking to or of their slaves. *CIL*,
VI, 21100 is interesting in this regard because of its use of the more Greek
sounding "Chrestos." It would be helpful to know where this man, incidently, not
a slave, placed the accent on his name.

easterner but also of a slave resident in Rome. In the latter case, there is no reason to assume that he had come from the Hellenized East, for a Roman master habitually utilizing Greek names for slaves was entirely likely to employ *Chrestus* for his Gaul. As Baumgart expresses it, "Die aus dem Ausland gekommenen Sklaven erhielten in der Regel einen neuen griech. oder lat. Namen. Nur selten behielten sie ihren heimischen Namen bei."[30]

Under these circumstances, any Chrestus attested as present in Rome might have been a free Greek or other free easterner but also, just as the Latin inscriptions of Rome in fact do make clear, a slave[31] perhaps from Gaul and therefore of western, but perhaps also from Greece, Asia Minor, Egypt, Syria, or Judea[32] and therefore of eastern

---

[30]Baumgart, *Sklavennamen*, p. 75. Frank ("Race Mixture," p. 700) argues that slaves with Greek names tended to be of eastern origin, but, in addition to the reasons already mentioned as well as Frank's own caveats, the good observations of Mary L. Gordon ("The Nationality of Slaves under the Early Roman Empire," *Journal of Roman Studies* 14 [1924]:93-111) and Solin (*Beiträge zur Kenntnis der griechischen Personennamen*, pp. 146-158) make this uncertain.

[31]*CIL*, VI contains the Latin inscriptions of Rome including a very important index of cognomina. Many of these inscriptions witness Chresti who were or, as their contemporary status as *libertini* indicates, had been slaves: *CIL*, VI, 668, 880, 1929, 1949, 3555, 5645, 6228/6385/6398, 7460, 7846, 7924, 11707, 12930, 14058, 14756, 14757, 14761, 14805, 16837, 18975, 20750, 20770, 20775, 21531, 22837, 26157, 28324, 28659, 31218, 33472, 33772, 37672.

[32]Except as an anachronism based on contemporary Nazi interest in forcing Jews to identify themselves by "Jewish" names, it is difficult to understand Baumgart's remark (*Sklavennamen*, p. 75; cf. Raul Hilberg, *The Destruction of the European Jews: Student Edition* [New York: Holmes & Meier Publishers, Inc., 1985], p. 56) that concerns of racial differentiation ("Rassenunterschied") might explain why Semitic slaves in Republican Rome were identified by Semitic name. More helpful is his alternative (p. 75, n. 72) that such names might be accounted for by the large number of slaves drawn under the Republic from Asia Minor and Syria. For the early empire he notes that these names decreased (cf. Solin, "Juden und Syrer" in *ANRW*, 2.29²:635, and his "Die Namen der orientalischen Sklaven in Rom" in *L'Onomastique latine: Paris 13-15 octobre 1975*, ed. Noël Duval, Colloques internationaux du Centre national de la recherche scientifique, 564 [Paris: Éditions du Centre national de la recherche scientifique, 1977], pp. 205-220, on the rarity of Semitic names in the West). This situation is mirrored in Rome's Jewish population, for its inscriptions show 78 percent of Jews having purely Latin (46%) or purely Greek (32%) names as opposed to thirteen percent with purely Semitic ones (Leon, *Jews of Ancient Rome*, p. 107; cf. Juster, *Les Juifs*, 2:221-234; Solin, "Juden und Syrer" in *ANRW*, 2.29²:711-713). As to what portion of Jews were slaves or *libertini*, we can only guess. Leon (p. 237) claims wrongly (so already Solin, "Juden und Syrer" in *ANRW*, 2.29²:714, n. 282; cf. *CII*, 256 and 462) that "there is not a single mention in our catacomb inscriptions of either

origin. There is, for example, a slave named Chrestus who, in response to an answered prayer, set up a votive tablet to the god Silvanus.[33] Another prepared an epitaph for his slave wife and children (*CIL*, VI, 14757), and a third had an epitaph prepared for him by the woman with whom he had lived for eighteen years (16837).[34] Which of these Chresti were Jews? Which were Egyptians, Syrians, Gauls, or Asians? Which were simply born into slavery in Rome itself? We have no way of knowing.

Equally important, the other thing not discernible from the name itself is the potential influence of any of these persons within Roman society, for, while we may assume that many slaves were practically invisible, others who exercised significant roles in the homes and the occupations of their powerful masters were no doubt perceived quite differently.[35] Specifically, there is the Chrestus (*CIL*, VI, 33472) who

---

slaves or freedmen." Still, his view in the same place that "by the time of our inscriptions there were no Jewish slaves within the Jewish community" may be generally accurate. If we follow the late date of these epitaphs which is proposed by Rutgers ("Überlegungen zu den jüdischen Katakomben Roms," *Jahrbuch für Antike und Christentum* 33 [1990]:142-154; cf. Leon, *Jews of Ancient Rome*, pp. 65-66), we must also recall Cicero's claim (*Pro Flacco* 28.66) according to which many Jews were in the city by 50 BCE and Philo's opinion that already under Augustus large numbers of these "were Roman citizens emancipated" (*Legatio* 155). In fact, depending upon how late we date them, by the time these epitaphs were prepared most of the descendants of Jewish slaves created by the events of 66-70 (Josephus *War* 6.414-419), 115-117, and even 132-135 CE were perhaps long integrated into the citizenship. As will be discussed later, *Chrestus* does not appear on any Roman or other Jewish inscription.

[33]*CIL*, VI, 668: "Silvano sancto v s l m Chrestus Orosiae Tullirae." Solin (*Die griechischen Personennamen*, 2:929) typically considers this Chrestus either a slave or freedman, but Sandys (*Latin Epigraphy*, p. 219) takes a single name followed by the genitive of possession to indicate slave status.

[34]As we might expect, these Chresti bore only the single name typical of a slave. Others bearing the single name and likely from details within the inscription to have been slaves include those mentioned in *CIL*, VI, 14757, 14759, 18975, and 32480 (2). On the other hand, the single-named Chresti in *CIL*, VI, 1871, 5716, 11707, 14756, and 20775 were evidently citizens mostly of the freedman class. *CIL*, VI, 5716 may refer to a freeborn foreigner.

[35]Alföldy, *Social History*, p. 148: "In the determination of social realities in the Roman world it was by no means *only* the fixed positions within a social hierarchy that mattered, but also the personal relations between individuals placed higher and lower, which were always of the greatest importance–for example, within the *familia*, between a slave and his master." See also his helpful figure on p. 146. Similarly, Garnsey and Saller (*Roman Empire*, p. 119) write that "even within the category of slaves, wealth could confer power over others. Responsibility within

held the financial position of *dispensator* for Norbanus Balbus and Norbanus Flaccus, both of whom appear to have been consuls about 20 CE.[36] Another ostensible slave, Chrestus Auctianus (6228, 6385, 6398), had indeed "increased" his own possessions to include many slaves (*vicarii*), and Chrestus "caesaris" (5645) belonged to a member of the imperial family.[37] But most interesting is "Chrestus aug[usti] cubicularius" (33772),[38] the chamberlain of some unspecified emperor perhaps of the second or the third century.[39] We shall return to him because the Alexandrian slave Helicon in that role under the emperor Gaius had wielded very much power against the Jewish people. After all, this Helicon "was with him when he was going to bed...so that he alone had convenient and leisurely audiences of the emperor."[40] So, though *Chrestus* reveals itself to have been the name of many Roman slaves, we should not conclude automatically from this that these Chresti were "just" slaves, for resourceful persons of that class were certainly in positions where their influence and power could be felt.

Of course someone with the name *Chrestus* need not have been either a free foreigner of eastern origin or a slave of undetermined provenance. Like the Ianuarius already noted, many of the Chresti in the Latin inscriptions of Rome bore not only the designation *libertus* of the freedman class but also the desirable *tria nomina* which marked them as citizens of Rome.[41] For example, Quintus Lucretius Chrestus

---

the master's household also conferred power, which varied with the size and status of the household."

[36]Cf. Attilio Degrassi, *I fasti consolari dell'impero romano dal 30 avanti Cristo al 613 dopo Cristo*, Sussidi eruditi, vol. 3 (Rome: Edizioni di storia e letteratura, 1952), pp. 7 and 8 (respectively, C. Norbanus Flaccus, 15 CE; L. Norbanus Flaccus, 19 CE).

[37]Heikki Solin (*Die griechischen Personennamen*, 2:930) dates this Chrestus to the first or second century.

[38]The reference to a wife indicates perhaps that this Chrestus had the status of imperial freedman.

[39]So, without explanation, Solin (*Die griechischen Personennamen*, 2:930).

[40]Philo *Legatio* 175; cf. *Legatio* 166-177. Much has been written about the tremendous influence and power of both imperial slaves and freedmen. Cf. Jerome Carcopino, *Daily Life in Ancient Rome: The People and the City at the Height of the Empire*, trans. E. O. Lorimer (1941; reprint ed., Harmondsworth, Eng.: Penguin Books, 1981), pp. 75-77; Alföldy, *Social History*, pp. 94-156; Garnsey and Saller, *Roman Empire*, pp.107-125.

[41]Most of the Chresti on p. 186 (n. 31) belonged to this category.

("Q[uintus] Lucretius Q[uinti] l[ibertus] Chrestus") had been freed from servitude by his former master, Quintus Lucretius Gemellus, himself by the way the *libertus* of some other Quintus Lucretius (*CIL*, VI, 1929). Then, to cite a few more examples, there are Marcus Pilius Chrestus ("M[arcus] Pilius M[arci] l[ibertus] Chrestus," 7460), Tiberius Antonius Chrestus ("T[iberius] Antonius T[iberii] l[ibertus] Chrestus," 14058), Gaius Cincius Chrestus ("C[aius] Cincius C[aii] l[ibertus] Chrestus," 14805), and likewise Lucius Crimillius Chrestus ("L[ucius] Crimill[i]us L[ucii] l[ibertus] Chrestus," 20750), i.e., Chrestus, the former slave of Lucius Crimillus, but now his freedman and a Roman citizen. It was natural in all of these cases that such men should have continued to be called Chrestus. This means, therefore, that otherwise unexplained Roman Chresti might have been either free foreigners of eastern origin or slaves of unknown derivation. Also, however, they might have been Roman citizens of the *libertinus* class. Moreover, as citizens these last normally[42] maintained a strong bond with their former masters and now patrons. This association, depending upon both the nature of the freedman's relationship with the patron and the magnitude of the patron's own influence, often gave the freedman a very real share in that influence.[43]

Furthermore, someone bearing the name *Chrestus* may just as well have belonged to the class of freeborn Roman citizens, that is, to the *ingenui*. Kajanto stresses the significant point, for example, that "a study of the transmission of cognomina reveals that persons with Greek cognomina...gave their children Greek and Latin cognomina in the ratio 4.6:4. This implies that a number of the bearers of Greek cognomina were likewise natives of Rome. Allowing for the many uncertainties of the calculations, it seems reasonable to conclude that a considerable proportion of the persons recorded in the Greek epitaphs were born in Rome."[44] And, as Solin explains, there is no reason that this should surprise us at the level of abstract either: "Man könnte a priori annehmen, dass die ständige Orientalisierung der römischen

---

[42]Peter Garnsey ("Independent Freedmen and the Economy of Roman Italy under the Principate," *Klio* 63 [1981]:359-371) points out the large number of successful freedmen with no ties to their former masters. "Wealthy freedmen abound in the sources" (p. 359).

[43]Cf. A. M. Duff, *Freedmen in the Early Roman Empire* (1928; reprint ed., New York: Barnes & Noble, 1958), passim; Susan Treggiari, *Roman Freedmen during the Late Republic* (Oxford: Clarendon Press, 1969), passim.

[44]Kajanto, *Greek Epitaphs*, p. 5. Similarly, Leslie F. Smith ("The Significance of Greek *Cognomina* in Italy," *Classical Philology* 29 [1934]:145-147) provides examples to show the early use of Greek cognomina by municipal magistrates who were necessarily freeborn citizens.

Bevölkerung durch die seit der mittleren Republik immer häufiger werdenden Freilassungen auch in der Namengebung der Freigeborenen ihre Spuren hinterlassen hätte."[45] One excellent illustration of all these things is the base of a statue which preserves both a dedication to the new Roman emperor Vespasian (69-79 CE) and a register in eight columns providing the praenomina, nomina, and cognomina of the several hundred citizens who were members of the Roman tribe making the dedication.[46] The samples below are taken from those two portions of columns on which the cognomen *Chrestus* is engraved:

---

[45]Solin, *Beiträge zur Kenntnis der griechischen Personennamen*, p. 96. Because the thesis of Solin's study is that Roman society linked Greek names with slaves, he ignores Kajanto's statistics as well his own statement and immediately denies that, as the empire began, even *libertini* gave these socially inferior names to their Roman citizen children. Still, in addition to the fact that an absolute position is inherently suspect, his own study shows, insofar as any one name is concerned, the problematic nature of this thesis. First, he soon softens it by noting that, during the first two imperial centuries, Greek cognomina normally served *libertini* and their offspring (p. 123). Hence, as Kajanto says, freeborn Roman citizens used Greek names, evidence of which appears in Solin's statistic (p. 133) that even Roman parents both of whom bore *Latin* cognomina (itself an uncommon situation occurring 17 percent of the time) chose *Greek* names for children one time in nine. Second, since 63 percent of Roman names were Greek, he admits these had a life of their own in Rome (p. 112). Given the city's bilingualism, this is not surprising. Third, he realizes his theory of socially isolated Greek names seems to contradict a Roman penchant for them and to require the unlikely conclusion that 70 percent of Romans were born into slavery (pp. 135-136; cf. Treggiari, *Roman Freedmen*, pp. 231-232). Fourth, stating that the tendency of freed persons to replace servile cognomina would demonstrate the inferior status of these names, he then oddly acknowledges that this tendency did not exist: "Tausende von Freigelassenen noch griechische Sklave-Cognomina führen" (p. 134). Equally important, on the basis of his differentiation in attitude between the beginning of the empire and the second century, he discovers a growing tendency of these cognomina to lose their servile sense and to be adopted by all levels of society (pp. 99, 124-126; cf. P. R. C. Weaver, "*Cognomina ingenua*: A Note," *Classical Quarterly* 14 [1964]:311-315, who deals with this change among Latin cognomina), a view quite ambiguous in terms of the Chrestus of interest to us, for he appeared neither at the beginning nor the end of this development. Most important, therefore, are two statements with which Solin might have introduced his study: first, generalities aside, the social status of individual Greek names varied greatly; second, the manner of their reporting makes the social status of these cognomina unclear (p. 137). In sum, a priori assumptions concerning the servile status of the very many Roman Chresti are inappropriate. A posteriori, as we shall soon see, they are simply wrong.

[46]*CIL*, VI, 200. It is their membership in the "trib suc iunior," i.e., in the *tribus suburana iunior* (cf. Sandys, *Latin Epigraphy*, p. 215) which reveals that the persons named on the inscription were Roman citizens.

Col 1, 2-11	Col 5, 37-46
C. Acilius Abascantus	Q. Fabius Primigenius
D. Annius Crescens	C. Fundanius Castus
T. Asinius Apollonius	Q. Fabius Faustio
D. Annius Ampliatus	C. Fundilius Crescens
C. Asinius Chrestus	T. Flavius Agathangelus
D. Annius Firmus	*C. Gallio Chrestus*
D. Annius Ampliatus	L. Gellius Mithridas
L. Aponius Libycus	D. Haterius Thyrsus
L. Ambivius Amarantus	M. Hirrius Martialis
D. Annius Onesimus	D. Iunius Felix

Chrestus does fit right in among these Latin and Greek derived cognomina of Rome and shows itself at home within this context. Like most other names it did not attain the popularity of *Crescens*, *Felix*, or *Secundus*, nor of other common names like *Primigenius*, *Iucundus*, *Iustus*, *Vitalis*, *Firmus*, nor of the theophoric *Martialis*, but it was certainly more common than *Facilis* and *Faustio*, and not far, if at all, behind both *Castus* and *Ampliatus*.[47] In addition, it exhibits greater frequency than more than half of all cognomina obtained from strictly Latin roots,[48] something which, given the claim that the previously

---

[47]As the third name in *tria nomina*, *Chrestus* appears fifty-four times* within the Latin inscriptions of Rome and by itself twenty-seven times,** in both cases with some references to the freedman status of the person so named. Among the Greek inscriptions of Rome collected in *IG*, XIV, the name Χρῆστος is clearly attested in 1272 and 2115 (misspelled). It may be present also in 2114 and 2116. For purposes of the present observation I have compared the frequency of the Latin form *Chrestus* only as part of *tria nomina* with the frequency of *Ampliatus* and so forth as furnished by Kajanto's *Cognomina*. Because he drew upon a much larger but unspecified pool of sources for his numbers (pp. 12-13), the comparison is only a rough one, and it is no doubt very low on the *Chrestus* side. (*That is, in *CIL*, VI, 200 [2], 880, 1833b, 1929, 1949, 3555, 4329, 5640, 6208, 6406, 6561, 7460, 7846, 7921, 7924, 10233, 11034, 11823, 12242, 12574, 12815, 12930, 14058, 14761, 14805, 15891, 16178, 17831, 18021, 18022 [2], 18249, 19208, 20750, 20770, 21100, 21531, 22052, 22837, 24255, 24605, 25449, 26157, 26421, 27255, 28324, 28659, 29094, 31218, 32923, 37460, 37672, 37811a.) (**In *CIL*, VI, 668, 1871, 5645, 5716, 6228/6385/6398, 6402, 10046 [2], 11707, 14756, 14757, 14759, 14760, 15384, 16837, 18975, 20276, 20775, 32480, 32543, 32923, 32997, 33472, 33772, 34623 [2], and 37377.)

[48]According to Kajanto (*Cognomina*, p. 29), Latin names as he defines them (p. 11) appear on the average twenty-three (23) times in inscriptions and literature. As just indicated, however, *Chrestus* surfaces more than twice as often as this just within the *tria nomina* of Rome. In other words, it is much more common than the majority of the etymologically Latin names with which his study deals. Similarly, Solin (*Die griechischen Personennamen*, 3:1438-1497) indicates that Chrestus is roughly the fiftieth most frequent out of a total of the six thousand Roman names with which he deals. In terms of the city of Rome at least, therefore, Linck ("De

referred to Roman bilingualism preceded the general use of cognomina there,[49] we may not consider strange.

Whether it was the fathers, or the grandfathers, or the great grandfathers[50] of Gaius Asinius Chrestus and Gaius Gallio Chrestus

---

antiquissimis testimoniis," p. 106) is quite right when he indicates that Chrestus was a "most familiar and pleasing" ("usitatissimum gratissimumque") name.

[49]Kajanto, *Cognomina*, p. 9 (cf. p. 19): "The cognomina came into general use at a time when Roman might had extended over the Mediterranean and far into the areas of Northern and North-Eastern barbarians, and the cognomina met in Latin inscriptions and literary documents were consequently of a mixed origin. Greek names were the largest single, non-Latin contingent, attesting the influence primarily of Greek-speaking slaves." Solin (*Beiträge zur Kenntnis der griechischen Personennamen*, p. 95), affirming the same chronology, employs it to support his previously mentioned view that the association of Greek names with slave status caused Roman citizens to avoid them as they began to use cognomina.

[50]For statistical purposes Solin considers as freeborn citizens of Rome (*ingenui*) only those persons whose names are recorded according to both their *tria nomina* and their filiation. As a good example of the latter, the Marcus Claudius Marci *filius* Marcelus (Marcus Claudius Marcelus, son of Marcus) whom Gordon (*Latin Epigraphy* #10 [p. 86]) discusses is by this definition a freeborn Roman citizen. Others bearing the *tria nomina* of citizenship but lacking the reference to filiation Solin is unwilling to treat in this way. Instead, they are *incerti*, i.e., either freed slave citizens (*libertini*) or *ingenui* (Solin, *Beiträge zur Kenntnis der griechischen Personennamen*, pp. 39-40, 124-126; cf. Lily Ross Taylor, "Freedmen and Freeborn in the Epitaphs of Imperial Rome," *American Journal of Philology* 82 [1961]:113-132). By definition, therefore, Solin cannot consider the two Chresti of this clearly first century inscription to have been *ingenui*, but this has nothing to do with the fact they may well have been exactly that. Specifically, the same principle would preclude treating two early imperial Roman consuls (Gordon, *Latin Epigraphy* #27 [pp. 102-103]) as freeborn citizens, and it does the same thing in terms of the nearly one thousand other similarly designated Roman citizens accounted for alongside of Gaius Asinius Chrestus and Gaius Gallio Chrestus within the present inscription, something in itself most improbable and, given the popularity there of the nomen-praenomen combination *Gaius Iulius* now to be discussed, in reality impossible. In addition, for the period of interest to us it disregards the important statistics of Kajanto (*Onomastic Studies in the Early Christian Inscriptions of Rome and Carthage*, Acta Instituti Romani Finlandiae, vol. 2.1 [Helsinki: Tilgmann, 1963], pp. 5-6) which demonstrate that, while freedmen were normally so identified on their inscriptions, *ingenui* recorded that status by means of filiation only 6.5 percent of the time. Therefore, though some caution is required, Frank's methodology in these matters appears to be more realistic. Treating filiation alone as definite proof of freeborn status, he normally recognizes as also belonging to this group those not otherwise designated as *liberti* (Frank, "Race Mixture," p. 691, n. 3, and p. 702). Smith ("Greek *Cognomina*," p. 145) is similar. In sum, to phrase the matter in its most conservative form, nothing precludes the possibility that Gaius Asinius and Gaius Gallio Chrestus were *ingenui*, and the same thing is true of several other Chresti whom we are about to meet.

who first achieved Roman citizenship we have no way of knowing. We may suppose that various of the families[51] of their tribal colleagues Gaius Iulius Facilis (Col 1, 68), Gaius Iulius Paris (1, 69), Gaius Iulius Eubiltus (2, 45), Gaius Iulius Strato, Gaius Iulius Primigenius, Gaius Iulius Justus, Gaius Iulius Methodicus, Gaius Iulius Menander (3, 50-54), Gaius Iulius Euphron (4, 56), Gaius Iulius Poemen (5, 48), Gaius Iulius Primigenius (5, 51), as well as of the other Gaii Iulii in the inscription[52] could trace their citizenship back to the patronage of Gaius Julius Caesar or perhaps more likely to that of his adopted son, Augustus, more than a half century before.[53]

The Latin inscriptions of Rome also testify to the presence in that city of about thirty other Chresti as well who, exactly like the two in CIL, VI, 200, bore the tria nomina of the citizenship without being identified as libertini, several of whom may well have been freeborn citizens of Rome.[54] To mention some of these Chresti about whom we know practically nothing more than the name itself, there are, for example, Ateius Chrestus (12574), Marcus Valerius Chrestus (19208), Marcus Marcius Chrestus (22052), Quintus Plarius Chrestus (24255), and Quintus Pomponius Chrestus (24605).

More interesting is Titus Flavius Chrestus. He gave his son the same name and called his daughter Chreste (CIL, VI, 18022), both of whom therefore were at least second generation Roman citizens, that is, ingenui.[55] In addition, the same Titus Flavius Chrestus, father or

---

[51]Not, according to Solin ("Juden und Syrer" in ANRW, 2.29^2:714-715), all.

[52]Gaius Iulius Argaeus, Anteros (Col 5, 54 and 55), Eucharistus, Primigenius, Vitalis, Iucundus, Atimetus, Octaianuarius (6, 43-50), Hestimus (7, 60), Secundus (7, 62), and Paederos (8, 54).

[53]Sandys, Latin Epigraphy, p. 218; Solin, Beiträge zur Kenntnis der griechischen Personennamen, p. 37 (cf. 130, n. 1); Chantraine, Freigelassene und Sklaven, p. 4. "Various" because the freed slave of any Gaius Iulius might have the same praenomen and nomen (Sandys, p. 219). A good example is CIL, XIII, 1. 1041 where Gaius Iulius Primulus honored his former master, Gaius Iulius Agedillus. In spite of his praenomen and nomen, therefore, Primulus was of the libertinus class rather than one of the ingenui who could trace their family citizenship back to Julius Caesar or Augustus.

[54]CIL, VI, 1833b, 1871, 4329, 5640, 6208/6406/6561, 7921, 10233, 11034-11038, 11823, 12242, 12574, 12815, 15891/17831, 16178, 18021, 18022 (2)=18249?, 19208, 21100 (Chrestos), 22052, 24255, 24605, 25449 (=18021?), 26421, 27255, 29094, 32923, 37460, and 37811a. Keeping in mind what was said on p. 192 (n. 50), we need not think that they were all ingenui.

[55]If we keep in mind the warning of Solin (Beiträge zur Kenntnis der griechischen Personennamen, p. 125, n. 1), the case (20276) of the freed persons A[ulus]

son, seems to appear in 18249 as the parent of a Titus Flavius Victor who died in infancy. Another interesting case is the Chrestus who identified himself on the epitaph of his twelve-year-old daughter only as Cocceius Chrestus, husband of Cocceia Magna (17831). Then, when he died, his wife and two sons, Lucius Cocceius Priscus and Lucius Cocceius Apollinaris, put his complete Roman name, Lucius Cocceius Chrestus, on a large marble monument (15891).

Other Chresti on the Latin inscriptions of Rome also appear to have been fairly well established. Gaius Octavius Chrestus was the patron of his freed slave Parthenio, the latter a banker (*argentarius*) who had no doubt worked in that trade on behalf of his master (*CIL*, VI, 4329). Gaius Nonius Chrestus had also freed at least one slave (7921) as had the long-living Publius Flavius Chrestus (18021) who may have been the person of the same name with the means to set up an elegant funerary urn for a good friend (25449). Judging by their impressive inscription, Publius Aelius Chrestus and his wife Cornelia Paula were well to do (10233). Marcus Aemilius Chrestus played the leading part in one of Rome's burial societies (11034-11038). Gaius Cornelius Chrestus and his wife Cornelia were in possession of several slaves and freed persons (16178), and the same is true also of Aulus Larcius Chrestos (21100).

Moreover, there existed a variety of Chresti who held prominent positions in Roman society.[56] In its first edition, for example, the *Prosopographia Imperii Romani* referred to two of these, one who held the highly important post of praetorian prefect in the early third century and the other who was the Roman author to be dealt with shortly.[57] By the time of its second edition, however, more recent inscriptional discoveries had not only uncovered the more complete form of the prefect's name—both the nomen and cognomen included, he was called Geminius Chrestus—but had likewise brought to light the distinguished Claudius Chrestus of Hadrumetum in North Africa.[58] In addition, and according to Philostratus (*Lives of the Sophists* 2.11), there was the previously mentioned Chrestus (Χρῆστος) of the second

---

Lucilius Idaeus and his wife Laudica is a bit more ambiguous. Their son's name was Chrestus, but, since he died at age nineteen, it may be that he had been born to them while they were slaves. If this is so, he also was born into slavery. If not, both he and his sister Chryseis were freeborn citizens of Rome.

[56]Not including the mid-first-century BCE criminal of perhaps minor stature about whom Cicero (*Epistulae ad familiares* 2.8.1) had received news while in Athens.

[57]*PIR* C 599 and C 600.

[58]*PIR*² G 144 and C 833 respectively.

century whose students had petitioned Rome that he be awarded the imperial chair of rhetoric in the city of Athens. This Chrestus was an internationally recognized sophist. A Roman philosopher of the late first century bore the same name. Martial wrote two epigrams (7.55 and 9.27) sharply critical of him, and from these we may assume that he was both well educated and a person of some means.

Two other cases deserve our special attention. The first is that of Gaius Iulius Chrestus. His name appears on the highly interesting, seven-line inscription from Syrian Antioch published by Victor Chapot in 1902.[59] The column on the left represents Chapot's transcription of the text, that on the right his interpretation:

[1]	....
[2] xvirstiliudic	xvir(o) stil(itibus) iudic(andis)
[3] qgermanici	q(uaestori) Germanici
[4] caesaris	Caesaris
[5] lecticaesarisaug	leg(ato) Ti. Caesaris Aug(usti)
[6] ciuliuschristus	C. Iulius Christus
[7] dioch...eqduplic	Dioch...? eq(ues) duplic(iarius).

Set up by this Chrestus,[60] the inscription is honorary in character,[61] praising its recipient by the recollection of his senatorial *cursus honorum*, presumably to date.

Most unfortunately, the name of the honoree has been lost from the top of the inscription. From what remains, we know that he began in normal fashion as one of the *decemviri stlitibus iudicandis*, i.e., as a member of the civil court system.[62] Typically again, he next became a *quaestor*, but in this case of the Germanicus ("quaestor Germanici Caesaris") who became the adopted son and likely successor of the emperor Tiberius. Then, at the time when Chrestus honored him with this dedication, he was *legatus*. Alfred Von Domaszewski takes this to signify that he was an army commander (*legatus legionis*) of the emperor Tiberius ("Ti[berius] Caesar Aug[ustus]") in Syrian Antioch

---

[59]Victor Chapot, "Antiquités de la Syrie du Nord," *Bulletin de correspondance hellénique* 26 (1902):161-162. A very fragmentary form of the inscription ("x vir stl iudi") was first brought to the attention of scholarship by Richard Förster, "Skulpturen von Antiochia," *Jahrbuch des kaiserlich deutschen Archäologischen Instituts* 13 (1898):191, and was then reproduced during 1902 in *CIL*, III, Supplement, 14165[14].

[60]Since *Christus* is not a cognomen, orthography requires *Chrestus* here (cf. *ILS*, 8967).

[61]Sandys, *Latin Epigraphy*, pp. 104-117.

[62]Ibid., pp. 110 and 222.

where Chrestus set up this inscription to him,[63] but M. P. Speidel indicates that *legatus* might better point to the higher position of provincial governor.[64] In any case, since Germanicus died in Antioch in 19 CE, that was the latest year in which our anonymous *quaestor* could have served him in that capacity. Given the interval between offices in the *cursus honorum*,[65] he would then have become *legatus* at some point prior to the death of Tiberius in 37 CE.[66] While holding that office, therefore, he was honored by Gaius Iulius Chrestus. Hence, this Chrestus and the Chrestus of *Claudius* 25.4 were contemporaries.

Concerning the identity of the inscription's honoree, Chapot[67] understands that he had been the *quaestor* of Germanicus specifically during this latter's 18-19 CE consular journeys in the East ("fut questeur de Germanicus, en Syrie, suivant toute apparence, et de 18 à 19"), and the interpretation of von Domaszewski is the same.[68] Still, Germanicus was consul in Rome in 12 CE, proconsul in 14 CE in Gaul, and then again consul in 18 CE during his special assignment to the East[69] where he referred to himself in an important primary source as the proconsul (ἀνθύπατος).[70] It appears, therefore, that Germanicus had occasion to be served by at least three quaestors during his career, two while consul in Rome, and one evidently in the East.[71] As a result, we may not be certain that the *quaestor* in our inscription was the one who served under Germanicus in 18-19 CE.

---

[63]A. von Domaszewski, "Eine Inschrift des P. Suillius Rufus," *Rheinisches Museum* 67 (1911):151; also, Ronald Syme, *History in Ovid* (Oxford: Clarendon Press, 1978), p. 89; cf. Sandys, *Latin Epigraphy*, p. 111. *Quaestor* of Germanicus, he would have become *legatus legionis*, the next office in the senatorial *cursus honorum*, shortly thereafter.

[64]Based on personal correspondence between Professor M. P. Speidel and the writer, November 11, 1993.

[65]Anthony R. Birley, *The FASTI of Roman Britain* (Oxford: Clarendon Press, 1981), pp. 4-35; cf. Sandys, *Latin Epigraphy*, p. 110.

[66]The *terminus ante quem* is fixed by the inscription.

[67]Chapot, "Antiquités," p. 162.

[68]Von Domaszewski, "Inschrift," p. 151.

[69]So Wilhelm Kroll in *PW* 10 (1919) 438, 439, 442, 450; similarly, *PIR*² I 221.

[70]Von Wilamowitz-Moellendorff and Zucker, "Zwei Edikte," p. 797.

[71]This is to be extrapolated from Mommsen (*Römisches Staatsrecht*, 3d ed., 3 vols. [1887; reprint ed., Graz: Akademische Druck- u. Verlagsanstalt, 1952-1969], 2:562, 568) and, following him, Gunter Wesener in *PW* 47 (1963) 810, 815, 818.

Nonetheless, significant circumstantial evidence does support this identification. First, Mommsen observes that inscriptions rarely include the lesser role of consular *quaestor* in Rome and that, when they do, the specific title *quaestor consulis* or *quaestor consulum* appears.[72] Second, he indicates that

> zwischen dem Oberfeldherrn und seinem Quästor besteht ein enges gewissermassen persönliches Verhältniss, wie es sonst zwischen Beamten nicht vorkommt; nach alter auch rechtlich anerkannter Sitte werden hier ähnliche Pflichten wie zwischen Vater und Sohn angenommen und äussern ihre Wirkung selbt noch nach Auflösung des Verhältnisses.[73]

So, when the present inscription introduces the honoree as "Quaestor Germanici Caesaris," it implies he was *quaestor* of Germanicus in the special sense evidently[74] possible only in 18-19 CE.

It appears quite probable that von Domaszewski has correctly identified this person.[75] He was Publius Suillius Rufus, the only man whom Tacitus some one hundred years later recognized as *quaestor* of Germanicus,[76] and, hence, quite likely, his *quaestor* par excellence. More important is the contemporary evidence of Ovid who directed a letter (*Ex Ponto* 4.8) to this son-in-law Suillius during the period of interest to us. Having been exiled by Augustus in 8 CE, Ovid later[77] wrote Suillius begging him to use his influence with Germanicus in order to end the banishment:

> Do you, if you hope that anything can be accomplished by petition, beseech with a suppliant's prayer the gods you worship. Your gods are–the young Caesar [Germanicus]. Propitiate your divinity. No altar surely is more familiar to you than this. That altar never permits

---

[72]Mommsen, *Staatsrecht*, 2:568, n. 3; 2:570, n. 2.

[73]Ibid., 2:563-564.

[74]As proconsul (*Oberfeldherr*) in Gaul, Germanicus seems not to have had such a *quaestor* (von Domaszewski, "Inschrift," p. 151).

[75]Von Domaszewski, "Inschrift," p. 151.

[76]Tacitus, *Annals* 4.31: "P. Suillium, quaestorem quondam Germanici." In *Annals* 13.42 Suillius refers to himself ("se quaestorem Germanici fuisse") in just that capacity.

[77]Syme (*History in Ovid*, p. 89) indicates that *Ex Ponto* 4 was written between shortly before 13 CE and shortly after 16 CE. Harry B. Evans (*Publica carmina* [Lincoln, NE: University of Nebraska Press, 1983], p. 153) suggests between 13 and 15 CE.

the supplications of its priest to be in vain: seek from it succor for my fate.[78]

These words demonstrate clearly the nature of Suillius' relationship with Germanicus. Couched in the terms of extreme religious devotion, they describe precisely what Mommsen mentions above as the "enges gewissermassen persönliches Verhältniss" that existed between *the quaestor* in this special sense and his superior. Therefore, it is hard to imagine otherwise than that von Domaszewski has correctly identified Publius Suillius Rufus to be the *quaestor* of Germanicus during the 18-19 CE eastern tour of the latter.

What more do we know about this man?[79] Influential if for no other reason than because of his attachment to Germanicus, he lost this patron in 19 CE. Then, about 25 CE and for reasons of judicial corruption, Tiberius exiled him.[80] However, "Suillius returned, and the succeeding generation viewed him in the plenitude of power, the venal favourite of Claudius, exploiting the imperial friendship long profitably, never well."[81] Not in favor with Tiberius, Suillius perhaps returned from exile when Germanicus' son, Gaius, became emperor in 37 CE. He then became a wealthy lawyer under Germanicus' brother, Claudius, but, as an old man, was exiled again by Nero.[82] Because he was governor of Asia,[83] it is also likely that Suillius had served as consul. In his dedication, then, Chrestus paid honor to a man closely connected to the most important persons within the imperial family. Certainly *quaestor* to Germanicus, the most illustrious member of that family until and even following death in 19 CE, and likely his *quaestor* par excellence, P. Suillius Rufus, certainly a *legatus* of the emperor Tiberius, he was, again, probably that Suillius who later possessed extreme influence under Germanicus' brother, the emperor Claudius.

---

[78]Ovid *Ex Ponto* 4.8.21-24 (LCL translation by Arthur Leslie Wheeler). That the reference is to Germanicus becomes particularly clear as the addressee of the poem changes from Suillius to Germanicus.

[79]The following information including textual references derives from *PIR* S 700, *PW* 7 (1931) 719-722, and Cichorius, *Römische Studien*, pp. 431-432. Further details are available there.

[80]Tacitus *Annals* 4.31.

[81]Ibid. For his relative place among the advisors of Claudius, see Thomas A. Dorey, "Claudius und seine Ratgeber," *Das Altertum* 12 (1966):149-150.

[82]Tacitus *Annals* 11.1-7 and 13.42-43. This exile occurred in 58 CE.

[83]Tacitus *Annals* 13.42-43. The proconsulate of Asia came evidently in 52 or 53 CE (*PW* 7 [1931] 721; *PIR* S 700).

What do we know about Gaius Iulius Chrestus? First, judging by the many men in *CIL*, VI, 200 whose *tria nomina* began with *Gaius Iulius*, he too was a Roman citizen.[84] Second, he identified himself on the inscription as "dioch eques duplicarius." While the first word, *dioch*, is uncertain,[85] *eques duplicarius* means that Chrestus served in the mounted guard of the provincial governor (*legatus*) in whose honor the dedication was prepared.[86] Third, and as von Domaszewski

---

[84]In a telephone conversation on November 30, 1992, M. P. Speidel indicated to me that Chrestus was probably–though, given the eastern provenance of the inscription, not necessarily–a Roman citizen.

[85]Von Domaszewski ("Inschrift," p. 152) proposes that it be completed as the word *diogmita*, i.e., as "diogmita eques duplicarius," but he himself sees problems with this explanation. He writes, "Merkwürdig ist es auch, dass ein *diogmita eques duplicarius* die Statue errichtet hat. Es ist das älteste Zeugnis für diese Polizeisoldaten, die beritten waren. Sie stammen bereits aus der Organization der hellenistischen Reiche. Dass ein einfacher Wachtmeister dieser Polizei Grund und Mittel hatte, ein solches Denkmal zu errichten, erklärt sich, wenn er ein Werkzeug [of the honoree] gewesen war." In other words, von Domaszewski indicates that his interpretation suffers from two basic difficulties, first, that there are no contemporary parallels for *diogmita eques duplicarius* and, second, that it would be unusual for a person of this minor rank to have either the reason for or the means of dedicating a monument to his superior. More likely, then, "dioch" is a second cognomen indicative, as M. P. Speidel suggests (cf. the previous note), of Chrestus' place of origin.

[86]Professor Speidel in personal correspondence of November 24, 1993, with the author. *Eques duplicarius* has exact parallels in two other Latin inscriptions, "L. Antonius M. f. Gal[eria] Pudens eq dupl..." (*CIL*, II, 2912) and "eq d Cest[ius] Silvanus" (*CIL*,sup*III*, 1.11180), but neither of these advances our knowledge of its significance. Nevertheless, *duplicarius alae*, i.e., the *duplicarius* of an auxiliary cavalry wing, appears often and quite clearly in the inscriptions as "die Bezeichnung für den in den einzelnen Turmen dem Decurio unterstellten zweiten Reiterbefehlshaber" (*PW* 5 [1905] 1843; *CIL*, III, 1.2016, 3223, 3252, 3394, 3677, 4278, 5899, 7644, 10609, and 15154; cf. in particular 7644 and 10609 showing the mark of the *duplicarius alae* as his possession of two horses). In other words, this rank falls between those of *decurio* and *sesquiplicarius*. Von Domaszewski (*Die Rangordnung des römischen Heeres*, ed. Brian Dobson, Beihefte der bonner Jahrbücher, vol. 14 [Cologne: Böhlau Verlag, 1967], pp. 35-36 and 50-51) refers, for example, to a wing of about 450 riders divided into ten units of forty-two men, the officers of which included five *decuriones*, one *duplicarius*, and four *sesquiplicarii*, each one of whom was in command of a single unit. Robert Saxer (*Untersuchungen zu den Vexillationen des römischen Kaiserheeres von Augustus bis Diokletian*, Epigraphische Studien, vol. 1 [Cologne: Böhlau Verlag, 1967], pp. 97-98) indicates in addition that the *decurio* of a cavalry wing stood next in rank below a *centurio legionis* (pp. 80-81) and received promotion to that important position on the recommendation of the governor (p. 53). This is significant for our purposes because the *duplicarius* was eligible for promotion to the rank of *decurio* (p. 54).

says, he must have had both the motive for honoring and the financial means to honor his superior in this fashion.[87] In sum, this inscription brings to light a Chrestus who, through his own relationship with its honoree, stood only a single person away from the innermost circles of the imperial family. It does so, moreover, according to a chronology consistent with that Claudian expulsion of Rome's Jewish population in which the *impulsor* Chrestus also participated. Thus, as a concrete example of the possibilities which lurk behind the name *Chrestus*, the chance survival of the Gaius Iulius with this cognomen stands out in a remarkable manner.

The same is true of the Chrestus who was a famous writer and traveller. Like the one of interest to the present study, he also exists for us only through the chance remains of a single reference, this time within the sixth century *De mensibus* written in the Constantinople of the emperor Justinian by the classical scholar Ioannes Laurentiou Philadelpheus Lydos, i.e., Lydus.[88] This Chrestus seems to have been active in the first or the second century.[89] Moreover, he was a Roman ("Χρῆστος δὲ ὁ 'Ρωμαῖος") whose work was of sufficient import to have been preserved for quotation at length several centuries later. Here then is a well-known Roman Chrestus perhaps contemporary with the Chrestus of interest to us. Are they the same person? This is not impossible.[90] Still, it is primarily by way of analogy that *De mensibus*

For example, a certain Annius Martialis was promoted from *duplicarius alae* to *decurio alae* and thence to *centurio legionis* (Brian Dobson and David J. Breeze, "The Roman Cohorts and the Legionary Centurionate" in *Epigraphische Studien* 8 [Düsseldorf: Rheinland-Verlag, 1969], p. 103).

[87]See p. 199, n. 85. Von Domaszewski ("Inschrift," p. 152) assumes a statue was involved, and Chapot ("Antiquités," p. 161) mentions a monument. As to the reason for the dedication, von Domaszewski ("Inschrift," p. 152) suggests Chrestus had profited from personal services rendered to the legate.

[88]Ioannes Laurentius Lydus *De mensibus*, ed. Guilielmus Roether (Darmstadt: n.p., 1827) 4.68. For purposes of an introduction to Lydus and his work consult Anastasius C. Bandy, *Ioannes Lydus on Powers or the Magistracies of the Roman State*, Memoirs Series, vol. 149 (Philadelphia: American Philosophical Society, 1983), pp. ix-lxxiv.

[89]*PIR* C 600, though without explanation, dates him from the time of Claudius or later. *OCD*[2] 630 indicates that Lydus' sources "go back directly or indirectly to the authoritative antiquarians of the first century B.C. and of the first two centuries A.D."

[90]Given the surviving circumstantial evidence, it may be that Suetonius and Lydus were writing about the same Chrestus who might be supposed to have had influence in the councils of Claudius. Were *Chrestus* a rare name in Rome or one

is relevant, for this text introduces a once famous Roman Chrestus lost otherwise to modernity and so gives us all the more reason to think the same thing true of the Suetonian Chrestus in *Claudius* 25.4.

It is only accidental that information has been preserved for us concerning any of the more prominent Chresti. We are fortunate in two cases to have both their nomen and cognomen, Geminius Chrestus and Claudius Chrestus. Though it may well be that the praenomen of the latter was Tiberius,[91] we are in fact missing this first part of both men's names. As regards the others, the Chrestus quoted by Lydus as well as the philosopher certainly bore the traditional three-part name, but their cognomen was, typically, sufficient to identify them. If, given his reputation, the Athenian sophist was a Roman citizen, we possess nothing but his cognomen also. Hence, although chance has preserved the praenomen of Gaius Iulius Chrestus alone and the nomina of only a few others, all these men attest to the fact that behind *Chrestus* may be found both the traditional Roman *tria nomina* and some person of distinction within Roman society. Obviously, just as in the cases for example of Cicero (Marcus Tullius Cicero), Martial (Marcus Valerius Martialis), Agrippa (Marcus Vipsanius Agrippa), the better known the person, the less need for recourse to anything but this cognomen.

Keeping these things in mind, we must be careful not to draw unwarranted conclusions from our inability to identify the Chrestus who makes his appearance in *Claudius* 25.4. Behind this name, in other words, may stand a slave of unknown origin but, likewise, of unknown influence, or a free foreigner, or a foreigner granted Roman citizenship by a Roman patron, or a freedman and new Roman citizen, or a freeborn Roman citizen with or without means, with or without significant authority. In such a light, we have all the more reason to suspect that it was the ancient prominence of this Chrestus rather than the carelessness of Suetonius which accounts for the modern anonymity of the man.

---

otherwise employed exclusively of persons without status, we could have some confidence in this identification. Nonetheless, since the evidence is not compelling and we know of various important Chresti, such an identification remains only an interesting possibility.

[91]Tiberius Claudius would be the typical praenomen and nomen of a foreigner granted Roman citizenship under the emperor Tiberius Claudius Caesar, that is, Claudius; see Sandys, *Latin Epigraphy*, pp. 217-218. Not without good reason, for example, did the city of Alexandria send as its petitioners to the emperor Claudius three of these persons, Tiberius Claudius Barbillus, Tiberius Claudius Phanias, and Tiberius Claudius Apollonius, all of whom are alluded to in Claudius' letter (P. Lond. 1912, lines 16-19) by their full Roman names. *CIL*, VI, 200 also lists a large number of Tiberii Claudii with their various cognomina.

Chapter Ten

Chrestus and the Christus

Having reached this point, we are in a position to indicate one person whom this prominent Chrestus was not. Specifically, Paulus Orosius is the father of views which link Chrestus with Christus, i.e, Jesus Christ. As indicated earlier,[1] he was sometimes untrustworthy in these matters, especially since this is not the only occasion revealing a tendency towards the Christianization of happenings within Jewish history.[2] Even so, his understanding persists into the modern period. Smallwood writes, for example, "the only reasonable interpretation of Suetonius' sentence is that the reference is to Christianity."[3] Her evidence is the reference to Momigliano's statement, "those who deny that the 'Chrestus' of Suetonius is Christ must undertake the onus of proving their view,"[4] a stance which he too fails to support.

---

[1]Pp. 123-129.

[2]In the same context (*Historiarum* 7.6.12) he did this with the Jewess Helena of Adiabene recast as a Christian. Benoit Lacroix (*Orose et ses idées*, Université de Montréal publications de l'Institut d'études médiévales, vol. 18 [Paris: Librairie philosophique J. Vrin, 1965], p. 157) refers here to Orosius' confusion of things Jewish and Christian. *Historiarum* 7.4.6 is more complicated: its Christianization of Tiberius' expulsion of Roman Jews follows earlier Christian reinterpretations but also stands side-by-side with the more original account in *Historiarum* 7.4.17 to which Orosius gave his usual twist of Jewish punishment resulting from abuse of Jesus. In terms of the sources, see Zangemeister's edition, pp. 441 and 450.

[3]Smallwood, *Jews under Roman Rule*, p. 211.

[4]Momigliano, *Claudius*, p. 33.

When we carefully sort out the actual arguments in favor of the *interpretatio christiana*, it becomes clear that the most common of these focuses on evidence that *Chrestus* is sometimes an alternative form of *Christus*. The reason for the centrality of this argumentation is that, unless *Chrestus* may mean *Christus*, there exists no basis whatsoever for the attempt to associate *Claudius* 25.4 with any aspect of Christianity. Momigliano and Smallwood are manifestly in error, therefore, when they assert that the onus falls upon those who would reject the Christian understanding of the text. In other words, this interpretation first enters the realm of possibility only after it has been demonstrated that, when Suetonius penned *Chrestus,* he could have meant *Christus.*

In this matter the testimony is quite clear. Tacitus did write "chrestianos" within his *Annals* 15.44 ("quos...vulgus chrestianos appellabat. Auctor nominis eius christus"), and we possess very much evidence elsewhere of *Chrestus, Chrestianus,* and their respective Greek equivalents being used to allude to the Christian messiah or people.[5] Nonetheless, it is Suetonius who interests us, and in his case this explanation flounders. Concretely, in *Nero* 16.2 he wrote that "punishment was inflicted on the Christians [Christiani], a class of men given to a new and mischievous superstition." Hence, Suetonius, who was hardly an associate of Tacitus' *vulgus,* did not mistake the word *Chrestianus* for *Christianus.* As a result, the claim of confusion applies poorly to *Claudius* 25.4. Moreover, *Nero* 16.2 reads as if it was the first time that Suetonius referred to the new religion.[6] For both of these reasons, it is practically impossible to treat his employment of *Chrestus* within any Christian context.

From the very beginning, therefore, the *interpretatio christiana* is beset by a fundamental difficulty, the only way around which would

---

[5]Harald Fuchs, "Tacitus über die Christen," *Vigiliae christianae* 4 (1950):65, 69-74. He interprets Tacitus in the sense that, though the historian himself knew better, *chrestianus* was the form of pronunciation used by the *vulgus* in referring to Christians. Hence, Baldwin (*Suetonius,* p. 355) writes, "It is *Christus* in Tacitus, also in Pliny, which suggests that this was the orthography known to educated Romans of Suetonius' own day." Erich Koestermann ("Ein folgenschwerer Irrtum des Tacitus (Ann. 15,44,2ff.)?" *Historia* 16 [1967]:460, 463, 465-466; following him, Solin, "Juden und Syrer" in *ANRW,* 2.29²:659) believes that Tacitus may have confused two different religious phenomena. According to his interesting but groundless thesis, the Chrestus of Suetonius was a Jewish activist whose still-extant followers appear as the Chrestiani of Tacitus. In his view the historian erroneously introduced his references to Christ and Christianity into the persecution of 64 CE.

[6]So too Robert Graves and Joshua Podro, *Jesus in Rome: A Historical Conjecture* (London: Cassell and Company, 1957), p. 40.

be to propose the highly doubtful conjecture of undocumented scribal activity changing an original *Christus* to *Chrestus*.[7] In support of that remote possibility the remainder of *Claudius* 25.4 is silent. By way of comparison, *Nero* 16.2 is revealing: even if Suetonius had utilized *chrestiani* here, we would still have no choice but to recognize it as a reference to things Christian. First, more obvious explanations of the word *chrestianus* do not exist; second, the subject matter is a new superstition; third, there is the clearly Christian parallel in Tacitus' *Annals* 15.44. This last passage is also instructive in its own right. It describes "a class of men, loathed for their vices, whom the crowd styled Christians [chrestianos]" and adds that "Christus [Christus], the founder of the name, had undergone the death penalty in the reign of Tiberius, by sentence of the procurator Pontius Pilatus."[8] Here too the context makes clear that the reference is to things Christian. In *Claudius* 25.4 we find nothing comparable. The result: from its very beginning this modern *interpretatio christiana* is just as dubious as the fifth-century Orosian prototype.[9]

---

[7]Salomon Reinach ("La première allusion au christianisme," p. 117) does make the interesting point that our earliest witness to the text of Suetonius is the fifth-century Orosius, who cites the manuscript of Suetonius before him as registering *Christus* instead of *Chrestus*. However, the implication that this manuscript contained the former reading is rightly rejected by Janne ("Impulsore Chresto," p. 541, n. 4) on the grounds that *Christus* is too close a reflection of Orosius' own interpretation of the passage. Janne's second argument, that Orosius perhaps wrote *Chrestus* only to have it later altered by Christian scribes, is superfluous. He is nevertheless correct in implying that Reinach's view fails to take account of the fact that the manuscript tradition of Orosius has no less of a history than that of Suetonius. Insofar as his Christian interpretation of the word is concerned, the position of Reinach also fails to account for the fact that *Nero* 16.2 reads as Suetonius' first allusion to the new religion in Rome.

[8]The LCL translation of Jackson does not concern itself with the preferable reading "chrestianos."

[9]A variation of the *interpretatio christiana* associates *Claudius* 25.4 not with Jesus Christus but with some other Jewish messianic pretender. Thus, Zielinski ("L'empereur Claude," p. 143) also changes *Chrestus* to *Christus* and so interprets Suetonius as if he had meant to write, "Claude chassa de Rome les Juifs, qui, sous l'impulsion *de leur Messie*, s'étaient livrés à de graves troubles." Chrestus is for him either a would-be Jewish messiah or the Roman Jewish preaching about such a figure. Roth (*History of the Jews*, p. 11) writes therefore that Chrestus could have been a false messiah, and Borg ("New Context for Romans XIII," pp. 211-212) understands the reference to be to "Jewish messianic agitation in Rome." Eisler is more precise. Depending upon the same variation, he changes Zielinski's "de leur Messie" to "d'un Messie" and then personalizes it so as to mean that Chrestus (=Christus) was in all likelihood Simon Magus who appeared in Rome at this time in the role of "*Jesus redivivus*" (ΙΗΣΟΥΣ ΒΑΣΙΛΕΥΣ, 1:132, n. 5; 1:133,

A second argument fundamental to the Christian interpretation of *Claudius* 25.4 shows again just how problematic it is. Typically, Bruce writes,

> He [Suetonius] intended his readers to understand that Chrestus who, as a matter of general knowledge, was the founder of Christianity. To be sure, Christ was not in Rome in the time of Claudius; but Suetonius, writing seventy years later, may have thought that he was. If his sources indicated that the riots which provoked Claudius's edict of expulsion were due to the introduction and propagation of Christianity in the capital, he could well have drawn the mistaken inference that it had been introduced there by Christ in person. Tacitus was better informed; he knew that Christ was crucified under Tiberius; but such accuracy required a degree of research for which others had neither the interest nor the inclination.[10]

Two basic difficulties stand in the way of this treatment. In the first place, it presupposes a translation/interpretation of *Claudius* 25.4 like that of the LCL: "Since the Jews constantly made disturbances at the instigation of Chrestus, he [Claudius] expelled them from Rome." That is, it presupposes the ablative absolute "impulsore Chresto" was intended to modify the participial/adjectival "tumultuantes" rather than the genuine predicate of the sentence, "expulit." It takes for granted, in other words, that the Chrestus element caused the Jewish riots which in turn caused the emperor to resort to the expulsion. As chapter 7 made clear, however, this is but a single, and not the most likely, interpretation of Suetonius' grammar.

---

n. 1; 1:133). In his view, then, Chrestus was a very specific messianic pretender whose appearance in Rome sparked commotion, an opinion mentioned by Bammel ("Judenverfolgung," p. 299) with approval, by both Maurice Goguel (*The Life of Jesus*, trans. Olive Wyon [New York: Macmillan Company, 1949], p. 97, n. 4) and Janne ("Impulsore Chresto," p. 542, n. 4) as interesting but not believable, and by Graves and Podro (*Jesus in Rome*, p. 40) as, given Simon's Samaritan origins, impossible. In any case, and regardless of their particular permutation of the *interpretatio christiana*, these explanations suffer from the same fundamental liability as it does, for they depend upon the same insupportable proposition that when Suetonius penned *Chrestus* he actually meant *Christus*. Consequently, these explanations have no life of their own. Instead, hardly obvious as independent readings of *Claudius* 25.4, they are an extension of the *interpretatio christiana*. In addition, they are further complicated by the necessary but far from certain presupposition that the already demonstrated use of *Chrestus/Chrestianus* for *Christus/Christianus* in reference to things Christian translates equally well into the realm of things Jewish.

[10]Bruce, "Christianity," p. 316. Insofar as "impulsore Chresto" is concerned, Vogelstein and Rieger (*Geschichte*, 1:19, n. 5) had already taken it to signify "christliche Predigten."

Second, and exactly as Bruce indicates, the text of Suetonius reads as if the *impulsor* Chrestus was in Rome at the time of the events described by it. Aware of the normative views that Jesus was no longer on the scene by the time of Claudius and that he had in any case never been to Rome, Bruce does several things. Most obviously, as the "may have," "if," and "could well have" demonstrate, he moves immediately to conjecture. On this basis he then changes *Chrestus* to *Christus*, posits errors in Suetonius' understanding not only of his source but of Christian origins as well, and reinterprets *Chrestus* so that it no longer signifies even *Christus* but refers instead to "the introduction and propagation of Christianity." The net result, Bruce stretches "impulsore Chresto" a very long distance to provide it with a meaning far from the natural or obvious one.

Still, he is far from alone in this cavalier reading of *Claudius* 25.4. For example, Hoerber writes, "we may conjecture that Suetonius, misinterpreting his source, as he seems to do not infrequently, thought Christus...was present in person to stir up trouble."[11] Again, in the judgment of Wiefel, "der Irrtum des Berichterstatters liegt darin, dass er den Kultheros für den Anführer einer religiösen Gruppe gehalten hat,"[12] an opinion which is expressed in a slightly different way by Luedemann: "Suetonius's mistake is that he considers the cult hero to be an earthly person who was present in Rome."[13] Again, and in the view of Jewett, "It is widely assumed that the 'Chrestus' in question was Christ, who Suetonius thought must have been present to provoke such a tumult. In this instance it was probably the Christian instigators who were banned."[14] Stern states similarly that "the words of Suetonius could convey the impression that Christus himself was present at Rome at that time, and that the disturbances were instigated by him personally, while Tacitus, indeed, was better informed."[15] Finally, Smallwood makes the claim that "the reference is to Christianity, though he [Suetonius] was apparently under the misap-

---

[11]Hoerber, "Decree of Claudius," p. 690. Similarly, Leon (*Jews of Ancient Rome*, pp. 25-26) writes that, provided Janne was accurate about Christianity having reached Rome by 40 CE, "we may suppose that Suetonius, misinterpreting his source, as he not infrequently did, apparently thought that Christus (or Chrestus) was there in person to stir up trouble."

[12]Wiefel, "Die jüdische Gemeinschaft," p. 76.

[13]Luedemann, *Paul*, p. 169.

[14]Jewett, *Chronology of Paul's Life*, p. 37.

[15]Stern, *Authors*, 2:116. He expressed similar views in the appendix to his "Jewish Diaspora" in *Jewish People*, 1:181.

prehension that "Chrestus" was a rabble-rouser present in person. In other words...disorder had been provoked by the arrival of Christian missionaries in Rome."[16]

A variation of the hypothesis according to which Suetonius had misunderstood his sources appears in the opinion that he was not directly at fault but had been led astray by police or archival reports themselves guilty of the misinterpretation of events.[17] For example, S. Reinach makes the claim that "Chrestus" really means those Jewish Christians "qui, au nom du Christ, pris par la police pour un agitateur (*impulsor*), provoquaient continuellement des troubles."[18] Likewise, Janne writes that "le *Chrestus impulsor* se trouvait dans un document officiel contemporain des faits et l'erreur a été commise par les 'bureaux' de l'époque claudienne."[19] Similarly, May supposes that the error of Suetonius arose from his consultation of police records in Roman archives which had taken Christian doctrinal disputes to mean Christ was actually present in Rome as both a "chef de bande" and "perturbateur professionel."[20]

As absolutely necessary as these views are to the *interpretatio christiana*, scholarship has provided little evidence which would justify their possibility and nothing to confirm them. First, having in mind

---

[16]Smallwood, *Jews under Roman Rule*, p. 211. However, unlike the previously mentioned scholars who assume that Suetonius associated the word *Chrestus* with Christianity, Smallwood may perhaps mean here that he erred even further by disassociating it entirely from its originally religious context. Seston ("L'Empereur Claude," p. 299) corrects "Chrestus" to the Christian "agitation messianique" but is also unclear if Suetonius realized that this was, as Seston claims, the real meaning of his source. In this regard the following statement of Smallwood ("Jews and Romans," p. 236) is also ambiguous: "There can be no reasonable doubt that 'Chrestus' is a mistake for 'Christus,' and quite obviously the trouble on this occasion was disturbances in the synagogue caused by the arrival of Christianity."

[17]As the following statement shows, Meyer (*Ursprung*, 3:463) is uncertain as to whether the misunderstanding belonged to Suetonius or to his source: "Die Unruhen sind nach Sueton durch einen gewissen Chrestus veranlasst; es ist längst erkannt, dass darin der Name Christus steckt, der ja von den Heiden durchweg in Chrestus umgestaltet wurde, und dass die Angabe, dass die Verkündung von Christus den Anlass gab, dahin entstellt worden ist, dass dieser selbst die Unruhen angestiftet habe."

[18]S. Reinach, "La première allusion au christianisme," p. 117. It is possible to read him to mean that the police failed to associate *Christus* with Christianity. In any case, he fails to state how Suetonius understood the word.

[19]Janne, "Impulsore Chresto," p. 546.

[20]May, "Politique religieuse," p. 40.

the expression "to preach Christ" from Philippians 1:15, Huidekoper translates "impulsore Chresto" by "under the impulse of Christianity," and he does so with the statement that "the use of the word 'Christ' for 'Christianity' is common enough."[21] Nevertheless, because Paul was using Christian lingo and in fact meant "Christ" rather than "Christianity," this is not a legitimate parallel to *Claudius* 25.4. Second, on the basis of Acts 25:19 Janne argues that the erroneous police report had taken the Christian claim of the living Jesus to mean he was currently active as *impulsor* in Rome,[22] but this is a supposition incapable of demonstration.

As indicated above, both Bruce and Stern provide an argument from silence based on what they suppose Suetonius did not know, but, in the absence of evidence to the contrary, it is in fact most likely that he shared Tacitus' knowledge of Christian origins. That is, Suetonius was an early second century contemporary and acquaintance certainly of Pliny and almost certainly of Pliny's good friend Tacitus as well,[23] each of whom did possess definite knowledge–*Letters* 10.96, 97 and *Annals* 15.44 above, respectively–about these matters. Thus, it is not feasible to proceed on the assumption that Suetonius' own *Nero* 16.2 expresses all he knew about the subject.[24] In any case, even if it were true that Suetonius knew absolutely nothing concerning Christianity, that would contribute no evidence for the Christian interpretation of *Claudius* 25.4.

The problematic character of this treatment becomes apparent another time when Bruce finds himself forced to recognize that "it is just conceivable that the riots mentioned by Suetonius were caused by the activity of an otherwise unknown Chrestus" and when Luedemann recognizes the possibility that "Chrestus was the name of a Jewish disturber in Rome."[25] Equally indicative of the inherent weakness of this argument is the odd position of Graves and Podro. Wanting to preserve both the natural sense of the passage that Chrestus was at

---

[21]Huidekoper, *Judaism at Rome*, p. 229.

[22]Janne, "Impulsore Chresto," p. 546. At the same time he repudiates the possibility that the error of Suetonius had arisen from Christian and, perhaps, Jewish traditions about Jesus' death under Claudius (pp. 545-546).

[23]Macé, *Essai sur Suétone*, pp. 80-81.

[24]This is essentially the point of Baldwin (*Suetonius*, p. 355).

[25]Bruce, "Christianity," p. 316; Luedemann, *Paul*, p. 169. Similarly, Penna ("Les Juifs a Rome," p. 331) asserts that, "Quant au nom de *Chrestus*, tout en admettant théoriquement qu'il soit celui d'un suborneur juif, il se comprend mieux en référence à Jésus-Christ." To these considerations we shall return shortly.

work in Rome as well as the inference that *Chrestus* signifies Jesus *Christus*, they take Suetonius literally to mean that Jesus, having escaped death on the cross, went off to Rome.[26] Depending as it does upon the two very improbable propositions that the *Chrestus* within Suetonius may be assumed to mean *Christus* and that Jesus did reach Rome, this view has no merit except to make clear once again that the onus rests upon scholars who favor the *interpretatio Christiana* to undergird it with credible evidence.

That is an impossible task. In a passage the context of which provides no other clear reason for assuming it, a Chrestus appears who, among all of the Roman Chresti, is supposed to be Jesus Christ and who, though this particular Christus never did visit the city, was responsible for the tumults leading to the expulsion of Roman Jewry. Manifestly, therefore, the onus does fall upon those who support the Chrestus/Jesus Christus identification to provide grounds sufficient to overcome such major obstacles to it.

Resultantly, and as if it did provide these grounds, attention has come to be focused on Acts 18:1-3:

> After this Paul left Athens and went to Corinth. There he found a Jew named Aquila, a native of Pontus, who had recently come from Italy with his wife Priscilla, because Claudius had ordered all Jews to leave Rome. Paul went to see them, and, because he was of the same trade, he stayed with them, and they worked together–by trade they were tentmakers.

That is, assuming this text and *Claudius* 25.4 refer to the same event, several scholars use an *interpretatio christiana* of the expulsion in Acts to justify the same interpretation of the Suetonian account.

Significant difficulties stand in the way of this approach. First, it presupposes the trustworthiness of Acts 18:1-3 in synchronizing the arrival of Aquila at Corinth with the Claudian expulsion of the Roman Jews. In fact, however, Luke-Acts has the tendency to create arbitrary associations between world-historical events and the intra-Christian history.[27] Hence, of the way in which Acts ties together the arrival of Aquila and the expulsion, Loisy writes, "Ce pourrait fort bien être un de ces synchronismes arbitrairement établis par le rédacteur avec les ressources de son érudition trop facile."[28] Luedemann expresses

---

[26]Graves and Podro, *Jesus in Rome*, pp. 39-42.

[27]Alfred Loisy, *Les Actes des Apotres* (Paris: Émile Nourry, 1920), p. 686; Luedemann, *Paul*, pp. 8-11, 174; Slingerland, "Acts 18:1-17 and Luedemann's Pauline Chronology," pp. 686-687.

[28]Loisy, *Les Actes*, p. 686.

himself analogously: "Luke's reason for their [Aquila and Priscilla] coming to Corinth, the edict of Claudius, could derive from Luke's penchant for meshing salvation history with world history."[29] As a result, although for the sake of his own thesis Luedemann is finally forced to accept the historical reliability of Acts both in terms of its Claudian expulsion within 18:1-3 and of Paul's appearance before the governor of Achaia in 18:12, the fact remains that we have difficulty trusting this document in such contexts.[30] It may well be, therefore, that the world historical happening which Acts summarizes–"Claudius had ordered all Jews to leave Rome"–had no original association with Aquila and Priscilla.[31]

A second difficulty arises from the use of free emendation. Jewett transforms the text of Acts so as to make it read, "when Paul arrived in Corinth he encountered Aquila and Priscilla who had recently come from Rome because of Claudius' edict banning the Christians [!] from that city."[32] Only a bit less blatant is Loisy's similarly unsupported suggestion that the original text had described Aquila as a "Christian" or "disciple" rather than a "Jew."[33] For a variety of reasons, such an approach fails. In the first place, unaware of Philo's likely reference to the same expulsion in *Legatio* 157, it is equally unaware that this contemporary text places the ejection within the context of a whole series of measures directed specifically against the Roman Jewish community. Second, the fact of a single Christian disturbed by the expulsion would establish a very thin thread upon which to hang any Christian interpretation. More particularly, even if we could show that Aquila had been a Christian already in Rome, it would be unsuitable to generalize from this that the expulsion was directed principally against things Christian in the city. That is, had he been a member

---

[29]Luedemann, *Paul*, p. 174. Earlier (pp. 8-9) he had rejected "the propriety of accepting any absolute datum of world history from Luke."

[30]Slingerland, "Acts 18:1-17 and Luedemann's Pauline Chronology," p. 687; "Acts 18:1-18, The Gallio Inscription, and Absolute Pauline Chronology," p. 441.

[31]If Romans 16 belongs to the letter which Paul sent to Rome, it does place Prisca and Aquila there. My sense (cf. p. 120, n. 33) is that this chapter was originally a note addressed to Ephesus and that the house church of Romans 16:3-5 is the Ephesian one mentioned in 1 Corinthians 16:19.

[32]Jewett, *Chronology of Paul's Life*, p. 36. This parallels the groundless claim of S. Reinach ("La première allusion au christianisme," pp. 108-122), most recently repeated by Luedemann (*Paul*, p. 168), that the letter of Claudius, P. Lond. 1912, dealt with the arrival of Christianity in Alexandria.

[33]Loisy, *Les Actes*, p. 686.

of the new sect, he would have been so as a Jewish Christian, i.e., as a Pontian Jew living in Rome who thought Jesus to be the messiah. Thus, since it may be assumed that the expulsion of all Roman Jews included those with zealot leanings, Pharisees, people of the land, those favorably disposed towards Qumran and so forth, there is no reason to suppose that Jewish Christians, provided they existed by this time in Rome, would have been treated any differently.

Moreover, the concrete evidence suggested in favor of Aquila's Roman Christianity is not convincing. Though Acts 18:18 implies that he was a Christian when he left Corinth with Paul and Acts 18:26 indicates that he was certainly one thereafter in Ephesus, the text is silent as to precisely when he joined the new sect. Janne interprets this failure to report Aquila's Pauline conversion in Corinth to mean that he was not so converted but had become a Christian previous to his expulsion from Rome: "Il est évident qu'Aquila était converti au christianisme avant de rencontrer Paul: l'apôtre, en effet, s'associe *immédiatement* à lui et pour la propagande et pour les affaires."[34]

Nevertheless, maintaining that Paul attached himself to Aquila for reasons of both faith and business, Janne reads into the text of Acts a religious motivation simply not present in it,[35] for in Acts 18:3 Paul attaches himself to Aquila "because he was of the same trade."[36] When he maintains in addition that Acts could not have passed over in silence the conversion of so significant a personage,[37] he fails to mention that Acts nowhere explicitly reports that event. Relatedly, he

---

[34]Janne, "Impulsore Chresto," p. 536, n. 1. Bruce ("Christianity," pp. 316-317) refers simply to "our independent inference from the New Testament that Aquila and Priscilla were Christians before they came to Corinth," a position shared as well by Luedemann (*Paul*, p. 174). Loisy (*Les Actes*, p. 685) bases his view that Prisca and Aquila were apostles independent of Paul on the high regard which the latter expressed towards them in Romans 16:3-4 and 1 Corinthians 16:19. Still, since, by way of example, Paul had a similar regard for the Philippian Christians whom he did convert, this argument is not convincing.

[35]As I have indicated elsewhere ("'The Jews' in the Pauline Portion of Acts," pp. 305-314), it is important to the intention of Acts that Paul be presented as a faithful Jew seeking out fellow Jews. So, if Acts 18:1-3 intends to insinuate any religious link between Aquila and Paul, it is their common bond as Jews.

[36]This is also the interpretation of Theodor Zahn, *Die Apostelgeschichte des Lucas*, Kommentar zum Neuen Testament, 2 vols. (Leipzig: A. Deichertsche Verlagsbuchhandlung, 1919-1921), 2:634-636.

[37]Janne, "Impulsore Chresto," p. 536, n. 1. Haenchen (*Apostelgeschichte*, p. 469, n. 4) provides the corollary that the Acts of the Apostles could not have failed to credit Paul with this important occurrence if, in fact, he had been responsible for Aquila's conversion.

ignores the fact that the order in Acts–Aquila as a Jew from Pontus (18:2), then a business partner of Paul (18:3), and, finally, a Christian (18:18?, 18:26)–does imply conversion, for it traces Aquila's movement at Corinth from Jew to Christian through Paul's instrumentality.[38]

Furthermore, though Haenchen is perhaps correct that it would "schlecht in das lukanische Geschichtsbild passen, wenn er zugeben müsste, dass schon vor Paulus Christen in Korinth waren," this is no evidence that the author of Acts was aware of but did in fact hide from readers Aquila's pre-Corinthian Christianity. In other words, this may just as well be an instance where what the author thought to be the case, i.e., that Aquila was a Jew rather than a Christian upon arrival in Corinth, corresponded of itself to the author's intentions.[39] More interesting is Janne's certainly correct view that the author of Acts was unlikely to attract attention to fundamentally Christian-associated disturbances in Rome.[40] Still, as a motive for changing the religious orientation of Aquila from a Christian to a Jewish one, this argument backfires. In other words, had the author of Acts thought the imperial expulsion from Rome to have been Christian-related or so interpretable, it would have been omitted.

Overall, therefore, the plain sense of Acts is that Aquila was not a Christian at the time he arrived in Corinth from Italy, for Loisy and Haenchen are quite correct about the intention of the author of Acts to stress that he was a Jew.[41] At best, in other words, Acts may be

---

[38]This aside, the author would appear to have had no notion of when or where Aquila became a Christian. Hence, even were it possible to show that the writer of Acts assumed Aquila to have been a Christian prior to his arrival in Corinth, this would not demonstrate that the writer thought Aquila had become a member of the new cult prior to the time he was expelled from Rome.

[39]Haenchen, *Apostelgeschichte*, p. 469, n. 4. For the same reason, according to Loisy (*Les Actes*, p. 685), a redactor perhaps turned the originally Christian Aquila into a Jew. Both Haenchen and Loisy propose alternatively that the switch might have come about so as to explain why Aquila was expelled from Rome in an action against Jews. Still, all explanations of the change are gratuitous until after it has been demonstrated that one actually occurred.

[40]Janne, "Impulsore Chresto," p. 539.

[41]At this point the issue is the meaning rather than the honesty of the author of Acts. Loisy and Haenchen recognize from the plain sense of the text that the writer, in Loisy's view, the redactor, was claiming Aquila for Judaism rather than for Christianity, and the same is apparently true of Eusebius as well: he writes that "Claudius banished the Jews from Rome, and Aquila and Priscilla, with the other Jews, left Rome" (*Ecclesiastical History* 2.18.9, LCL translation by Kirsopp Lake). That the claim might be bogus is entirely possible, but no one has so far shown either this or that Aquila was a Christian prior to his arrival in Corinth.

used only to provide evidence for exactly what it says, in other words, that Aquila was a Jew from Pontus expelled along with all other Jews from the city of Rome. Conjecture alone facilitates the introduction of a single Christian into this account of a Claudian expulsion of Roman Jews, and even its correctness would be no justification for the leap to the conclusion that the expulsion was basically Christian related. By way of summary, under no circumstances may we use the illegitimate *interpretatio christiana* of Acts 18:1-3 to support the *interpretatio christiana* of *Claudius* 25.4.

Another Acts-associated argument supportive of this Christian interpretation functions no better. Specifically, it happened often according to Acts that, when Paul arrived in a city to proclaim the gospel, he soon met very hostile Jewish actions which ended in riots. In Thessalonica, for example, "the Jews became jealous, and with the help of some ruffians in the marketplaces they formed a mob and set the city in an uproar" (Acts 17:5), and to Beroea they came also "to stir up and incite the crowds" (Acts 17:13), events paralleled as well for Antioch (13:50), Iconium (14:2), Corinth (18:12), and Jerusalem (21:27). As a consequence, Smallwood argues that the preaching of the gospel concerning Jesus, i.e., "impulsore Chresto," caused the same thing to occur in Rome:

> It can well be imagined that Christian preaching in Rome, directed in the first instance to the Jews, aroused the same sort of opposition and uproar there as St Paul's did among the Jewish communities in Asia Minor and Greece, and that the resultant disturbances formed a serious threat to public order.[42]

For various reasons this analogy is not convincing. In the first place, it depends entirely upon the credibility of Acts, but Acts tends to slander non-Christian Jews precisely in this way by painting them as rabble-rousers, troublemakers, disturbers of the peace, and would-be murderers. This means that the repeated image of Jews instigating crowds at the appearance of Paul is, as I have shown elsewhere,[43] a creation of the author of Acts. Resultantly, historical analogies drawn from Acts are without merit. Second, it depends upon Suetonius' own veracity in this matter, for we have observed that his reference to "Iudaeos assidue tumultuantes" represents a similar image. Third, it

---

Also, and as pointed out earlier, "Pre-Corinthian" and "Roman" may or may not be synonyms.

[42]Smallwood, *Jews under Roman Rule*, p. 212. Similarly, Bruce ("Christianity," pp. 322-323) and May ("Politique religieuse," p. 39).

[43]Slingerland, "'The Jews' in the Pauline Portion of Acts," pp. 312-317.

assumes without evidence that Christianity was already present in Rome by the time of the expulsion. Fourth, it assumes a rather ugly picture of Jews resorting to major violence over questions of the identification of the messiah. Most important, it ignores the genuine historical analogy that the Roman Jewish community had by this time experienced many difficulties, expulsion included, entirely independent of any association with Christianity. Particularly in light of this last observation it is superfluous to explain *Claudius* 25.4 on the basis of any supposed analogy with the Acts of the Apostles.

Still to be noted are the last few arguments in support of the Chrestus/Jesus Christus identification. The most popular of these is the one proposed by Janne that, if Chrestus had been some unknown man, we might expect Suetonius to have written "Chresto quodam," i.e., "a certain Chrestus:" "Si *Chrestus* avait été un simple affranchi, donc, peu connu, Suétone aurait accolé *quidam* à son nom: *impulsore Chresto quodam*; l'historien parle d'un *Chrestus* généralement connu à son époque."[44] We have seen already that the form of expression in *Claudius* 25.4 implies exactly what Janne writes, that this Chrestus was someone generally recognized after his own generation. Even so, with the subsequent jump to the conclusion that such a well-known Chrestus could only have been Jesus, i.e., the one sort-of-Chrestus whom we moderns are generally aware of or interested in, the logic of Janne and those who follow him fails completely.

What remains in support of the *interpretatio christiana* are two unconvincing arguments from silence. The first depends upon both a fact, i.e., that Josephus did not mention the Claudian expulsion,[45] and an assumption, i.e., that the tendency of Josephus was to avoid making reference to things Christian. Bringing these two together, Janne comes to the conclusion that Josephus must have neglected the expulsion because of its association with Christianity.[46] Nonetheless, the authentic conclusion to be drawn here concerns the incredible lengths to which Janne is willing to go for the sake of the Christian interpretation of *Claudius* 25.4.[47] Specifically, expressed without any

---

[44]Janne, "Impulsore Chresto," p. 540. So too, Stern, *Authors*, 2:116; Bruce, *Commentary*, p. 368, and his "Christianity," p. 316; Graves and Podro, *Jesus in Rome*, p. 39.

[45]Contrary, as we have seen, to Paulus Orosius.

[46]Janne, "Impulsore Chresto," p. 551.

[47]It is unnecessary to discuss Janne's groundless claim ("Impulsore Chresto," pp. 544 and 547) that the adverb *assidue* in *Claudius* 25.4 is a sign of Christian involvement in the events described there. No more worthy of consideration is his *interpretatio christiana* of even Dio 60.6.6 (pp. 533-534, 548-550).

controls, this approach is ridiculous because it would signify that Christianity lurked behind every reference which Josephus did *not* make to the new Jewish sect. Again, it provides no evidence for the existence of the Josephan tendency upon which it is built.[48] Finally, if we are seeking a motive for the failure of Josephus to refer to this happening, we have seen already that the fact of the Jewish expulsion alone is cause enough to make sense of why he, a Roman Jew himself and principal apologist for his people, should have chosen to pass over not only it but also all other Claudian anti-Jewish measures.[49] In sum, there is no justification for the manipulation of Josephan silence in order to support the *interpretatio christiana* of *Claudius* 25.4.

Luedemann introduces the second argument from silence. On the basis of the opinion that Suetonius and Dio Cassius were dependent upon some common source for their descriptions of Claudius' punitive action against Roman Jews,[50] he wishes to make the case that the Jewish disturbances behind the action were Christian related. Directly standing in the way of the interpretation is the fact, as Luedemann recognizes, that Dio made no reference to Christian involvement in this matter. To circumvent this major stumbling block to his thesis, Luedemann applies the same argument from silence to the text of Dio as Janne had to Josephus. That is, since Dio also tended to avoid reference to Christianity, his silence about its role in the Roman disturbances confirms that the common source material behind Dio and Suetonius implicated the new religion. In other words, because Suetonius used the same source, his reference to Chrestus is really to Christianity.[51] Still, this line of argumentation is as unconvincing as is that of Janne. In the first place, no consensus exists on the question of whether or not Suetonius and the later Dio Cassius relied upon common sources.[52] In the second, to posit the absence of reference as

---

[48]For all they wrote, Josephus, Tacitus, Suetonius, Pliny, and Dio had very little to say about Christianity. Perhaps they found the subject unimportant.

[49]We have seen that this is not how he handled the earlier expulsion under Tiberius (*Antiquities* 18.65-84). He did describe that banishment but only for the purpose of explaining it away.

[50]Luedemann, *Paul*, p. 166.

[51]Ibid., p. 169.

[52]Momigliano ("Osservazioni sulle fonti per la storia di Caligola, Claudio, Nerone," *Rendiconti della R. Accademia Nazionale dei Lincei, Classe di scienze morali, storiche e filologiche* 8 [1932]:307, 311), although having less evidence available than in the case of Gaius, argues that, where their materials agree, Suetonius and Cassius Dio did utilize common sources on Claudius. In support of

proof of its presence makes no more sense here than in the instance of Janne. Finally, and most important, we have observed already that Suetonius and Dio were reflecting separate events.[53]

In sum, all of the evidence intended to establish the *interpretatio christiana* of *Claudius* 25.4 proves itself to be irrelevant, fallacious, or supportive of the opposite conclusion. Thus, to the long list of Roman Chresti with whom we might find it possible to identify the Chrestus of Suetonius, the addition of Jesus Christus and related permutations reveals itself to be quite baseless. As a result, in order to identify the *impulsor* Chrestus and so permit that information to illuminate both *Claudius* 25.4 and the broader policies of the emperor Claudius vis-à-vis Roman Jewry, we must now turn to a more sensible context.

---

such a view, he does not draw upon Suetonius *Claudius* 25.4/Dio 60.6.6. In terms of the more readily compared Gaius, Balsdon (*Gaius*, pp. 227-228) asserts the weakness of Momigliano's evidence for any common source, a position already taken by Frank Burr Marsh (*The Reign of Tiberius* [1931; reprint ed., New York: Barnes & Noble, Inc., 1959], pp. 272, 277) who supposes that "in the main" Suetonius and Dio employed different sources, the former reading a variety of materials, the latter perhaps following one writer in particular. As Momigliano, Balsdon, and Marsh make clear, however, it is not ultimately general theories but the individual case which counts. Insofar as the equally unresolved question of Dio's dependency upon Suetonius is concerned, see p. 107, n. 63.

[53]Pp. 104-109.

Chapter Eleven

Claudius in the Company of His Predecessors and Cronies

To this point in our analysis of the Suetonian comment that Claudius "Iudaeos impulsore Chresto assidue tumultuantes Roma expulit," we have found it necessary to proceed in a thoroughly contextual manner. In so doing, we have discovered among other things that the Christian interpretation of the passage is simply out of context. Specifically, having concluded that Suetonius assumed his second century readers would be competent to identify Chrestus, we also recognized the non sequitur of jumping from this conclusion to the anachronistic one that the man was the only "sort-of" Chrestus, i.e., Jesus Christus, with whom modernity is familiar.

In other words, besides the just examined contortions necessary to the establishment of the Christian interpretation, our foregoing analysis of the name *Chrestus* and of its usage in Rome established that this was a popular name and one associated with various strata of Roman society including free foreigners, slaves, freedmen Roman citizens, multiple generation Roman citizens, intellectuals, and also magistrates. Furthermore, we found that persons even on the lowest social rungs, i.e., the slaves and freedmen, wielded power completely disproportionate to their social status depending upon whose slave or freedman they became. That is, we encountered several contextually sensible candidates for the Suetonian Chrestus, the identity of whom was common knowledge at least into the early second century.

Just as important, we reminded ourselves of the fundamental realities of imperial power within which the Claudian expulsion of Roman Jews assumes credibility. By way of example, we may recall

219

two primary sources that provide us with glimpses of these realities. More generally, the Ankaran title to the *Res gestae* of Augustus reads, "Concerning the Accomplishments of the Divine Augustus by which He subjected the World to the Mastery of the Roman people."[1] The emperor, in other words, is the subject who subjects; all others are objects subjected to this absolute imperial power.

Similar but more pertinent is the letter which Claudius himself sent to Alexandria toward the end of 41 CE. In it he menaced all of the inhabitants of the city with the threat that he might be "forced to show what a benevolent ruler can be when he is turned to righteous indignation."[2] Then, turning specifically to the Jews of Alexandria, Claudius raised the even more frightening possibility that he might "proceed against them in every way as fomenting a common plague for the whole world."[3] The point is, we may treat neither of these as an empty threat because the absolute reality of imperial power makes them entirely believable. Consequently, this reality, so obvious that discussion of *Claudius* 25.4 has tended to overlook it, furnishes the ultimate foundation for any accurate comprehension of the Suetonian statement. More precise explanations aside, in other words, Claudius expelled Roman Jews because it was within his power to do so.

Here, therefore, we might appropriately return to our previous discussion of imperial whim or, to employ the expression of Mommsen, "Willkür."[4] Nonetheless, and although this phenomenon ought not to be ignored, it is perhaps more worthwhile to consider Claudius' own choice of vocabulary, for he couched his deadly threats against the people of Alexandria not in the language of imperial caprice but of benevolence and righteousness. Since very few absolute rulers have assessed themselves differently, there is neither cause to doubt that Claudius considered himself to be a humane autocrat nor reason to deny that he thought his wrath entirely justified. Again, therefore, more detailed explanations aside, Claudius used his absolute power to expel Roman Jews for what he thought to be good reason.

Good reason, at least from his perspective, there certainly was. Regardless or perhaps in part because of Seneca's complaint about the widespread popularity of Judaism in Rome,[5] influential persons there,

---

[1] Cf. p. 31.

[2] P. Lond. 1912, lines 79-82.

[3] Lines 98-100.

[4] Mommsen, "Religionsfrevel" in *Gesammelte Schriften*, 3:397; cf. p. 141.

[5] In Augustine *City of God* 6.11; cf. p. 30.

explicitly, both its writers and emperors, shared absolutely outrageous attitudes towards Jews and their cult. Cicero had called it a "barbaric superstition,"[6] and Augustus, according to Suetonius, also held it in contempt.[7] Much later Tacitus was still referring to "the absurd and filthy Jewish way of life."[8] He was even able to assure his readers that Jews were "hateful to the gods." This was so because, among the other preposterous theories, they owed their beginnings to a plague of leprosy; their god was an ass the gilded image of which resided in the holy of holies in Jerusalem; their cult involved both human sacrifice and cannibalism; their Sabbath observance conjured up not only dingy dinners but also hideous afflictions of the groin; and their dietary practices conflicted with traditional Roman ones.[9]

From the perspective of its likely victims, this combination of righteous indignation and absolute power was extremely dangerous. Having no great appreciation of the Isiac cult, we easily overlook the hazard posed by this combination for its Roman priests whom Tiberius ordered to be crucified.[10] No more appreciative of Druidic religion, we are not surprised that, provoked no doubt by righteous indignation, the philanthropic emperor Claudius had "utterly abolished the cruel and inhuman religion of the Druids among the Gauls."[11] Likewise, in the very same text Suetonius wrote that this emperor expelled Jews from Rome.

Therefore, keeping in mind their plague-ridden and god-forsaken *superstitio* with its own rites of human sacrifice, and not knowing any better, we might suppose Claudius to have been equally justified in expelling the practitioners of that cult from Rome. Then too, at least as Tacitus evaluated them, the Roman Christians who were executed under Nero received no more than they had coming on account of their disgraceful behavior ("flagitia") and their deadly cult ("exitiabilis superstitio").[12] Similarly, knowing no better than what Pliny wrote to the emperor Trajan about the Bithynian Christians and their own *flagitia*, we might be in a position to appreciate how the combination

---

[6]*Pro Flacco* 28.67; cf. p. 16.

[7]*Augustus* 93; cf. p. 47.

[8]*Histories* 5.5; cf. p. 16.

[9]Cf. pp. 16-27.

[10]*Antiquities* 18.79; cf. p. 51, n. 44.

[11]*Claudius* 25.5.

[12]*Annals* 15.44; cf. p. 8.

of righteous indignation and absolute power rationalized the capital measures which this outstanding imperial governor utilized against them.[13] In fact, however, we do know better because, at least insofar as the Jewish and Christian cults are concerned, it was undeniably religious prejudice rather than righteous indignation that combined with absolute power and resulted in great hardship for the adherents of both communities.

Within this general context we may now turn to two eyewitness descriptions which permit us to glimpse what such prejudice and the imperial authority behind it looked like from the perspective of its potential Jewish victims. First, we may recall[14] Seneca's explanation for why he had abandoned his vegetarian diet during the early years of the emperor Tiberius:

> Do you ask how I came to abandon the practice? It was this way: The days of my youth coincided with the early part of the reign of Tiberius Caesar. Some foreign rites were at that time being expelled, and abstinence from certain kinds of animal food was set down among evidence of the superstition. So at the request of my father, who did not fear prosecution, but who detested philosophy, I returned to my previous habits.

Soon after becoming emperor, Tiberius initiated the expulsion of the practitioners of Jewish and other *sacra*. Resultantly, even those persons of the highest social standing were in fear of being charged with participation in these *sacra* and were thus forced to modify any of their own customary practices which might have left them open to false prosecution. Here we do not behold matters directly through the eyes of the intended victims of the expulsion, but no imagination is required in order to appreciate how things must have looked to them. That is, if the upper-class and innocent Seneca was at risk merely on account of his diet, this was much more so for those who could claim neither social status nor innocence and who refused to forswear the practices which characterized faithfulness to their religion.

The second of these eyewitness accounts does come directly from the pen of a Jew as he described his own personal encounter with the emperor Gaius in Rome. This, as we saw, was a terrifying experience. What Philo and the other Alexandrian Jewish delegates had expected was a basically neutral hearing on the subject of the political situation of Alexandrian Jewry.[15] What they in fact encountered, however, was

---

[13]Pliny *Letters* 10.96.

[14]*Epistulae morales* 108.22; cf. pp. 21-22, 50-62.

[15]*Legatio* 349.

"a ruthless tyrant with a menacing frown on his despotic brow,"[16] that is, an absolute ruler, who soon turned menacingly to the subject of Jewish religiosity. Thus, having acknowledged Gaius most piously as "Σεβαστὸν Αὐτοκράτορα," the August Emperor, Philo observed that

> the mildness and kindness with which he replied to our greeting was such that we gave up not only our case but our lives for lost! In a sneering, snarling way he said, "Are you the god-haters who do not believe me to be a god...?" And stretching out his hands towards heaven he gave utterance to an invocatory address which it was a sin even to listen to, much more to reproduce in the actual words.[17]

Gaius next confronted Jewish delegates with the fact that their cultic practices had permitted them to sacrifice on behalf of but not to him. Realizing that the supposedly impartial judge had become their accuser and forced to silence by his absolute power, they responded with a "visibly deep shudder."[18] Thereafter, just before returning to the political issue, Gaius attacked them on the grounds of the very same religious practice which Tiberius had previously used: "Why do you refuse to eat pork?" he asked.[19] The interview completed, Philo and his colleagues waited to be executed but were in fact spared that fate simply because the emperor concluded otherwise.[20] Here, then, from the rare eyewitness perspective of one who actually experienced it, we see just how terrifying the combination of absolute power and prejudice could be, for the fate of Philo and his Jewish co-religionists depended entirely upon the whim of a single, hostile person.

It is the secondary Jewish and Gentile sources which provide the most information about the circumstances within which Roman Jews found themselves. Consistent not only among themselves but also with the primary witness of Seneca and Philo, these too paint a picture of Roman political authority hostile towards and directed in particular against the practice of Judaism in the city. More generally, we may recall how the third-century Dio characterized this earlier situation:

> I do not know the origins of this name [Jews] for them, but it also refers to the other persons, even foreigners, who eagerly pursue their customs. And this people is even among the Romans. Though often

---

[16]*Legatio* 350.

[17]Ibid., 352-353.

[18]Ibid., 357-360.

[19]Ibid., 361.

[20]Ibid., 366-367.

curtailed, it increased to the greatest extent so as to win by force the
freedom of its religious belief.[21]

It was on these explicitly religious grounds that the Jewish cult had
been "often curtailed."

Concerning the precise repressions of religion to which he was
alluding, Dio definitely had in mind at least the two that he himself
described in 57.18.5a and 60.6.6. The first of these was the expulsion
under Tiberius: "As the Jews had flocked to Rome in great numbers
and were converting many of the natives to their ways, he [Tiberius]
banished most of them."[22] The second was the work of Claudius. Just
after becoming emperor, he of course had ordered "the practicing-the-
traditional-life Jews not to gather."[23]

The other measures behind which explicit motives are visible
also had as their goal the repression of Roman Judaism. In *Legatio*
159-161, Philo let slip that at the time of Sejanus' death in 31 CE
Tiberius was in the process of acting against the practice of customs
associated with that cult both in Rome and other cities of Italy.[24]
Again, we see from *Annals* 2.85, *Tiberius* 36, Dio 57.18.5a, as well as
Antiquities 18.65-84 that this emperor had already turned to expulsion
to curtail these practices in Rome,[25] and from his protégé Valerius
Maximus we discover that Republican magistrates had used expulsion
for the same purpose.[26] Especially significant in this regard is Philo's
Legatio 157 where another, very probably Claudian, banishment also
receives an explicitly religious explanation.

For the sake of situating *Claudius* 25.4 within the context in
which it actually belongs, the above details are vital. In general, they
connect governmental actions against Roman Jewry with attempts to
repress the religious practices associated with this people, and they
illustrate, just as Dio affirmed, that the attempts were part of a
continuum. In particular, they demonstrate that Claudius himself was
an exemplary participant in the same process. Specifically, Dio 60.6.6
makes perfectly clear that, soon after becoming emperor, Claudius too
interfered with the practice of Jewish rites in Rome, and *Legatio* 157

---

[21]Dio 37.16.5-17.1; cf. pp. 62-63.

[22]Cf. pp. 55-59.

[23]Cf. pp. 131-134.

[24]Cf. pp. 69-77.

[25]Cf. pp. 50-60, 67-69.

[26]*Factorum* 1.3; cf. pp. 39-46.

ascribes a similar motivation to the apparently Claudian expulsion to which it refers.

Within this context it becomes practically impossible to interpret *Claudius* 25.4 as anything but one additional measure intended to rid Rome of the same foreign *superstitio*. More generally, and by way of analogy, we may consider the claim of Acts 18:2 that "Claudius had ordered all Jews to leave Rome." Ignoring the emperor's motivation altogether, this statement nevertheless makes perfectly good sense within the context of the long-term religious hostility just described. The same thing is true therefore of *Claudius* 25.4, for we have already observed how its central assertion that Claudius "expelled the Jews from Rome" is identical to the assertion of Acts. To express it a bit differently, regardless of scholarship's preoccupation with the *impulsor* Chrestus and images of trouble-making Jews, neither the ambiguous "impulsore Chresto" nor "assidue tumultuantes" amounts to anything more than a secondary element, i.e., a modifier, in a sentence the actual subject of which is Roman authority and the actual object of which is Roman Jews. Given this particular combination of subject and object, it takes very little guesswork to imagine either the kind of verb by which Suetonius united the two or the implicit motivation for the action of that verb.

There is however an important difference between Acts 18:2 and the core of *Claudius* 25.4: the latter implies a religious motivation behind this expulsion.[27] Specifically, we saw that within Suetonian usage the word *Iudaeus* had a fixed religious connotation.[28] In his view, that is, the persons whom Claudius expelled from the city were practitioners of the Jewish *sacra*. Furthermore, we observed also that *Claudius* 22-25, the larger unit into which Suetonius incorporated this expulsion, featured as one of its essential components the Claudian measures associated with just such sundry religious rites.[29] Thus, combining these observations with the report of Dio that the same emperor had already taken measures against the practice of Judaism in Rome, that the explicitly religion-based expulsion of *Legatio* 157 is almost certainly Claudian and therefore likely identical with the one referred to by both Suetonius and Acts, and that these actions were not unique to Claudius, we have every reason to think this emperor was simply following the precedent of his uncle Tiberius who likewise on religious grounds had expelled Jews from the city. Hence, contrary

---

[27]The implication is Suetonius' own. Its credibility is nevertheless secured by the fact that it matches the consensus of ancient writers, Jewish and Gentile.

[28]Pp. 154-155.

[29]P. 152.

to his opinion elsewhere, Benko suggests the present expulsion might have been "a renewal of Tiberius' edict" of 19 CE.[30]

According to Dio, after all, Claudius took action in 41 CE not against Roman Jews per se but against the corporate aspects of their cult, and this echoes the 19 CE measures of the emperor Tiberius, who gave Roman Jews the option of abandoning their religion, i.e., their religious practices, or leaving the city. Furthermore, and as already indicated, there is no evidence that Claudius ever repealed his own 41 CE prohibition. Instead, these superstitious rites ceased all together when the practitioners themselves were later excluded from the city. Thus, looked at within the broader context of Roman Jewish life under the early empire, the primary assertion of Suetonius that Claudius "expelled the Jews from Rome" appears to be entirely reasonable, for what it describes is one more authoritative measure intended to rid the city of this particular "barbaric superstition."

This established, it might appear the better part of wisdom to conclude our analysis of *Claudius* 25.4 at the present point since, whatever the more exact meaning of "impulsore Chresto" and "assidue tumultuantes," these secondary details can do no more than provide ancillary light on what is the primary factum of religious repression. Furthermore, their very introduction runs the risk of obscuring this one factum, for the history of interpretation has been governed by these secondary elements, "impulsore Chresto" principally insofar as it was thought to shed light on the *Christus* of Christianity, "assidue tumultuantes" as the archetypal enterprise by which scholarship has tended to identify Roman Jewry. Nevertheless, having restored both of these to their appropriate context within the subjective context of Suetonius and the objective history of religious repression, we would be ill-advised to ignore the contribution either might make to our more complete understanding of the Claudian expulsion of Roman Jews.

Insofar as the "assidue tumultuantes" is concerned, it adds little to our historical understanding. That is, this Suetonian modifier of "Iudaeos" tells us more about the subjective context of Suetonius than it does about the objective history of religious repression at Rome. In any literal way the expression is plainly incredible because according to Suetonian usage these words conjure up the image of a continuous civil war in the city.[31] Figuratively, however, they might make a bit more sense. In other words, supposing the continued validity of the 41 CE prohibitions against the Jewish cult and the resultantly difficult position of devotees caught between obeying their heavenly god and

---

[30] Benko, "Edict of Claudius," p. 407.

[31] Cf. pp. 155-159.

earthly master, we might conjecture that these Jews had attempted to circumvent the interdictions. As a result, it is not impossible that Suetonius referred to these hypothetical acts of disobedience by means of the verb *tumultuare*. If so, of course, he was dependent upon the language of anachronism and hence composed hyperbolically because behind the image of constantly rebelling Jews lay his consciousness of the 66-70 CE Jewish war.[32]

Still, even treated in this way, "assidue tumultuantes" remains suspicious. First, it smacks too much of Suetonius' own tendentious characterization of Jews. Second, its image of a disorderly Jewry in Rome is historically anomalous: excluding the modern reconstructions, we have no analogy for any kind of corporate Jewish misbehavior in the city.[33] In other words, the "assidue tumultuantes" attached to "Iudaeos" looks much more like an anachronistic explicative than a source-based detail of Roman Jewish history. Consequently, we should perhaps paraphrase the Suetonian statement as "Chrestus caused the emperor Claudius to expel those so-and-so Jews from Rome." They and their foreign *superstitio*, as also the Druidic cult of the Gauls, wrote he with pleasure, received their just deserts under Claudius.[34]

Because it does not betray to us the fingerprints of Suetonius, "impulsore Chresto" is different. That he should have supposed his second century readers able to recognize the identity of a person sufficiently influential to have played a named part in the imperial expulsion of Roman Jews makes unqualified good sense. For the same reason, Suetonius had no need to be explicit about the specifics of that part. Unfortunately, the very fact that he was in a position to assume the comprehension of his readers resulted in a shorthand manner of expression which leaves modern inquirers in the dark.

In order to shed light on this matter, we need recall how from a strictly grammatical angle Suetonius meant that, whatever his specific

---

[32]Cf. p. 153.

[33]During the uneasy last years of the Republic, Cicero feared the forensic clout of the Roman Jews. Dio 60.6.6 brings up the thought of potential Roman Jewish disturbances only to indicate that they did not occur. The Acts of the Apostles does go out of its way to characterize Jews just about everywhere as troublemakers and murders, but neither Acts 18:2 nor 28:11-31 appears able to make any mention of the like disturbances in Rome.

[34]*Claudius* 25.5 expresses Suetonius' pleasure that this emperor acted more severely against the Druidic cult than had Augustus. Comparing the Claudian anti-Jewish measure in *Claudius* 25.4 with the Augustan one in *Augustus* 93 (cf. pp. 47-50), we may also see an implicit heightening. While Augustus commended the snub of Gaius against the Jewish cult in Jerusalem, he did not prohibit the cult, something which the expulsion obviously accomplished in Rome.

part, Chrestus played it in regard either to the Roman Jewish activity, i.e., to the *tumultuare*, or to the Claudian one, i.e., to the *expellere*. Respectively, in other words, he meant either that "Claudius expelled from Rome the Jews whom Chrestus caused to rebel continuously" or that "Chrestus caused Claudius to expel from Rome the continuously rebelling Jews." Various considerations, including both the "Chrestus impulit/Claudius expulit" parallelism as well as the consideration that *tumultuare* was likely the product of his own tendentiousness, have led us to the conclusion that Suetonius intended "impulsore Chresto" to modify *expellere*. Unable to demonstrate this unconditionally, however, we are forced to interpret the ablative absolute in both ways beginning with the possibility that Suetonius did intend it to modify the participle.

Here the question becomes how Chrestus might be supposed to have produced a Jewish reaction. To propose tentative answers we return to our previous discussion of the ways in which Suetonius used the idea behind *impulsor*. We observed that this might be a friend producing a particular course of action likely by means of verbal encouragement or an enemy producing the same course but likely by means of physical force. The first of these, i.e., and paraphrasing, "Chrestus encouraging them, the Jews rebelled, and Claudius [therefore] expelled them from the city," would force us into complicated suppositions about causation. That is, in addition to the explicit element associated with Chrestus, i.e., "Chrestus being the cause," as well as the implicit but obvious one associated with *tumultuare*, i.e, and so the LCL above, "*Since* the Jews constantly made disturbances," there would have to have been a third, implicit element of causation operative here as well. Specifically, if they had had no reason for doing so, Roman Jews would hardly have responded to the encouragement of Chrestus. To express it a bit differently, this interpretation would demand some primary cause of Roman Jewish discontent which made them vulnerable to the urging of Chrestus.

Now, as to the nature of this potential cause of unhappiness, we need only repeat that Claudius' anti-Jewish measures of 41 CE must have been a tremendous burden for Roman Jewry caught between god and emperor.[35] Supposing these remained in place, we might perhaps

---

[35]Cf. Alföldy, *Social History*, p. 155: "Even in the Early Empire there were occasional instances of social unrest and even open political conflicts without any social relevance: they were isolated from each other in time and space and their motivations were different. These conflicts can only be reduced to a common denominator in one respect, a common denominator which is important for an understanding of the social conflicts of the Empire: these uprisings originated for the most part among groups in the population who were, for specific reasons, under a pressure that was especially heavy and generally atypical."

conjecture that a Jewish Chrestus had led co-religionists in illegal actions intended to maintain their pious way of life. Though we are absolutely ignorant of any analogous person or actions, a scenario like this may not be entirely out of the question. As a result, not to be rejected out of hand is the idea of Friedrich Blass that there could have been "damals in Rom einen unruhigen Juden dieses Namens." In a similar way Linck refers to the likelihood that Chrestus was some forgotten Jewish "instigator," Radin writes of "the machinations of a certain [Jewish] Chrestus," Penna claims it is theoretically possible he was a "suborneur juif," and Luedemann also mentions the possibility of what he calls a "Jewish disturber."[36] Indeed, for Koestermann this is not a possibility but a certainty: "für jeden unvoreingenommenen Leser kann das entsprechend sonstigem lateinischen Sprachgebrauch nur heissen: Claudius verjagte die Juden aus Rom, weil sie es auf Anstiften eines [jüdischen] Chrestus ständig zu Ausschreitungen in der Stadt kommen liessen."[37]

In order to provide evidence that our Chrestus was a Jew, Radin maintains the name itself would have been fashionable among Jews "since it was a fairly good rendering of such a frequently occurring name as Zadok."[38] So too, Reinach claims *Chrestus*, a name common among freed slaves, was suitable to Jews because they belonged to that class.[39] Nonetheless, since *Chrestus* was widely used in part because of its positive meaning for the Greco-Roman world as a whole, we may not derive its meaning from the Hebrew *Zadok* or limit its usage to Jews. Moreover, among all of the remnants of Jewish-related papyri, inscriptions, and literary witnesses surviving from antiquity, *Chrestus* or Χρῆστος does not appear as the name of a single person otherwise identifiably Jewish. The large quantities of Greek papyri from Egypt in the *CPJ* do not contain it,[40] and the same is also true of the *CII* as well as of the Greco-Roman literary texts accumulated

---

[36]Friedrich Blass,"ΧΡΗΣΤΙΑΝΟΙ-ΧΡΙΣΤΙΑΝΟΙ," *Hermes* 30 (1895):467-468; Linck, "De antiquissimis testimoniis," pp. 106-107; Radin, *Jews among Greeks and Romans*, p. 313; Penna, "Les Juifs a Rome," p. 331; Luedemann, *Paul*, p. 169. See also Michael Grant, *The Jews in the Roman World* (New York: Charles Scribner's Sons, 1973), p. 146; Roth, *History of the Jews*, p. 11; and May, "Politique religieuse," p. 38.

[37]Koestermann, "Ein folgenschwerer Irrtum," p. 457.

[38]Radin, *Jews among Greeks and Romans*, p. 313.

[39]Th. Reinach, *Textes*, p. 329, n. 2.

[40]Cf. the individual indices to the three volumes and appendix 2, "Prosopography of the Jews in Egypt," 3:167-196.

in Stern's *Authors*.[41] Insofar as Rome itself is concerned, *Chrestus* is absent from the relatively lengthy list of names available within the Jewish catacombs of the city.[42] This is not to deny that Roman Jews were called Chrestus. As intimated already, it may well be that among large numbers of Chresti in the Latin (*CIL*, VI) and of the Χρῆστοι in the Greek inscriptions of Rome (*IG*, XIV) are Jews not so identified.[43] The point is, instead, that within the name itself specifically Jewish associations are absent.

Benko's method of demonstrating that Chrestus was "a rabble-rouser who incited the Jews to various riots" is to identify him as a zealot, one of those "emotionally high-strung people, violently anti-Roman, whose primary purpose was removal of the Roman rule from Palestine." He was, moreover, "an extremist who took an aggressive attitude toward his Greco-Roman neighbors and believed that in particular the emperor was the personification of all evils that befell the Jews."[44] It is correct, as we have seen before,[45] that events of principal concern to Judea could reverberate in Rome. Josephus tells us in *War* 2.80-81 and *Antiquities* 17.300-301 that following directly upon extremely serious disturbances in Judea, eight thousand Jews at Rome gathered in the temple of the Palatine Apollo to demonstrate before Augustus their strong opposition to Archelaus' rule of Judea. Similarly, in both *War* 2.105 and *Antiquities* 17.330-331 we read of the related case in which a man insisting he was the Hasmonean prince Alexander had arrived in the city with a large retinue: the entire Jewish population of Rome did crowd the streets to glimpse the man. Nevertheless, at least insofar as Josephus informs us, neither of these highly charged, Judea-associated events had resulted in disorders necessitating imperial measures against Roman Jews. In other words, our only analogies by which to evaluate Benko's conjecture do not support his thesis.

---

[41]Martial's earlier noted *Epigram* 7.55 (p. 195) is addressed to Chrestus and contains a reference to contemporary events within Jewish history, but of the possibility that he was a Jew there is not the slightest hint.

[42]So already Leon, *Jews of Ancient Rome*, p. 25, n. 2: "the name Chrestus does not appear among the several hundred known names of Roman Jews."

[43]Cf. pp. 182, 184 (n. 22), 186 (n. 32), 187. *CII*, 683 from north of the Black Sea provides us the analogy of a woman, Χρῆστη, whom Schürer (*History*, 3¹:36) and Stern (*Authors*, 2:116) assume to be Jewish. Especially in light of its last line, nothing in the inscription compels this interpretation.

[44]Benko, "Edict of Claudius," pp. 412, 413-414, 415.

[45]P. 116, n. 15.

Equally without historical analogy is the Roman Jewish zealot whose profile Benko traces so clearly. Of such a specific individual we know absolutely nothing elsewhere. But, of such a characterization of Jews, however, we are well informed, for by this point in our study we have heard much of rabble-rousing Jews and their plots against well intended imperial order. Furthermore, though Benko provides us with no clue as to what exactly it might have been in Judea which caused this particular Jewish extremist to rally Roman Jewry to civil war, we do know that Claudius himself had already taken gratuitous, to use Smallwood's characterization, action against the practice of Judaism within Rome. As a result, there is no need to go so far afield as Benko does in order to imagine that some devout Roman Jew perhaps rallied his co-religionists within the city to disobey imperial orders against the public practices of the Roman Jewish community. Instead, were we to proceed along these lines, the truth would be better served by Wieseler's more neutral identification of Chrestus as a "sonst nicht weiter bekannten römischen Juden."[46] In other words, the individual represented by the language of "Jewish disturbers" was more likely, given the context of Roman Jewish life after 41 CE, to have been some person of piety unable to ignore the requirements of his religion.

Returning to the element of triple causation which is inherent in interpretations of Suetonius that make the *impulsor* Chrestus an ally of the "Iudaeos assidue tumultuantes," we must suppose Claudius' order banning the public rites of Judaism caused grave hardship for devout Roman Jews. Hence, though anomalous, it is not absolutely impossible that a Jewish leader might have led in the circumvention of these orders and that this in turn had caused the emperor to expel the city's Jewry.

Alternatively, it might be that Suetonius associated *impulsore Chresto* with the participial phrase in order to imply not that Chrestus was an ally of Roman Jews but that he was their enemy who moved them probably by violent means to a state of religious disobedience. In other words, and again paraphrasing, "Chrestus attacking them, the Jews rebelled, and Claudius [therefore] expelled them from the city." This would have the immediate advantage of being much less complicated than the previous interpretation. To be precise, it obviates the triple causation necessary to that interpretation and therefore corresponds to the double causation inherent within the passage of Suetonius. In other words, under these circumstances there would be no need to speculate about what caused Jewish vulnerability to the admonitions of a allied *impulsor*, for if Chrestus were their enemy who forced [*impulit*] them into acts of disobedience, the necessity of any

---

[46]Wieseler, *Chronologie*, p. 122, n. 3.

additional implicit cause would automatically disappear. Here, that is, Chrestus struck so severe a blow against the members of the Roman Jewish community that disobedience resulted, and this in turn caused Claudius to expel it.

Furthermore, though reconstructions based upon the existence of a Jewish *impulsor* rest upon purely hypothetical foundations and hardly account for Suetonius' expectation that contemporary readers were familiar with his name, the present one would eliminate both of these difficulties. Specifically, and as we shall soon consider at length, there is nothing at all hypothetical about the *impulsor* Sejanus under Tiberius who did act against Roman and other Jewry. Thus, it might be that Suetonius knew Chrestus as the person in charge of measures against Jewish practices in Rome. He perhaps enforced the imperial order against the gatherings for religious purposes and so provoked disobedience. Such status could easily account for why Suetonius had no need to identify him except by cognomen. In sum, it is unlikely Suetonius intended "impulsore Chresto" to modify "Iudaeos assidue tumultuantes." Still, within the context of religious repression at the center of Suetonius' statement about the Claudian expulsion of Roman Jewry, in either of the above two ways this interpretation would make good sense.

Nevertheless, if we take seriously the likelihood that "assidue tumultuantes" is but a non-historical, Suetonian aspersion and that "impulsore Chresto" in any case modifies *expellere*, we achieve more convincing results. Here too we begin by recalling that Suetonius used *impulsor* in two different ways, i.e., in reference both to a friend causing action on the basis of verbal encouragement and to an enemy employing violence. For our present purposes, the second alternative has little to commend it. This is because a Chrestus attacking the emperor and so causing him to expel the Roman Jewish population is hard to imagine. However, since the early second century could easily have been familiar with an influential friend of Claudius, the first alternative is entirely plausible.[47]

In fact, imperial history just prior to the time of Claudius provides us with information about two other *impulsores* associated with the Jewish people. These are Tiberius' praetorian prefect Sejanus and Gaius' slave Helicon. Though well known from various sources for

---

[47]Cf. Raymond E. Brown and John P. Meier, *Antioch and Rome: New Testament Cradles of Catholic Christianity* (New York: Paulist Press, 1983), p. 100: "The name [Chrestus] is attested as a Roman name, but how would a pagan Roman have caused such internal friction among Jews as to cause expulsion?" Because the presupposition of "internal friction" depends upon a misreading of Suetonius, a "pagan Roman" did not cause it.

many other reasons, Sejanus-the-anti-Jewish-*impulsor* survives by a Philonic thread about as thin as the Suetonian one which preserves Chrestus.[48] Similarly, important though he also was, Helicon, exactly like Chrestus, has no existence whatsoever outside a single report, in this case again, of Philo.[49]

Insofar as the former is concerned, we noticed[50] how in *Legatio* 159-161 Philo had claimed that under Tiberius

> matters in Italy became troublesome when Sejanus was organizing his onslaughts. For Tiberius knew the truth, he knew at once after Sejanus's death that the accusations made against the Jewish inhabitants of Rome were false slanders, invented by him because he wished to make away with the nation.

Or, and as Eusebius paraphrased the affair, "Sejanus, the prefect of Tiberius, who had very much influence with him, encouraged greatly that he destroy the Jewish people."[51] Sejanus was then the *impulsor* who moved Tiberius against Roman Jewry.

Equally or perhaps even more revealing than Sejanus is Helicon. Again, knowing only that he was a slave, we might well presume his insignificance. Realizing also, however, that he "held the post of chamberlain and Captain of the Guard in the [emperor Gaius'] house, a post greater than any that was given to anyone else,"[52] that he advised the emperor,[53] and that, while in Rome, Philo was entirely conscious of the great authority which he had with his master, we immediately recognize in Helicon an extremely influential imperial *impulsor*. His part in the account of the Alexandrian Jewish embassy to Gaius commences as Philo informed his readers that the Egyptian household slaves ("οἰκέτας"), led by this Helicon, had encouraged the emperor to take pleasure in the abuse of the Alexandrian houses of prayer (*Legatio* 165-166). Persuasive and often in the private company of the emperor, Helicon was well equipped in matters anti-Jewish by

---

[48]He so appears only in *Flaccus* 1-2 and *Legatio* 159-161.

[49]*Legatio* 166-178, 203-206 (cf. *PIR*[2] H 49). For the thread in Tacitus by which our knowledge of Agricola hangs, see Mellor, *Tacitus*, p. 14. He also notes (p. 138) that Tacitus himself had nearly disappeared by the end of antiquity.

[50]P. 69.

[51]*Ecclesiastical History* 2.5.6-7; cf. p. 70, n. 18.

[52]*Legatio* 175.

[53]Ibid., 203-204. This text also makes mention of another such figure, the actor Apelles of Ascalon.

his familiarity with the accusations against Jews and their religious traditions ("κατὰ ' Ιουδαίων καί τῶν ' Ιουδαϊκῶν ἐΘῶν," *Legatio* 170). Consequently, "he assembled a string of indictments one after the other. And the impression made on Gaius's mind grew firmer so that his memory of the charges was ineffaceable" (*Legatio* 177). Helicon was, in other words, "always *instigating* and training the ruler... against the [Jewish] people."[54] Furthermore, his name then recurs in association with the Gaian plans for the temple in Jerusalem.[55]

Impulsore Sejano, at the instigation of Sejanus, Tiberius made an attack upon Roman Jewry; *impulsore Helicone*, at the instigation of Helicon, Gaius encouraged measures against Alexandrian houses of prayer and prepared for the desecration of Judaism's cult center in Jerusalem. *Impulsore Chresto*, at the instigation of Chrestus, the next emperor expelled the Roman Jews. Quirks of historical reporting and manuscript transmission make us aware that knowledge of Chrestus survived at least into the second century, for this is when Suetonius referred to him. Nonetheless, powerful though he was, Helicon owes his continued existence to the chance survival of a single first century text, the *Legatio*. Likewise, the important detail that the powerful praetorian prefect Sejanus had any part whatsoever in the measures against Roman and other Jews depends upon that very same single source.[56] In other words, the fact that Chrestus survives in only one ancient writer has no bearing on the question of his significance, for we at least know that he, unlike either Helicon or Sejanus-the-anti-Jewish-*impulsor*, remained identifiable to Suetonius and his readers into the early second century.

This fact combined with the considerations, first, that behind *Chrestus* might have stood a person from nearly any rank in Roman society, and, second, that Suetonius presupposed his readers could identify him, makes it reasonable to search for Chrestus-the-impulsor among those who had significant influence with the emperor Claudius. Furthermore, Josephus provides the explicit justification for such a procedure. Narrating events associated with the dispute between Jews and Samaritans at the time when Cumanus served as the procurator of Claudius in Judea (*War* 2.232-246), Josephus ranged Cumanus with the Samaritans as an enemy of Jews. Near the end of the account and describing the resultant hearing before Claudius, Josephus indicated Agrippa II was present to defend the Jewish position. Even so, "many

---

[54]*Legatio* 178, my translation.

[55]*Legatio* 203-205. It also refers to Apelles of Ascalon, who was an imperial *impulsor* in this matter.

[56]From the reference in the *Flaccus* it is impossible to draw specific details.

of the powerful" ("πολλοὶ τῶν δυνατῶν," *War* 2.245) were on Cumanus'
side in Rome. Who were these persons? Since power in the city was
determined by proximity to the fountain of that power, i.e., to the
emperor, it becomes reasonable to conclude that Josephus had in mind
figures exactly like those whom we have met in the persons of Sejanus
and Helicon. This would then signify in turn that within the company
which Claudius kept there were–and it is hardly surprising, given his
own attitudes–many who were prepared to take a stand against Jews,
just as Cumanus himself, another personal appointee of the emperor,
had chosen to do.

Fortunately, we are not required to settle for guesswork in the
present matter because in the parallel account of *Antiquities* 20.118-
136 Josephus explicitly identified these powerful, anti-Jewish allies of
Cumanus as the emperor's very own freedmen and friends. According
to *Antiquities* 20.135,

> Caesar's freedmen [ἀπελευθέρων] and friends [φίλων] displayed the
> greatest partiality [σπουδή] for Cumanus and the Samaritans, and
> they would have got the better of the Jews, had not Agrippa the
> Younger, who was in Rome and saw that the Jewish leaders were
> losing the race for influence [literally, "being dismayed"], urgently
> entreated Agrippina....

This is a vital passage, for it makes explicit what has been implicit so
far, that Claudius was surrounded by his own anti-Jewish, Sejanus-
like friends and anti-Jewish, Helicon-like[57] freedmen who were more
than able to use their association with the emperor to bring calamity
upon their Jewish targets.

Thus, it is reasonable to conjecture, for example, that the Gaius
Iulius Chrestus contemporary with Claudius had worked his way into
imperial circles through the influence of Publius Suillius Rufus, his
own patron and good friend of the emperor.[58] Hence, we might desire
perhaps to identify him with the Chrestus *impulsor* who served as the
immediate source behind the decision of Claudius to expel the Jewish
population from Rome. Alternatively, the sixth-century Lydus has also
preserved an otherwise anonymous Roman Chrestus who was actually
a well-known author contemporary or roughly so with the Chrestus of
interest to us.[59] It requires no imagination whatsoever to suppose a
writer such as this one might have harbored the typical anti-Jewish

---

[57]Helicon was the slave of Gaius, but manumitted to freedman status, his fundamental role and influence would not have changed; cf. p. 187, n. 35.

[58]*ILS*, 8967; cf. pp. 195-200.

[59]*De mensibus* 4.68; cf. pp. 200-201.

feelings of his class and at the same time found a place of influence among the closest friends of Claudius. Likewise, Chrestus could just as well have been an anti-Jewish Alexandrian contemporary with those more famous ones, Apion and Chaeremon, whom we know to have been active at Rome in this period,[60] or with those, perhaps including Chaeremon, so generously noted by Claudius in his letter to that city.[61] It is impossible to prove any of these suggestions, and they are in fact no more than that. Their value lies instead in the context which they establish for the Suetonian *impulsor* Chrestus.

Available also, however, is an even more probable scenario along these same lines. If either Gaius Iulius Chrestus, or the Roman author Chrestus, or someone by that name in Alexandria might be supposed to have reflected a more upper-class imperial influence analogous in general to that of Sejanus with Tiberius, we have previously noted the two other Roman Chresti at the opposite end of the social ladder who clearly did have contact with the imperial family.[62] Concerning the former of these we know nothing more than what his apparently first- or second-century epitaph claims, for the Chrestus "caesaris" of *CIL*, VI, 5645 was a slave belonging to a member of the imperial family. Of which Caesar might have owned him or of how much, if any, influence he at one time or another had,[63] we are ignorant.

Much more tantalizing is the latter imperial Chrestus. For his deceased spouse Secunda he provided a marble tablet, identifying himself thereon as "Chrestus aug[usti] cubicularius" (*CIL*, VI, 33772), i.e., as the chamberlain of some unidentified emperor. What this of course means is that he held the same position as Helicon and likely exercised at least some degree of influence over the emperor whose slave or freedman he was. Helicon, after all, had been present with Gaius "when he was going to bed...so that he alone had convenient and leisurely audiences of the emperor,"[64] and the same thing would no doubt have applied equally in the instance of the *cubicularius* Chrestus too. As Duff quite reasonably estimates, "the most prominent and influential of the Emperor's purely domestic servants were the

---

[60]Cf. pp. 17-18, 25.

[61]P. Lond. 1912, lines 16-20. Cf. Baldwin (*Suetonius*, p. 356) who makes the provocative suggestion, but then rejects it, that "*Chrestus* could have been some Greek anti-semite, attempting to import the troubles of Alexandria to Rome."

[62]P. 188.

[63]Judging by the epitaph itself, this particular Chrestus was perhaps of little significance at the time of his death, but so was Helicon (*Legatio* 206).

[64]*Legatio* 175.

chamberlains."[65] Unfortunately, we possess his wife's rather than his own epitaph, for that latter might be expected to correspond to some degree with the appropriately boastful one of the extremely powerful Claudian freedman Pallas.[66] Was this imperial Chrestus the Helicon-like *impulsor* who convinced Claudius to banish Roman Jews? Given the fact that the name itself was popular in Rome, that the city's surviving inscriptions represent the mere fragments of antiquity, and that this particular epitaph tells us very little about the Chrestus on it, there is no way of knowing.[67]

Even so, that *Claudius* 25.4 points to some imperial freedman named *Chrestus* is very likely, for Suetonius himself implied as much. Specifically, we observed that one main component of *Claudius* 22 to 25.5b is Claudian measures associated with sundry religious practices and cults.[68] For present purposes, therefore, *Claudius* 25.5c becomes particularly important as the transitional bridge between the old unit *Claudius* 22 to 25.5b and the new one that starts in *Claudius* 26.1.

The transition begins with the crucial words "Sed et haec," i.e., "but these things:"[69]

> But he [Claudius] administered these and the other things and even to a great extent his entire government not so much by his own as by the decision making of his wives and freedmen. So he was everywhere and for the most part, being of such a nature that it were either advantageous to them or pleasing [for them].[70]

"But Claudius administered these things...by the decision making of his wives and freedmen." In itself, the *sed* is no more than a transition

---

[65]Duff, *Freedmen*, p. 145.

[66]Known to us from Pliny the Younger, chance did not preserve that inscription either (cf. Sandys, *Latin Epigraphy*, p. 11).

[67]Solin, as already indicated (p. 188, n. 37), suggests dating this Chrestus to the second or third century.

[68]Cf. p. 225.

[69]The traditional division between these units makes the "sed et haec" into the conclusion of the first unit. If this were correct, it would provide additional evidence in support of the case being made here. In fact, however, "sed et haec" makes better sense as the introduction to the second unit. Even so, the presence of the *haec* means that these last words of *Claudius* 25 do form a bridge between the two units.

[70]My translation of "Sed et haec et cetera totumque adeo ex parte magna principatum non tam suo quam uxorum libertorumque arbitrio administravit, talis ubique plerumque, qualem esse eum aut expediret illis aut liberet."

from the unit *Claudius* 22-25 to the fresh section about the wives and freedmen of the emperor in *Claudius* 26-29.[71] Still, it was Suetonius himself who decided to order these two units in this distinctive way, and, more important, it was he again who established the direct link between them with the key word *haec.* In other words, here Suetonius himself maintained that the emperor's wives and freedmen did play a *causal* role in the just-referred-to events. For this reason it makes good sense that he introduced causality only lines before in reference to that *impulsor* with whom he associated the Claudian expulsion of Roman Jews. Indisputably not one of the emperor's wives, Chrestus therefore fits suitably between the other two imperial Chresti whose names the inscriptions of Rome preserve, and this certainly appears to be how Suetonius identified him in *Claudius* 25.5c.[72]

---

[71]Suetonius discussed the wives in *Claudius* 26, their children in *Claudius* 27, and the freedmen in *Claudius* 28. *Claudius* 29 then concludes discussion of these persons in the same terms with which Suetonius had introduced it: "Wholly under the control of these [freedmen] and of his wives, as I have said, he [Claudius] played the part, not of a prince, but of a servant, lavishing honours, the command of armies, pardons or punishments, according to the interests of each of them, or even their wish or whim; and that too for the most part in ignorance and blindly" (*Claudius* 29.1). That is, whether for the sake of their advantage or pleasure, their interests, or wish and whim, Claudius acted according to the inclinations of his wives and freedmen.

[72]Vis-à-vis the dominance of imperial freedmen under Claudius see Duff, *Freedmen*, pp. 143-186 and 221-228 (appendix 3). In the view of Garnsey and Saller (*Roman Empire*, p. 24), "some emperors, most notably Claudius (but also Nero and Commodus), aroused the aristocracy's anger by allowing themselves to be swayed by imperial freedmen, slaves or wives. In the case of freedmen and slaves, their power was a natural result of the access they gained to the emperor while helping him carry out routine duties." Relatedly, Martin (*Tacitus*, p. 144) writes that "according to Suetonius, reflecting the senatorial tradition, Claudius was wholly under the thumb of his wives and freedmen, who dictated imperial policy. It is clear that Tacitus worked within the framework of the same tradition." Martin (p. 160) affirms the worth of this tradition. A primary source is the *Apocolocyntosis* of Seneca (cf. Michael Coffey, "Seneca, Apocolocyntosis 1922-1958," *Lustrum* 6 [1961]:239-271). In it the freedmen of Claudius appear regularly (6, 13). Among his wives only Messalina is mentioned but as her husband's victim (11, 13). For the influence of Claudius' freedman Narcissus, concerning whom the sources preserve some detail, see Jean Melmoux, "L'action politique de l'affranchi impérial Narcisse: un exemple de la place des affranchis dans les entourages impériaux au milieu du 1ᵉʳ siècle," *Studii clasice* 17 (1975):61-69. In terms of Chrestus, his last sentence is interesting: "L'ensemble de sa [Narcissus'] carrière politique...contribue à prouver que les grands affranchis du milieu du premier siècle valaient mieux–et de loin–que le médiocre tableau laissé par les sources dont nous disposons." Still, from the perspective of this study, Momigliano (*Claudius*, p. 43) is essential: "Their [freedmen's] importance has led ancients and

At this point, we may return to what Josephus told readers. He claimed that the "powerful," i.e., the emperor's own Roman friends and freedmen, were associated with just such interests antagonistic to the Jewish people. At the time during which he was writing, Agrippa had succeeded against the anti-Jewish influences in Rome[73] and so been able to avert a disaster for the Judean delegates and perhaps also for Judea itself, but this changed nothing in terms of the reality of those forces and their inclination to bring hardship upon Jews. Thus, it is not inconceivable Chrestus was either a Jew who encouraged the other Roman Jews to disobey the 41 CE Claudian prohibitions against the public practices of their Roman cult or, a bit more likely, the Roman official who either enforced these prohibitions or encouraged the later expulsion itself. Nevertheless, the evidence at our disposal does point rather clearly in the direction of some once conspicuous but no longer identifiable imperial freedman who pursued his anti-Jewish interests with Claudius and in this way, as *impulsor*, caused the emperor to expel Roman Jews and, with them, their *superstitio* from the city.

Considering the attention which scholarship has devoted to the problem of the identity of Chrestus, we might assume that its solution would significantly advance our understanding of the Suetonian claim that Claudius "Iudaeos impulsore Chresto assidue tumultuantes Roma expulit." Only in a very limited way is this true. Specifically, we commenced our present discussion by reminding ourselves that both "assidue tumultuantes" and "impulsore Chresto" are but modifiers in a sentence the real subject of which is the emperor Claudius and the real object of which is Roman Jews. Furthermore, we are aware that analogous juxtapositions of this particular subject-object combination occur consistently within the context of the religious repression of Roman Jewry and that *Claudius* 25.4 itself bears other marks of that same context.

Ultimately, in other words, the likely identity of Chrestus as a once famous freedman of Claudius turns out to be less significant than might otherwise have been thought. That is, drawing attention to the supposedly turbulence-prone character of Roman Jews, the previous

---

moderns alike to suppose that the government must have fallen entirely into their hands. The baselessness of this supposition is obvious; the fact that Claudius was the organizer of this ministry is proof enough that his personality dominated it." Again, Dorey ("Ratgeber," pp. 144, 152-155) insists freedman influence on is not the same thing as freedman control over Claudius.

[73]This is as Josephus told the story, for he carefully avoided any reference which might have implied personal hostility on Claudius' part against Jews. Thus, Josephus ignored the 41 CE measures reported by Dio and the expulsion noted by Philo, the Acts of the Apostles, and Suetonius.

interpretation of *Claudius* 25.4 has tended to exonerate the autocrat Claudius at the expense of his Jewish subjects. Therefore, placing responsibility for the expulsion on the freedman who manipulated Claudius into that action, the present interpretation could also be utilized to exonerate the emperor. Philo himself would supply the precedent because, for purposes of sparing the emperor Tiberius, his report concerning the barrage of ca 31 CE anti-Jewish measures does blame the praetorian prefect Sejanus.

Nonetheless, as made clear already, Philo's apologetic attempt to disassociate Tiberius' own inclinations from those of his prefect is a failure,[74] for in both the presence and the absence of his prefect Tiberius pursued a similar anti-Jewish policy. Consequently, while the officially influential *impulsor* Sejanus no doubt encouraged and aided Tiberius in some of his measures against Roman and other Jews, the emperor himself was obviously disposed already to move in the same direction. In other words, that disposition rather than the *impulsor* Sejanus was the primary cause of the measures which Tiberius took against Roman Jewish religiosity.

Furthermore, it was Tiberius himself who had made the decision to give Sejanus a position of great authority. Not likely to have chosen a person whose views were much different from his own, the emperor listened well to his appointee, something hardly surprising, when the latter suggested courses of action in accord with imperial views. As has been indicated already,[75] the Auillius Flaccus of *Flaccus* 1-2 provides an excellent parallel:

> the policy of attacking the Jews begun by Sejanus was taken over by Flaccus Avillius. He had not like his predecessor the power to ill-treat outright the whole nation, for he had less opportunities of doing so, but those whom he reached suffered the direct misery from the stabs which he dealt to them one and all.... This Flaccus, then, who had been given a place in the suite of Tiberius Caesar was...made prefect of Alexandria and the country round it.

Similarly, that Gaius had been any more the innocent dupe of Helicon than Tiberius had been of Sejanus, Philo denied outright. In his view Gaius himself was the implacable enemy of the Jewish people (*Legatio* 180, 201). He, as we noticed, attacked Jews in various places and on a variety of fronts.[76] Likewise, keeping in mind the insistence of Josephus that the friends and freedmen of Claudius took an anti-

---

[74]Pp. 71-72.

[75]Ibid.

[76]Pp. 77-86.

Jewish stance, we may not forget that the emperor himself chose all these persons. This is true whether he was a genius or a fool, whether he did indeed allow wives and, in particular, freedmen to order him around, or whether his choice of counselors was well calculated to serve what he thought were his own best interests.

Consequently, we may not give this freedman Chrestus any more credit than is his due. We have traced a long history of upper-class and imperial bad attitudes towards Roman Jews and, in particular, Roman Judaism, and we have scrutinized how these attitudes worked themselves out in a whole series of concrete imperial measures taken against them. Again, we have seen already how Tiberius was moved by his anti-Jewish praetorian prefect to act against Roman and other Jews, but we know also that Tiberius himself had a mind set which made him entirely capable of taking action on his own. Both with and without Sejanus, in other words, under Tiberius Roman Jews were not safe. Similar is Gaius, for if his slave Helicon encouraged him in his support for various measures against the Jewish houses of prayer in Alexandria, he nonetheless listened to Helicon because they shared a common, virulent anti-Jewish attitude. Again, then, and this scarcely needs to be written, even without Helicon, Jews under Gaius were not safe. In particular, unless we are to believe that Chrestus was the ghost writer behind Claudius' 41 CE letter to Alexandria and also that he plotted the measures of the very same year against the practice of Judaism at Rome, it was Claudius himself who acted the traditional imperial role when he responded in a positive way to the freedman encouragement reported by Suetonius. Again, in other words, with or without the anti-Jewish freedman Chrestus as the *impulsor*, under Claudius Roman Jews were not safe.

Returning, then, to the basic considerations of grammar, the real subject of *Claudius* 25.4 is Claudius, the real object is Roman Jewry, and the real connection between them is a hardly unique activity devised to repress Jewish religious life at Rome. Rightly therefore did Suetonius make the *impulsor* Chrestus a grammatically subsidiary element. Everything considered, after all, this man played but a minor role in the periodic subjugation of Roman Jewish religiosity under the early empire.

Conclusion

The emperor Claudius is always worthy of our attention; so of course is Rome, the city from which he ruled the world; so are the significant numbers of Jews who helped shape the Roman population; and so also therefore is the claim of Suetonius that "Chrestus caused Claudius to expel from Rome the continuously rebelling Jews." Here, after all, the three proper nouns *Claudius*, *Rome*, and *Jews* come together in such a way that, placed within an appropriate historical context, *Claudius* 25.4 may be expected to yield significant information about all three. As long, however, as the interpretation of this text was governed by its fourth proper noun, the problematic *Chrestus*, little could have been expected of it. Unfortunately, since the time of the fifth-century historian Paulus Orosius, the latter has been the situation. That is, with Chrestus identified as Jesus Christus, and the entire passage explained on the basis of this *interpretatio christiana*, *Claudius* 25.4 has been relegated to a footnote largely within early Christian history.

Thus, if for no other reason than that it liberated *Claudius* 25.4 from the Orosian ghetto, the present study would be of value. In fact, however, this is only a beginning point, for the real worth of the work lies in its permitting the freed text to assume a rightful place among the several other significant accounts clustering around a point where the terms *Claudius*, *Rome*, and *Jews* intersect. Within some of these materials the late Republican and early imperial predecessors of Claudius encounter Roman Jews; in others they challenge diaspora Jews of various Italian cities as well as of both Syrian Antioch and Alexandria; and in still others they confront the members of sundry foreign *superstitiones* at Rome. Interesting in their own right, these accounts have been particularly useful for our purposes because they provide the historical context within which we were able to make sense of Claudius' own policymaking vis-à-vis the foreign *superstitio* of Roman Jews.

Hence, although the working title of the present volume read "Roman Jewry under the Early Empire," this had to be eliminated because we now realize that these particular Romans, except perhaps as corporate straw persons, could hardly have been the main subject of research the actual focus of which turned out to be the imperial repression of a particular foreign religious sect. Expressed a bit differently, this inquiry teaches at least as much about the dangers inherent in the mixture of power, self-righteousness, and prejudice as it does about the so-victimized Roman Jews.

By way of summary, our analysis began with the exposition of tendencies distorting the view of actual relationships between early imperial power and Roman Jewry. Concretely, it disclosed how the apologetic needs of Philo and Josephus masked the imperial hostility towards Jews and their religious way of life. Likewise, it demonstrated how the imperial sources consistently slandered Jews in terms of their foreign *superstitio*. No less significantly, it also made clear the tendency of modern scholarship to take these ancient distortions for granted and so to draw the false conclusion from them that trouble-making Roman Jews were in great measure responsible for their own repeated difficulties.

Then, within the context of Gentile and Jewish sources available for the reconstruction of Roman Jewish history prior to the time of Claudius, it became quite apparent that, rather than any presupposed inclination to disorder or violence, the regular object of governmental hostility was Jewish religiosity. In other words, we discovered that hypothetical Roman Jewish rabble-rousing failed to provide a real background for the later Claudian expulsion of Roman Jewry. What did was the very real upper-class and imperial prejudice manifested prior to Claudius in concrete actions intended to drive Judaism from the city.

We then discovered that Claudius was, at least in this regard, the faithful heir of his predecessors. Specifically, Tacitus indicated how in "externae superstitiones" this emperor perceived dangers for the traditional Roman religion. Philo's *Legatio* 155-158 pointed in a similar direction. Again, Dio referred to the measures which, as soon as he became emperor, Claudius had taken against the assemblies of Roman Jews. Likewise, Acts 18:2, *Claudius* 25.4, and *Legatio* 157 all revealed how, sometime later, he also expelled this segment of the city's population.

Closer examination of our resources for the year 41 CE proved especially useful. P. Lond. 1912, the highly revealing letter which Claudius addressed to the city of Alexandria, demonstrated not only the potential danger associated with imperial self-righteousness but also the tangible hostility directed towards the already repressed

Alexandrian Jewish community. More importantly, Dio 60.6.6 as well as its parallel in *Legatio* 155-158 presented the new emperor as he immediately set out to curtail the practice of the Jewish cult at Rome.

Analogy from 41 CE in place, we then turned to the analysis of Suetonius' statement that Claudius sometime later "Iudaeos impulsore Chresto assidue tumultuantes Roma expulit" and, hence, to the conclusions of the previous chapter. That is, though apparently identified by Suetonius as a once well-known slave or freedman of Claudius, whatever his identity, the Chrestus of this text was nothing more than a secondary actor, i.e., a secondary grammatical element, in a short sentence the real subject of which is an emperor, Claudius, the real object Roman Jews in the practice of their religious way of life, and the real predicate but one more hardly uncommon action of the former against the latter.

What, then, have we found out? Among other things, that at the expense of those Jews historiography ancient and modern has been rather charitable to Claudius. That, insofar as he harbored highly prejudicial, hostile attitudes towards the participants in the rites of Roman Jews, this emperor fit in very amicably among his imperial predecessors. That he, like they, acted more than once on the basis of these attitudes. That, consequently, Roman Jewish life under the early empire must always have been unpredictable and, on some occasions, difficult or impossible. That Claudius, following the example of his uncle Tiberius, ultimately expelled the Jewish cult from the city.

In sum, we may recall the dual claim of Momigliano, first, that analysis of Claudian religious policy best reveals the ideals governing his entire administration and, second, that, because of the nature of the sources, this religious policy becomes clearest in Claudius' attitude towards Jews and Judaism. Granting even a modicum of truth to this claim, we shall have to conclude that, in many cases where the dearth of ancient sources makes them otherwise difficult to detect, absolute power, outrageously prejudicial attitudes, self-righteous certitude, and whim lie behind the policymaking not only of Claudius but of his imperial predecessors as well.

Appendices

1. Roman Synagogues

Philo's word for the house of prayer was προσευχή (*proseuche*; cf. the Latin *proseucha* with precisely the same meaning in the scholium to Juvenal's *Satire* 3.296 [*Scholia in Iuvenalem*, ad loc.]: "*Proseucha*: Locus Iudaeorum, ubi orant.*"*), and he envisioned a variety of such *buildings* in the Rome of his own day (*Legatio* 156, 157). Moreover, based on the Jewish epitaphs from Rome it is possible to posit the existence of at least eleven separate synagogues (συναγωγή in these inscriptions) in the city (Leon, *Jews of Ancient Rome*, pp. 135-166; cf. La Piana, "Foreign Groups," pp. 351-359; Collon, "Remarques sur les quartiers juifs," pp. 72-94; Penna, "Les Juifs a Rome," p. 327).

Because of the modern use of the term *synagogue* it is easy to read into these inscriptions the idea of eleven buildings. Thus, La Piana (pp. 353-354; cf. Collon, p. 73) seems to envision "synagogues" comparable to the temples of Greco-Roman religion dotting Rome's ancient landscape. Terminologically of course we must be cautious, for a distinction often exists between the congregation of worshippers, i.e., the συναγωγή, and the place where they worship, i.e., the προσευχή or οἶκος (Schürer, *History* 2.425, 429-431, 439-440; cf. Juster, *Les Juifs* 1.414, n. 8 and 1.456b, n. 3; La Piana, pp. 347-348; Leon, p. 139). A good example of this distinction is found in *CII*, 738, which provides an inscription from Phocaea in Asia Minor that reads, "Tation...having built for his co-religionists this house (*oikos*) and the colonnade of the atrium has made it a gift to the Jews. The community (*synagogue*) of Jews has honored Tation...."

Again, by way of analogy from German usage, the word *Kirche* signifies *church* in the sense of the building with that name, and *Gemeinde* designates the congregation of the faithful which uses this structure. Difficulties arise in English because, although the words *church* and *synagogue* might refer to either the building or the congregation, they both bring to mind primarily the structure. As Philo made clear in *Legatio* 157, however, the idea behind the Greek term *synagogue* (συνάγεσθαι) is that of the gathering itself, i.e., of the *Gemeinde* or congregation, and the word *proseuche* then corresponds to *Kirche*, i.e., to the place where the gathering takes place. Thus, although Philo indicated the existence of more than one *proseuche* in Rome and Josephus did apply *synagogue* in reference to the structure (*Antiquities* 19.300; cf. *Life* 277, 280, 293 for his synonymous use of *proseuche*), the inscriptional references to the synagogues of Rome are misleading when compelled to conjure up images of buildings set aside for the purposes of religion (Penna, p. 327; cf. May, "Politique religieuse," p. 15).

Given, after all, the ex-slave status and poverty of many Roman Jews, it is probable that synagogues met in private homes or rented halls like those used by early Christian communities (Romans 16:5, 1 Corinthians 16:19, Acts 19:9). Perhaps it is partially for this reason, though in the Roman port city of Ostia a *proseuche* was discovered (Maria Floriani Squarciapino, "The Synagogue at Ostia," *Archeology* 16 [1963]:194-203; Alf Thomas Kraabel, "The Diaspora Synagogue: Archeological and Epigraphic Evidence since Sukenik" in *ANRW*, 2.19[1]: 497-500, as well as his "Social Systems of Six Diaspora Synagogues" in *Ancient Synagogues: The State of Research*, ed. Joseph Gutmann, Brown Judaic Studies, vol. 22 [Chico, California: Scholars Press, 1981], pp. 79-91), that Rome itself has yielded nothing in this regard. On the other hand, the both magnificent and magnificently preserved house of prayer in the Asian city of Sardis (Kraabel, "Diaspora Synagogue" in *ANRW*, 2.19[1]:483-488; Andrew R. Seager and A. Thomas Kraabel, "The Synagogue and the Jewish Community" in George M. A. Hanfmann, *Sardis from Prehistoric to Roman Times: Results of the Archeological Exploration of Sardis 1958-1975* [Cambridge: Harvard University Press, 1983], pp. 168-190) serves to remind us of the part chance has played in the survival of these structures.

2. The Order of Occurrences in *Claudius* 25.3-5

It might appear to be possible to establish a relative date for the anti-Jewish measure of *Claudius* 25.4 on the basis of its place in the order of other occurrences referred to in *Claudius* 25.3-5. Nevertheless, what follows–cf. Smilda (*C. Suetonii Tranquilli*, ad loc.) as the source of both parallels and chronological data–reveals that Suetonius' order is not chronological but topical by foreign nationality (*Claudius* 22.1):
1. "Peregrinae condicionis homines vetuit"
   no dateable parallel
2. "Civitatem R. usurpantes...percussit"
   no dateable parallel
3. "Provincias Achaiam et Macedoniam...senatui reddidit"
   44 CE = Dio 60.24.1
4. "Lyciis...libertatem ademit"
   43 CE = Dio 60.17.3
5. "Rhodiis... [libertatem] reddidit"
   53 CE = Tacitus *Annals* 12.58 (combined with the next event [Ilium] and Bononia, so a chronological unit)
   51 CE = Suetonius *Nero* 7 (the same event as is in Suetonius

Claudius and Tacitus; clearly dated by Suetonius *Nero* to 51 CE)
6. "Iliensibus...tributa remisit"
     53 CE = Tacitus *Annals* 12.58 (and contemporary with Rhodes
     above and Bononia)
     51 CE = Suetonius *Nero* 7 (the same event as is in Suetonius
     Claudius and Tacitus; clearly dated by Suetonius *Nero* to 51 CE)
7. "Iudaeos...expulit"
8. "Germanorum legatis...permisit"
     58 CE = Tacitus *Annals* 13.54 (Smilda claims Suetonius erred
     and really described an event which happened under Nero.
     Otherwise, it must be attached to
     47 CE = Tacitus *Annals* 11.10 and the continuation of the event
     in
     49 CE = Tacitus *Annals* 12.10. I see no reason to reject an event
     under Claudius, so we may place it in 47-49 CE. Otherwise, we
     must assume another Parthian delegation coming to Rome under
     Claudius. The problem is that the event under Nero in Tacitus
     appears very much like the one under Claudius in Suetonius,
     except that the Parthians are not referred to by name in the
     former. If they are the same event, it may well be that the event
     happened under Claudius. In other words, perhaps Tacitus erred
     rather than Suetonius.)
9. "Druidarum religionem...abolevit"
     No dateable parallel
In sum, the chronological disorder of *Claudius* 25.3-5 prohibits even
relative chronological conclusions about the date of the expulsion in
Suetonius.

Bibliography

Abel, Ernest L. "Were the Jews Banished from Rome in 19 A.D.?" *Revue des études juives* 127 (1968):383-386.

Adler, Ada, ed. *Suidae Lexicon.* 5 parts. Leipzig: B. G. Teubner, 1928-1938.

Alessandrí, Salvatore. "La presunta cacciata dei Giudei da Roma nel 139 a. Cr." *Studi classici e orientali* 17 (1968):187-198.

Alföldy, Géza. *The Social History of Rome.* Translated by David Braund and Frank Pollock. Baltimore: Johns Hopkins University Press, 1991.

Applebaum, S[himon]. "The Legal Status of the Jewish Communities in the Diaspora." In *The Jewish People in the First Century: Historical Geography, Political History, Social, Cultural and Religious Life and Institutions.* Edited by S. Safrai and M. Stern. Compendia Rerum Iudaicarum ad Novum Testamentum: Section One. 2 vols. Philadelphia: Fortress Press, 1974-1987.

Baldwin, Barry. *Suetonius.* Amsterdam: Adolf M. Hakkert, 1983.

Balsdon, J. P. V. D. *The Emperor Gaius (Caligula).* Oxford: Clarendon Press, 1934.

Balsdon, J. P. V. D. "Notes concerning the Principate of Gaius." *Journal of Roman Studies* 24 (1934):13-24.

Balsdon, J. P. V. D. *Romans and Aliens.* Chapel Hill: University of North Carolina Press, 1979.

Bammel, Ernst. "Judenverfolgung und Naherwartung: Zur Eschatologie des Ersten Thessalonicherbriefs." *Zeitschrift für Theologie und Kirche* 56 (1959): 294-315.

Bandy, Anastasius C. *Ioannes Lydus on Powers or the Magistracies of the Roman State.* Memoirs Series, vol. 149. Philadelphia: American Philosophical Society, 1983.

Barrett, Anthony A. *Caligula: The Corruption of Power.* 1989. Reprint. New York: Simon & Schuster, 1991.

Baumgart, Julius. *Die römischen Sklavennamen.* Breslau: R. Nischkowsky, 1936.

Bell, H. Idris. "Egypt under the Early Principate." In *CAH,* 10:284-315.

Bell, H. Idris. *Jews and Christians in Egypt: The Jewish Troubles in Alexandria and the Athanasian Controversy Illustrated by Texts from Greek Papyri in the British Museum.* 1924. Reprint. Westport, CT: Greenwood Press, 1976.

Benko, Stephen. "The Edict of Claudius of A.D. 49 and the Instigator Chrestus." *Theologische Zeitschrift* 25 (1969):406-418.

Berliner, A. *Geschichte der Juden in Rom von der ältesten Zeit bis zur Gegenwart.* 2 vols. Frankfurt: J. Kaufmann, 1893.

Beyer, Hermann W., and Lietzmann, Hans. *Jüdische Denkmäler I: Die jüdische Katakombe der Villa Torlonia in Rom.* Berlin: Walter de Gruyter & Co., 1930.

Bikerman [Bickerman], Élie. "Une question d'authenticité: Les privilèges juifs." *Annuaire de l'Institut de philologie et d'histoire orientales et slaves* 13 = *Mélanges Isidore Lévy* (1953):11-34.

Birley, Anthony R. *The FASTI of Roman Britain.* Oxford: Clarendon Press, 1981.

Blass, Friedrich. "ΧΡΗΣΤΙΑΝΟΙ-ΧΡΙΣΤΙΑΝΟΙ." *Hermes* 30 (1895):465-470.

Bludau, A. "Die Juden Roms im ersten christlichen Jahrhundert." *Katholik* 1 (1903):113-134, 193-229.

Boissevain, Ursulus Philippus, ed. *Cassii Dionis Cocceiani: Historiarum romanarum quae supersunt.* 5 vols. Berlin: Weidmannsche Buchhandlung, 1895-1931.

Borg, Marcus. "A New Context for Romans XIII." *New Testament Studies* 19 (1972-1973):205-218.

Box, Herbert, ed. *Philonis Alexandrini: IN FLACCUM.* London: Oxford University Press, 1939.

Brown, Raymond E., and Meier, John P. *Antioch and Rome: New Testament Cradles of Catholic Christianity.* New York: Paulist Press, 1983.

Bruce, F. F. "Christianity under Claudius." *Bulletin of the John Rylands Library* 44 (1962):309-326.

Bruce, F. F. *Commentary on the Book of Acts.* 1954. Reprint. Grand Rapids: Wm. B. Eerdmans Publishing Co., 1966.

Bruce, F. F. "Tacitus on Jewish History." *Journal of Semitic Studies* 29 (1984): 33-44.

Campbell, Jim. "America's Long History of Burning Black Churches." *The Plain Dealer* (Cleveland), 19 June 1996.

Carcopino, Jerome. *Daily Life in Ancient Rome: The People and the City at the Height of the Empire.* Translated by E. O. Lorimer. 1941. Reprint. Harmondsworth, Eng.: Penguin Books, 1981.

Chantraine, Heinrich. *Freigelassene und Sklaven im Dienst der römischen Kaiser.* Forschungen zur antiken Sklaverei, vol. 1. Wiesbaden: Franz Steiner Verlag, 1967.

Chapot, Victor. "Antiquités de la Syrie du Nord." *Bulletin de correspondance hellénique* 26 (1902):161-208.

Cichorius, Conrad. *Römische Studien: Historisches, Epigraphisches, Literargeschichtliches aus vier Jahrhunderten Roms.* 2d ed. Darmstadt: Wissenschaftliche Buchgesellschaft, 1961.

Coffey, Michael. "Seneca, Apocolocyntosis 1922-1958." *Lustrum* 6 (1961):239-271.

Cohen, Shaye J. D. *Josephus in Galilee and Rome: His Vita and Development as a Historian.* Columbia Studies in the Classical Tradition, vol. 8. Leiden: E. J. Brill, 1979.

Collon, Suzanne. "Remarques sur les quartiers juifs de la Rome antique." *Mélanges d'archéologie et d'histoire de l'École française de Rome* 57 (1940): 72-94.

Constant, Pierre, ed. *Valère Maxime: actions et paroles mémorables.* 2 vols. Paris: Librairie Garnier Frères, 1935.

Cumont, Franz. *The Oriental Religions in Roman Paganism.* 1911. Reprint. New York: Dover Publications, 1956.

Cumont, Franz. *Recherches sur le symbolisme funéraire des romains.* Paris: Librairie orientaliste Paul Geuthner, 1942.

Daniel, Jerry L. "Anti-Semitism in the Hellenistic-Roman Period." *Journal of Biblical Literature* 98 (1979):45-65.

Davis, S. *Race-Relations in Ancient Egypt: Greek, Egyptian, Hebrew, Roman.* New York: Philosophical Library, 1952.

Deferrari, Roy J., trans. *Paulus Orosius: The Seven Books of History against the Pagans.* Washington: Catholic University of America, 1964.

Degrassi, Attilio. *I fasti consolari dell'impero romano dal 30 avanti Cristo al 613 dopo Cristo.* Sussidi eruditi, vol. 3. Rome: Edizioni di storia e letteratura, 1952.

Dinkler, Erich. "Schalom–Eirene–Pax: Jüdische Sepulkralinschriften und ihr Verhältnis zum frühen Christentum." *Rivista di archeologia cristiana* 50 (1974):121-144.

Dobson, Brian, and Breeze, David J. "The Roman Cohorts and the Legionary Centurionate." In *Epigraphische Studien*, vol. 8. Düsseldorf: RheinlandVerlag, 1969.

Domaszewski, A[lfred] von. "Eine Inschrift des P. Suillius Rufus." *Rheinisches Museum* 67 (1911):151-152.

Domaszewski, A[lfred] von. *Die Rangordnung des römischen Heeres*. Edited by Brian Dobson. Beihefte der bonner Jahrbücher, vol. 14. 2d ed. Cologne: Böhlau Verlag, 1967.

Dorey, Thomas A. "Claudius und seine Ratgeber." *Das Altertum* 12 (1966):144-155.

Duff, A. M. *Freedmen in the Early Roman Empire*. 1928. Reprint. New York: Barnes & Noble, 1958.

Eisler, Robert. ΙΗΣΟΥΣ ΒΑΣΙΛΕΥΣ ΟΥ ΒΑΣΙΛΕΥΣΑΣ. Religionswissenschaftliche Bibliothek, vol. 9. 2 vols. Heidelberg: Carl Winters Universitätsbuchhandlung, 1929.

Engers, Maurits. "Der Brief des Kaisers Claudius an die Alexandriner." *Klio* 20 (1926):168-178.

Evans, Harry B. *Publica carmina*. Lincoln, NE: University of Nebraska Press, 1983.

Feldman, Louis H. "Flavius Josephus Revisited: The Man, His Writings, and His Significance." In *ANRW*, 2.21^2:763-862.

Feldman, Louis, trans. *Josephus: The Life, Against Apion, The Jewish War, Jewish Antiquities*. Translated by H. St. J. Thackeray et al. LCL. 10 vols. Cambridge: Harvard University Press, 1926-1965.

Fick, August. *Die griechischen Personennamen nach ihrer Bildung erklärt und systematisch geordnet*. Edited by Fritz Bechtel and August Fick. 2d ed. Göttingen: Vandenhoeck & Ruprecht, 1894.

Flusser, David. "Paganism in Palestine." In *The Jewish People in the First Century: Historical Geography, Political History, Social, Cultural and Religious Life and Institutions*. Edited by S. Safrai and M. Stern. Compendia Rerum Iudaicarum ad Novum Testamentum: Section One. 2 vols. Philadelphia: Fortress Press, 1974-1987.

Förster, Richard. "Skulpturen von Antiochia." *Jahrbuch des kaiserlich deutschen Archäologischen Instituts* 13 (1898):177-191.

Frank, Tenney. "Race Mixture in the Roman Empire." *American Historical Review* 21 (1915-1916):689-708.

Frend, W. H. C. *Martyrdom and Persecution in the Early Church: A Study of a Conflict from the Maccabees to Donatus*. Garden City: Anchor Books, 1967.

Fuchs, Harald. "Tacitus über die Christen." *Vigiliae christianae* 4 (1950):65-93.

Fuks, Alexander. "Aspects of the Jewish Revolt in A.D. 115-117." *Journal of Roman Studies* 51 (1961):98-104.

Gager, John G. *The Origins of Anti-Semitism: Attitudes toward Judaism in Pagan and Christian Antiquity.* New York: Oxford University Press, 1985.

Gallego-Blanco, E., ed. *Historia contra los paganos.* Barcelona: Puvill libros, n.d.

Garnsey, Peter. "Independent Freedmen and the Economy of Roman Italy under the Principate." *Klio* 63 [1981]:359-371.

Garnsey, Peter, and Saller, Richard. *The Roman Empire: Economy, Society and Culture.* Berkeley and Los Angeles: University of California Press, 1987.

Garzetti, Albino. *From Tiberius to the Antonines.* Translated by J. R. Foster. London: Methuen, 1974.

The Gods Delight: The Human Figure in Classical Bronze. Organized by Arielle P. Kozloff and David Gordon Mitten. Cleveland: The Cleveland Museum of Art, 1988.

Goetz, Hans-Werner. *Die Geschichtstheologie des Orosius.* Darmstadt: Wissenschaftliche Buchgesellschaft, 1980.

Goguel, Maurice. *The Life of Jesus.* Translated by Olive Wyon. New York: Macmillan Company, 1949.

Goodenough, Erwin R. *An Introduction to Philo Judaeus.* 2d ed. Oxford: Basil Blackwell, 1962.

Goodenough, Erwin R. *Jewish Symbols in the Greco-Roman Period.* Bollingen Series, vol. 37. 13 vols. New York: Pantheon Books, 1953-1965.

Gordon, Arthur E. *Illustrated Introduction to Latin Epigraphy.* Berkeley and Los Angeles: University of California Press, 1983.

Gordon, Mary L. "The Nationality of Slaves under the Early Roman Empire." *Journal of Roman Studies* 14 (1924):93-111.

Graetz, Heinrich. *History of the Jews.* Edited and translated by Bella Lowy. 6 vols. Philadelphia: The Jewish Publication Society of America, 1891-1898.

Grant, Michael. *The Jews in the Roman World.* New York: Charles Scribner's Sons, 1973.

Graves, Robert, and Podro, Joshua. *Jesus in Rome: A Historical Conjecture.* London: Cassell and Company, 1957.

Gressmann, Hugo. "Jewish Life in Ancient Rome." In *Jewish Studies in Memory of Israel Abrahams.* Edited by George Alexander Kohut. New York: Press of the Jewish Institute of Religion, 1927.

Guterman, Simeon L. *Religious Toleration and Persecution in Ancient Rome*. London: Aiglon Press Ltd., 1951.

Gutmann, Joseph. "Early Synagogue and Jewish Catacomb Art and its Relation to Christian Art." In *ANRW*, 2.21²:1313-1342.

Haenchen, Ernst. *Die Apostelgeschichte*. Kritisch-exegetischer Kommentar über das Neue Testament. 14th ed. Göttingen: Vandenhoeck & Ruprecht, 1965.

Hardy, E. G. *Studies in Roman History*. New York: Macmillan Company, 1906.

Harnack, Adolf. "Chronologische Berechnung des 'Tags von Damaskus.'" *Sitzungsberichte der preussischen Akademie der Wissenschaften* 34 (1912):673-682.

Harnack, Adolf. *The Mission and Expansion of Christianity in the First Three Centuries*. Edited and translated by James Moffatt. 2d ed. 2 vols. New York: Putnam's Sons, 1908.

Heidel, W. A. "Why Were the Jews Banished from Italy in 19 A.D.?" *American Journal of Philology* 41 (1920):38-47.

Helm, Rudolf, ed. *Die Chronik des Hieronymus: Hieronymi Chronicon: Eusebius Werke* 7. GCS, vol. 47, 2d ed. Berlin: Akademie-Verlag, 1956.

Hengel, Martin. *Judaism and Hellenism: Studies in Their Encounter in Palestine during the Early Hellenistic Period*. Translated by John Bowden. 2 vols. Philadelphia: Fortress Press, 1981.

Hennig, Dieter. "Zu neuveröffentlichten Bruchstücken der <Acta Alexandrinorum>." *Chiron* 5 (1975):317-335.

Hilberg, Raul. *The Destruction of the European Jews: Student Edition*. New York: Holmes & Meier Publishers, Inc., 1985.

Hoerber, Robert O. "The Decree of Claudius in Acts 18:2." *Concordia Theological Monthly* 31 (1960):690-694.

Howard, Albertus Andreas, and Jackson, Carolus Newell. *Index verborum C. Suetoni Tranquilli*. Cambridge: Harvard University Press, 1922.

Huidekoper, Frederic. *Judaism at Rome B.C. 76 to A.D. 140*. 3d ed. New York: James Miller, 1880.

Hunt, A. S., and Edgar, C. C., trans. *Select Papyri*. LCL. 5 vols. Cambridge: Harvard University Press, 1963.

Janne, Henri. "Impulsore Chresto." *Annuaire de l'Institut de philologie et d'histoire orientales* 2 (1933-1934):531-553.

Jewett, Robert. *A Chronology of Paul's Life*. Philadelphia: Fortress Press, 1979.

Johnston, Patricia A. "The Concept of Empire in Vergil's *Eclogues*: Immigrants, Emigrants, and a Child to Guide Them." *Humanitas: Newsletter of the Ohio Classical Conference* 15 (1990-1991):26-41.

Jones, H. Stuart. "Claudius and the Jewish Question at Alexandria." *Journal of Roman Studies* 16 (1926):17-35.

Juster, Jean. *Les Juifs dans l'Empire romain: leur condition juridique, économique et sociale.* 2 vols. Paris: Librairie Paul Geuthner, 1914.

Kajanto, Iiro. *The Latin Cognomina.* Commentationes Humanarum Litterarum, vol. 36.2. Helsinki: Societas Scientiarum Fennica, 1965.

Kajanto, Iiro. *Onomastic Studies in the Early Christian Inscriptions of Rome and Carthage.* Acta Instituti Romani Finlandiae, vol. 2.1. Helsinki: Tilgmann, 1963.

Kajanto, Iiro. *A Study of the Greek Epitaphs of Rome.* Acta Instituti Romani Finlandiae, vol. 2.3. Helsinki: Tilgmann, 1963.

Karst, Josef, ed. *Die Chronik aus dem armenischen übersetzt mit textkritischem Commentar: Eusebius Werke 5.* GCS, vol. 20. Leipzig: J. C. Hinrichs'sche Buchhandlung, 1911.

Kasher, A. "The Jewish Attitude to the Alexandrian Gymnasium in the First Century A.D." *American Journal of Ancient History* 1 (1976):148-161.

Kempf, Carolus, ed. *Valerii Maximi: Factorvm et dictorvm memorabilivm libri novem cvm Ivlii Paridis et Ianvarii Nepotiani epitomis.* 2d ed. 2 vols. 1888. Reprint. Stuttgart: B. G. Teubner, 1982.

Koestermann, Erich. "Ein folgenschwerer Irrtum des Tacitus (Ann. 15,44,2ff.)?" *Historia* 16 (1967):456-469.

Konikoff, Adia. *Sarcophagi from the Jewish Catacombs of Ancient Rome: A Catalogue Raisonne.* 2d ed. Stuttgart: Franz Steiner, 1990.

Kraabel, Alf Thomas. "The Diaspora Synagogue: Archeological and Epigraphic Evidence since Sukenik." In *ANRW*, 2.19[1]:477-510.

Kraabel, Alf Thomas. "Social Systems of Six Diaspora Synagogues." In *Ancient Synagogues: The State of Research.* Edited by Joseph Gutmann. Brown Judaic Studies, vol. 22. Chico, California: Scholars Press, 1981.

Kraeling, Carl H. "The Jewish Community at Antioch." *Journal of Biblical Literature* 51 (1932):130-160.

Kraemer, Ross S. "Jewish Women in the Diaspora World of Late Antiquity." In *Jewish Women in Historical Perspective.* Edited by Judith R. Baskin. Detroit: Wayne State University Press, 1991.

Kümmel, Werner Georg. *Introduction to the New Testament*. Translated by Howard Clark Kee. Nashville: Abingdon Press, 1975.

Lacroix, Benoit. *Orose et ses idées*. Université de Montréal publications de l'Institut d'études médiévales, vol. 18. Paris: Librairie philosophique J. Vrin, 1965.

Lake, Kirsopp. "The Chronology of Acts." In *The Beginnings of Christianity*. Edited by F. J. Foakes Jackson and Kirsopp Lake. 5 vols. London: Macmillan, 1920-1933.

Lambertz, Max. *Die griechischen Sklavennamen*. Vienna: n.p., 1907.

Lane, Eugene N. "Sabazius and the Jews in Valerius Maximus: A Re-examination." *Journal of Roman Studies* 69 (1979):35-38.

La Piana, George. "Foreign Groups in Rome during the First Centuries of the Empire." *Harvard Theological Review* 20 (1927):183-403.

Latte, Kurt. *Römische Religionsgeschichte*. Handbuch der Altertumswissenschaft, vol. 5.4. Munich: C. H. Beck'sche Verlagsbuchhandlung, 1960.

Leon, Harry J[oshua]. *The Jews of Ancient Rome*. 1960. Reprint with new Introduction by Carolyn A. Osiek. Peabody, MA: Hendrickson Publishers, Inc., 1995.

Levick, Barbara. *Claudius*. New Haven: Yale University Press, 1990.

Lévy, Isidore. "Tacite et l'origine du peuple juif." *Latomus* 5 (1946):331-340.

Lewin, Thomas. *Fasti Sacri or A Key to the Chronology of the New Testament*. London: Longmans, Green, and Co., 1865.

Lieberman, Saul. *Greek in Jewish Palestine: Studies in the Life and Manners of Jewish Palestine in the II-IV Centuries C.E.* 2d ed. New York: Philipp Feldheim, Inc., 1965.

Linck, Kurt. "De antiquissimis veterum quae ad Iesum Nazarenum spectant testimoniis." *Religionsgeschichtliche Versuche und Vorarbeiten* 14 (1913-1914):1-115.

Loisy, Alfred. *Les Actes des Apotres*. Paris: Émile Nourry, 1920.

Luedemann, Gerd. *Paul: Apostle to the Gentiles: Studies in Chronology*. Translated by F. Stanley Jones. Philadelphia: Fortress Press, 1984.

Lydus, Ioannes Laurentius. *De mensibus*. Edited by Guilielmus Roether. Darmstadt: n.p., 1827.

Macé, Alcide. *Essai sur Suétone*. Paris: Ancienne librairie Thorin et fils, 1900.

Malaise, Michel. *Les conditions de pénétration et de diffusion des cultes égyptiens en Italie*. Études préliminaires aux religions orientales dans l'empire Romain, vol. 22. Leiden: E. J. Brill, 1972.

Marsh, Frank Burr. *The Reign of Tiberius*. 1931. Reprint. New York: Barnes & Noble, Inc., 1959.

Marshall, Anthony J. "Flaccus and the Jews of Asia (Cicero *Pro Flacco* 28.67-69)." *Phoenix* 29 (1975):139-154.

Martin, Ronald. *Tacitus*. Berkeley and Los Angeles: University of California Press, 1981.

May, Gaston. "L'activité juridique de l'Empereur Claude." *Revue historique de droit français et étranger* 15 (1936):55-97, 213-254.

May, Gaston. "Notes complémentaires sur les actes de l'Empereur Claude." *Revue historique de droit français et étranger* 22 (1943):101-114.

May, Gaston. "La politique religieuse de l'Empereur Claude." *Revue historique de droit français et étranger* 17 (1938):1-46.

Mellor, Ronald. *Tacitus*. New York: Routledge, 1993.

Melmoux, Jean. "L'action politique de l'affranchi impérial Narcisse: un exemple de la place des affranchis dans les entourages impériaux au milieu du 1er siècle." *Studii clasice* 17 (1975):61-69.

Merrill, Elmer Truesdell. *Essays in Early Christian History*. London: Macmillan and Co., 1924.

Merrill, Elmer Truesdell. "The Expulsion of Jews from Rome under Tiberius." *Classical Philology* 14 (1919):366-372.

Metzger, Bruce M. "The Nazareth Inscription Once Again." In *Jesus und Paulus: Festschrift für Werner Georg Kümmel zum 70. Geburtstag*. Edited by E. Earle Ellis and Erich Grässer. 2d ed. Göttingen: Vandenhoeck & Ruprecht, 1978.

Meyer, Eduard. *Ursprung und Anfänge des Christentums*. 3 vols. Stuttgart: J. G. Cotta'sche Buchhandlung Nachfolger, 1923.

Millar, Fergus. *A Study of Cassius Dio*. Oxford: Clarendon Press, 1964.

Moehring, Horst R. "The *Acta pro Judaeis* in the *Antiquities* of Flavius Josephus: A Study in Hellenistic and Modern Apologetic Historiography" in *Christianity, Judaism and Other Greco-Roman Cults: Studies for Morton Smith at Sixty: Judaism before 70*. Edited by Jacob Neusner. Studies in Judaism in Late Antiquity, vol. 12.3. Leiden: E. J. Brill, 1975.

Moehring, Horst R. "Joseph ben Matthia and Flavius Josephus: The Jewish Prophet and the Roman Historian." In *ANRW*, 2.21²:864-944.

Moehring, Horst R. "The Persecution of the Jews and the Adherents of the Isis Cult at Rome A.D. 19." *Novum Testamentum* 3 (1959):293-304.

Momigliano, Arnaldo. *Claudius: The Emperor and His Achievement.* 1943. New preface, 1961. Reprint. Westport, CT: Greenwood Press, 1981.

Momigliano, Arnaldo. "Osservazioni sulle fonti per la storia di Caligola, Claudio, Nerone." *Rendiconti della R. Accademia Nazionale dei Lincei, Classe di scienze morali, storiche e filologiche* 8 (1932):293-336.

Mommsen, Theodor. "Der Religionsfrevel nach römischen Recht" in *Gesammelte Schriften.* 8 vols. 1905-1913. Reprint. Berlin: Weidmannsche Verlagsbuchhandlung, 1965.

Mommsen, Theodor. *Römisches Staatsrecht.* 3d ed. 3 vols. 1887. Reprint. Graz: Akademische Druck- u. Verlagsanstalt, 1952-1969.

Mommsen, Theodor. *Römisches Strafrecht.* Systematisches Handbuch der Deutschen Rechtswissenschaft, vol. 1.4. Leipzig: Duncker und Humblot, 1899.

Mommsen, Theodor. "Zeitalter des Scholiasten Juvenals" in *Gesammelte Schriften.* 8 vols. 1905-1913. Reprint. Berlin: Weidmannsche Verlagsbuchhandlung, 1965.

Murphy-O'Connor, Jerome. "Paul and Gallio." *Journal of Biblical Literature* 112 (1993):315-317.

Musurillo, Herbert A., ed. *The Acts of the Pagan Martyrs: Acta Alexandrinorum.* 1954. Reprint. New York: Arno Press, 1979.

Nash, Ernest. *Pictorial Dictionary of Ancient Rome.* 2d ed. 2 vols. New York: Frederick A. Praeger, 1961-1962.

Ohlemutz, Erwin. *Die Kulte und Heiligtümer der Götter in Pergamon.* 1940. Reprint. Darmstadt: Wissenschaftliche Buchgesellschaft, 1968.

Pape, W., and Benseler, G. *Wörterbuch der griechischen Eigennamen.* 3d ed. 2 vols. 1911. Reprint. Graz: Akademische Druck- u. Verlagsanstalt, 1959.

Penna, Romano. "Les Juifs a Rome au temps de l'Apotre Paul." *New Testament Studies* 28 (1982):321-347.

Platner, Samuel Ball. *A Topographical Dictionary of Ancient Rome.* Completed and revised by Thomas Ashby. 1929. Reprint. Rome: "L'Erma" di Bretschneider, 1965.

Prete, Serafino. "Un episodio del sacco gotico di Roma del 410: Hieron., *Ep.* 127,13–Oros., *Histor.*, VII 39." In *Storiografia e storia: Studi in onore di Eugenio Duprè Theseider*. Edited by Massimo Petrocchi. 2 vols. Rome: Bulzoni editore, 1974.

Rabello, Alfredo Mordechai. "The Legal Condition of the Jews in the Roman Empire." In *ANRW*, 2.30:662-762.

Radin, Max. *The Jews among the Greeks and Romans*. Philadelphia: Jewish Publication Society, 1915.

Ramsay, W. M. *Pauline and Other Studies in Early Christian History*. London: Hodder and Stoughton, 1906.

Reinach, Salomon. "La première allusion au christianisme dans l'histoire: sur un passage énigmatique d'une lettre de Claude." *Revue de l'histoire des religions* 90 (1924):108-122.

Reinach, Théodore. "L'empereur Claude et les Juifs d'après un nouveau document." *Revue des études juives* 79 (1924):113-144.

Reinach, Théodore. *Textes d'auteurs grecs et romains relatifs au Judaïsme réunis, traduits et annotés*. 1895. Reprint. Hildesheim: Georg Olms Verlagsbuchhandlung, 1963.

Richardson, Lawrence, Jr. *A New Topographical Dictionary of Ancient Rome*. Baltimore and London: The Johns Hopkins University Press, 1992.

Rolfe, John C., trans. *Suetonius: Lives of the Caesars, Lives of Illustrious Men*. LCL. 2 vols. Cambridge: Harvard University Press, 1913-1914.

Roth, Cecil. *The History of the Jews of Italy*. Philadelphia: Jewish Publication Society of America, 1946.

Rutgers, Leonard Victor. "Archaeological Evidence for the Interaction of Jews and Non-Jews in Late Antiquity." *American Journal of Archeology* 96 (1992): 101-118.

Rutgers, Leonard Victor. *The Jews in Late Ancient Rome: Evidence of Cultural Interaction in the Roman Diaspora*. Religions in the Graeco-Roman World, vol. 126. Leiden: E. J. Brill, 1995.

Rutgers, Leonard Victor. "Überlegungen zu den jüdischen Katakomben Roms." *Jahrbuch für Antike und Christentum* 33 (1990): 140-157.

Salmon, Edward T. *A History of the Roman World from 30 B.C. to A.D. 138*. 6th ed. 1968. Reprint. London: Routledge, 1989.

Sandys, Sir John Edwin. *Latin Epigraphy: An Introduction to the Study of Latin Inscriptions*. 2d ed. 1927. Reprint. Chicago: Ares Publishers Inc., 1974.

Saxer, Robert. *Untersuchungen zu den Vexillationen des römischen Kaiserheeres von Augustus bis Diokletian.* Epigraphische Studien, vol. 1. Cologne: Böhlau Verlag, 1967.

Schürer, Emil. *The History of the Jewish People in the Age of Jesus Christ.* Edited by Geza Vermes, Fergus Millar, Matthew Black, and Martin Goodman. 3 vols. Edinburgh: T. and T. Clark, 1973-1987.

Schwartz, Barry. "Tolerance: Should We Approve of It, Put Up with It, or Tolerate It?" *Academe* 82 (1996):24-28.

Schwartz, J. "Note sur la famille de Philon d'Alexandrie." *Annuaire de l'Institut de philologie et d'histoire orientales et slaves* 13 = *Mélanges Isidore Lévy* (1953):591-602.

Scramuzza, Vincent M. *The Emperor Claudius.* Cambridge: Harvard University Press, 1940.

Scramuzza, Vincent M. "The Policy of the Early Roman Emperors towards Judaism." In *The Beginnings of Christianity.* Edited by F. J. Foakes Jackson and Kirsopp Lake. 5 vols. London: Macmillan, 1920-1933.

Seager, Andrew R., and Kraabel, A. Thomas. "The Synagogue and the Jewish Community." In George M. A. Hanfmann, *Sardis from Prehistoric to Roman Times: Results of the Archeological Exploration of Sardis 1958-1975.* Cambridge: Harvard University Press, 1983.

Seager, Robin. *Tiberius.* Berkeley and Los Angeles: University of California Press, 1972.

Seel, Otto, ed. *M. Iuniani Iustini epitoma historiarum Philippicarum Pompei Trogi.* Leipzig: B. G. Teubner, 1935.

Seston, W. "L'Empereur Claude et les Chrétiens." *Revue d'histoire et de philosophie religieuses* 11 (1931):275-304.

Sevenster, J. N. *The Roots of Pagan Anti-Semitism in the Ancient World.* Supplements to Novum Testamentum, vol. 41. Leiden: E. J. Brill, 1975.

Sherwin-White, A. N. *The Letters of Pliny: A Historical and Social Commentary.* Oxford: Clarendon Press, 1966.

Sherwin-White, A. N. *Racial Prejudice in Imperial Rome.* Cambridge: Cambridge University Press, 1967.

Simon, Marcel. "Jupiter-Yahvé: Sur un essai de théologie pagano-juive." *Numen* 23 (1976):40-66.

Slingerland, Dixon. "Acts 18:1-17 and Luedemann's Pauline Chronology." *Journal of Biblical Literature* 109 (1990):686-690.

Slingerland, Dixon. "Acts 18:1-18, the Gallio Inscription, and Absolute Pauline Chronology." *Journal of Biblical Literature* 110 (1991):439-449.

Slingerland, Dixon. "Chrestus: Christus?" In *The Literature of Early Rabbinic Judaism: Issues in Talmudic Redaction and Interpretation*. Edited by Alan J. Avery-Peck. Studies in Judaism: New Perspectives on Ancient Judaism, vol. 4. Lanham, MD: University Press of America, 1989.

Slingerland, Dixon. "The Composition of Acts: Some Redaction-critical Observations." *Journal of the American Academy of Religion* 56 (1988): 99-113.

Slingerland, Dixon. "'The Jews' in the Pauline Portion of Acts." *Journal of the American Academy of Religion* 54 (1986):305-321.

Slingerland, Dixon. "Suetonius *Claudius* 25.4, Acts 18, and Paulus Orosius' *Historiarum adversum paganos libri VII*: Dating the Claudian Expulsion(s) of Roman Jews." *Jewish Quarterly Review* 83 (1992):127-144.

Slingerland, Dixon. "Suetonius *Claudius* 25.4 and the Account in Cassius Dio." *Jewish Quarterly Review* 79 (1989):305-322.

Smallwood, E. Mary. "The Chronology of Gaius' Attempt to Desecrate the Temple." *Latomus* 16 (1957):3-17.

Smallwood, E. Mary. "Jews and Romans in the Early Empire." *History Today* 15 (1965):232-239, 313-319.

Smallwood, E. Mary. *The Jews under Roman Rule from Pompey to Diocletian: A Study in Political Relations*. Studies in Judaism in Late Antiquity, 2d ed., vol. 20. Leiden: E. J. Brill, 1981.

Smallwood, E. Mary, ed. *Philonis Alexandrini: LEGATIO AD GAIUM*. 2d ed. Leiden: Brill, 1970.

Smallwood, E. Mary. "Some Notes on the Jews under Tiberius." *Latomus* 15 (1956): 314-329.

Smilda, Henricus. *C. Suetonii Tranquilli: Vita Divi Claudii*. Groningen: J. B. Wolters, 1896.

Smith, Leslie F. "The Significance of Greek *Cognomina* in Italy." *Classical Philology* 29 (1934):145-147.

Smith, Morton. "Goodenough's *Jewish Symbols* in Retrospect." *Journal of Biblical Literature* 86 (1967):53-68.

Solin, Heikki. *Beiträge zur Kenntnis der griechischen Personennamen in Rom*. Commentationes Humanarum Litterarum, vol. 48. Helsinki: Societas Scientiarum Fennica, 1971.

Solin, Heikki. *Die griechischen Personennamen in Rom: Ein Namenbuch.* 3 vols. Berlin and New York: Walter de Gruyter & Co., 1982.

Solin, Heikki. "Juden und Syrer im westlichen Teil der römischen Welt. Eine ethnisch-demographische Studie mit besonderer Berücksichtigung der sprachlichen Zustände." In *ANRW*, 2.29²:587-789.

Solin, Heikki. "Die Namen der orientalischen Sklaven in Rom." In *L'Onomastique latine: Paris 13-15 octobre 1975*, edited by Noël Duval. Colloques internationaux du Centre national de la recherche scientifique, 564. Paris: Éditions du Centre national de la recherche scientifique, 1977.

Spinka, Matthew, and Downey, Glanville, trans. *Chronicle of John Malalas: Books VIII-XVIII.* Chicago: University of Chicago Press, 1940.

Squarciapino, Maria Floriani. "The Synagogue at Ostia." *Archeology* 16 (1963): 194-203.

Stauffenberg, Alexander Schenk Graf von, ed. *Die römische Kaisergeschichte bei Malalas: Griechischer Text der Bücher IX-XII und Untersuchungen.* Stuttgart: W. Kohlhammer Verlag, 1931.

Stern, Menahem. "Antisemitism in Rome." In *Antisemitism through the Ages.* Edited by Shmuel Almog. Oxford: Pergamon Press, 1988.

Stern, Menahem. *Greek and Latin Authors on Jews and Judaism.* 3 vols. Jerusalem: Israel Academy of Sciences and Humanities, 1976-1984.

Stern, Menahem. "The Jewish Diaspora." In *The Jewish People in the First Century: Historical Geography, Political History, Social, Cultural and Religious Life and Institutions.* Edited by S. Safrai and M. Stern. Compendia Rerum Iudaicarum ad Novum Testamentum: Section One. 2 vols. Philadelphia: Fortress Press, 1974-1987.

Stern, Menahem. "The Jews in Greek and Latin Literature." In *The Jewish People in the First Century: Historical Geography, Political History, Social, Cultural and Religious Life and Institutions.* Edited by S. Safrai and M. Stern. Compendia Rerum Iudaicarum ad Novum Testamentum: Section One. 2 vols. Philadelphia: Fortress Press, 1974-1987.

Styger, Paul. "Heidnische und christliche Katakomben." *Pisciculi: Studien zur Religion und Kultur des Altertums, Franz Joseph Dölger zum sechzigsten Geburtstage dargeboten von Freunden, Verehrern und Schülern.* Ergänzungsband 1. Edited by Theodor Klausner and Adolf Rücker. Münster: Verlag Aschendorf, 1939.

Suhl, Alfred. *Paulus und seine Briefe: Ein Beitrag zur paulinischen Chronologie.* Studien zum Neuen Testament, vol. 11. Gütersloh: Gerd Mohn, 1975.

Syme, Ronald. *History in Ovid.* Oxford: Clarendon Press, 1978.

Taylor, Lily Ross. "Freedmen and Freeborn in the Epitaphs of Imperial Rome."
    American Journal of Philology 82 (1961):113-132.

Tcherikover, Victor. *Hellenistic Civilization and the Jews.* Translated by S. Apple-
    baum. New York: Atheneum, 1959.

Treggiari, Susan. *Roman Freedmen during the Late Republic.* Oxford: Clarendon
    Press, 1969.

Turner, E. G. "Tiberivs Ivlivs Alexander." *Journal of Roman Studies* 44 (1954):
    54-64.

Vogelstein, Hermann, and Rieger, Paul. *Geschichte der Juden in Rom.* 2 vols.
    Berlin: Mayer und Müller, 1896.

Volkmar, Gustav. "Die Religionsverfolgung unter Kaiser Tiberius und die Chro-
    nologie des Fl. Josephus in der Pilatus-Periode." *Jahrbücher für pro-
    testantische Theologie* 11 (1885):136-143.

Wallace-Hadrill, Andrew. *Suetonius: The Scholar and His Caesars.* London: Duck-
    worth, 1983.

Weaver, P. R. C. "*Cognomina ingenua*: A Note." *Classical Quarterly* 14 (1964):
    311-315.

Wessner, Paul, ed. *Scholia in Iuvenalem vetustiora.* 1931. Reprint. Stuttgart: B.
    G. Teubner, 1967.

Wiefel, Wolfgang. "Die jüdische Gemeinschaft im antiken Rom und die Anfänge
    des römischen Christentums: Bemerkungen zu Anlass und Zweck des
    Römerbriefs." *Judaica* 26 (1970):65-88.

Wieseler, Karl. *Chronologie des apostolischen Zeitalters bis zum Tode der Apostel
    Paulus und Petrus.* Göttingen: Vandenhoeck und Ruprecht, 1848.

Wilamowitz-Moellendorff, Ulrich von, and Zucker, F. "Zwei Edikte des Germanicus
    auf einem Papyrus des Berliner Museums." *Sitzungsberichte der preuss-
    ischen Akademie der Wissenschaften* 33 (1911):794-821.

Williams, Margaret H. "The Expulsion of the Jews from Rome in A.D. 19." *La-
    tomus* 48 (1989):765-784.

Williams, Margaret H. "The Organization of Jewish Burials in Ancient Rome in
    the Light of Evidence from Palestine and the Diaspora." *Zeitschrift für
    Papyrologie und Epigraphik* 101 (1994):165-182.

Willrich, Hugo. "Caligula." *Klio* 3 (1903):397-470.

Zahn, Theodor. *Die Apostelgeschichte des Lucas.* Kommentar zum Neuen Testa-
    ment. 2 vols. Leipzig: A. Deichertsche Verlagsbuchhandlung, 1919-1921.

Zaidman, Louise Bruit, and Pantel, Pauline Schmitt. *Religion in the Ancient Greek City*. Translated by Paul Cartledge. Cambridge: Cambridge University Press, 1992.

Zangemeister, Carolus, ed. *Historiarum adversum paganos libri vii: accedit eiusdem liber apologeticus. CSEL*, vol. 5. 1882. Reprint. Hildesheim: Georg Olms Verlagbuchhandlung, 1967.

Zielinski, Thaddée. "L'empereur Claude et L'idée de la domination mondiale des Juifs." *Revue de l'Université de Bruxelles* 32 (1926-1927):128-148.

Indices

1. Subjects

Absolutism: Augustan, 220; Claudian, 5, 95, 134, 145, 150, 220, 221; Gaian, 86, 95, 223; imperial, 28-29, 30-31, 86, 220, 221-223, 245; Trajanic, 221-222

Agrippa, Marcus, 48

Agrippa I (Herod), 62, 73, 77, 78, 80, 91, 94, 99, 102, 103, 112, 138, 155; Claudian friendship with, 99, 103, 113, 138 (*see also* Claudius); Tiberian imprisonment of, 62, 77. *See also* Cult, Jewish (at Jerusalem); Gaius (emperor); Jews, Alexandrian

Agrippa II (Herod), 103, 112, 113, 114, 234-235, 239. *See also* Claudius

Alexander Lysimachus (alabarch): brother of Philo, 79, 104; friend of Claudius, 78, 81, 102, 104, 146 (*see also* Claudius); prisoner of Gaius, 78, 79, 81 (*see also* Gaius [emperor]). *See also* Jews, Alexandrian

Alexander, Tiberius, 103, 144, 150

Alexandria. *See* Jews, Alexandrian

Antioch, John of, 51, 55, 60. S *ee also* Antioch, Syrian

Antioch, Syrian, 195-196, 214. *See also* Antioch, John of; Gaius (emperor); Jews, of Syrian Antioch; Malalas, John; Synagogues

Antiochus Epiphanes, 18, 19, 24, 62, 83

Apion, 17-19, 25, 66, 136, 183, 236

Apologetics, ancient Jewish and Christian. *See* Tendentiousness

Aquila/Priscilla, 90, 96, 117, 120, 122, 210-214

Aricia, 89, 90, 110, 118, 129, 151

Ass, the image of the Jewish god supposedly an, 19-20, 142, 221

Astrology. *See* Cult, astrological

Attitudes, negative upper-class/imperial: towards Jews, 10, 16, 25, 26, 27, 47, 65, 66, 82, 83-84, 87, 89, 93, 119, 133, 140, 233-236, 239, 240, 241, Augustan, 49, Claudian, 1, 89, 112, 139, 149, 235, 245; towards Judaism, 10, 16-27, 47, 49, 63, 65, 72, 76, 84, 110, 133, 143, 151, Augustan, 47, 49, Claudian, 1, 110, 151, 245; towards Roman Jews, 87, 112, 220-221, 241; towards Roman Judaism, 89, 100, 110, 112, 134, 151, 220-221, 241, 245, Claudian, 89, 100, 110, 134, 245. *See also* Augustus; Cicero; Dio Cassius; Hostility, upper-class/imperial; Philo-Judaism; Prejudice, upper-class/imperial; Seneca; Suetonius; Tacitus

Augustus: and the abolition of the Jewish ethnarchy in Alexandria, 65 (*see also* Jews, Alexandrian); and his supposed approval of the Roman Jewish cult, 69, 74, 91-92, 134-135, 142 (*see also* Attitudes, negative upper-class/imperial; Philo-Judaism); cult of, 31, 32, 48, 81, 91, 94, 100, 146; and dietary law, 21; and Druidism, 141, 227 (*see also* Druidism); fascism of, 30-31, 220; and his hostility to Jews and/or Judaism, 49, 221; and the Jerusalem cult, 47-49, 227 (*see also* Cult, Jewish [at Jerusalem]); and the Jewish population of Rome, 187; and his supposed Roman Jewish ghetto, 92; and the sabbath, 21 (*see also* Sabbath, upper-class/imperial hostility to)

Barbillus, Claudius, 102, 146, 147, 201

Caesar, Julius, and supposed favor of Roman Jews, 46-47

272 *Claudian Policymaking*

59; towards Jews and/or Judaism, 11, 21, 23, 24, 25, 27, 28, 31, 32, 44, 45, 55-57, 63, 66, 68, 72, 74, 76, 81, 86-87, 89, 99, 101, 102, 110, 133, 143, 145, 148, 150, 223, 225, 239, 244-245. See also Attitudes, negative upper-class/ imperial; Augustus; Claudius; Cult, Jewish (at Rome); Gaius (emperor); Kashrut; Philo-Judaism; Prejudice, upper-class/ imperial; Proselyte/proselytizer; Sabbath, upper-class/imperial hostility to; Tacitus; Valerius Maximus
Houses of prayer. See Synagogues
Impulsor. See Chrestus
Interpretatio christiana. See Chrestus
Jamnia, 85
Jerusalem. See Cult, Jewish (at Jerusalem)
Jew: in Dio Cassius, 62-63, 155, 169; in Suetonius, 54, 63, 152, 153-156, 169, 225
Jews: supposed blame of, 9-10, 27, 28, 32, 77, 83, 84, 125-126, 137; as supposedly diseased, 25-26 (*see also* Claudius; Plague); and their early presence in Rome, 43-45; as supposedly hated by the gods, 26; supposed isolationism of, 34; and the Jewish aristocracy, 62, 93, 150 (*see also* Agrippa I; Agrippa II; Alexander Lysimachus; Alexander, Tiberius; Philo); as popularly respected, 29-30; as supposed troublemakers, 10, 16, 27-29, 45, 58-59, 60, 63, 77, 97, 115-116, 132, 136-139, 142, 143, 148, 149, 155, 156-159, 225, 226-227, 228-231, 239-240. See also Prejudice, upper-class/imperial; Tendentiousness
Jews, Alexandrian: and the alabarch Alexander, 78, 79, 81, 102, 104, 150 (*see also* Alexander Lysimachus); and Augustan abolition of the Jewish ethnarchy, 65; and citizenship, 36, 66; and clashes with Gentiles, 23-25, 77, 79, 80,

81, 143-147; and the supposed Claudian edict for, 14, 65, 83, 99, 101 (*see also* Edicts, Josephan); and Claudius, 79, 80-81, 100-102, 113, 114, 143-150, 220, 245 (*see also* Claudius; 41 CE); and Claudius' genuine Alexandrian letter (P. Lond. 1912), *see* the index Biblical and Classical Sources; and their delegation to Gaius, 23-25, 85, 222-223, 233-234 (*see also* Gaius [emperor]); and events in Rome, 147-149; and the famine of 19 CE, 65-67, 76-77, 86 (*see also* Dole; Germanicus); Gaian measures against, 23-25, 77-83, 87, 91, 92, 94, 222-223, 233-234, 241 (*see also* Gaius [emperor]); the legal rights of, 23-25, 80-81, 86, 100-101, 150; and Philo, 10, 23-25 (*see also* Philo); and the pogrom of 38 CE, *see* 38 CE; and the post-Claudian period, 150; and the visit of Agrippa I to, 80. See also Apion; Ass; Augustus; Barbillus, Claudius; Chaeremon; Chrestus; Cult, Isiac; Cult, Jewish (at Rome); Egypt; Flaccus; Manetho; Synagogues; Tiberius
Jews, Diasporan: Gaian measures against, 82-83; 31 CE Tiberian measures against, 72, 69-77, 244
Jews, Egyptian. See Egypt; Jews, Alexandrian
Jews, of Jerusalem. See Cult, Jewish (at Jerusalem)
Jews, Roman: and citizenship stipulations, 139-142; and their unknown provenance, 52. See also Aquila/Priscilla; Aricia; Attitudes, negative upper-class/imperial; Augustus; Caesar, Julius; Campus Martius; Catacombs; Chrestus; Cicero; Claudius; Collegia; Cults, foreign; Cult, Jewish (at Rome); Dole; Expulsion, Claudian; Expulsion, 19 CE Tiberian; Expulsion, Republican; 52 CE; 41 CE; Freedmen; Gaius (emperor); Hostility, upper-class/ imperial; Jews; Juvenal; Nero; Onomastics; Persius;

Indices

2. Modern Authors

Indices

3. Biblical and Classical Sources
(select)

Acta Isidori   24, 112-113
Acts of the Apostles
  9:23-25   9
  18:1-18   2, 8, 96, 116-119, 120,
    121-122, 129, 151, 210-214, 225
  23:26-30   8-9
Augustine *City of God*
  6.11   30, 220
Cicero *Epistulae ad familiares*
  2.8.1   194
Cicero *Pro Flacco*
  28.67   16-17, 221
Dio Cassius
  37.16.5-17.1   62-63, 132, 223-224
  52.35-36   132
  57.18.5   55-60, 108, 120, 132,
    133, 224
  60.6.6-7   28, 29, 31, 96, 97-110,
    111, 112, 113-114, 120, 131-139,
    142-143, 147-150, 215, 216-217,
    224, 245
Diodorus Siculus
  34/35.1.1   25
  34/35.1.3   18
  34/35.1.5   19
Eusebius *Chronicle*
  year 21 of Tiberius   71
  year 2 of Vespasian   124
  years of Claudius   127-128
Eusebius *Ecclesiastical History*
  2.5.6-7   70-71, 233
  2.18.9   213
1 Maccabees
  8-15   45
Inscriptions
  CII, 683   230
  CII, 738   247
  CII, 741   37
  CIL, VI, 200   190-193, 199, 201
  CIL, VI, 200, 668, etc.   191
  CIL, VI, 668, 880, etc.   186
  CIL, VI, 1833b, 1871, etc.   193
  CIL, VI, 1871, 5716, etc.   187
  CIL, VI, 1929, 5645, etc.   188-189
  CIL, VI, 4329, 7921, etc.   194
  CIL, VI, 5645   187, 188, 236

CIL, VI, 33772   187, 188, 236
IG, XIV, 1639, 1859   179-180
ILS, 8967   195-200, 235
SEG 8.13   122
Josephus *Antiquities*
  2.207   32
  12.22   33
  12-20   12-14, 45
  14.186-267   14, 46-47
  17.300-301   116, 230
  17.330-331   116, 230
  18.65-84   67-69, 221, 224
  18.257-260   18, 81
  18.261-309   83
  18.276-283   11-12
  19.276   78, 81
  19.278-279   79, 81, 82
  19.279-291   14-15, 65, 99-102,
    138
  19.326-327   103
  20.118-136   235
Josephus *Apion*
  1.227-250   25
  1.289-290   25
  2.21   25-26
  2.63   66
  2.80   19
  2.94-95   18
Josephus *War*
  2.80-81   116, 230
  2.105   116, 230
  2.184-203   83-84
  2.232-246   234-235
Juvenal *Satires*
  3.296 (scholium)   247
  3.60-65   185
  4.117 (scholium)   89-90, 118,
    151
Letter of Aristeas
  15   33
Lydus *De mensibus*
  4.68   200-201, 235-236
Macrobius *Saturnalia*
  2.4.11   21
Malalas *Chronicle*
  10.244.22-245.2   82-83

South Florida Studies in the History of Judaism

South Florida Academic Commentary Series

243001	The Talmud of Babylonia, An Academic Commentary, Volume XI, Bavli Tractate Moed Qatan	Neusner
243002	The Talmud of Babylonia, An Academic Commentary, Volume XXXIV, Bavli Tractate Keritot	Neusner
243003	The Talmud of Babylonia, An Academic Commentary, Volume XVII, Bavli Tractate Sotah	Neusner
243004	The Talmud of Babylonia, An Academic Commentary, Volume XXIV, Bavli Tractate Makkot	Neusner
243005	The Talmud of Babylonia, An Academic Commentary, Volume XXXII, Bavli Tractate Arakhin	Neusner
243006	The Talmud of Babylonia, An Academic Commentary, Volume VI, Bavli Tractate Sukkah	Neusner
243007	The Talmud of Babylonia, An Academic Commentary, Volume XII, Bavli Tractate Hagigah	Neusner
243008	The Talmud of Babylonia, An Academic Commentary, Volume XXVI, Bavli Tractate Horayot	Neusner
243009	The Talmud of Babylonia, An Academic Commentary, Volume XXVII, Bavli Tractate Shebuot	Neusner
243010	The Talmud of Babylonia, An Academic Commentary, Volume XXXIII, Bavli Tractate Temurah	Neusner
243011	The Talmud of Babylonia, An Academic Commentary, Volume XXXV, Bavli Tractates Meilah and Tamid	Neusner
243012	The Talmud of Babylonia, An Academic Commentary, Volume VIII, Bavli Tractate Rosh Hashanah	Neusner
243013	The Talmud of Babylonia, An Academic Commentary, Volume V, Bavli Tractate Yoma	Neusner
243014	The Talmud of Babylonia, An Academic Commentary, Volume XXXVI, Bavli Tractate Niddah	Neusner
243015	The Talmud of Babylonia, An Academic Commentary, Volume XX, Bavli Tractate Baba Qamma	Neusner
243016	The Talmud of Babylonia, An Academic Commentary, Volume XXXI, Bavli Tractate Bekhorot	Neusner
243017	The Talmud of Babylonia, An Academic Commentary, Volume XXX, Bavli Tractate Hullin	Neusner
243018	The Talmud of Babylonia, An Academic Commentary, Volume VII, Bavli Tractate Besah	Neusner
243019	The Talmud of Babylonia, An Academic Commentary, Volume X, Bavli Tractate Megillah	Neusner
243020	The Talmud of Babylonia, An Academic Commentary, Volume XXVIII, Bavli Tractate Zebahim A. Chapters I through VII	Neusner
243021	The Talmud of Babylonia, An Academic Commentary, Volume XXI, Bavli Tractate Baba Mesia, A. Chapters I through VI	Neusner
243022	The Talmud of Babylonia, An Academic Commentary, Volume XXII, Bavli Tractate Baba Batra, A. Chapters I through VI	Neusner

South Florida International Studies in Formative Christianity and Judaism

South Florida-Rochester-Saint Louis
Studies on Religion and the Social Order